W9-CLZ-393

ARNPRIOR PUBLIC LIBRARY
21 Madawaska Street
Arnprior, Ontario
K7S 1R6

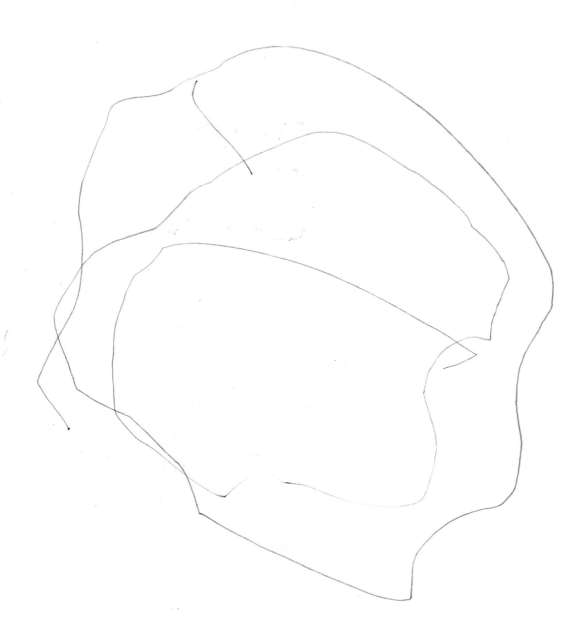

THE ILLUSTRATED ENCYCLOPEDIA OF
WEAPONRY

THE ILLUSTRATED ENCYCLOPEDIA OF
WEAPONRY

From Flint Axes to Automatic Weapons

Chuck Wills

In Association with the Berman Museum of World History

THUNDER BAY
P·R·E·S·S
San Diego, California

ARNPRIOR PUBLIC LIBRARY
21 Madawaska Street
Arnprior, Ontario
K7S 1R6

Thunder Bay Press
An imprint of the Baker & Taylor Publishing Group
10350 Barnes Canyon Road, San Diego, CA 92121
www.thunderbaybooks.com

Publisher: Peter Norton

Moseley Road Inc.
123, Main Street Irvington, New York 10533
www.moseleyroad.com

Moseley Road
Publisher: Sean Moore
General Manager: Karen Prince
Art Director: Tina Vaughan
Production Director: Adam Moore

Editorial
Lisa Purcell, Jo Weeks, Jill Hamilton, James Harrison,
Frank Ritter, Phil Hunt, Damien Moore
Index: Nancy Ball

Design
Heather McCarry, Mark Johnson-Davies

Photography
Jonathan Conklin, Sean Moore, Assisted by Kira Tidmore
Additional photography by Richard McCaffrey

Picture research
Jo Walton

Berman Museum of World Hostory
Adam Cleveland, Susan Doss, David Ford

North American Compilation Copyright © 2012, Thunder Bay Press
Copyright © 2012, Moseley Road Inc.

Copyright under International, Pan American, and Universal Copyright
Conventions. All rights reserved. No part of this book may be reproduced or
transmitted in any form or by any means, electronic or mechanical, including
photocopying, recording, or by any information storage-and-retrieval system,
without written permission from the copyright holder. Brief passages (not to
exceed 1,000 words) may be quoted for reviews.

"Thunder Bay" is a registered trademark of Baker & Taylor. All rights reserved.

All notations of errors or omissions should be addressed to
Thunder Bay Press, Editorial Department, at the above address.
All other correspondence (author inquiries, permissions) concerning
the content of this book should be addressed to
Moseley Road Inc., info@moseleyroad.com

ISBN-13: 978-1-60710-501-5
ISBN-10: 1-60710-501-2

Library of Congress Cataloging-in-Publication Data available upon request.

Printed in China
1 2 3 4 5 16 15 14 13 12

CONTENTS

PART V
THE WORLD AT WAR
20TH CENTURY AND BEYOND

RESOURCES

"THE GREATEST JOY A MAN CAN KNOW IS
TO CONQUER HIS ENEMIES AND DRIVE THEM
BEFORE HIM. TO RIDE THEIR HORSES AND TAKE
AWAY THEIR POSSESSIONS. TO SEE THE FACES
OF THOSE WHO WERE DEAR TO THEM BEDEWED
WITH TEARS, AND TO CLASP THEIR WIVES AND
DAUGHTERS IN HIS ARMS."

—Genghis Khan

FOREWORD

FROM THE ROCK FIRST HELD in the hands of Paleolithic man to the twenty-first century assault rifle, weapons have been an integral component in human history. As early humans evolved, so did their technology. Small rocks became specialized tools and weapons. These early innovations helped man in his quest for food, and eventually in protecting both family and territory. Stone technology gave way to metallurgy and as humans passed through each period of history—copper, bronze, and iron—their use and development of weapons increased. With the advent of agriculture and animal domestication, the reliance on weapons shifted from hunting food to protection from wild animals and other humans. Newly acquired possessions—food, animals, and shelter—carried intrinsic wealth and brought status. Humans used weapons to protect both.

Early weapons were effective only in hand-to-hand combat. The introduction of gunpowder into Europe brought radical change in weaponry and warfare. Its military use was first recorded in 919 c.e., and by the eleventh century explosive bombs filled with gunpowder were fired from catapults in China. Europe's initial use of gunpowder in the thirteenth century was recorded by the English philosopher Roger Bacon, and cannons were made in Florence, Italy, around 1326 with technology used by bell makers. By the later fourteenth century, hand-held firearms made an appearance. When metal projectiles could pierce armor, chain mail became a necessity, yet often was a poor defense against gunpowder and lead. Soon hand-to-hand combat was used only as a last means of defense.

"THE ROOT OF THE EVIL IS NOT THE CONSTRUCTION OF NEW, MORE DREADFUL WEAPONS. IT IS THE SPIRIT OF CONQUEST."

—Ludwig von Mises

The design of new weaponry was not left to the military. Leonardo da Vinci, the great Renaissance artist and inventor who hated war was, however, fascinated by structure and function and the beauty of design and utility. This must have been why his great genius was used in inventing numerous weapons, including missiles, multibarreled machine guns, grenades, mortars, and even a modern-style tank. As deadly as these early weapons were, it would be several centuries before technological advances allowed hand guns to fire more than one projectile at a time. Guns did not cause the obsolescence of other weapons; knives, swords, and other implements were still needed in combat. To overcome the deficiency of single-fire weapons, combination weapons—those that could perform more than one function—were developed. Single-fire guns were fitted with bayonets, and the fighting ax contained a gun in the handle. If the shot missed the target, its user had an alternate defense source. Combination weapons continue to be manufactured today. A recent example would be a cellular phone that contains a small .22 caliber pistol that could be used for assassinations or easily smuggled through security screening by terrorists.

Multishot weapons appeared in the nineteenth century. Early examples called "pepperboxes" shot from five to twenty times. Perhaps the most famous multishot weapon was the Gatling gun, capable of firing up to 800 rounds per minute, which—had it been introduced earlier—might have meant an earlier triumph by the Union Army during the U.S. Civil War. The twentieth century saw its share of multishot weapons; one of the best known was the Thompson submachine gun used by the likes of Roaring Twenties gangsters Dillinger and Bonnie and Clyde. Once it was adopted by the military, the multishooting machine gun changed warfare. With one-shot guns, advancement toward an enemy could be accomplished during reloading. With machine guns, movement on an open battlefield became more deadly, and gunplay was performed from entrenchments and behind barricades.

"POLITICAL POWER GROWS OUT OF THE BARREL OF A GUN."

—Mao Zedong

Technology changes were required to protect battlefield soldiers. Tanks and other armored vehicles were developed in the early twentieth century to reduce battle casualties by protecting soldiers as they advanced across an open battlefield.

In the modern era, technology continues to change the way weapons function in society, yet today's weapons technology has not made firearms obsolete. The military use of precision guided missiles has changed the way modern armies accomplish their goals and objectives. Yet, firearms and knives still play an important role in warfare.

In addition to their intrinsic value as property and the worth of the materials of which they were composed (the Persian scimitar owned by both Abbas I and Catherine the Great being a case in point—see pages 108-109), weapons throughout history have represented status in society, communicating one's prosperity and power. Many early weapons were costly, affordable only to the wealthy. Rulers in Europe and Asia had weapons constructed of gold or silver and encrusted with precious stones to flaunt their wealth, not only in their own society, but to those visiting their country.

> "A SWORD IS NEVER A KILLER, IT IS A TOOL IN THE KILLER'S HANDS."
> —Seneca

Many beautiful weapons come from the area around Persia—what is present-day Iran—and the Near East. Gold inlay, called damascene, embellished steel blades; hilts were decorated with rubies, emeralds, and other precious stones. Today, weapons reveal the status of their buyer, but in a different way. The country with the most weapons or the largest arsenal has the most military power, and military power symbolizes superior world status.

Aside from practical use, weapons have a unique appeal for collectors and museums because of their technology, materials, craftsmanship, and beauty. The most ordinary weapons tell the story of the time and the society in which they were made and used. Though they served and continue to serve deadly purposes, weapons allow a glimpse into human history.

Robert P. Lindley

ROBERT LINDLEY
Berman Museum of World History, Anniston, Alabama,

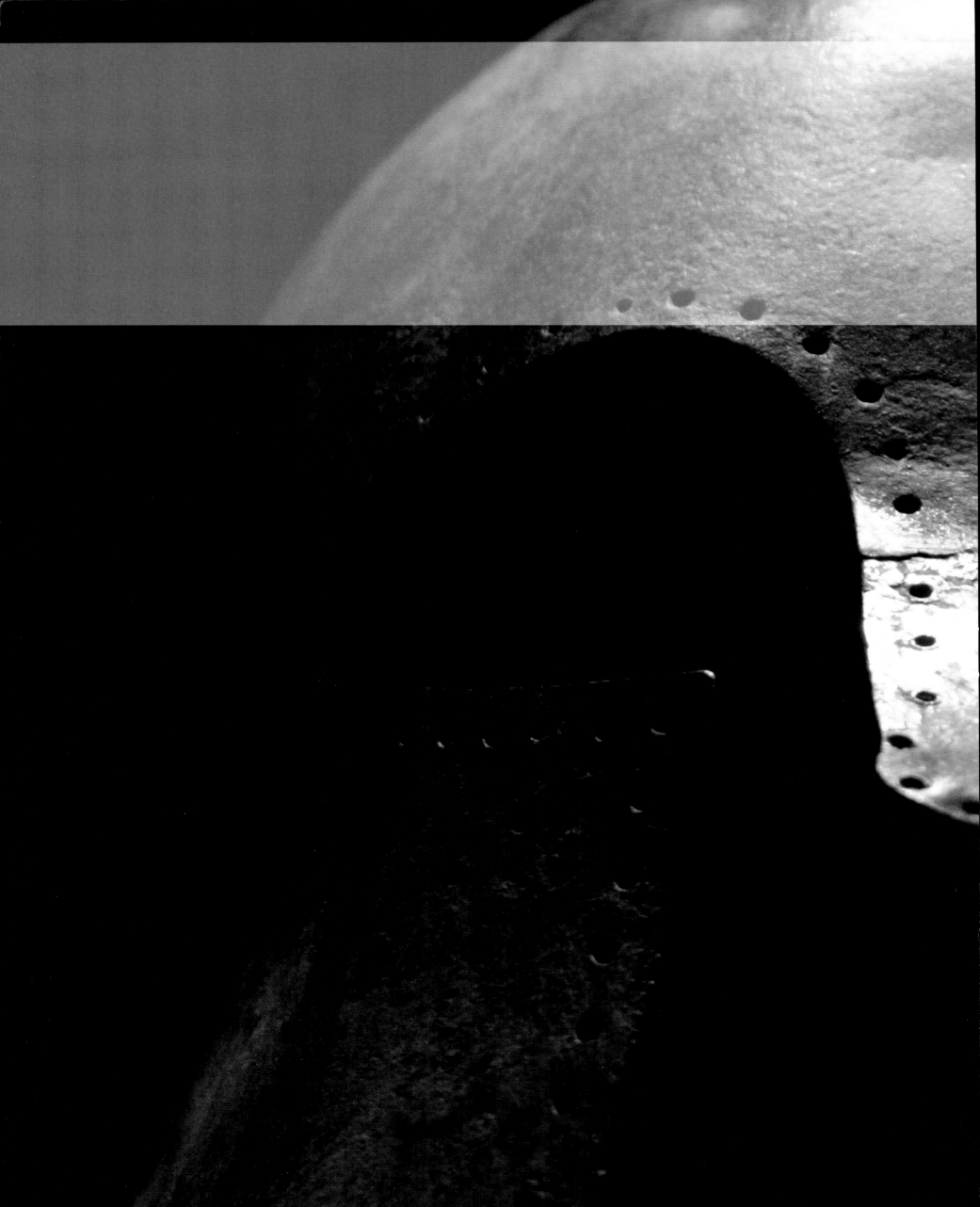

PREHISTORIC & ANCIENT WEAPONS
4500BC–AD100

From the earliest days humankind used a variety of weapons for hunting and defense

STONE AND BRONZE

The story of weapons begins with creation of the the first crude stone implements by early hominids, perhaps as long as 5 million years ago. At some point between 15,000 and 10,000BC, early modern humans refined the toolmaking process to craft axes, knives, and spear points. They used hard stones such as flint, knapped to achieve a sharp tip or cutting edge. These early weapons, along with specialized devices such as the atlatl (spear-thrower) and bolas (weighted throwing cords for entangling the legs of animals), were used in hunting; just when and where humans turned such weapons on each other in a way that we would recognize as warfare is still a matter of debate.

The next great advance in weapons technology came when humans discovered how to smelt mineral ore to produce metal—first copper, then bronze, allowing the creation of ever more durable blades and projectiles.

Early weapons timeline
In the space of 200,000 years, humankind's weaponry evolved from the roughly shaped stone hand axes of prehistoric man to beautiful, elaborately decorated bronze artifacts, which were themselves to give way to more durable weapons made of iron.

200,000–41,000 BC
Chipped hard stones used for hunting

40,000–22,000 BC
Sharpened stones lashed to handles to form axes.

HUNTING ANIMALS
Neolithic cave paintings such as this one depict male and female hunters using a variety of weapons, including bows and arrows and bolas.

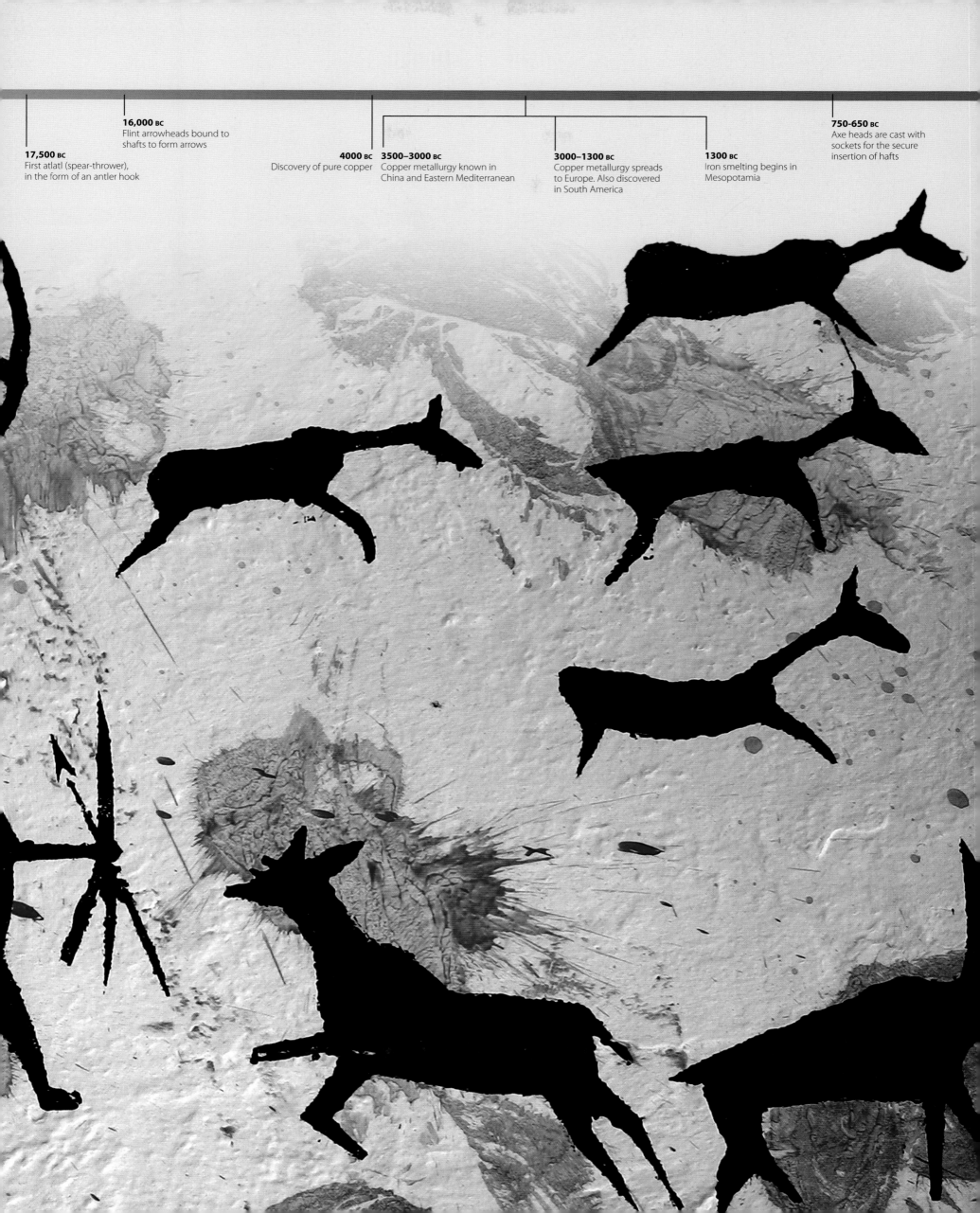

17,500 BC
First atlatl (spear-thrower),
in the form of an antler hook

16,000 BC
Flint arrowheads bound to
shafts to form arrows

4000 BC
Discovery of pure copper

3500–3000 BC
Copper metallurgy known in
China and Eastern Mediterranean

3000–1300 BC
Copper metallurgy spreads
to Europe. Also discovered
in South America

1300 BC
Iron smelting begins in
Mesopotamia

750-650 BC
Axe heads are cast with
sockets for the secure
insertion of hafts

THE FIRST WEAPONS

Between 5 million and 1.5 million years ago, the early hominids *Australopithecus* lived in Africa's Olduvai Gorge. At some point, one of them chipped a small rock against another to create a crude cutting edge—the first tool. This modest event was the "big bang" for human technology—including weaponry.

When the Stone Age began around 3 million years ago, the first modern humans learned to fashion basic tools from stone. Between 600,000 and 100,000 BCE, multipurpose tools like the hand-ax replaced cruder implements as humans developed techniques to "flake" blades from stone, especially flint.

FROM HUNTING TO WAR

How and when hunting weapons began to be used against humans rather than animals, and when warfare as an organized activity developed, are controversial questions. In anthropological circles, no subject is more hotly debated than whether human aggression toward other humans is "hardwired" in our DNA or if it is imparted culturally. But it's likely that prehistoric peoples fought over hunting territory, especially as the climatic changes that occurred throughout the period transformed landscapes.

In 1964, archaeologists found the bodies of more than fifty people—both men and women—at Jebel Sahaba, a site in what is now Egypt near the Sudanese border dating from between 12000 and 5000 BCE. They had been killed with stone-bladed weapons. To some archaeologists and historians, the number of bodies and the manner of their deaths seemed to be evidence that prehistoric warfare went beyond mere raiding and territorial clashes.

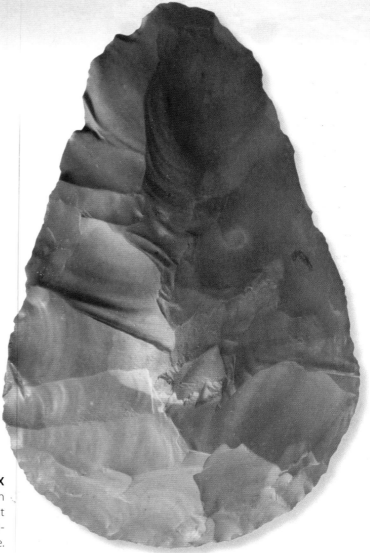

BASIC IMPLEMENT
A prehistoric stone tool from around 400,000 BCE, when humans were fashioning primitive hand-axes for general cutting and chopping purposes.

STONE HAND-AX
This Paleolithic hand-ax was discovered in gravel pits in southern England. Its near-heart shape reflects a more advanced stone-working style than the adjacent example.

FLINT AX
Uncovered in Denmark, this impressive example of a flint ax dates from around 10,000 BCE. By the time of this early Mesolithic (middle Stone Age) era, tools such as this were vital for the hunting activities that had become well established among the primitive peoples. Note the especially detailed chiseling on the ax edges.

In this pre-agricultural time, procuring a steady food supply was the main priority. Spears were the earliest weapons used to hunt mammals, and by 250,000–100,000 BCE hunters had hardened the ends of wooden spears or tipped them with edged stone. The development of the atlatl, or spear thrower, greatly increased the spear's range and power. The bow and arrow came on the scene around 10,000 BCE, as did the knife in its modern form.

The Stone Age ended in different parts of the world at varying times as copper, bronze, and then iron were discovered across the globe. These metals would lead to the birth of a whole new breed of tools and weapons.

CLOVIS POINTS

SPEAR AND ARROWHEADS

MAYA WEAPONS
A selection of blades from the Maya civilization, which was present in Central America from around 2,000 BCE until the 17th century. Made from stone such as flint and obsidian, the Mayas would use these as knives and as tips for spears.

STONE ARROWHEAD
Native American tribes crafted stone arrowheads such as this example for hunting. Later, the weapons would be used to defend themselves against white settlers.

EARLY HUNTERS
A prehistoric cave painting at the UNESCO World Heritage site in Bhimbetka, India, depicting hunters using a variety of weapons to catch their prey. The presence of a bow and arrow suggests that this particular drawing was created in the Mesolithic era, from between 10,000 and 5,000 BCE.

STONE AND WOOD

The characteristics of flint—predominantly the ease with which a sharp edge could be forged from it—meant that this was the stone of choice for the earliest implements. Nevertheless, as their skills developed, ancient peoples turned to other types of stone, as well as wood and even bone, to create tools and weapons.

STEATITE HOE
A hoe blade is made from steatite, a variety of soapstone with a high chalk content. Being fairly easy to shape, steatite was used for tools, decorative objects, and weapons by many early people. This example comes from the Mississippian Native American culture (c. 1000–1500 CE) in what is now the southeastern United States.

GREENSTONE CELT
Archaeologists use the term celt (from the late Latin *celtis*, meaning "chisel") to describe the stone (and later bronze) ax- and adze-heads used by early peoples. These celts, from North America, are made from greenstone. A very hard rock found in riverbeds, greenstone is hard to work, but its durability is similar to that of iron. While these celts were used as woodworking tools, they and similar blades are the early ancestors of weapons like the battle-ax.

ATLATL
One of the most effective early weapons was the atlatl, or spear thrower. This consisted of a grooved wooden shaft, into which the user placed a spear or dart; a hook-like projection at the end of the shaft held the projectile in place until the user was ready to "fire" by thrusting the atlatl toward the target. The additional force provided by the atlatl sent the spear flying with much more speed than if it had been thrown by hand, and thus increased its impact on the target. A refinement to the basic design added a small weight, or banner stone (like the one shown far right) to increase resistance.

AX HEAD
A full-grooved ax head dating from between 1000 and 1500 CE. The groove allowed the head to be mounted on a wooden handle.

JADEITE AX
This impressive Neolithic ax from 4,000–2,000 BCE was discovered in Canterbury, southern England. It was fashioned from jadeite, a material that was particularly challenging to work with due to its density.

BOLA
Like the atlatl, the bola or bolas (from the Spanish *boleadros,* or "balls") was a simple but elegant and highly effective weapon. First used by indigenous peoples of South America to hunt animals like guanaco, the bola, such as the one shown here, consisted of round weights—usually three, sometimes more—attached to cords. The user whirled the cords overhead and then launched the bola at the animal to entangle its legs. The bola's ability to immobilize an animal without wounding or killing it led to its later adoption by South American gauchos (cowboys) for rounding up cattle.

Banner stone

ANCIENT METALLURGY

Around six thousand years ago the discovery of pure copper in Anatolia—in present-day Turkey—opened up the possibility of weapons made, or partly made, of metal. Knowledge of copper smelting passed to Mesopotamia and Egypt, and by 3500 BC use of the metal for weapons had spread to Europe, India, and China. Copper was commonly smelted alongside tin and the two molten metals combined to form bronze.

Unlike iron, which was first used around 1300 BC, copper and bronze were relatively soft metals producing arrow tips and sword blades that did not long retain their sharpness. However, casting metal did allow strongly integrated weapons to be made; for example, in the late European Bronze Age (c. 750–760 BC), bronze axheads were cast with a socket to achieve a secure bond with their hafts, which were usually made of wood.

BRONZE IN ANCIENT EGYPT
In this stone carving at the early New Kingdom mortuary temple (c. 1490–1460 BC) of Queen Hatshepsut at Thebes, Egypt, axmen carry axes that have socketed bronze heads.

SHARPER BLADES

Whether intended for hunting animals or for human combat, weapons made from wood were always susceptible to breakage in use, as were the tips of flint arrowheads and spearheads, which had to be laboriously knapped with rudimentary tools. Despite their relative softness, copper blades could be relied upon to remain sharp for longer than flint or wood. When copper was combined with tin, the resulting bronze produced yet sharper blades. Other metals, including aluminum and silicone were also used. All such alloys produced sharper blades than copper alone.

INTEGRATED WEAPONS

The inherent weakness of a Stone Age weapon was the join between its sharpened stone head and its wooden haft. Stone axheads, for example, were tanged, or bound to their hafts using string or leather strips. The forces involved in chopping with an ax inevitably caused the head to loosen. Flint arrowheads were equally susceptible to such loosening and arrows would have been less reliable as a result. With the advent of casting in bronze, arrowheads and spearheads could be made with an integrated socket into which a shaped wooden arrow or spear was tightly inserted.

Some bronze arrowheads and spearheads featured a hole in the socket to enable a metal pin to further secure the join. Swords, too, were cast in a single piece, requiring only a comfortable grip to be bound to the hilt.

ORNAMENTATION

Stone Age weapons offered little scope for decoration but by the late Bronze Age craftsmen were making highly ornamented cutting weapons, shields, and helmets. The most impressive of these were wielded by chieftains, either on the battlefield or as powerful signs of office in tribal ceremonies.

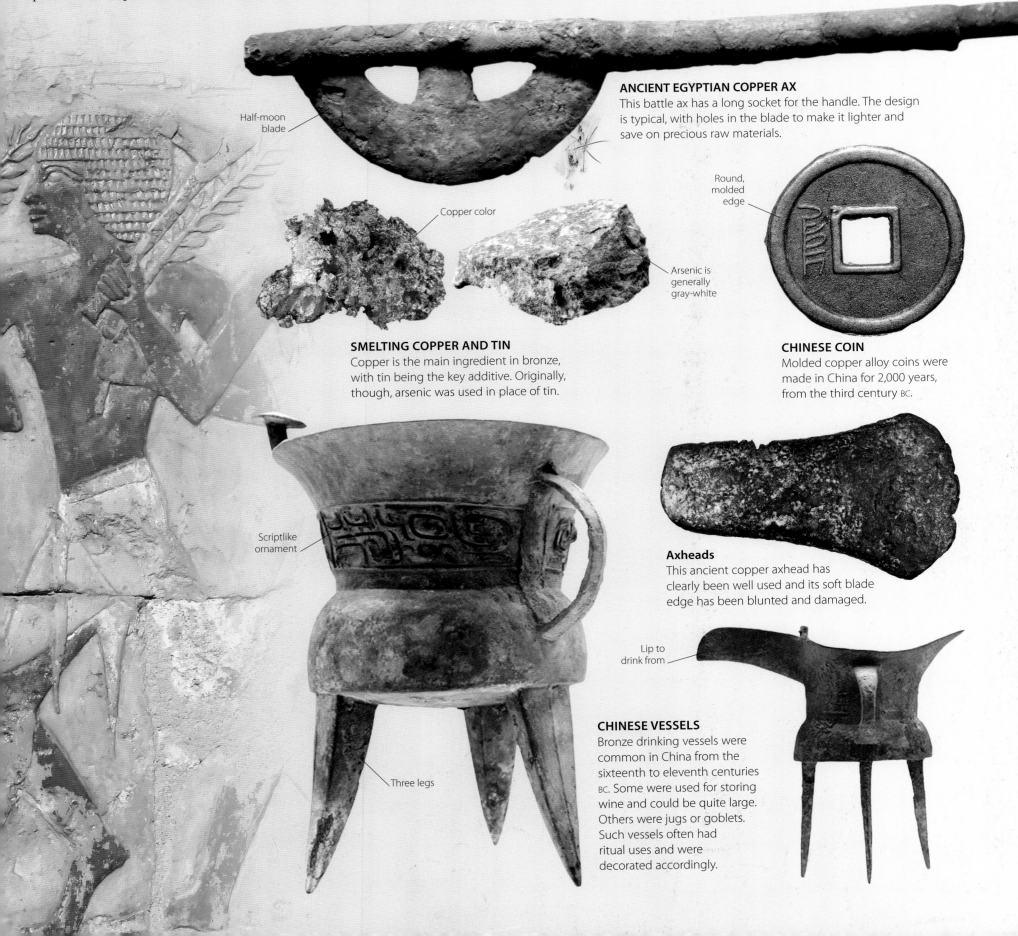

Half-moon blade

ANCIENT EGYPTIAN COPPER AX
This battle ax has a long socket for the handle. The design is typical, with holes in the blade to make it lighter and save on precious raw materials.

Copper color

Arsenic is generally gray-white

Round, molded edge

SMELTING COPPER AND TIN
Copper is the main ingredient in bronze, with tin being the key additive. Originally, though, arsenic was used in place of tin.

CHINESE COIN
Molded copper alloy coins were made in China for 2,000 years, from the third century BC.

Scriptlike ornament

Axheads
This ancient copper axhead has clearly been well used and its soft blade edge has been blunted and damaged.

Lip to drink from

CHINESE VESSELS
Bronze drinking vessels were common in China from the sixteenth to eleventh centuries BC. Some were used for storing wine and could be quite large. Others were jugs or goblets. Such vessels often had ritual uses and were decorated accordingly.

Three legs

EARLY METAL WEAPONS

The Bronze Age was a huge technological advance for humankind. During this period, people first learned how to create tools—and weapons—by refining, smelting, and casting metal ores. Because different cultures developed metalwork at different times, the term "Bronze Age" covers a wide time period. It is also something of a misnomer, because in its earliest phase, copper rather than true bronze (an alloy of about 90 percent copper and 10 percent tin) was used. This period is sometimes sub-categorized as the Chalcolithic Age. Copper metallurgy was known in China and the Eastern Mediterranean by 3500–3000

A NEWFOUND STRENGTH
Copper and especially bronze weapons offered vast advantages in strength, sharpness, and durability over stone weapons. So significant were these metals that historians credit their development with spurring the growth of urban civilizations by creating a class of skilled metalworkers, and with greater contact between scattered peoples as traders traveled far abroad in search of copper and tin deposits. Bronze and copper weapons also helped ancient armies overwhelm opponents who had not mastered the new technology. Bronze, however, had some disadvantages—chiefly that while copper was a fairly common ore, deposits of its other component, tin, were concentrated in just a few locations, like Britain and Central Europe.

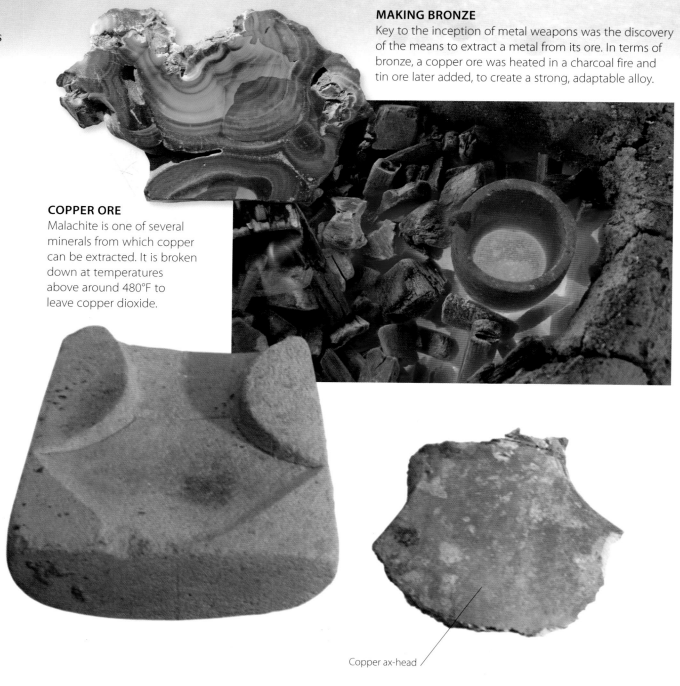

MAKING BRONZE
Key to the inception of metal weapons was the discovery of the means to extract a metal from its ore. In terms of bronze, a copper ore was heated in a charcoal fire and tin ore later added, to create a strong, adaptable alloy.

COPPER ORE
Malachite is one of several minerals from which copper can be extracted. It is broken down at temperatures above around 480°F to leave copper dioxide.

MOLDING THE MATERIAL
This mold was discovered near to a section of copper ax (far right) in Cát Tiên, southern Vietnam. The site was home to a civilization that dated from the 4th century CE, highlighting how copper was introduced across the world at different times.

Copper ax-head

ANCIENT EGYPTIAN COPPER AX
This battle-ax has a long socket for the handle. The design is typical, with holes in the blade to make it lighter and save on precious raw materials.

BCE, and over the next millennium or so the use of copper and, later, bronze spread into Europe and also developed independently in South America.

Once metalsmiths had figured out how to achieve the high temperatures needed to smelt iron ore by using charcoal, and how to fortify iron implements by hammering and tempering them in water, iron weapons began to replace those of copper and bronze. Historians generally date the start of the Iron Age to between 1200 and 1000 BCE. Around a thousand years later, Indian and Chinese metalsmiths learned how to combine iron with carbon to create an even stronger metal—steel.

AX HEADS
A pair of Bronze Age copper ax heads. Such an ax was carried by "Ötzi"—a mummified man whose remains, dating from about 3300 BCE, were found frozen into a glacier on the Austrian-Italian border in 1991. One theory about Ötzi's death holds that he died of wounds sustained from an attack by a band of hunters attempting to take his prized implement.

NATIVE AMERICAN DAGGER
A ceremonial dagger belonging to the native Kwakiutl people, who have lived in the Pacific Northwest region of British Columbia in Canada since around 7,000 BCE. As well as copper, the piece is made from wood, nails, bone and twine.

DECORATED HEAD
A detail of the copper head of the dagger (right), which features a depiction of a bear. The Kwakiutl have traditionally been renowned for their rituals and for ceremonies where gifts such as this would be bestowed.

BRONZE

As bronze began to be used by different cultures around the world, new types of weapons were fashioned. These implements also became more elaborate, with simple blades used for arrowheads and spears being followed by larger weapons such as daggers, swords, and scabbards.

FROM STONE TO METAL
Sickles were originally made from flint, but the advent of new metals led to sharper, more durable examples being made. This Bronze Age sickle would have been attached to a wooden handle and used for agricultural purposes such as cutting crops or clearing areas of vegetation.

EGYPTIAN FRIEZE
A stone-carved frieze in the Ramesseum at Luxor depicting Ramesses II firing a bow and arrow. By the time the Egyptian Pharaoh came to power in 1279 BCE, bronze weapons were commonplace in Ancient Egypt.

SPEARHEAD
This is a modern replica of a late Bronze Age spearhead from the Mycenaean Era—a period named for the Greek city-state that dominated much of the Mediterranean world from 3000 to about 1000 BCE. It has a fluted, leaf-shaped blade and an overall length of 27.5in/70cm.

PERSIAN ARROWHEAD
Made of solid bronze, this arrowhead was found in the Luristan Mountains of Persia (modern Iran) and dates from sometime between 1800 and 700 BCE. Exactly who made this weapon and similar objects is debated; they may have been brought to the site by nomadic tribes from what is now Russia, or created locally.

SHORT SWORD
A Greek short sword, with a blade made between 3200 and 1150 BCE. The decorated hilt and pommel were attached at a later point in history.

EUROPEAN BLADE
Made from bronze, this ornate blade is from the Hallstatt culture, which predominated in central Europe between the 8th and 6th centuries BCE. Though it may have been used as a knife, the circular holes indicate that it might also have served as a spearhead.

BRONZE DAGGER
An extremely rare Bronze Age dagger—one of the objects found in Luristan. Dating from between 1200 and 800 BCE, it has a double-edged blade 11in/28cm long and a finely wrought handle with finger grooves.

BRONZE AGE AX HEAD
This impressive bronze ax-head was among a number of 9th–8th century BCE items found at St Erth in Cornwall, southwest England. Measuring 5in/13cm, the piece would have been cast in a mold and attached to a wooden handle.

IRON

Following on from stone and bronze, iron was the last—and arguably the most important—of the three major toolmaking eras. Once the difficulties of extracting and then purifying iron from its ore had been overcome, an abundant new material was available that would eventually supersede bronze. When iron was turned into the tougher alloy of steel through the addition of carbon, it would transform the nature of weaponry and revolutionize societies around the world.

MIXTURE OF METALS
As this Iranian ax-head from the 9th century BCE illustrates, bronze was still being used for weaponry during the early Iron Age. Here, the iron blade is set in a bronze head decorated with feline imagery.

EARLY IRON AGE SWORD
This 3,000-year sword features an iron blade with a bronze handle. Note the high level of corrosion of the iron component as a result of the metal's oxidation process.

METEORITES, MYTHS AND MAGIC
The first human contact with iron was through the discovery of iron meteorites. Their celestial origins gave rise to the belief that iron was a magical element, and weapons forged from meteoric iron were given a mythical significance. Initially considered more valuable than gold, astral iron was used to make one of the two daggers discovered in Tutankhamun's tomb in 1924.

HAND PROTECTION
A Japanese *tsuba*, or sword guard, made from iron. This often-ornate element of a sword was positioned at the base of the blade to protect the hands during combat.

RITUAL DAGGER
This elaborate Tibetan ritual dagger features a three-sided iron blade. Its handle is adorned with silver, while a mythical aquatic creature at the hilt and an opened-mouthed deity at the end of the handle are made from gold.

MULTIPURPOSE TOOL
This iron dagger and sheath would have been carried by an individual working the land in early 16th-century Germany. With its additional smaller knife and skewer, it served a purpose as both a weapon and a general tool.

BARBED TIP
A barbed iron arrow point that would have commonly been seen across Medieval Europe. This example may have been an arrowhead for use with a longbow or the tip of a "javelin"-type weapon.

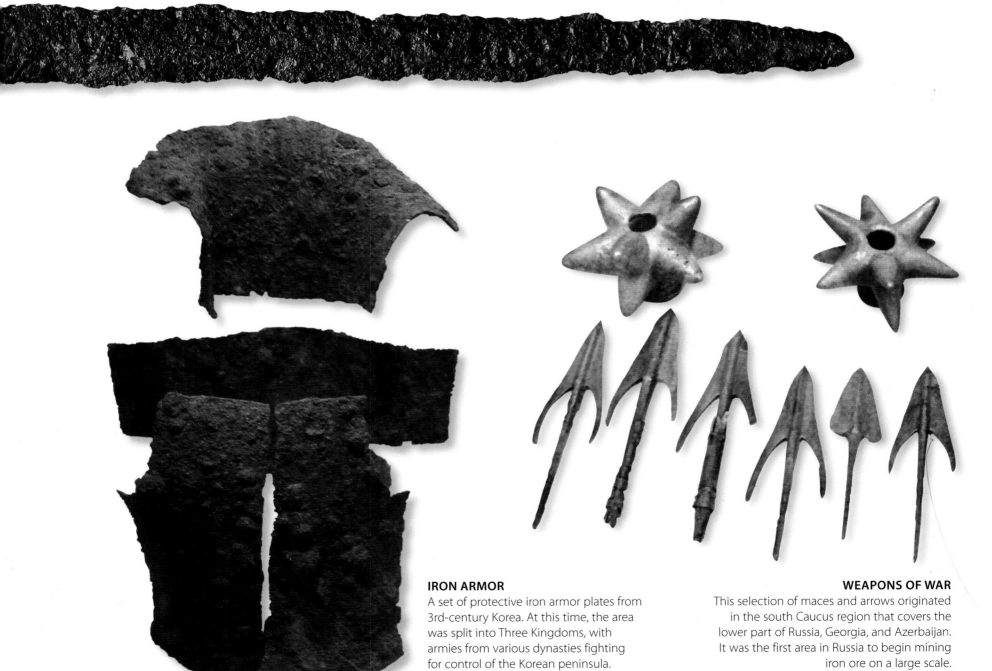

IRON ARMOR
A set of protective iron armor plates from 3rd-century Korea. At this time, the area was split into Three Kingdoms, with armies from various dynasties fighting for control of the Korean peninsula.

WEAPONS OF WAR
This selection of maces and arrows originated in the south Caucus region that covers the lower part of Russia, Georgia, and Azerbaijan. It was the first area in Russia to begin mining iron ore on a large scale.

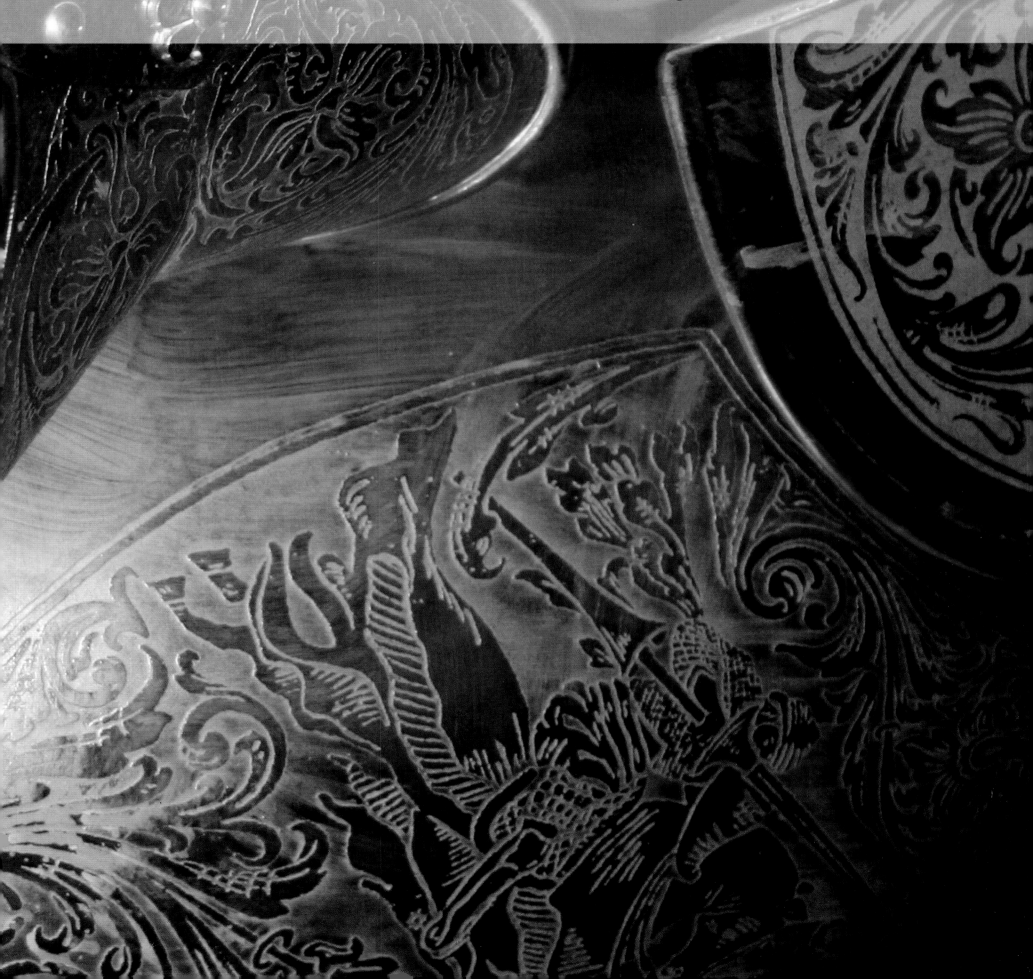

THE ORIGINS OF WARFARE

AD100–1500

For centuries bows and arrows and blades of many designs were the main weapons

BLADES AND ARMOR

Warfare between human beings required far more sophisticated weapons than those used to hunt animals. While crude bows and arrows developed into powerful longbows and crossbows, the discovery of ways to smelt iron around 3000 years ago inevitably brought a new generation of lethal weaponry. Hammered into sharp points and honed into razor-sharp blades, iron was fashioned into durable implements that, time and again, could be used to club, impale, or slice the enemy into submission. Evolving tactics of combat engendered specialized weapons, from the huge broadsword of the medieval period to African fighting knives. In terms of defense, iron was also shaped into helmets, shields, and suits of protective body armor. And as society grew in sophistication, so too did the weapons, becoming not only more effective for their purpose but also more beautiful as craftsmen vied to attract commissions from the richest and most powerful men.

Iron weapons timeline
The discovery of iron smelting, and later steel making, was followed by the appearance an extraordinary variety of weapons for stabbing, slashing, and clubbing. Only the spread of firearms would make such weapons largely obsolete.

1300 BC
Iron smelting begins in Mesopotamia

300 BC
Babylonians invent chain-mail armor

BATTLE OF TOURS
In France in AD732 the Battle of Tours was fought between the Franks and the Burgundians. Depicting the violence of the fight, this painting also shows the variety of weapons the soldiers had at their disposal.

AD 1–100
Romans produce armor from flattened strips of iron

AD 100
Chinese achieve carbon-intermediate steel

AD 400–900
Europeans further develop iron and steel spears, swords, axs, and knives

1100s
Flanged mace for penetrating armor

1300s
Halberd pole arm, incorporating a spike, hook, and ax-head

1400s
Two-handed broadsword

1500s
Firearms begin to challenge the supremacy of iron hand weapons

CLUBS AND SPEARS

In many indigenous societies, the warrior's priorities were to prove his personal courage (thus elevating his social status) or to seize loot or to capture the enemy for enslavement or (as in the Aztec Empire in Mexico) for ritual sacrifice. Traditional weapons—club and spear, along with a bow and arrows—were used because they required the user to get close to his opponent, which was more honorable. Combat was often highly ritualized and subject to strict rules—in parts of Polynesia, for example, the use of the bow and arrow was apparently forbidden in warfare but permitted in ceremonial competitions. The use of traditional weapons persisted

WAR: A WAY OF LIFE

For many of the indigenous peoples of what Europeans dubbed the "New World"—the Americas and the islands of the Pacific—warfare was a way of life. In some cultures, all neighboring peoples who weren't explicitly allies were considered enemies, and no young male was considered fully a man until he'd been tested in battle. At the same time, however, warfare in these areas differed in concept from what historian Victor Davis Hanson termed "the Western Way of War," in which the annihilation of the enemy was the goal.

Drumstick

Stylized faces and figures

TLINGIT CLUB AND DRUM

A ceremonial war club and drum of the Tlingit people of southern Alaska. Tlingit clubs were made of a variety of materials, including ivory and bone, and a special type of club was used in rituals to kill enemy captives taken in battle.

Simple linear artwork

Geometric designs

in some places even after traders arrived with guns to sell. Still, the indigenous peoples could see the effectiveness of firearms, especially as they began to lose their lives and lands to the white newcomers. A British sailor who encountered the Tlingit people of Alaska in the 1790s summed it up: "Their former weapons, Bows and Arrows, Spears and Clubs are now thrown aside & Forgotten. At Nootka . . . everyone had his musket. Thus they are supplied with weapons which they no sooner possess than they turn against their donors. Few ships have been on the coast that have not been attack'd . . . and in general many lives . . . lost on both sides."

NORTHWEST INDIAN CLUBS
The war club was a common weapon among many North American peoples; shown here are two distinct examples from the Pacific Northwest. The carving and decoration on the upper one indicate it might have been for ceremonial use.

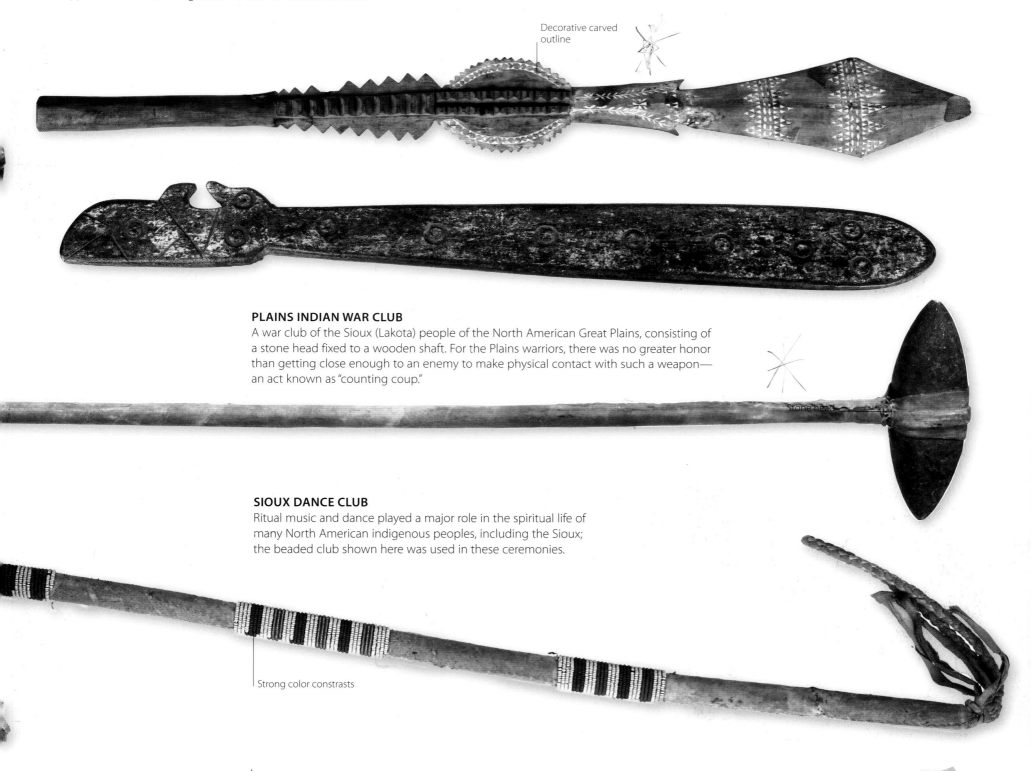

Decorative carved outline

PLAINS INDIAN WAR CLUB
A war club of the Sioux (Lakota) people of the North American Great Plains, consisting of a stone head fixed to a wooden shaft. For the Plains warriors, there was no greater honor than getting close enough to an enemy to make physical contact with such a weapon—an act known as "counting coup."

Stone head

SIOUX DANCE CLUB
Ritual music and dance played a major role in the spiritual life of many North American indigenous peoples, including the Sioux; the beaded club shown here was used in these ceremonies.

Strong color constrasts

CLUBS AND SPEARS CONTINUED . . .

Hole for wrist strap

MAORI PATU

The short-handled war club, or patu, was the principal
weapon of the Maori people of New Zealand. It could be
carved from the wood of the kauri tree, whalebone, or jade,
as in the example shown here. The hole in the handle would
have accommodated a leather thong attaching the weapon
to the warrior's wrist.

Scratched decoration
with pigment coloring

FIJIAN WAR CLUB

A Polynesian war club, made of wood and with blue
decoration. In some areas, especially the Hawaiian Islands,
such clubs were edged with shark's teeth.

Saw-toothed edge

FIJIAN CALACULA

A Fijian calacula, or club, with a saw-tooth "blade." Fijian
warriors used a wide variety of clubs and sometimes
decorated them with teeth taken from slain enemies.

INDIAN WOODEN CLUB

This wooden club from India has been carefully carved with plenty of decorative detailing
around the head and on the handle. Viewed from the top the head resembles a sunflower.
This amount of ornamentation suggests that the club had a use beyond mere protection
and warfare. It dates from the late nineteenth century.

Heavy ribbed head

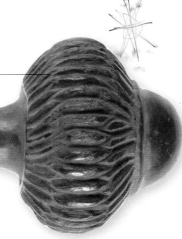

The club's hitting surface is the animal's snout

AFRICAN CLUB
This distinctive club is a simple representation of the head of a cow or bull. As symbols of a person's wealth, cattle have always been very important to African tribespeople so it is likely that this club belonged to an important member of the tribe and would have been used for ceremonial purposes. It was made in the nineteenth century.

IRON AFRICAN CLUB
Made in the early nineteenth century, this iron club is the work of a skilled artisan. Along with snakes on the handle, its head has an intricate plaited ribbon ornamentation.

Snakes twist up the handle

ZULU SPEAR
A Zulu *umKhonto* (spear), which is very similar to the famous Zulu assegai. The decision by the great Zulu leader Shaka (1787–1828) to equip his warriors with these stabbing spears—replacing longer and rather ineffective throwing spears—helped the Zulu forge a vast empire.

Macaw feathers

AMAZON SPEAR
A ceremonial spear of the Caraja people, who live on the banks of the Araguaia River, deep in the Brazilian rainforest. These spears are usually adorned with the feathers of birds like eagles and macaws.

Base of metal spear head where it would attached to wood or bamboo pole

JAPANESE SPEAR
The head of a Japanese spear (*yari*) from the eighteenth century. The weapon first came into widespread use in the fourteenth century, and several variations subsequently developed. Generally, Japanese infantry used a long version, which could be up to 20 feet in length, while Samurai carried a shorter model.

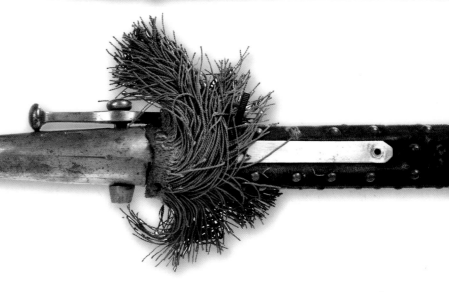

BOAR SPEAR
This European spear was used for hunting wild boar, a favorite pastime of the European nobility: A 1547 inventory of arms at the Tower of London lists a number of "Boar speres" owned by King Henry VIII of England. They could also be used on the battlefield.

BOWS AND CROSSBOWS

The bow and arrow date back to at least the Mesolithic Era (c. 8000–2700 BC) and the weapon is common to peoples in every part of the world. By providing a means of killing at a distance, the bow and arrow was a huge advance in hunting—and in warfare, especially after composite bows came into use around 3000 BC. Composite bows were constructed using layers of sinew and horn to reinforce the basic wooden structure, giving

SHORT BOWS

Mounted archers, often fighting from chariots, were an important component of the armies of empires like the Assyrians and Egyptians in ancient times. The Greeks and Romans, however, preferred the sword and spear, and when they were at their most influential the number of archers fell in European armies. The use of the bow revived in Europe during the medieval era in the form of the longbow and crossbow.

The bow and arrow remained the primary weapon of the nomadic "horse peoples" of Central Asia. Perhaps the greatest masters of the art of bow-and-arrow warfare were the Mongols who, starting in the early thirteenth century, conquered vast stretches of Asia and made inroads into Europe and the Middle East. They had short, composite recurved bows with an effective range of 1000 feet and a variety of specialized arrows—some for long-range targets, some for close-in fighting.

BOWS AND ARROWS

CENTRAL AMERICAN INDIAN BOW
The indigenous peoples of Central and South America made graceful bows for use in hunting, fishing, and warfare; arrows were often tipped with curare or other poisons. The bow shown here is from Panama.

FLAMING ARROWS
Once the tip was dipped in a flammable substance and set alight, flaming arrows were fired at fortifications in hopes of setting them afire, or into enemy formations. The arrow shown here came from Sempach, where Swiss and Austrian forces clashed in 1386.

Cloth soaked in flammable substance

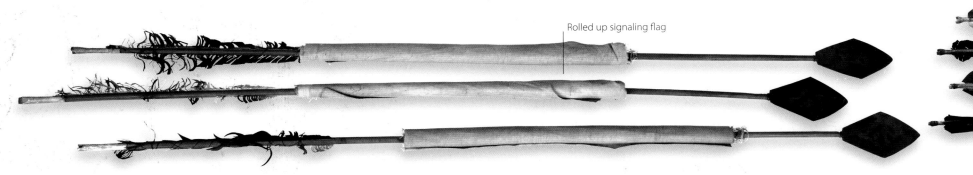

Rolled up signaling flag

JAPANESE SIGNAL ARROWS
Arrows have been used not only as combat projectiles but for signaling as well. These eighteenth-century Japanese arrows had a small cloth flag wound around the shaft, which opened upon firing.

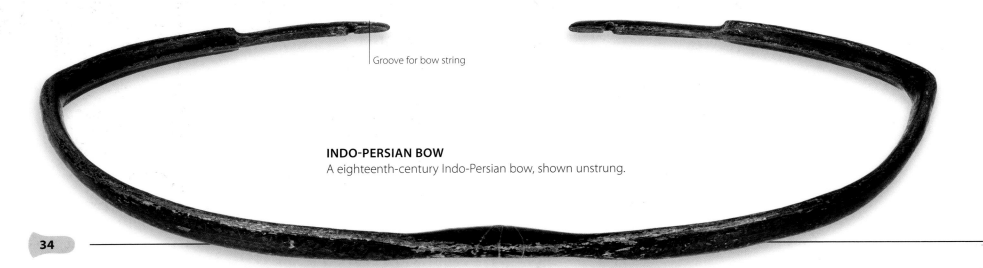

Groove for bow string

INDO-PERSIAN BOW
A eighteenth-century Indo-Persian bow, shown unstrung.

it greater strength, flexibility, and overall effectiveness. The development of the recurved bow, in which the tips of the bow face in the opposite direction from the user when the bow is drawn and fired, was another technical advance: Recurving allowed a more efficient application of energy. In addition, because recurved bows were shorter and more compact than "straight" bows, they were better suited to use on horseback.

AFRICAN BOWS

These bows reflect the geographic and ethnic diversity of the African continent. Some peoples, especially those who lived in jungle areas where hunting tended to be at short range, used relatively short bows; others, like those who lived in the highlands of what is now Kenya, used longer bows, similar to the pair made of pale wood above.

Darts have cotton "vanes"

Barbs helped the arrow to stay put

AFRICAN ARROWS

A variety of arrows used by the Wellengulu people of Kenya's Aberdare Mountains.

AFRICAN QUIVER

An African quiver (arrow holder) from around 1900. Made of wicker and waterproofed with resin, it held arrows and poison darts. The darts were used with a blowpipe and had cotton wadding instead of feather vanes.

LONGBOWS

Originally developed in Wales, the longbow was adopted by the English and used to deadly effect against the French during the battles of the Hundred Years War (1337–1453). Made of elm or yew and generally about six feet long, the weapon had a range of up to 600 feet. It was not always aimed directly at single targets; English longbowmen mastered the tactic of sending swarms of arrows raining down on the enemy from above. This proved devastating to French knights: One wrote that before the Battle of Agincourt in 1415, "The French were boasting that they would cut off the three fingers of the right hand of all the archers that should be taken prisoners [so] neither man nor horse should ever again be killed with their arrows." Among the longbow's disadvantages were that it required considerable strength and training to use effectively.

CROSSBOWS

The crossbow, chiefly used in Continental Europe, had a short bow attached at right angles to a wooden (sometimes metal) stock. It fired either arrows or metal bolts, known as quarrels, at a range of up to 1000 feet. Prior to the introduction of firearms, the crossbow was the most technically advanced weapon in European warfare—and one of the most feared, because its bolts could pierce even plate armor. The Church, in fact, tried to ban its use (at least by Christians against Christians) in 1139. It had a slow rate of fire, however, as drawing back the bowstring either with a winch-like device or by placing a foot on a "stirrup" fixed to the stock and pulling the weapon upward required considerable time and effort.

CROSSBOWS

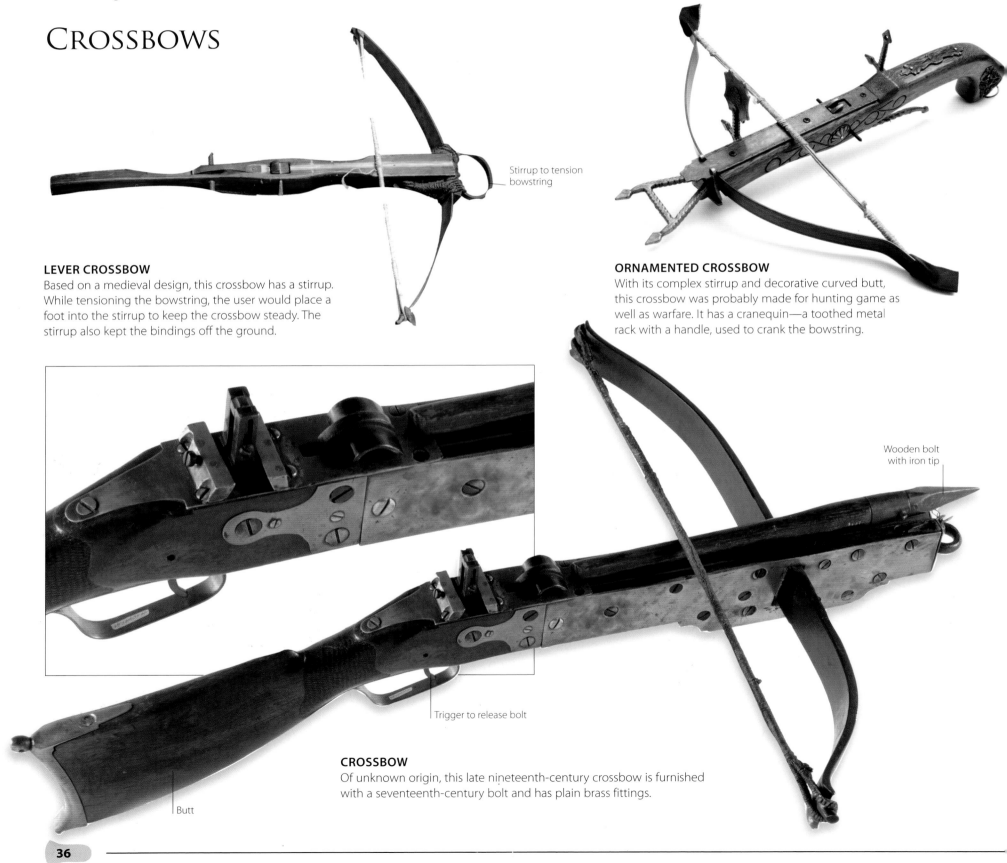

LEVER CROSSBOW
Based on a medieval design, this crossbow has a stirrup. While tensioning the bowstring, the user would place a foot into the stirrup to keep the crossbow steady. The stirrup also kept the bindings off the ground.

Stirrup to tension bowstring

ORNAMENTED CROSSBOW
With its complex stirrup and decorative curved butt, this crossbow was probably made for hunting game as well as warfare. It has a cranequin—a toothed metal rack with a handle, used to crank the bowstring.

Wooden bolt with iron tip

Trigger to release bolt

CROSSBOW
Of unknown origin, this late nineteenth-century crossbow is furnished with a seventeenth-century bolt and has plain brass fittings.

Butt

SPORTING CROSSBOW
A seventeenth-century sporting crossbow such as the one pictured proved excellent for shooting game or targets. The crossbow is still viable for military usage today, as a weapon for silent killing by special forces.

Nut to hold bowstring

CHILD'S CROSSBOW
A seventeenth-century toy crossbow.

Bowstring with looped ends

Firing lever

Box of bolts

CHINESE REPEATING CROSSBOW
A very rare example of the Chinese repeating crossbow, or *chukonu*. A box mounted on top of the frame held the bolts, which were fed into firing position by operating a lever. There are accounts of its use as far back as the second century, and reportedly some were used by Chinese troops as recently as the Sino-Japanese War (1894–95).

MACES AND FLAILS

The mace—a heavy club with a broad head often studded with spikes or knobs—has its roots in prehistory; the first known examples date from the Bronze Age (see pp 20–21) and the earliest depiction of its use in battle comes from the ancient Egyptian Narmer Palette dating from around 3100 BCE. While the use of mace-type weapons in the "Old World" declined in the Classical Era, they gained a new lease on life in Medieval Europe thanks to their effectiveness against armor. A variation on the mace was the flail, which had a heavy head attached to a shaft by a chain: infantry used a two-handed design, while horsemen used a shorter, single-handed variant.

MACES

The Medieval revival of the mace came in response to the increasing use of chain mail and, later, plate armor in warfare—not only in Europe, but also in Northern Africa and the Indian Subcontinent. The mace (now typically of iron or steel construction) didn't necessarily have to penetrate armor; a strong blow was often enough to break an opponent's limb or skull or otherwise stun or incapacitate him. Between the eleventh and thirteenth century, however, flanged maces appeared; these had heads with bladelike metal ridges that could penetrate armor. Other versions had spikes, which also had armor-piercing qualities.

Maces were most commonly used by foot soldiers, but shorter versions, more suited to mounted use, were often carried by knights. Cheap to make and simple to use, the mace was also a favorite weapon of peasant revolutionaries, like the Hussites (followers of the religious and political reformer Jan Hus) in early fifteenth-century Bohemia (now the Czech Republic).

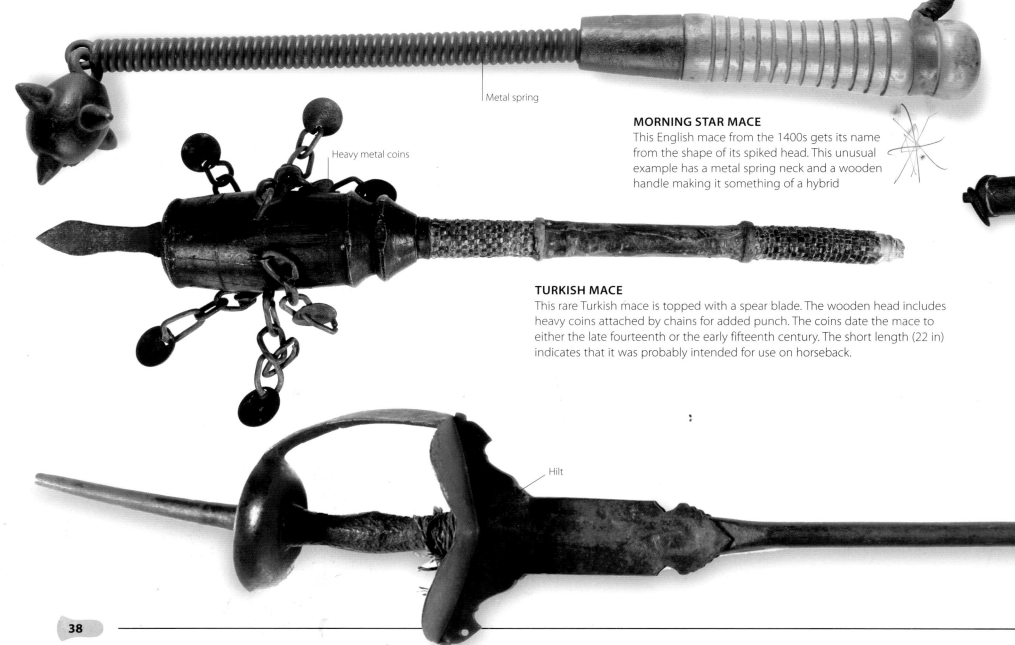

Leather thong

Metal spring

Heavy metal coins

MORNING STAR MACE
This English mace from the 1400s gets its name from the shape of its spiked head. This unusual example has a metal spring neck and a wooden handle making it something of a hybrid

TURKISH MACE
This rare Turkish mace is topped with a spear blade. The wooden head includes heavy coins attached by chains for added punch. The coins date the mace to either the late fourteenth or the early fifteenth century. The short length (22 in) indicates that it was probably intended for use on horseback.

Hilt

THE CEREMONIAL MACE

The mace was also a favorite weapon of fighting clergy, because unlike a sword or other edged weapon, it could wound or kill without shedding blood, which was forbidden by the canonical law of the Roman Catholic Church. (Modern historians, however, dispute whether the mace and similar weapons were used to any significant extent by Medieval churchmen—although the Bayeux Tapestry, which chronicles the Norman invasion of England in 1066, depicts Bishop Odo of Bayeux wielding a large mace.)

Like the halberd (see pp 40–45), over time the mace went from being a combat weapon to a ceremonial object and a symbol of authority. In England and Scotland, elaborately decorated maces have long been carried in civic and academic processions by "sergeants at arms," mayors, and other worthies. In the British Parliament's House of Commons, for example, a mace lies on the table in front of the Speaker during debates.

CEREMONIAL MACES
The mace as a real weapon went out of use with the disappearance of heavy armor. Ceremonial maces are often made from precious metals such as silver, sometimes with elaborate engravings.

RARE BULWA
A rare Caucasian Commander's *Bulwa* (Russian Mace) with an oval soapstone head capped with silver and a silver-mounted wooden shaft.

INDIAN MACE AND PISTOL
Dating from the mid-sixteenth century, this unusual mace is from Tanjore (Thanjavur), India. It has a hilt and a vaned head containing a percussion pistol, which was added at a later date.

Pistol flintlock

MACES AND FLAILS CONTINUED . . .

Flanged head

INDIAN MACE
The Indian mace shown here dates from about 1550. It has a flanged head, designed to penetrate—or at least dent—armor.

MORGENSTERN
One of the most common types of sixteenth-century European maces was the morgenstern, which had a spiked head attached to the shaft. The morgenstern was used extensively by the Habsburgs, and the name comes from either the German for "morning star," likely a reference to its sunlike spiked head, or as a grim joke based on the fact that the weapon was often used in dawn raids on enemy encampments.

Spiked head

FLAILS

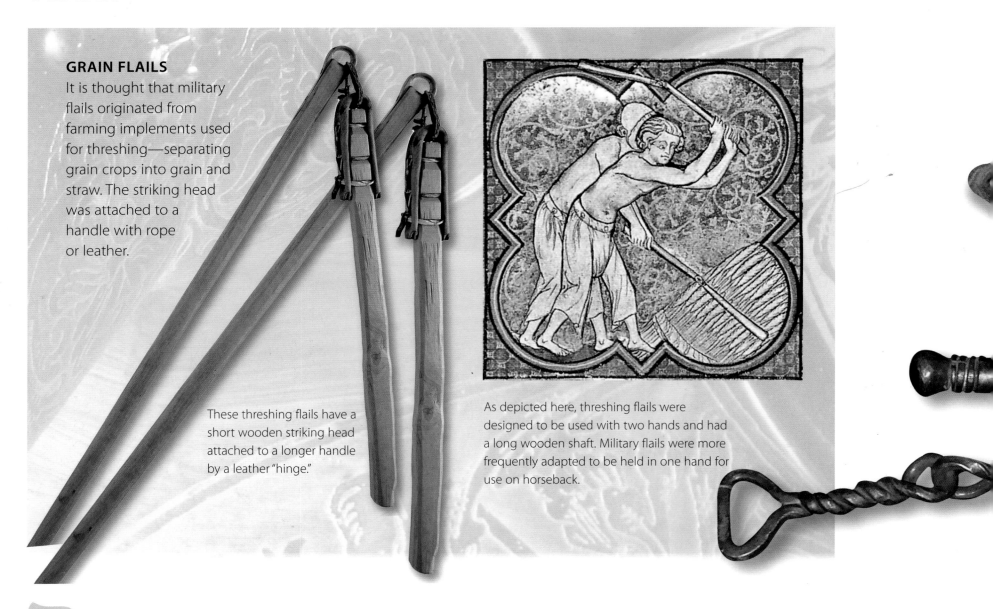

GRAIN FLAILS
It is thought that military flails originated from farming implements used for threshing—separating grain crops into grain and straw. The striking head was attached to a handle with rope or leather.

These threshing flails have a short wooden striking head attached to a longer handle by a leather "hinge."

As depicted here, threshing flails were designed to be used with two hands and had a long wooden shaft. Military flails were more frequently adapted to be held in one hand for use on horseback.

ENGLISH FLAIL

An English flail from the time of King Henry VII (r. 1485–1509). While similar to the morgenstern in design, flails usually had several lengths of chain or spiked balls attached to a shaft, although this example has only one. A major advantage of the flail was that it could be swung over or around a knight's shield.

Spiked head

ENGLISH FLAIL

This variation on the English flail has a wooden handle and a slender chain making it lighter to wield.

Slender chain

LEATHER FLAIL

An unusual flail with a knotted hardwood striking head attached to a wooden handle by leather straps. A leather thong secured the weapon to its owners wrist.

BONE FLAIL

A more "primitive" flail design using knotted leather for the handle and bone for the striking heads.

Leather handle

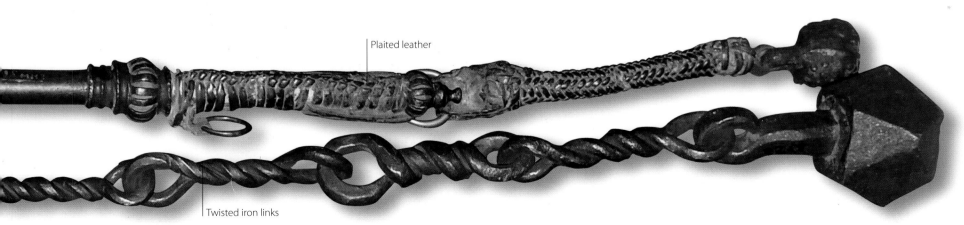

Plaited leather

Twisted iron links

RUSSIAN FLAILS

Military flails of 18th-century Russian insurgents.

THE CRUSADES

"Deus Vult!" ("God wills it!") proclaimed Pope Urban II at Clermont, France, in 1095. Instead of fighting each other, the Pope wanted the Christian nobility of Europe to unite in order to stem the tide of Islamic expansion in the East and restore the Holy Land to Christian rule. The result was the Crusades—a number of separate conflicts over several hundred years (the term derives from *crux*, or *crus*, Latin for "cross," and probably refers to the cross depicted on the cloth garment worn by the European Crusaders; eventually "Crusade" signified any "holy war"). Despite initial military successes, the Crusaders ultimately failed to achieve their objectives and fostered a deep hostility between the Western and Islamic worlds that persists today. However, they also led to a cultural exchange between West and East—an exchange that was reflected in weaponry and warfare.

THE CHRISTIAN ONSLAUGHT
A stained-glass window celebrates the "heroic" Crusader forcing Saracens into retreat. In reality, the Crusades were marked by brutality and mass slaughter of civilians.

CRUSADER VS. SARACEN

The invading Crusaders and their Islamic opponents (whom they dubbed "Saracens") had fundamentally different styles of fighting. In the words of British historian John Keegan, "Crusading warfare was a strange contest, which confronted the face-to-face warriors of the north European tradition with the evasive, harrying tactics of the steppe horsemen." The Saracens drew on the traditions of the "horse peoples" of Central Asia, with their highly mobile armies of mounted bowmen and hit-and-run tactics. Using a composite bow, a horseman could penetrate chain mail at up to 475 feet. In contrast, the European forces had at their epicenter a nucleus of knights—heavily loaded down with lances, swords, chain-mail armor, and metal helmets—who considered anything other than close combat with the enemy to be dishonorable, and whose preferred tactic was an all-out charge.

SIEGES IN THE HOLY LAND

While on the offensive, the Crusaders laid siege to cities like Jerusalem, which fell after a relatively brief military onslaught in 1099. Within a century, however, Jerusalem had been recaptured and the Crusaders driven into a handful of castles and other fortified positions on the Mediterranean coast. Now it was their turn to endure siege. They discovered that the Saracens were adept at this kind of warfare, particularly in their use of incendiary (flame-producing) weapons. While under siege themselves, the Saracens had used inflammable compounds to set fire to the siege towers used during Crusader attempts to scale castle walls or tunnel underneath them. Now the Saracens used trebuchets and other siege engines to hurl incendiaries. However, hunger, thirst, and disease were greater threats to the defenders.

Strengthened tip to protect sword

MAMELUKE SWORD AND SCABBARD
With its curved blade and simple cross-hilt, the Mameluke sword was derived from the sabers used by the Mamlukes of Eygpt. These warriors beat first the Mongols in 1260 and then the Crusaders in 1291, a success that led to the end of the Crusades in 1302.

Quillon block

Brass scabbard

ENGLISH FLAIL
Flails had one or more lengths of chain or spiked balls attached to a shaft. A major advantage of this type of weapon was that it could be swung over or around a knight's shield, delivering a severe body blow if well aimed.

Heavy, spiked ball

Head fully protected

Ferrule

CROSS DAGGER
This wooden cross from France conceals a deadly surprise: a dagger with a 9½-inch scalloped blade.

Spikes could dent or penetrate armor

Cross attached to the visor

Cruciform hilt

Marquetry-style woodwork

Blade hidden within

Narrow slits for the eyes

KNIGHTS OF MALTA SWORD
Also known as Knights Hospitaller and Order of St. John of Jerusalem, the Knights of Malta was an order of "warrior monks" founded to protect Christian pilgrims to the Holy Land during the Crusades.

HELMET AND ARMOR
The crusading knight was a forbidding sight with his full face helmet and chain mail body armor. However, these outfits had drawbacks: They were uncomfortable to wear and hindered movement.

POLE ARMS AND AXES

A pole arm is a weapon with a blade or pointed tip attached to a long shaft. While pole arms have existed in various forms since prehistoric times, they gained prominence in the Medieval and Renaissance eras in Europe and elsewhere as a means of dealing with cavalry; the length of pole arms like the halberd extended the foot soldier's "reach" by providing the means of attacking a mounted opponent while staying out of range of sword thrusts. The battle-ax was another ancient weapon that found a new usefulness when pitted against armored warriors. The introduction of firearms and the subsequent decline in the battlefield prominence of heavily armored horsemen downgraded pole arms to ceremonial use in the West, though the pike retained its usefulness—as a means of protecting firearm-equipped infantry—well into the gunpowder era.

THE HALBERD AND THE PIKE

While there were many different types of European pole arms, the "classic models" were the halberd and the pike.

First appearing in the fourteenth century and usually about 5 ft long, the halberd was a triple-threat weapon: it was topped with a spiky point to keep mounted opponents at bay; a hook that could be used to pull an opponent out of the saddle; and an ax-head that could penetrate armor.

The pike—a simple, spear-like weapon consisting of a metal head attached to a wooden shaft—came into widespread use in the twelfth century, and was originally used as a defensive weapon against cavalry. The Swiss, however, turned the pike into a formidable offensive weapon, arming phalanx-like infantry formations called *Gewalthaufen* with pikes as long as 22 ft.

POLE ARMS AROUND THE WORLD

Warriors in other cultures also made extensive use of pole arms, for the same reasons as Europeans—besides their effectiveness against cavalry, they were relatively simple to manufacture and didn't require lengthy training to use. While the Samurai of Medieval Japan, for example, are popularly associated with the sword (see pp 96–97), they were supported by foot soldiers who wielded *yari* (spears).

The spear—whether used as a thrown weapon or as a stabbing implement in close combat—remained a mainstay of warriors in many cultures until the spread of firearms around the world. Perhaps the greatest spearmen in history are the Zulu warriors of Southern Africa: formed into units called *impis* and armed with the short *assegai* spear, they conquered much of the region in the early nineteenth century.

The following five pages show an interesting sampling of pole arms and axes spanning the globe and dating from the sixteenth through nineteenth centuries.

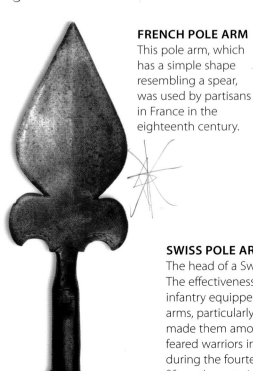

FRENCH POLE ARM
This pole arm, which has a simple shape resembling a spear, was used by partisans in France in the eighteenth century.

SWISS POLE ARM
The head of a Swiss pole arm. The effectiveness of Swiss infantry equipped with pole arms, particularly the pike, made them among the most feared warriors in Europe during the fourteenth and fifteenth centuries.

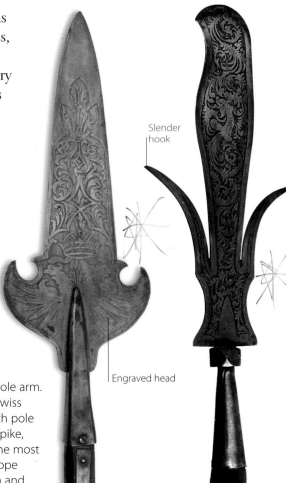

Slender hook

Engraved head

ITALIAN POLE ARM
The *glaive*, or *fouchard*, is a European pole arm with a single-edged knife-like blade, usually 18 in, fixed to a shaft of up to 7 ft in length. Some versions—like the Italian examples shown here—also had one or more hooks to snag riders from the saddle. As with the halberd, glaives took on a more ceremonial role as firearms changed European warfare.

ENGLISH POLE ARMS
Here are two examples of the English pike. While the introduction of the bayonet led to the decline of the pike in land battle, they were used in boarding actions in naval warfare into the nineteenth century.

INDO-PERSIAN LANCE HEAD

A twin-bladed Indo-Persian lance head, used during the Qajar Dynasty (1794–1925).

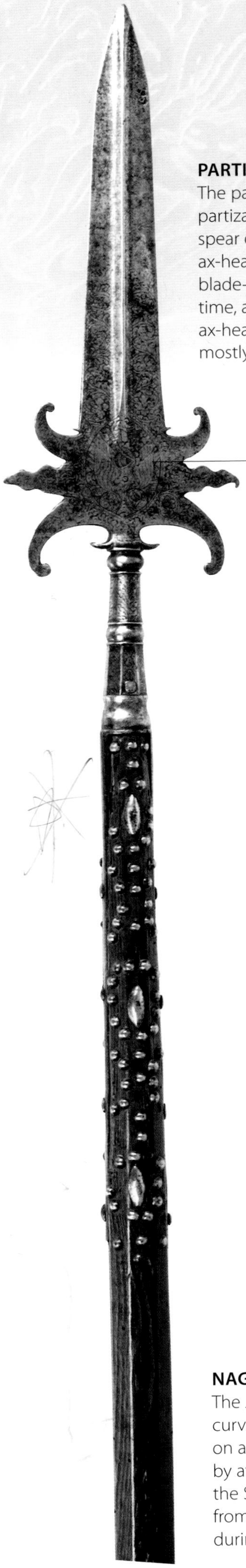

PARTISAN

The partisan, or partizan, was a type of spear or pike with ax-heads below the blade—though over time, as shown here, the ax-heads became mostly decorative.

decorative ax-head

NAGINATA POLE ARM

The Japanese *naginata* is a curved sword blade mounted on a long handle and was used by attendants and servants of the Samurai. This one dates from the eighteenth century, during the Late Edo Period.

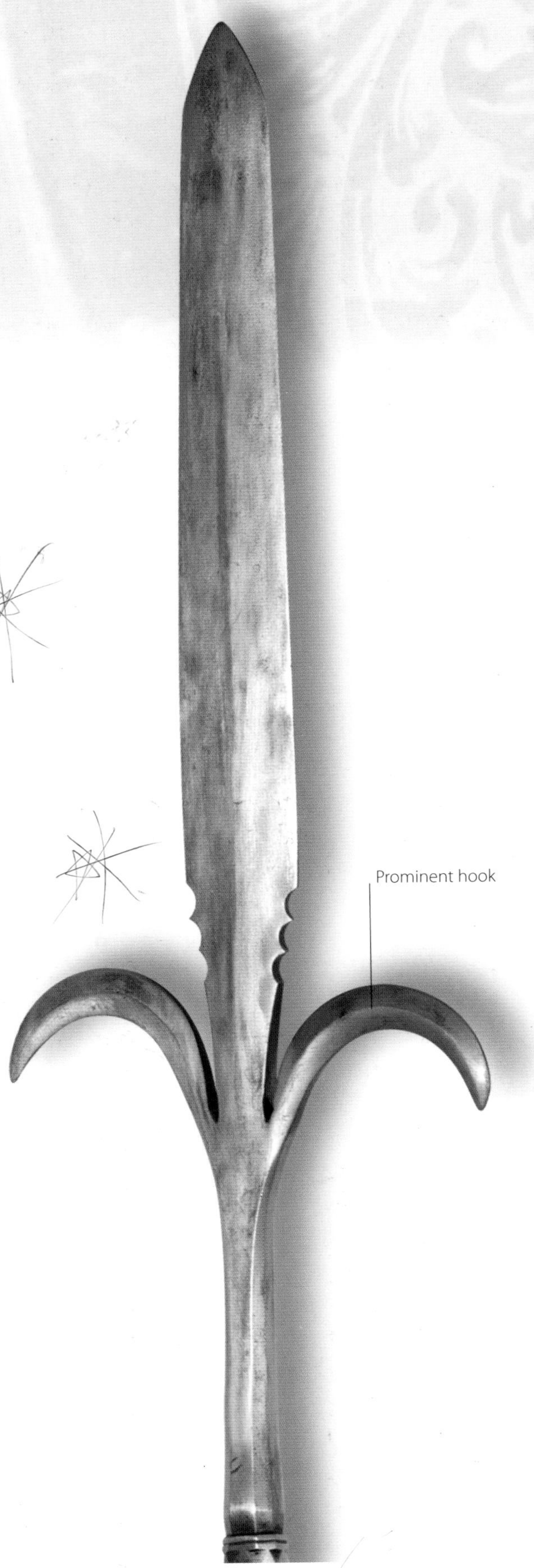

Curved blade

Prominent hook

CHINESE POLE ARMS

A late 18th century pole-arm head with a serrated sword base and prominent hooks that were used to dismount enemy horsemen.

POLE ARMS AND AXES CONTINUED . . .

ENGLISH HALBERD
A fine example of the halberd dating from the sixteenth century and probably of English origin, this weapon has a typically long, tapering blade, and a clearly defined ax-head.

SWISS HALBERD
This halberd, probably made in the early seventeenth century, is a classic example of this type of pole arm. In many European armies, halberds were carried by sergeants as symbols of authority well into the era of gunpowder warfare.

CHINESE HALBERD
This halberd dates from the eighteenth century Qing Dynasty and is known as a *ji*. Nowadays, ji are used in martial arts training.

CHINESE POLE ARM
A classic Chinese *fu pa* (tiger fork) gets its trident shape from a conjoining of the middle blade and a single curved outer component. The weapon is thought to have developed in Southern China for fighting tigers, and is still used today in certain schools of Chinese martial arts.

ax-head

Distinctive, crescent-shaped hooks

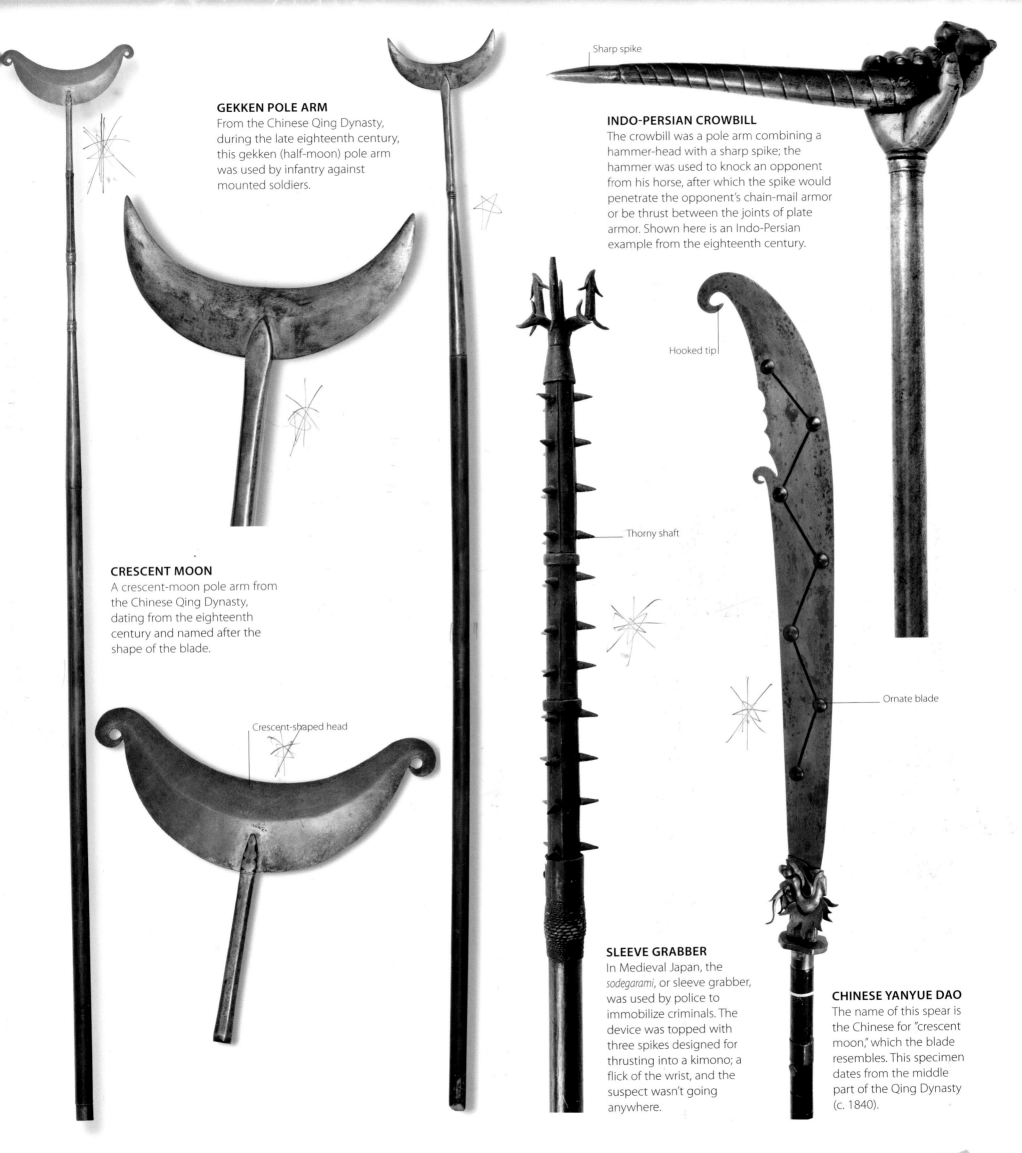

GEKKEN POLE ARM
From the Chinese Qing Dynasty, during the late eighteenth century, this gekken (half-moon) pole arm was used by infantry against mounted soldiers.

CRESCENT MOON
A crescent-moon pole arm from the Chinese Qing Dynasty, dating from the eighteenth century and named after the shape of the blade.

Crescent-shaped head

Thorny shaft

INDO-PERSIAN CROWBILL
The crowbill was a pole arm combining a hammer-head with a sharp spike; the hammer was used to knock an opponent from his horse, after which the spike would penetrate the opponent's chain-mail armor or be thrust between the joints of plate armor. Shown here is an Indo-Persian example from the eighteenth century.

Sharp spike

Hooked tip

Ornate blade

SLEEVE GRABBER
In Medieval Japan, the *sodegarami*, or sleeve grabber, was used by police to immobilize criminals. The device was topped with three spikes designed for thrusting into a kimono; a flick of the wrist, and the suspect wasn't going anywhere.

CHINESE YANYUE DAO
The name of this spear is the Chinese for "crescent moon," which the blade resembles. This specimen dates from the middle part of the Qing Dynasty (c. 1840).

ARMOR

The use of special clothing to protect the wearer from projectiles and blades goes back at least 10,000 years, when Chinese soldiers wore cloaks of rhinoceros hide, but warriors and hunters were probably wearing protective garments of leather and other materials long before this. Metal armor—first chain mail, and later plate armor—was used widely in Europe from ancient times into the late medieval period (and later, in other parts of the world), until the growing effectiveness of firearms led to its decline. In more recent times, the introduction of new synthetic materials has led to a revival in body armor.

HELMETS

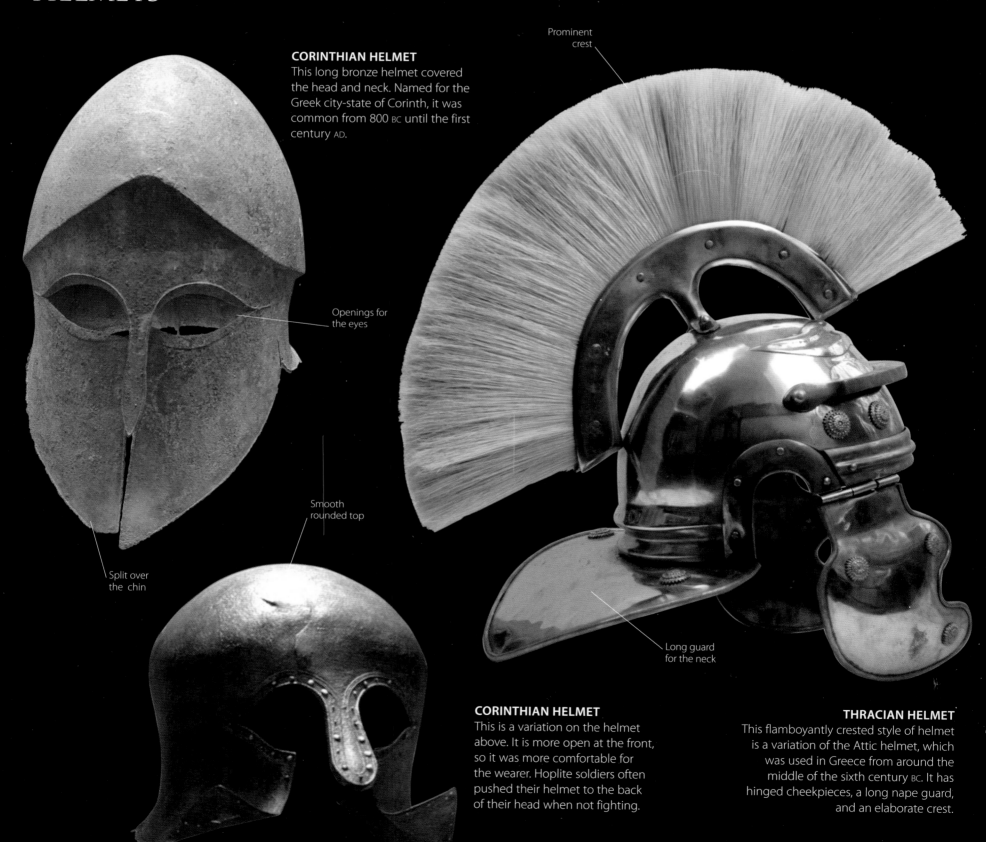

CORINTHIAN HELMET
This long bronze helmet covered the head and neck. Named for the Greek city-state of Corinth, it was common from 800 BC until the first century AD.

Openings for the eyes

Split over the chin

Smooth rounded top

Prominent crest

Long guard for the neck

CORINTHIAN HELMET
This is a variation on the helmet above. It is more open at the front, so it was more comfortable for the wearer. Hoplite soldiers often pushed their helmet to the back of their head when not fighting.

THRACIAN HELMET
This flamboyantly crested style of helmet is a variation of the Attic helmet, which was used in Greece from around the middle of the sixth century BC. It has hinged cheekpieces, a long nape guard, and an elaborate crest.

HOPLITES TO KNIGHTS

Ancient Greek infantry (hoplites) went into battle protected by a cuirass made of bronze, which protected the torso, as well as a helmet and greaves (shin protectors) of the same metal. The soldiers of Ancient Rome's legions also wore a cuirass, although their version consisted of a sort of leather vest covered in iron hoops, and they wore iron helmets.

Starting around the ninth century, European knights began to wear coats of chain mail—thousands of small iron rings riveted or welded together. Because chain mail by itself was often insufficient to deflect an arrowhead or spear point, coats of mail were usually worn over a leather tunic. Helmets came in a variety of styles, from simple conical iron affairs to more sophisticated models with articulated visors.

Chain mail was hardly lightweight (a typical coat weighed 30 pounds), but it offered the wearer relative freedom of movement. In the late medieval era, however, the introduction of weapons like the longbow and crossbow, whose arrows and bolts could penetrate mail, led European warriors to adopt armor made of overlapping plates of iron or steel. At their most sophisticated, suits of plate armor afforded the wearer full-body protection. The trade-off was their heavy weight—if a knight was knocked off his feet or his horse, he would be at a disadvantage.

AROUND THE WORLD

Variations on chain mail—usually consisting of overlapping metal plates—were worn by warriors in nations all over the world, from Persia and India to China and Japan. The suits of armor used by the samurai of medieval Japan were particularly fine and, like the best of European plate-armor suits, were magnificent examples of craftsmanship. In many cultures the wearing of armor was largely limited to the warrior elite (they were the only ones able to afford these expensive items, for one thing), but in India and elsewhere foot soldiers used garments of leather or heavily padded fabric for protection.

Among the most interesting nonmetal forms of armor were the raw silk shirts worn by Mongol horsemen. Because of silk's strength, if an enemy arrow pierced the horseman's body, the silk would be driven into the wound along with the arrowhead, allowing the arrow to be more easily removed than if it had torn through another type of material.

Long decorative spike

Inlaid with gold

INDO-PERSIAN HELMET
A beautifully made Indo-Persian kulah khud (helmet), topped with a spike and fringed with chain mail.

Finely worked chain mail protects the face

Riveted around the top

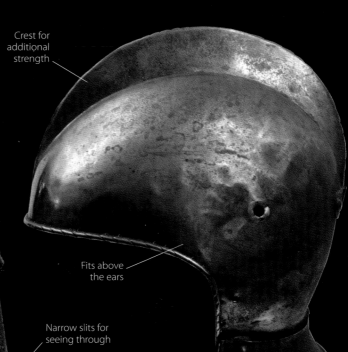

Crest for additional strength

Fits above the ears

Narrow slits for seeing through

ENGLISH HELMET
The first forged-steel helmets appeared in Europe in the tenth century. The sixteenth-century English helmet shown here is of a type known as a *burgonet*, which—while it did not offer the protection of earlier helmets that covered the entire head or face—gave the wearer greater visibility and freedom of movement.

GERMANIC HELMET
This ancient helmet from the Germanic area of Europe would have struck fear into the heart of any opponent. However, it must also have been very uncomfortable to wear with only a very narrow field of vision.

Fully protected cheeks

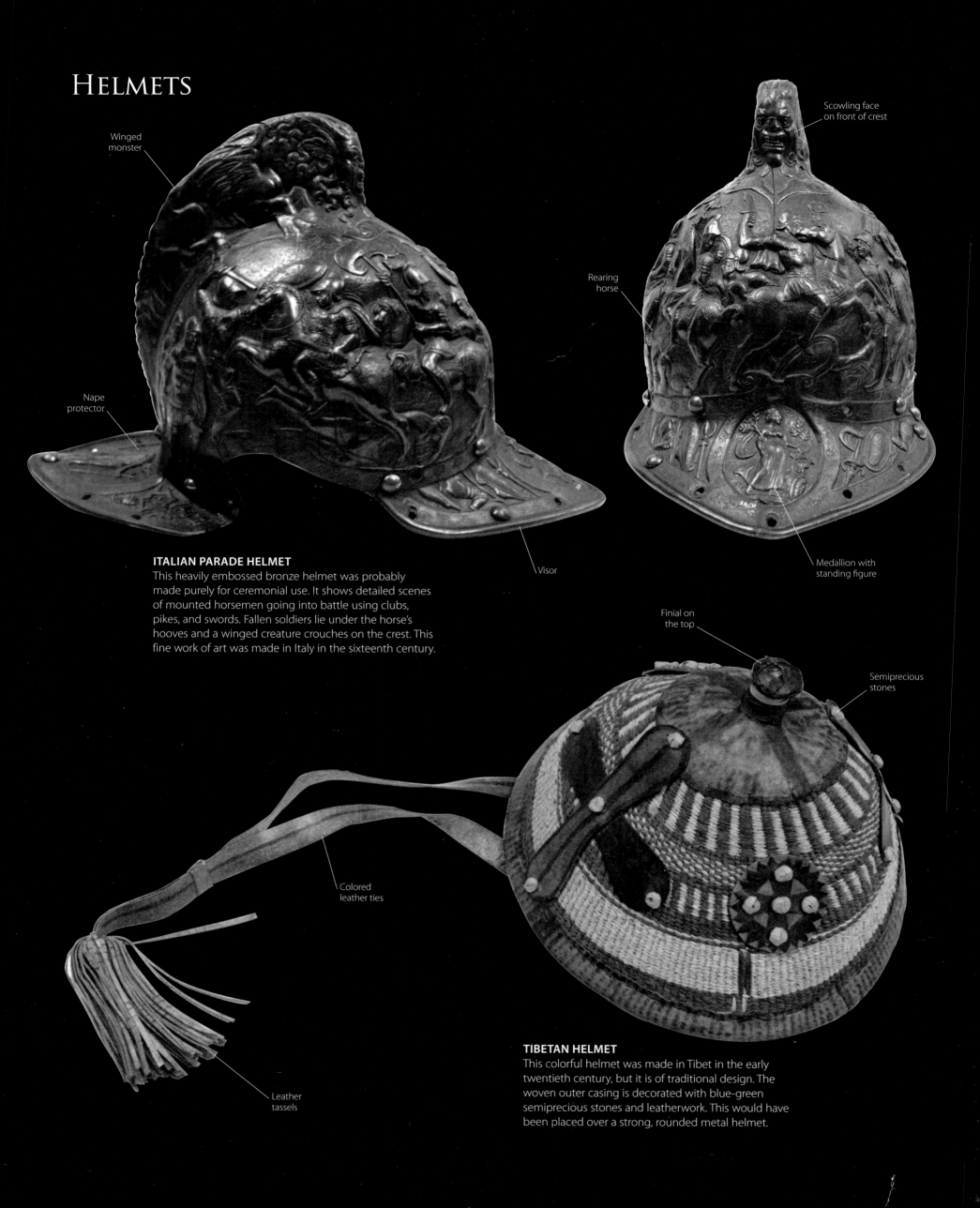

Helmets

Winged
monster

Nape
protector

Scowling face
on front of crest

Rearing
horse

Visor

Medallion with
standing figure

ITALIAN PARADE HELMET

This heavily embossed bronze helmet was probably
made purely for ceremonial use. It shows detailed scenes
of mounted horsemen going into battle using clubs,
pikes, and swords. Fallen soldiers lie under the horse's
hooves and a winged creature crouches on the crest. This
fine work of art was made in Italy in the sixteenth century.

Finial on
the top

Semiprecious
stones

Colored
leather ties

Leather
tassels

TIBETAN HELMET

This colorful helmet was made in Tibet in the early
twentieth century, but it is of traditional design. The
woven outer casing is decorated with blue-green
semiprecious stones and leatherwork. This would have
been placed over a strong, rounded metal helmet.

Traditional style
pith helmet

Wide rim

GORDON HIGHLANDER'S HELMET
This helmet dates from 1882. The Gordon
Highlander's were formed in 1794 and
disbanded in 1994. They saw active service
in many parts of the world, including India,
Afghanistan, and South Africa.

Strong steel
casing

STAHLHELM
The steel helmet that was used by the
Germans in both world wars has a
distinctive coal-scuttle shape recognizable
the world over. Several versions were made
for different situations.

Silver crest
over top

NAZI HELMET
This Nazi helmet has a silver-colored crest
over the top indicating that the wearer was
either in the fire bridage or part of the fire
protection police force.

JAPANESE HELMET
This is a Japanese helmet from World War II. It is very
similar to the British Brodie helmet. Given the name type
92, it was known as a tetsubo (steel cap) in Japanese, but
the soldiers also called it tetsukabuto (steel helmet). The
steel was poor quality and offered little protection.

Glory with
thirteen stars

Khaki wool
fabric

Gold braid

US ARMY OFFICER'S VISOR HAT
This visor hat dates from the Vietnam War
and has the spread-eagle insignia. The
eagle clutches an olive branch in one talon
and thirteen arrows in the other. The oak
leaves on the visor indicate that it
belonged to a senior officer.

Shields & Gun Shields

Brass rim strengthens the edge

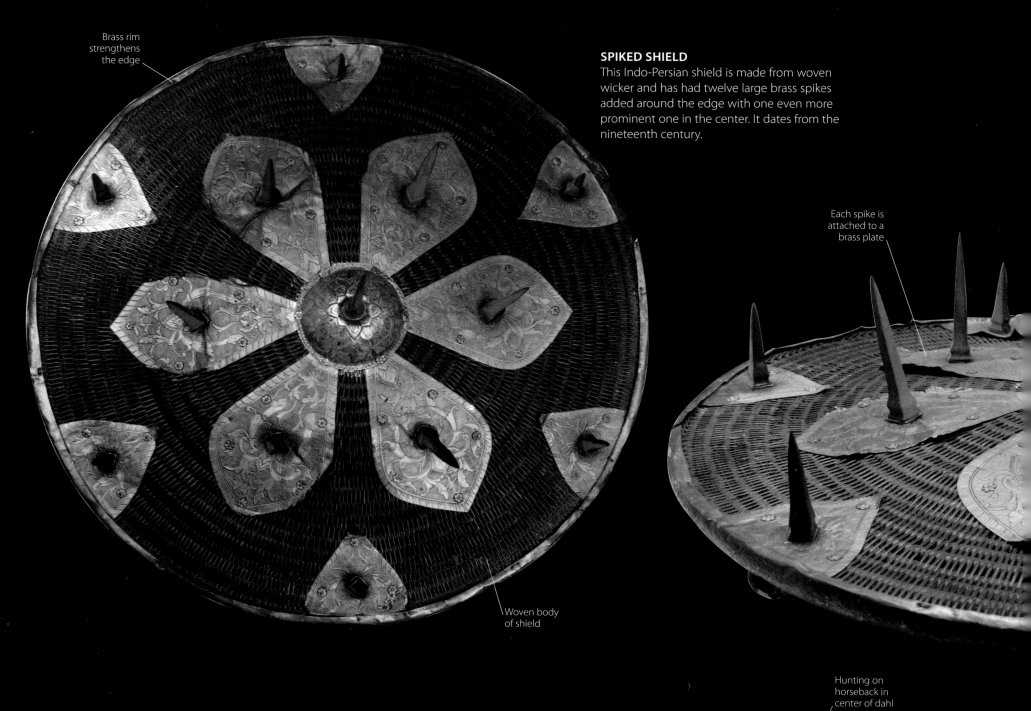

Woven body of shield

Each spike is attached to a brass plate

SPIKED SHIELD

This Indo-Persian shield is made from woven wicker and has had twelve large brass spikes added around the edge with one even more prominent one in the center. It dates from the nineteenth century.

Brass boss

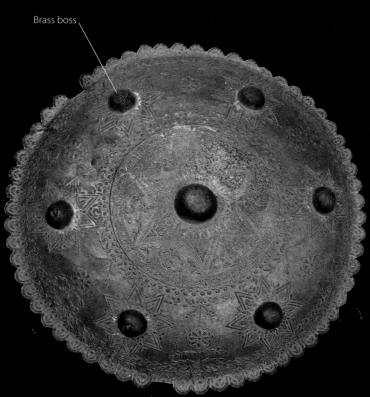

PERSIAN SHIELD

This shield is made of brass and has a scalloped rim. Each of the seven bosses forms the center of an embossed star and the surface has fine decorative detailing. It dates from the fifteenth century.

Hunting on horseback in center of dahl

DHAL

An Indo-Persian dhal (shield), beautifully painted with court and landscape scenes. Dhal were often covered with leather (including rhinoceros hide) and embellished with precious stones.

Scenes from everyday life

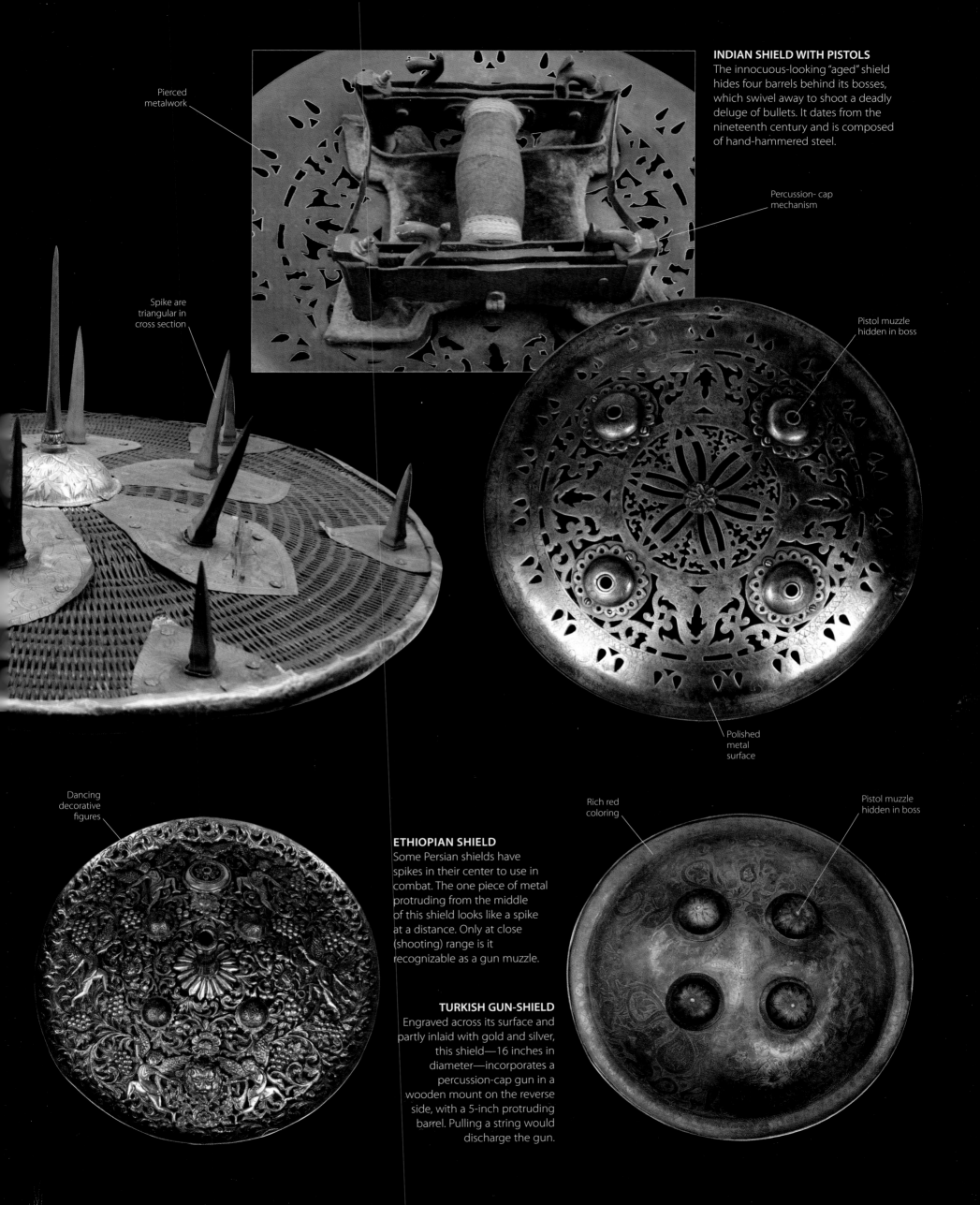

INDIAN SHIELD WITH PISTOLS
The innocuous-looking "aged" shield hides four barrels behind its bosses, which swivel away to shoot a deadly deluge of bullets. It dates from the nineteenth century and is composed of hand-hammered steel.

Pierced metalwork

Percussion- cap mechanism

Spike are triangular in cross section

Pistol muzzle hidden in boss

Polished metal surface

Dancing decorative figures

Rich red coloring

Pistol muzzle hidden in boss

ETHIOPIAN SHIELD
Some Persian shields have spikes in their center to use in combat. The one piece of metal protruding from the middle of this shield looks like a spike at a distance. Only at close (shooting) range is it recognizable as a gun muzzle.

TURKISH GUN-SHIELD
Engraved across its surface and partly inlaid with gold and silver, this shield—16 inches in diameter—incorporates a percussion-cap gun in a wooden mount on the reverse side, with a 5-inch protruding barrel. Pulling a string would discharge the gun.

Shields & Body Armor

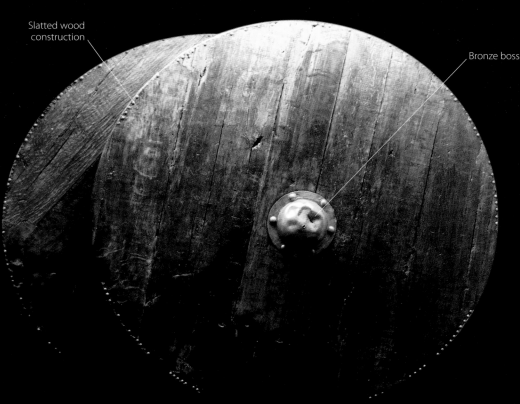

Slatted wood construction

Bronze boss

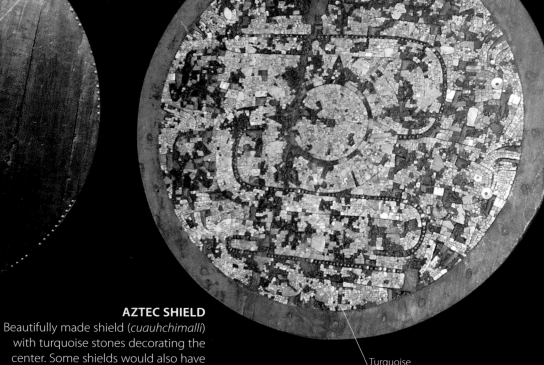

Wooden frame

Turquoise mozaic

THORSBERG SHIELDS

These comparatively plain wooden shields are decorated with bronze central bosses. Dating to the third century BC, they were found near Süderbrarup Anglia in Germany.

AZTEC SHIELD

Beautifully made shield (*cuauhchimalli*) with turquoise stones decorating the center. Some shields would also have feathers around the lower edge.

Tiny pieces of colored iron

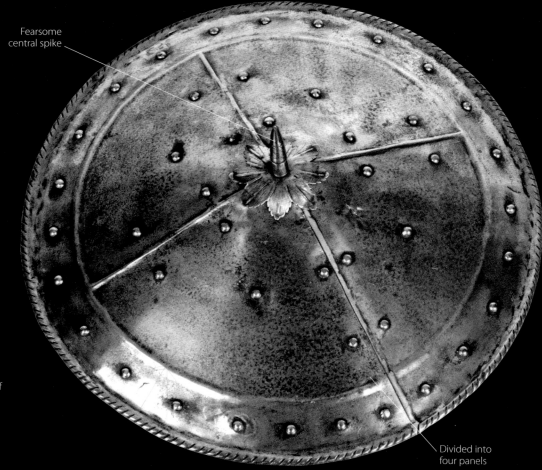

Fearsome central spike

Divided into four panels

NANYUE ARMOR

From the mausoleum of the Nanyue King, this is a reproduction of the king's body armor. It is made up of 709 pieces of iron fastened with silk thread, which allowed the wearer to move more easily. Nanyue is on the border of China and Vietnam.

SPIKE SHIELD

A sixteenth-century European shield with a spike in its center. During the medieval era, large shields gave way to the smaller, lighter buckler (apparently from an Old French word meaning "fist of metal"), which could be used to parry an opponent's sword or a blow from a mace.

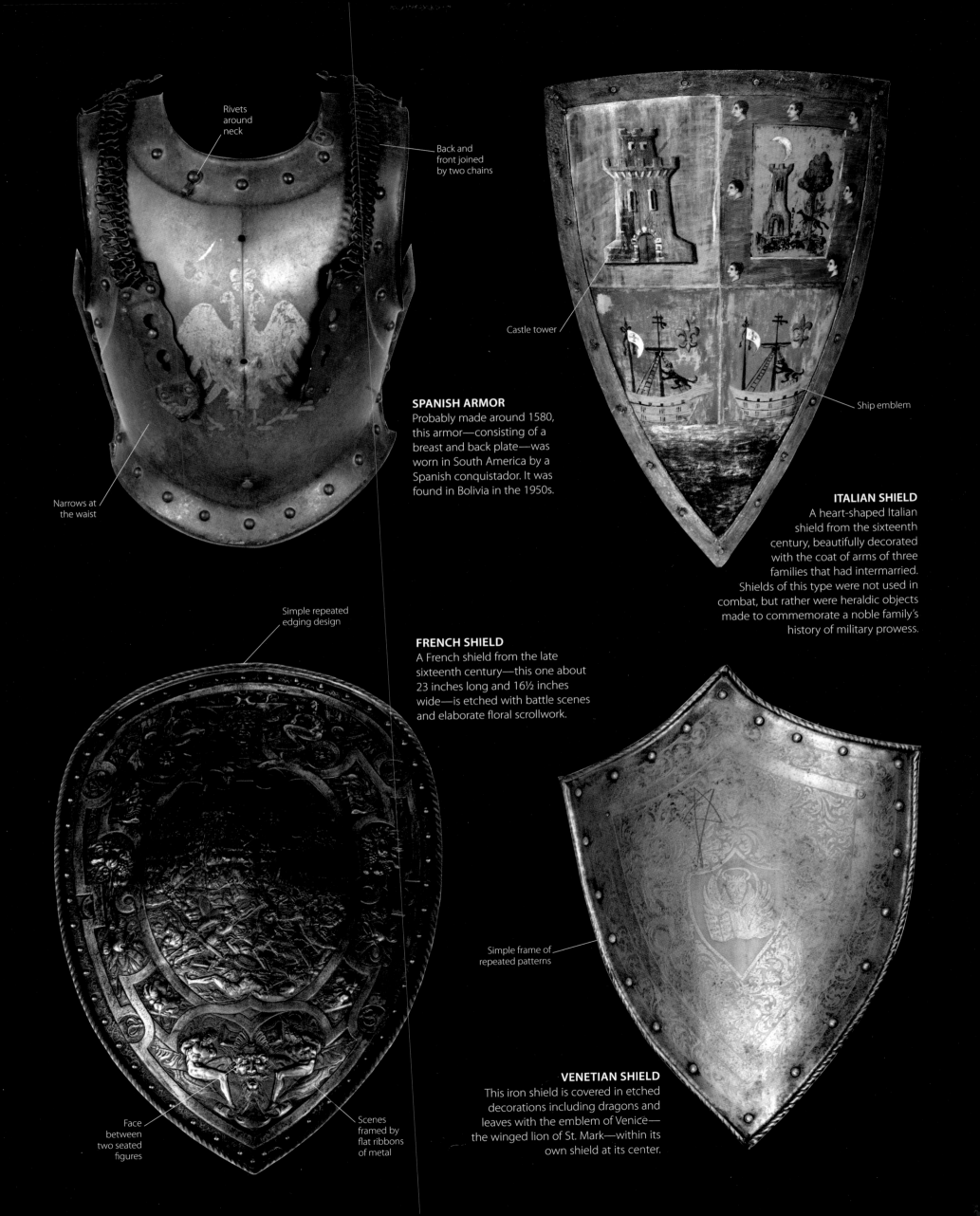

SPANISH ARMOR
Probably made around 1580, this armor—consisting of a breast and back plate—was worn in South America by a Spanish conquistador. It was found in Bolivia in the 1950s.

Rivets around neck

Back and front joined by two chains

Narrows at the waist

Castle tower

Ship emblem

ITALIAN SHIELD
A heart-shaped Italian shield from the sixteenth century, beautifully decorated with the coat of arms of three families that had intermarried. Shields of this type were not used in combat, but rather were heraldic objects made to commemorate a noble family's history of military prowess.

Simple repeated edging design

FRENCH SHIELD
A French shield from the late sixteenth century—this one about 23 inches long and 16½ inches wide—is etched with battle scenes and elaborate floral scrollwork.

Simple frame of repeated patterns

Face between two seated figures

Scenes framed by flat ribbons of metal

VENETIAN SHIELD
This iron shield is covered in etched decorations including dragons and leaves with the emblem of Venice—the winged lion of St. Mark—within its own shield at its center.

POLE ARMS AND AXES CONTINUED . . .

Bronze decoration

Round blade

QI BATTLE-AX
This unusually shaped battle-ax was used by warriors in Yunnan Province in China. It is made of bronze and has a round blade. Near the "eye", which is used to fix the ax to the haft, the socket is decorated with a bronze creature, perhaps for good luck.

Bronze ax-head

TURKISH BATTLE-AX
This battle-ax with its traditionally shaped head and spike was made in Turkey sometime in the sixteenth or seventeenth centuries, but the haft is likely to be more recent.

Shaped top

RUSSIAN POLE ARM
This eighteenth-century pole arm has a long ax blade with a pointed and shaped top. It has to attachments, one on either side of the haft each bound with leather.

INDIAN BATTLE-AX
An eighteenth-century Indian battle-ax with a beautifully etched blade, decorative fluke, and spiked tip.

Metal haft

Decorative tip

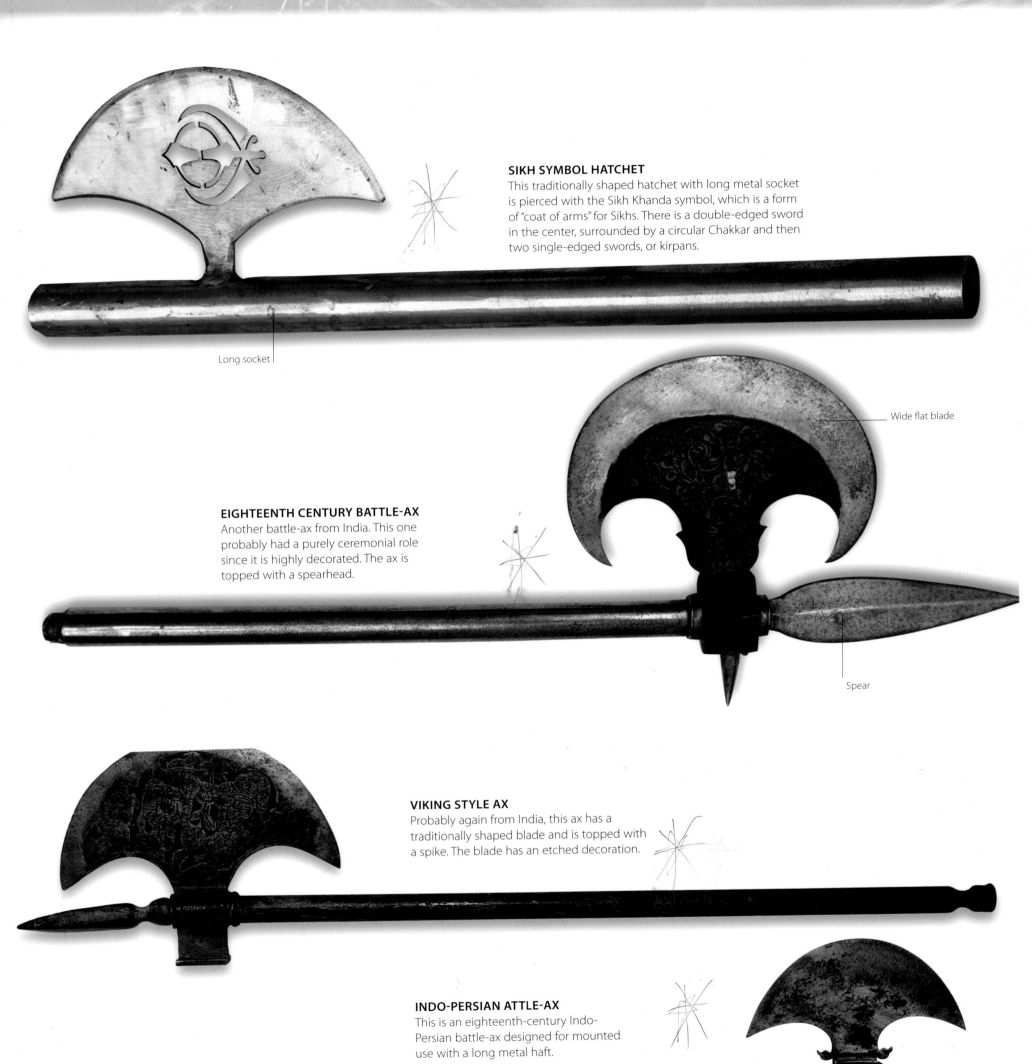

SIKH SYMBOL HATCHET
This traditionally shaped hatchet with long metal socket is pierced with the Sikh Khanda symbol, which is a form of "coat of arms" for Sikhs. There is a double-edged sword in the center, surrounded by a circular Chakkar and then two single-edged swords, or kirpans.

Long socket

Wide flat blade

EIGHTEENTH CENTURY BATTLE-AX
Another battle-ax from India. This one probably had a purely ceremonial role since it is highly decorated. The ax is topped with a spearhead.

Spear

VIKING STYLE AX
Probably again from India, this ax has a traditionally shaped blade and is topped with a spike. The blade has an etched decoration.

INDO-PERSIAN ATTLE-AX
This is an eighteenth-century Indo-Persian battle-ax designed for mounted use with a long metal haft.

POLE ARMS AND AXES CONTINUED . . .

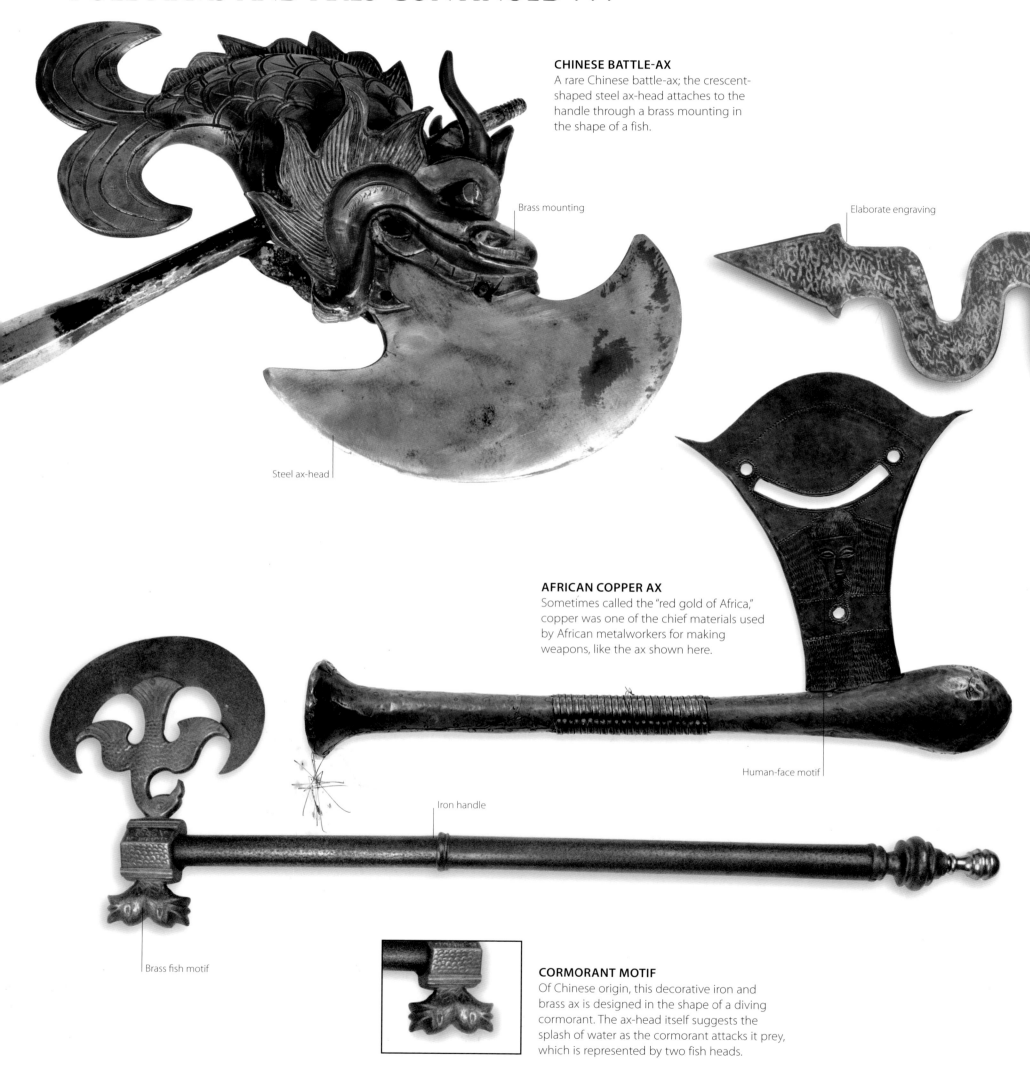

CHINESE BATTLE-AX
A rare Chinese battle-ax; the crescent-shaped steel ax-head attaches to the handle through a brass mounting in the shape of a fish.

Brass mounting

Elaborate engraving

Steel ax-head

AFRICAN COPPER AX
Sometimes called the "red gold of Africa," copper was one of the chief materials used by African metalworkers for making weapons, like the ax shown here.

Human-face motif

Iron handle

Brass fish motif

CORMORANT MOTIF
Of Chinese origin, this decorative iron and brass ax is designed in the shape of a diving cormorant. The ax-head itself suggests the splash of water as the cormorant attacks it prey, which is represented by two fish heads.

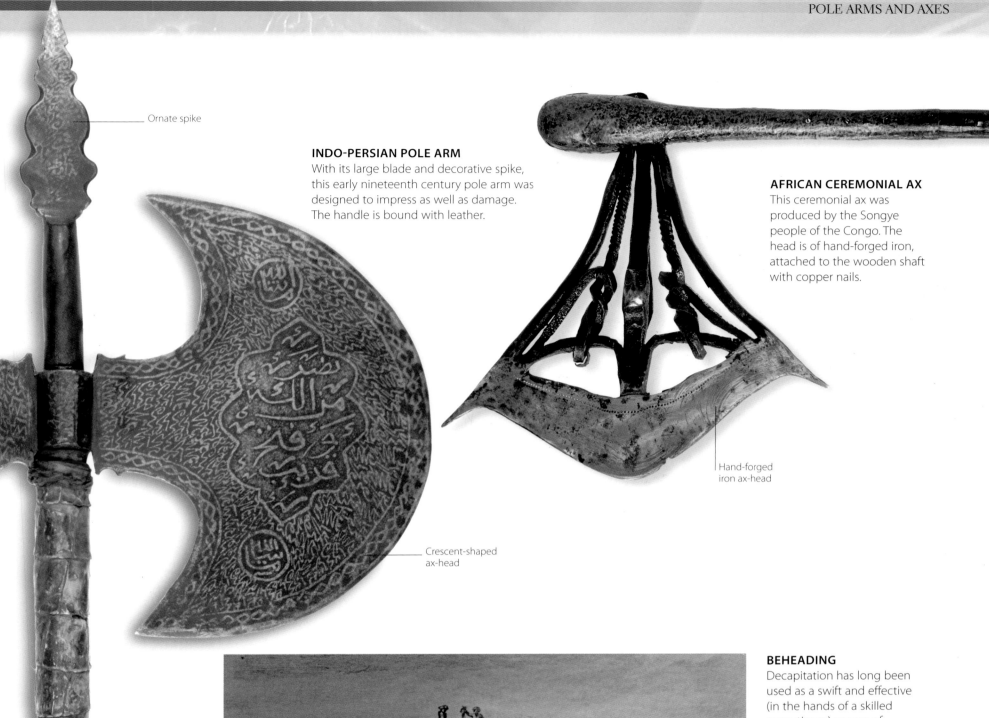

Ornate spike

INDO-PERSIAN POLE ARM
With its large blade and decorative spike, this early nineteenth century pole arm was designed to impress as well as damage. The handle is bound with leather.

AFRICAN CEREMONIAL AX
This ceremonial ax was produced by the Songye people of the Congo. The head is of hand-forged iron, attached to the wooden shaft with copper nails.

Hand-forged iron ax-head

Crescent-shaped ax-head

BEHEADING
Decapitation has long been used as a swift and effective (in the hands of a skilled executioner) means of despatching the death penalty. A large, crescent-shaped ax and a block are the usual tools of the trade; specialty swords are also employed (without a block).

INDONESIAN SWORD
Thought to be a beheading sword, the blade of this late nineteenth-century weapon has a hooked and serrated tip, sharpened on the opposite side. There are four holes in the blade.

Serated edge

KUKRI

The kukri, or *khukuri*, is a highly celebrated fighting knife. Developed by the Ghurkha people of Nepal, it has a blade of 12 inches or longer with a distinct "kink." Alhough relatively heavy—up to 2 pounds—the kukri is remarkably ergonomic. Said to be able to balance vertically on a finger, it is capable of taking off an opponent's head or arm with a single blow. The weapon first came to the attention of the West when British forces encountered it in the Anglo-Nepalese War (1814–16). Subsequently, Ghurkha warriors began serving with the British Army—a tradition that continues to this day. They brought with them their kukris—usually made by village craftsmen of a distinct caste—and used them to deadly effect in both world wars and in colonial conflicts.

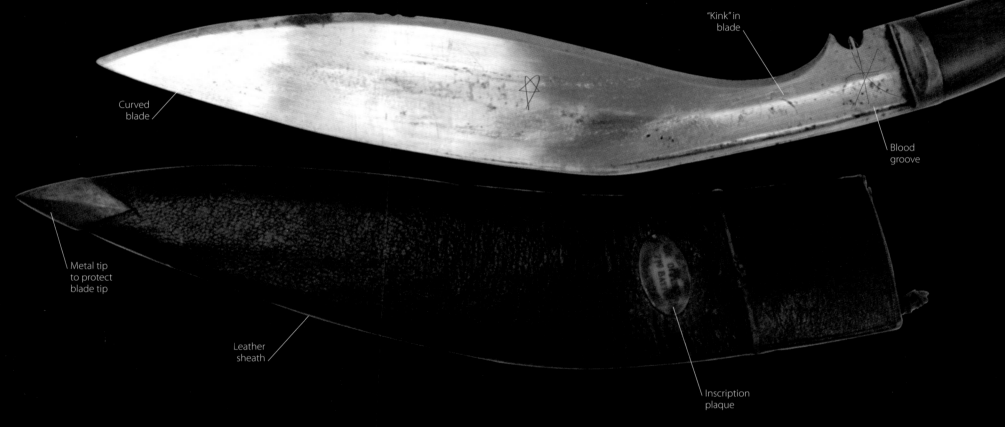

"Kink" in blade

Curved blade

Blood groove

Metal tip to protect blade tip

Leather sheath

Inscription plaque

NASIRI BATTALION
Two Nasiri battalions—eventually the 1st Gurkha rifles—were created from Gurkhas defeated in the Anglo-Nepalese War 1816, so beginning the Gurkha's long and loyal allegiance to the British. "Nasiri" means friendly, an allusion to the new relationship.

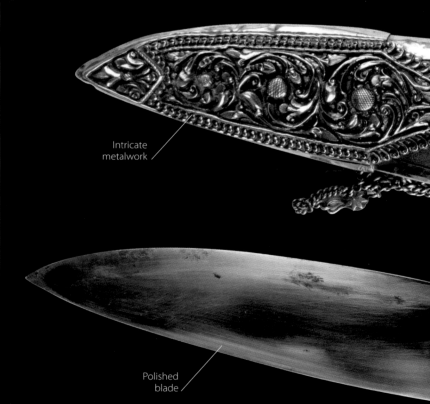

Intricate metalwork

Polished blade

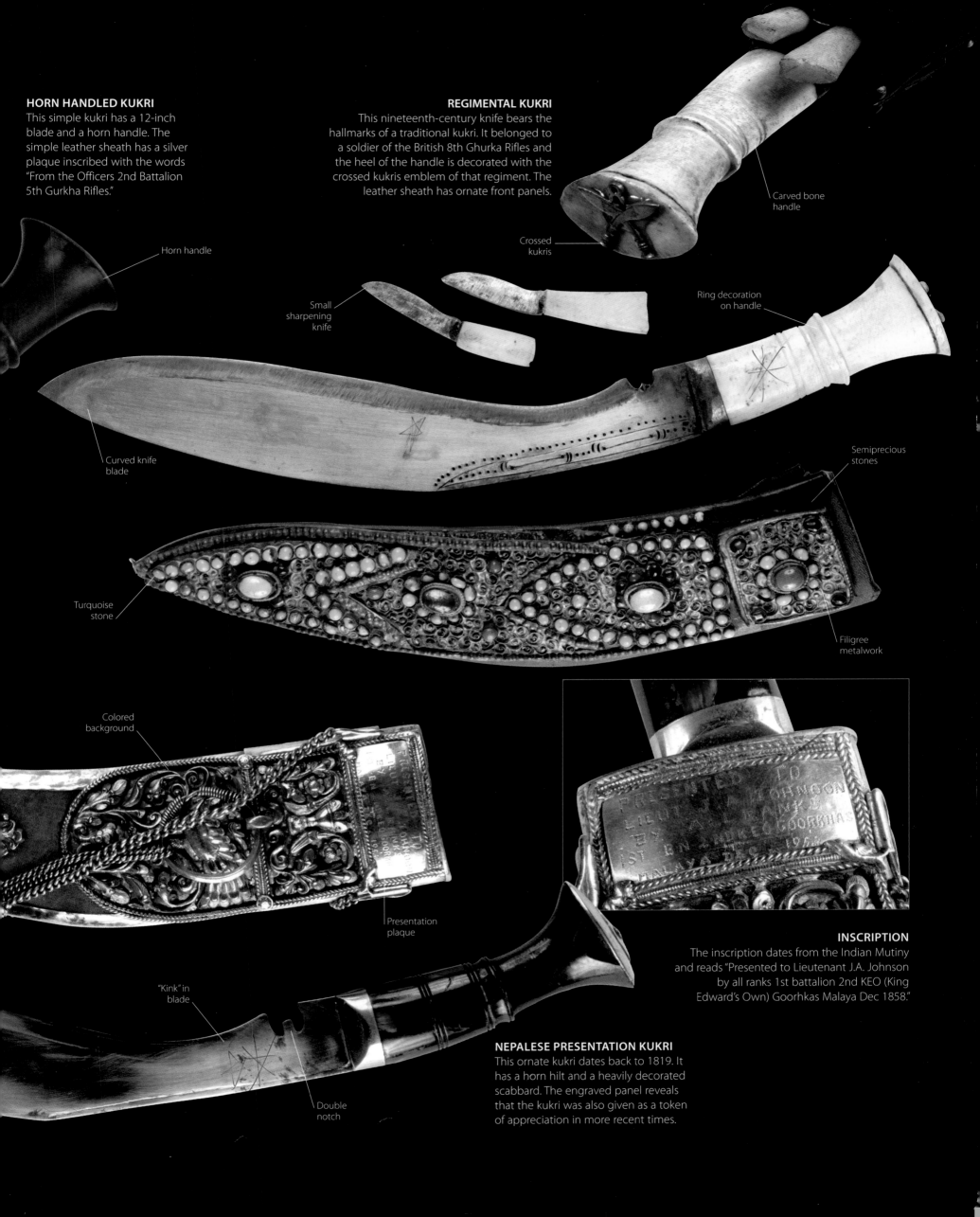

HORN HANDLED KUKRI

This simple kukri has a 12-inch blade and a horn handle. The simple leather sheath has a silver plaque inscribed with the words "From the Officers 2nd Battalion 5th Gurkha Rifles."

Horn handle

Curved knife blade

REGIMENTAL KUKRI

This nineteenth-century knife bears the hallmarks of a traditional kukri. It belonged to a soldier of the British 8th Ghurka Rifles and the heel of the handle is decorated with the crossed kukris emblem of that regiment. The leather sheath has ornate front panels.

Carved bone handle

Crossed kukris

Small sharpening knife

Ring decoration on handle

Semiprecious stones

Turquoise stone

Filigree metalwork

Colored background

Presentation plaque

"Kink" in blade

Double notch

INSCRIPTION

The inscription dates from the Indian Mutiny and reads "Presented to Lieutenant J.A. Johnson by all ranks 1st battalion 2nd KEO (King Edward's Own) Goorhkas Malaya Dec 1858."

NEPALESE PRESENTATION KUKRI

This ornate kukri dates back to 1819. It has a horn hilt and a heavily decorated scabbard. The engraved panel reveals that the kukri was also given as a token of appreciation in more recent times.

DAGGERS AND FIGHTING KNIVES

A dagger is simply a short-bladed knife, held in one hand and intended for stabbing. The name may come from the ancient Roman province of Dacia (now Romania) and probably originally meant "Dacian knife." Daggerlike weapons have been in use since prehistoric times; they predate the sword, and versions are found in cultures around the world. The dagger's small size limited its usefulness in warfare, but that same attribute—and the ease of concealment—made it a favorite of both criminals and assassins. Many cultures have also adopted knives of an intermediate size between the dagger and sword; these weapons are generally known as fighting knives.

THE DAGGER IN THE WEST

In medieval and Renaissance times, the dagger served a special function: It was used to penetrate armor where plates joined together or through other openings, like a helmet visor. If he was knocked off his horse or otherwise disabled, a knight became easy prey to a mere foot soldier with a dagger. One of the most famous types of dagger, the narrow-bladed Italian stiletto, was developed specifically for this purpose. In the sixteenth century, a new style of sword fighting gained popularity in Europe, in which a dagger was held in one hand (usually the left) and the sword in the other, with the dagger being used to parry the opponent's sword thrusts.

The growing popularity of the pistol as a personal defense (or offense) weapon in the 1700s led to a decline in the dagger's use, although some nations' military officers and members of paramilitary and political groups continued to wear them for ceremonial purposes. Fighting knives had a resurgence during the trench warfare of World War I and later they were an important weapon for special forces—for "silent elimination" of sentries, for example.

EUROPEAN

LEFT-HANDED DAGGER
A left-handed dagger, designed to be used in conjunction with a sword. These daggers, like the eighteenth-century French one shown, sometimes had substantial down-curved quillions that could be used to trap the opponent's blade long enough to get in a sword thrust.

NAVAL DIRK
A relatively long knife, the Scottish dirk (the word probably comes from the Gaelic *sgian dearg*, or "red knife," was often used in conjunction with the claymore broadsword. This example, with a gilt brass handle with ivory grips, is a British naval model from about 1770.

COSSACK KINDJAL
Sometimes called the "Circassian dagger," from its origin with the Circassian people of the Caucasus Mountains, the *kindjal* was adopted by the Cossacks of the Russian Empire from the eighteenth century onward. This nineteenth-century example has a 14-inch blade and a hilt inlaid with semiprecious stones. In the hands of Cossack warriors, it was used in conjunction with the *shashka* sword.

Down-curved quillons

Ivory grip

Decorated hilt

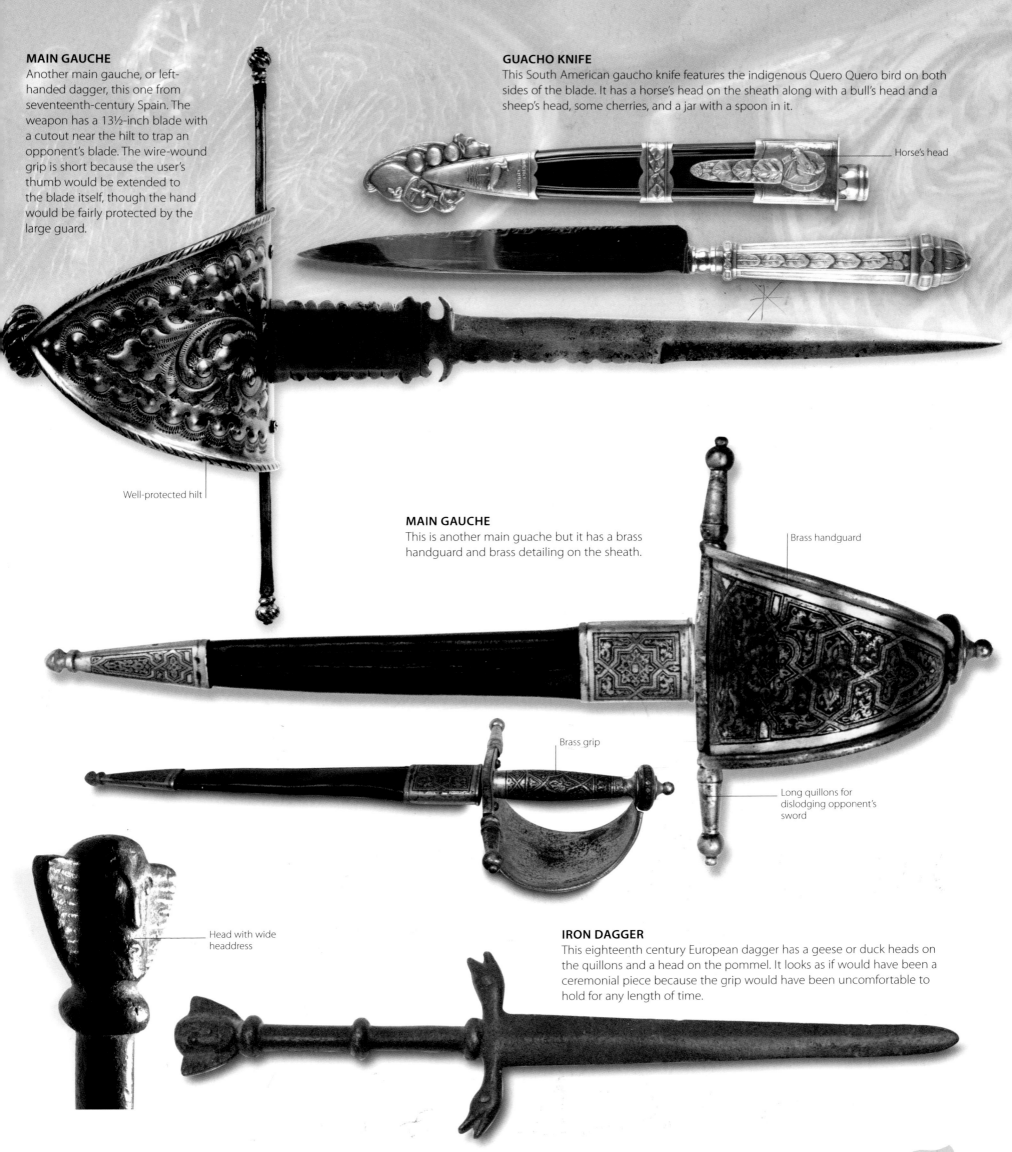

MAIN GAUCHE
Another main gauche, or left-handed dagger, this one from seventeenth-century Spain. The weapon has a 13½-inch blade with a cutout near the hilt to trap an opponent's blade. The wire-wound grip is short because the user's thumb would be extended to the blade itself, though the hand would be fairly protected by the large guard.

Well-protected hilt

GUACHO KNIFE
This South American gaucho knife features the indigenous Quero Quero bird on both sides of the blade. It has a horse's head on the sheath along with a bull's head and a sheep's head, some cherries, and a jar with a spoon in it.

Horse's head

MAIN GAUCHE
This is another main guache but it has a brass handguard and brass detailing on the sheath.

Brass handguard

Brass grip

Long quillons for dislodging opponent's sword

Head with wide headdress

IRON DAGGER
This eighteenth century European dagger has a geese or duck heads on the quillons and a head on the pommel. It looks as if would have been a ceremonial piece because the grip would have been uncomfortable to hold for any length of time.

EUROPEAN CONTINUED . . .

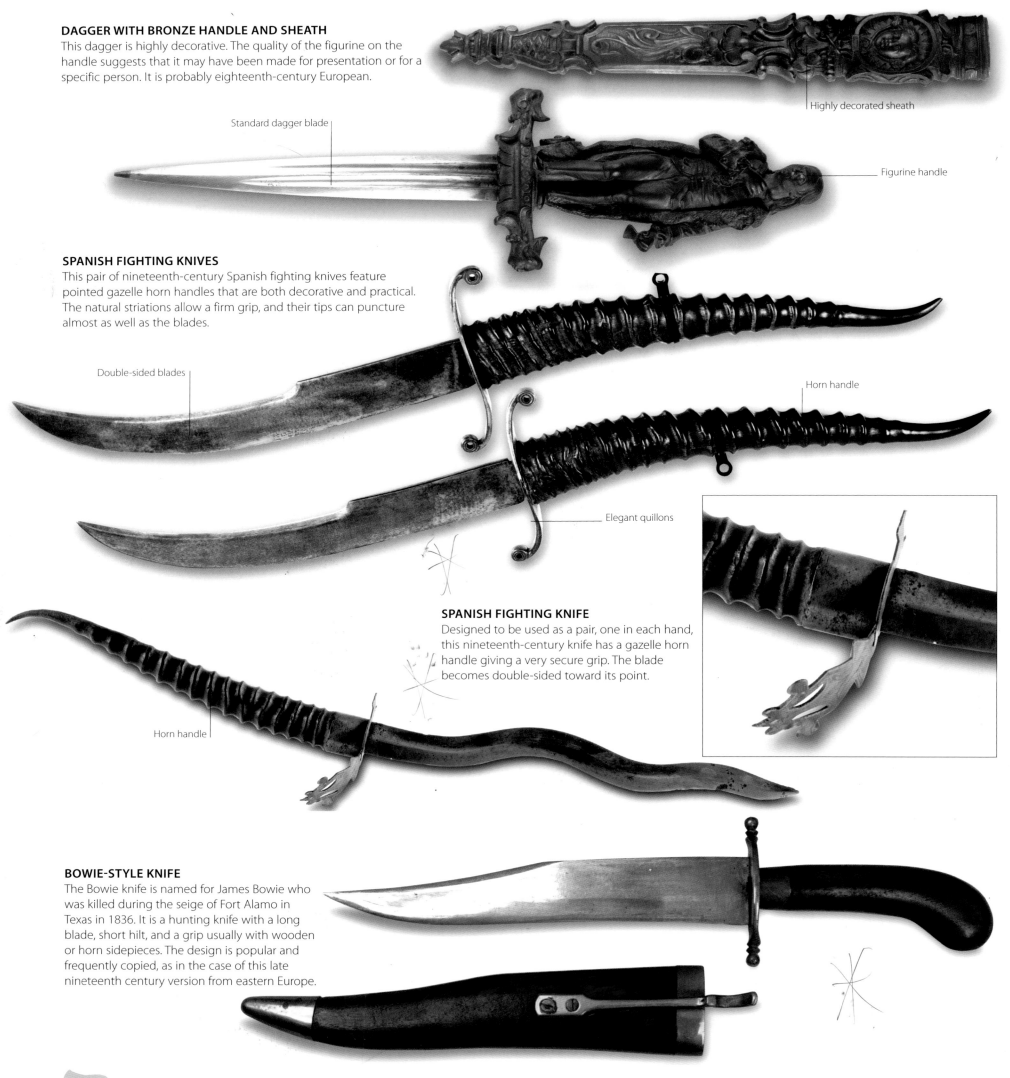

DAGGER WITH BRONZE HANDLE AND SHEATH
This dagger is highly decorative. The quality of the figurine on the handle suggests that it may have been made for presentation or for a specific person. It is probably eighteenth-century European.

Highly decorated sheath

Standard dagger blade

Figurine handle

SPANISH FIGHTING KNIVES
This pair of nineteenth-century Spanish fighting knives feature pointed gazelle horn handles that are both decorative and practical. The natural striations allow a firm grip, and their tips can puncture almost as well as the blades.

Double-sided blades

Horn handle

Elegant quillons

SPANISH FIGHTING KNIFE
Designed to be used as a pair, one in each hand, this nineteenth-century knife has a gazelle horn handle giving a very secure grip. The blade becomes double-sided toward its point.

Horn handle

BOWIE-STYLE KNIFE
The Bowie knife is named for James Bowie who was killed during the seige of Fort Alamo in Texas in 1836. It is a hunting knife with a long blade, short hilt, and a grip usually with wooden or horn sidepieces. The design is popular and frequently copied, as in the case of this late nineteenth century version from eastern Europe.

AFRICAN

NORTH AFRICAN DAGGER
A nineteenth-century North African dagger with a sinuous blade, perhaps influenced by Malaysian kris designs.

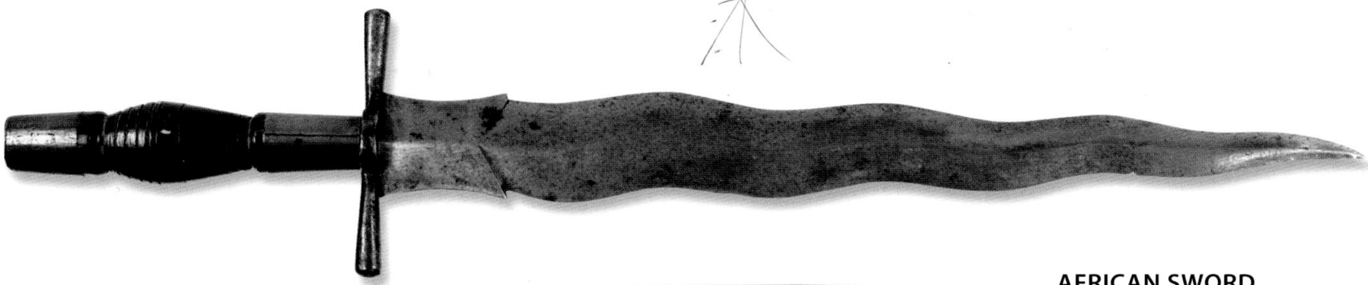

AFRICAN SWORD
A Masai *seme*, or lion knife, from East Africa. It has a double-edged blade that widens from the hilt until just before the tip. This item dates from the late nineteenth century. It would usually have a leather sheath dyed a traditional red color.

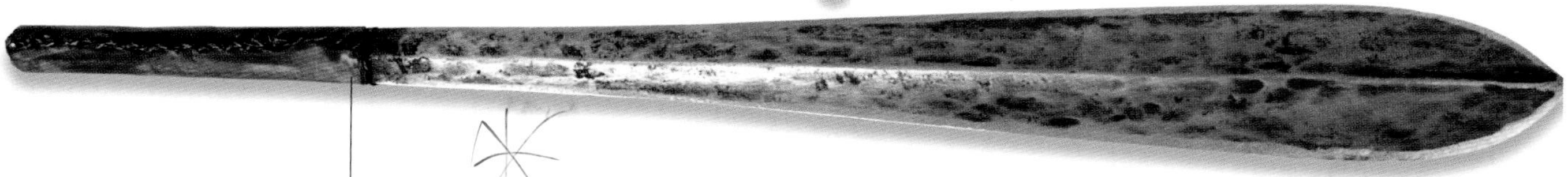

Red handle

WOODEN AFRICAN DAGGER
An example of a twentieth-century African wooden dagger with a fur-covered handle.

Animal hair

AFRICAN RITUAL KNIFE
This African knife, probably made early in the twentieth century, was used in ceremonial rituals. Its hilt is decorated with a tuft of animal hair.

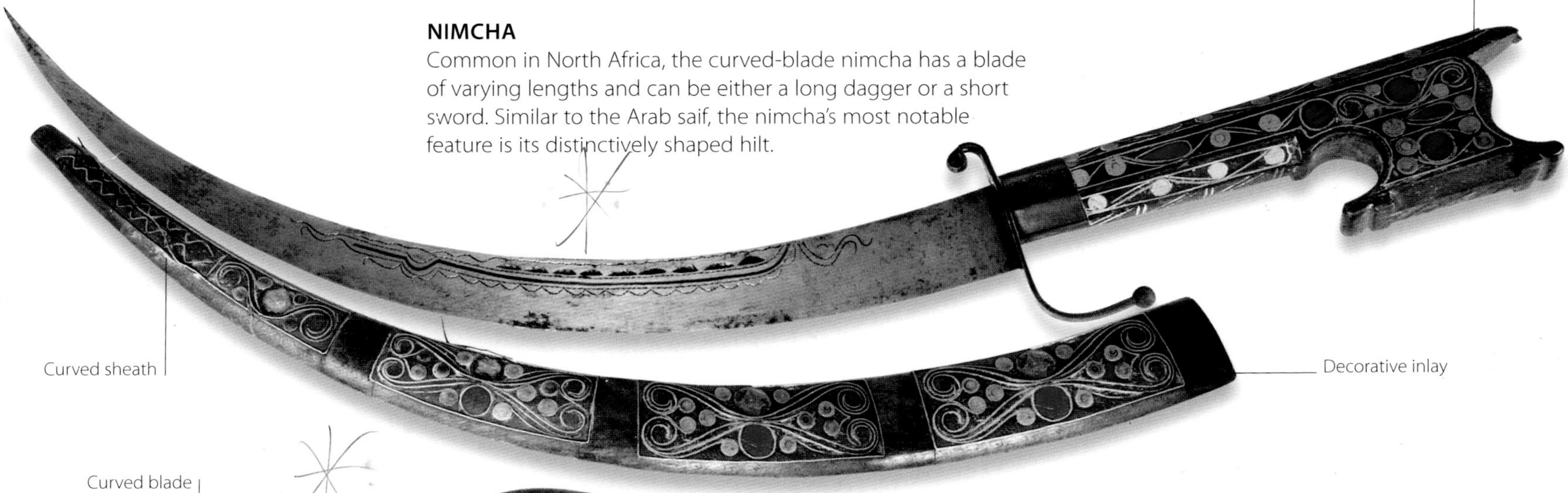

The hilt has a shaped and notched top

NIMCHA
Common in North Africa, the curved-blade nimcha has a blade of varying lengths and can be either a long dagger or a short sword. Similar to the Arab saif, the nimcha's most notable feature is its distinctively shaped hilt.

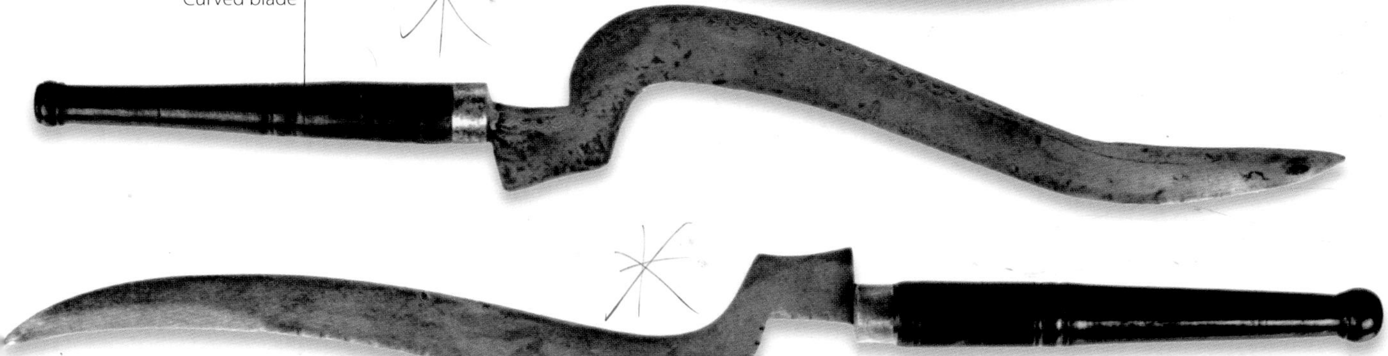

Decorative inlay

Curved sheath

Curved blade

AFRICAN FIGHTING KNIVES
This pair of North African fighting knives have ebony handles .

One of many blades

AFRICAN THROWING BLADE
Many African peoples made use of knives specially designed for throwing. Most had multiple blades to increase the chances of hitting an opponent; they were usually thrown horizontally, from right to left.

JAMBIYA

The jambiya—which may also be spelled jambia, janbiya, or janbia—is a short fighting knife of Middle Eastern origin with a curved, double-sided, steel blade. The people of South Arabia pass their jambiyas from generation to generation. Today they continue to be worn from the belt, especially by the men of Yemen, for whom the weapon is an integral part of status and identity. Etiquette dictates that the blades are removed from their sheaths only in extreme circumstances, or for use as an accessory in traditional dance. The quality of the hilt is understood as an important indicator of the significance of the wearer. Most jambiya hilts are made of wood or the horn of various animals, but the most prestigious are made from African rhinoceros horn.

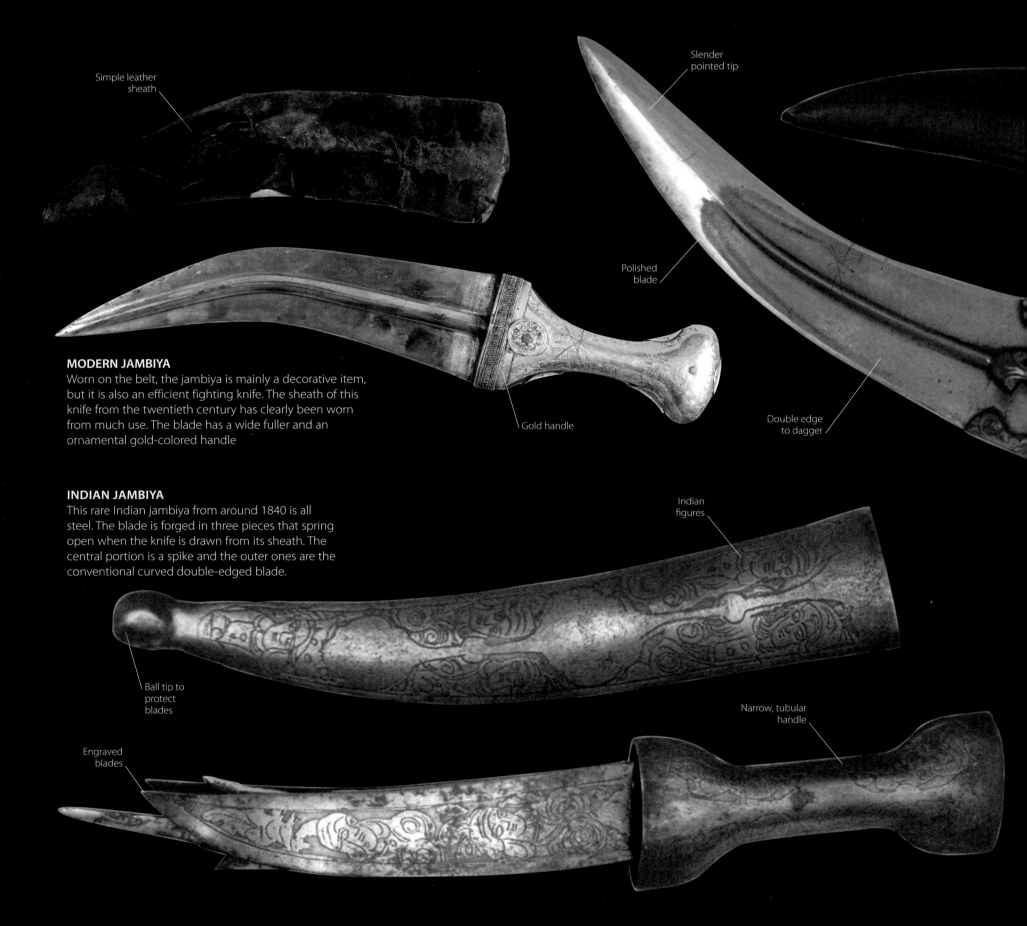

Simple leather sheath

Slender pointed tip

Polished blade

MODERN JAMBIYA
Worn on the belt, the jambiya is mainly a decorative item, but it is also an efficient fighting knife. The sheath of this knife from the twentieth century has clearly been worn from much use. The blade has a wide fuller and an ornamental gold-colored handle

Gold handle

Double edge to dagger

INDIAN JAMBIYA
This rare Indian jambiya from around 1840 is all steel. The blade is forged in three pieces that spring open when the knife is drawn from its sheath. The central portion is a spike and the outer ones are the conventional curved double-edged blade.

Indian figures

Ball tip to protect blades

Narrow, tubular handle

Engraved blades

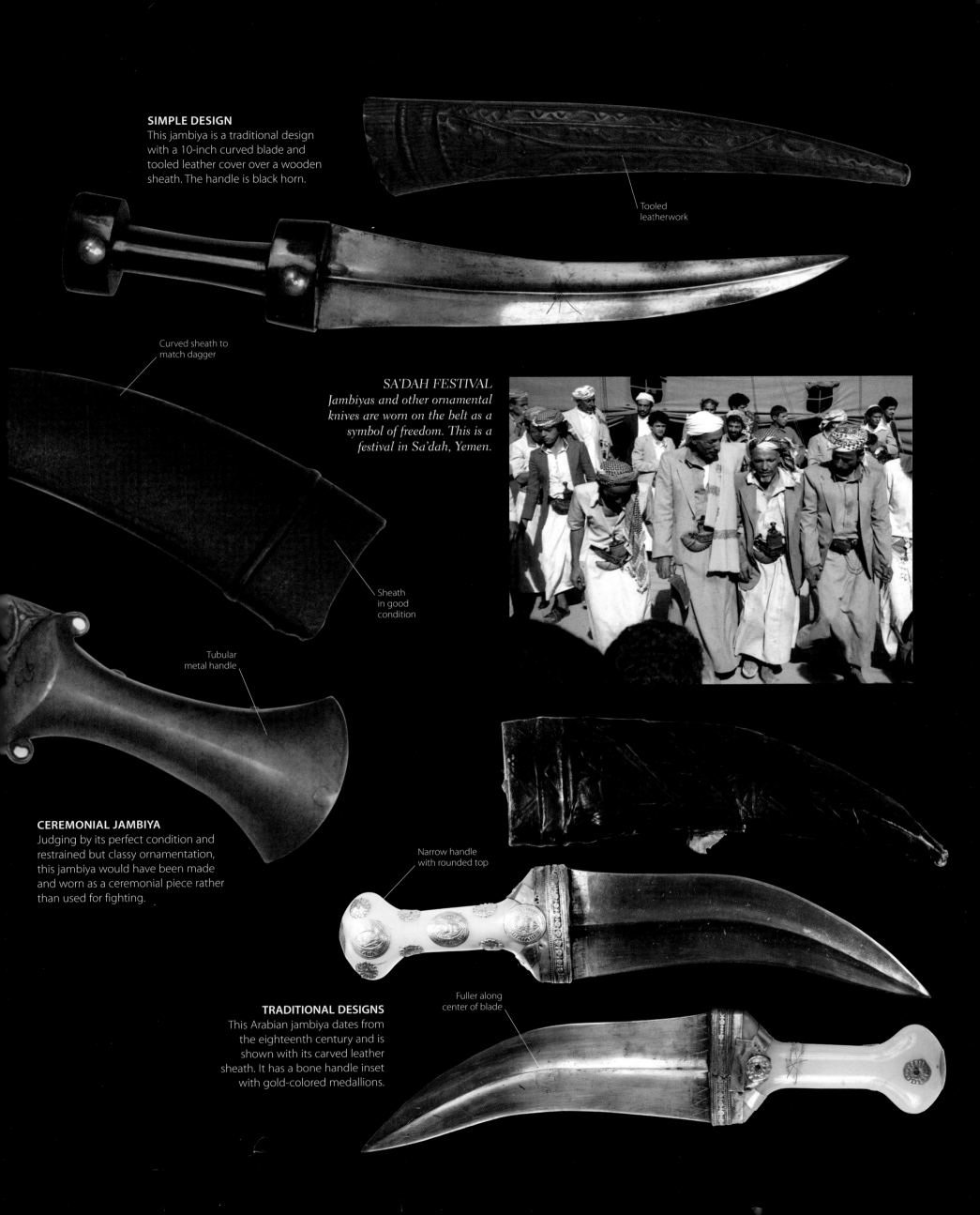

SIMPLE DESIGN
This jambiya is a traditional design with a 10-inch curved blade and tooled leather cover over a wooden sheath. The handle is black horn.

Tooled leatherwork

Curved sheath to match dagger

SA'DAH FESTIVAL
Jambiyas and other ornamental knives are worn on the belt as a symbol of freedom. This is a festival in Sa'dah, Yemen.

Sheath in good condition

Tubular metal handle

CEREMONIAL JAMBIYA
Judging by its perfect condition and restrained but classy ornamentation, this jambiya would have been made and worn as a ceremonial piece rather than used for fighting.

Narrow handle with rounded top

TRADITIONAL DESIGNS
This Arabian jambiya dates from the eighteenth century and is shown with its carved leather sheath. It has a bone handle inset with gold-colored medallions.

Fuller along center of blade

ASIA MINOR

Gold foliage design

Short, carved wood handle

ARABIAN KNIFE

This seventeenth-century Arabian knife has a carved wood handle. Gold ornamentation at the top of the blade gives an indication of how richly decorated it must once have been.

Simple undecorated handle

Each blade tapers to a fine point

PERSIAN THREE-BLADED DAGGERS

Persian three-bladed daggers—in these examples, the blade is made up of three leaves that spring apart when the weapon is pulled from its sheath. The blades are decorated with silver and gold damascening.

Ivory handle

AFGHAN

This eighteenth-century pesh kabz (blade tapering to a slender point) from Afghanistan features gold inlay on the blade.

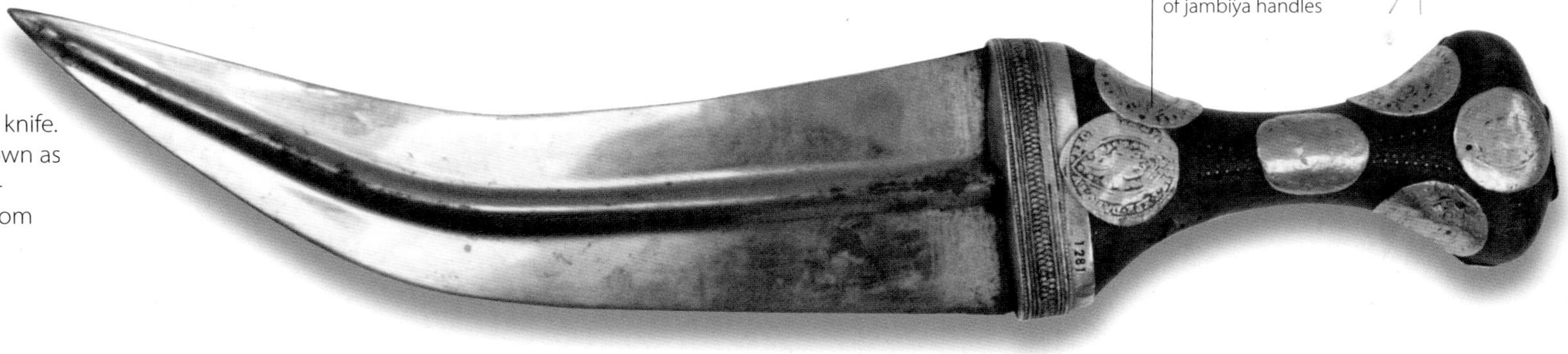

Gold medallions typical of jambiya handles

INDIAN KHANJAR

Khanjar is Arabic for dagger or knife. This style of dagger is also known as a jambiya. This one has a gold-decorated handle and dates from the eighteenth century..

DOUBLE-SPIKED KATARA

Lacking the usual straight handle and with spikes instead of blades, this is nevertheless a formidable weapon that was intended to intimidate as well as to wound.

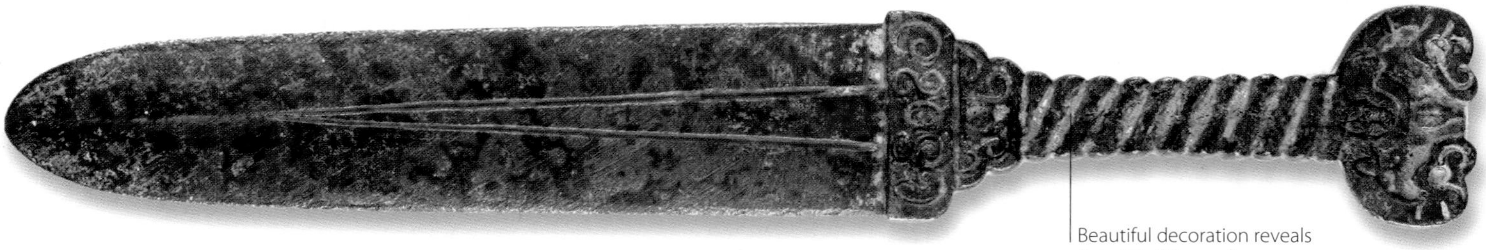

Wavy narrow blade

BRONZE KNIFE

Of an unknown date, this dagger is thought to have been used for display purposes and may be Celtic in origin.

Beautiful decoration reveals the skill of the craftsman

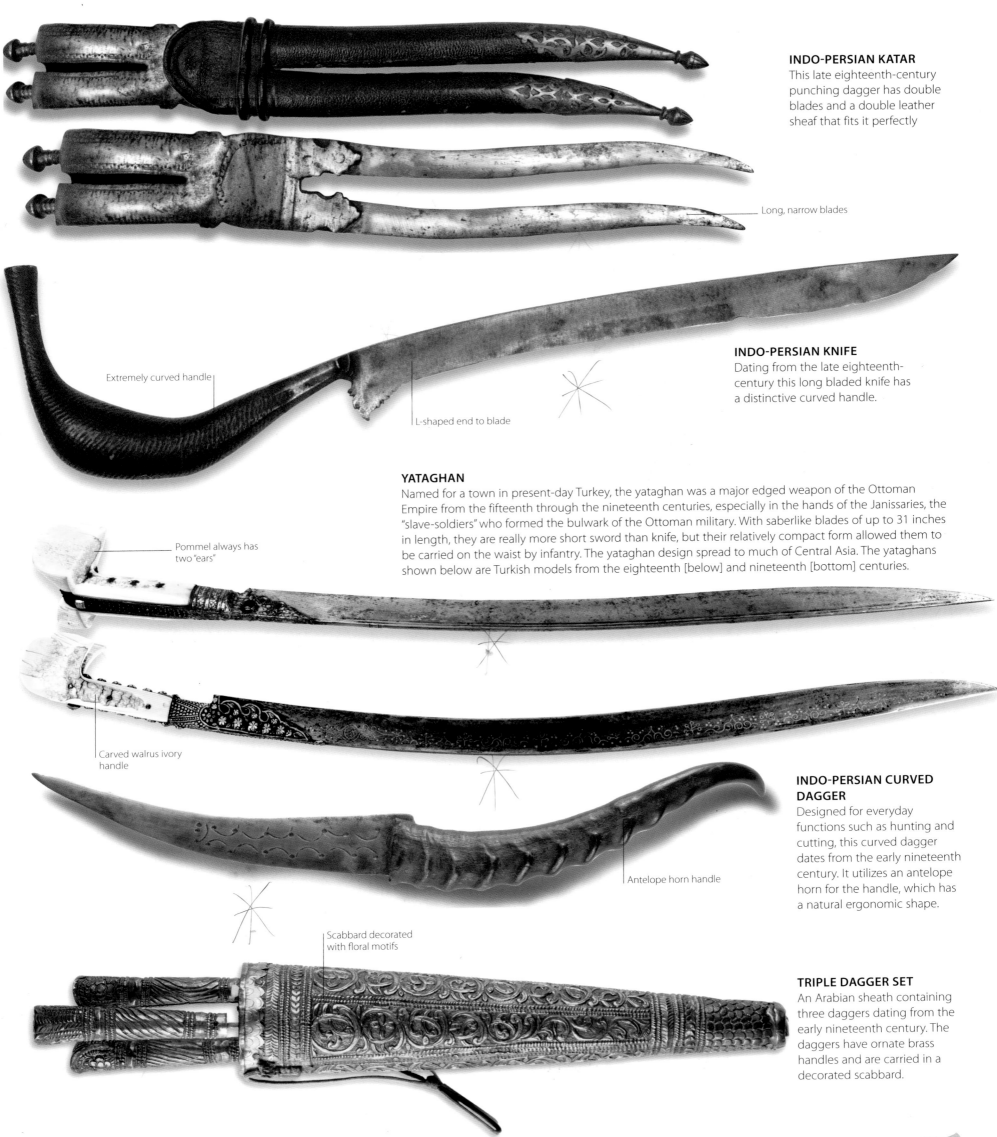

INDO-PERSIAN KATAR
This late eighteenth-century punching dagger has double blades and a double leather sheaf that fits it perfectly

Long, narrow blades

INDO-PERSIAN KNIFE
Dating from the late eighteenth-century this long bladed knife has a distinctive curved handle.

Extremely curved handle

L-shaped end to blade

YATAGHAN
Named for a town in present-day Turkey, the yataghan was a major edged weapon of the Ottoman Empire from the fifteenth through the nineteenth centuries, especially in the hands of the Janissaries, the "slave-soldiers" who formed the bulwark of the Ottoman military. With saberlike blades of up to 31 inches in length, they are really more short sword than knife, but their relatively compact form allowed them to be carried on the waist by infantry. The yataghan design spread to much of Central Asia. The yataghans shown below are Turkish models from the eighteenth [below] and nineteenth [bottom] centuries.

Pommel always has two "ears"

Carved walrus ivory handle

INDO-PERSIAN CURVED DAGGER
Designed for everyday functions such as hunting and cutting, this curved dagger dates from the early nineteenth century. It utilizes an antelope horn for the handle, which has a natural ergonomic shape.

Antelope horn handle

Scabbard decorated with floral motifs

TRIPLE DAGGER SET
An Arabian sheath containing three daggers dating from the early nineteenth century. The daggers have ornate brass handles and are carried in a decorated scabbard.

ASIA MINOR

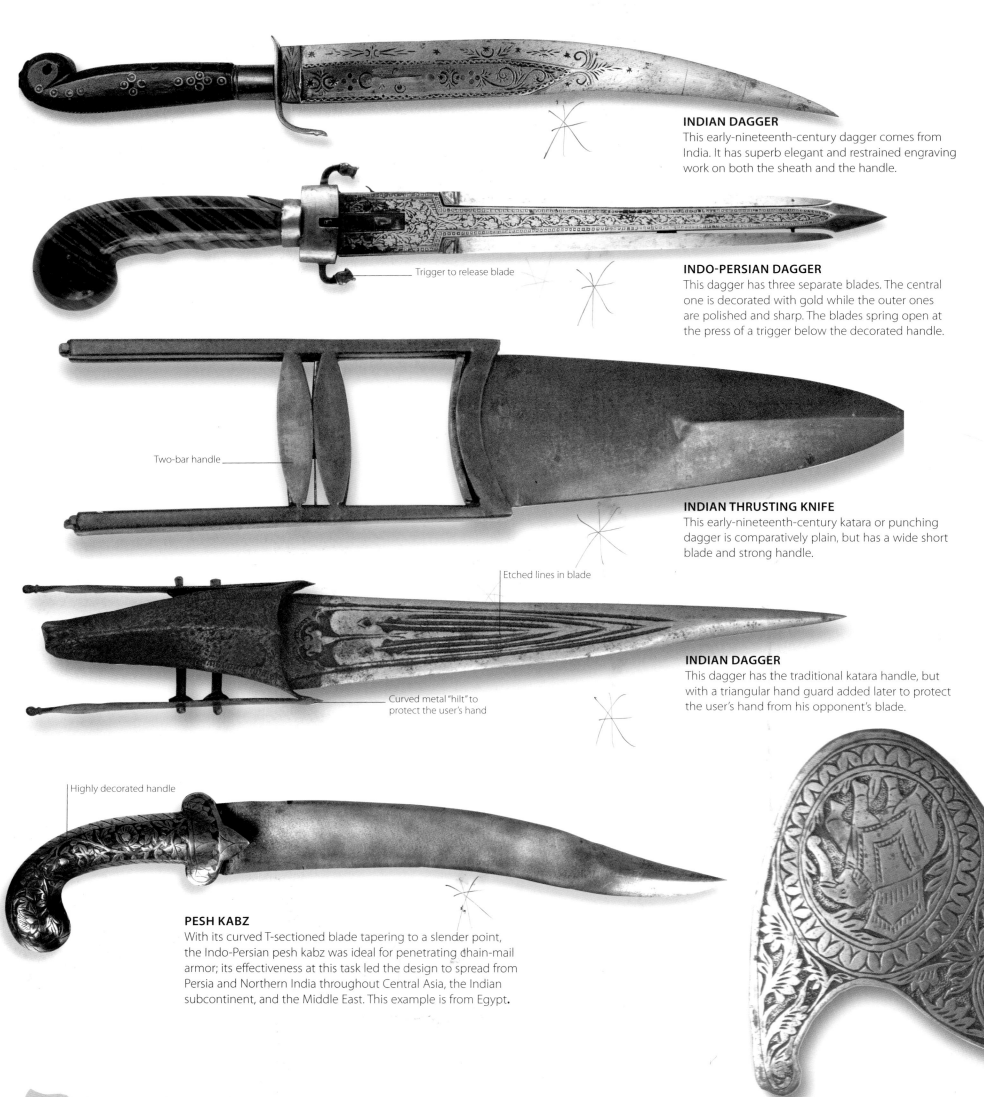

INDIAN DAGGER
This early-nineteenth-century dagger comes from India. It has superb elegant and restrained engraving work on both the sheath and the handle.

Trigger to release blade

INDO-PERSIAN DAGGER
This dagger has three separate blades. The central one is decorated with gold while the outer ones are polished and sharp. The blades spring open at the press of a trigger below the decorated handle.

Two-bar handle

INDIAN THRUSTING KNIFE
This early-nineteenth-century katara or punching dagger is comparatively plain, but has a wide short blade and strong handle.

Etched lines in blade

INDIAN DAGGER
This dagger has the traditional katara handle, but with a triangular hand guard added later to protect the user's hand from his opponent's blade.

Curved metal "hilt" to protect the user's hand

Highly decorated handle

PESH KABZ
With its curved T-sectioned blade tapering to a slender point, the Indo-Persian pesh kabz was ideal for penetrating chain-mail armor; its effectiveness at this task led the design to spread from Persia and Northern India throughout Central Asia, the Indian subcontinent, and the Middle East. This example is from Egypt.

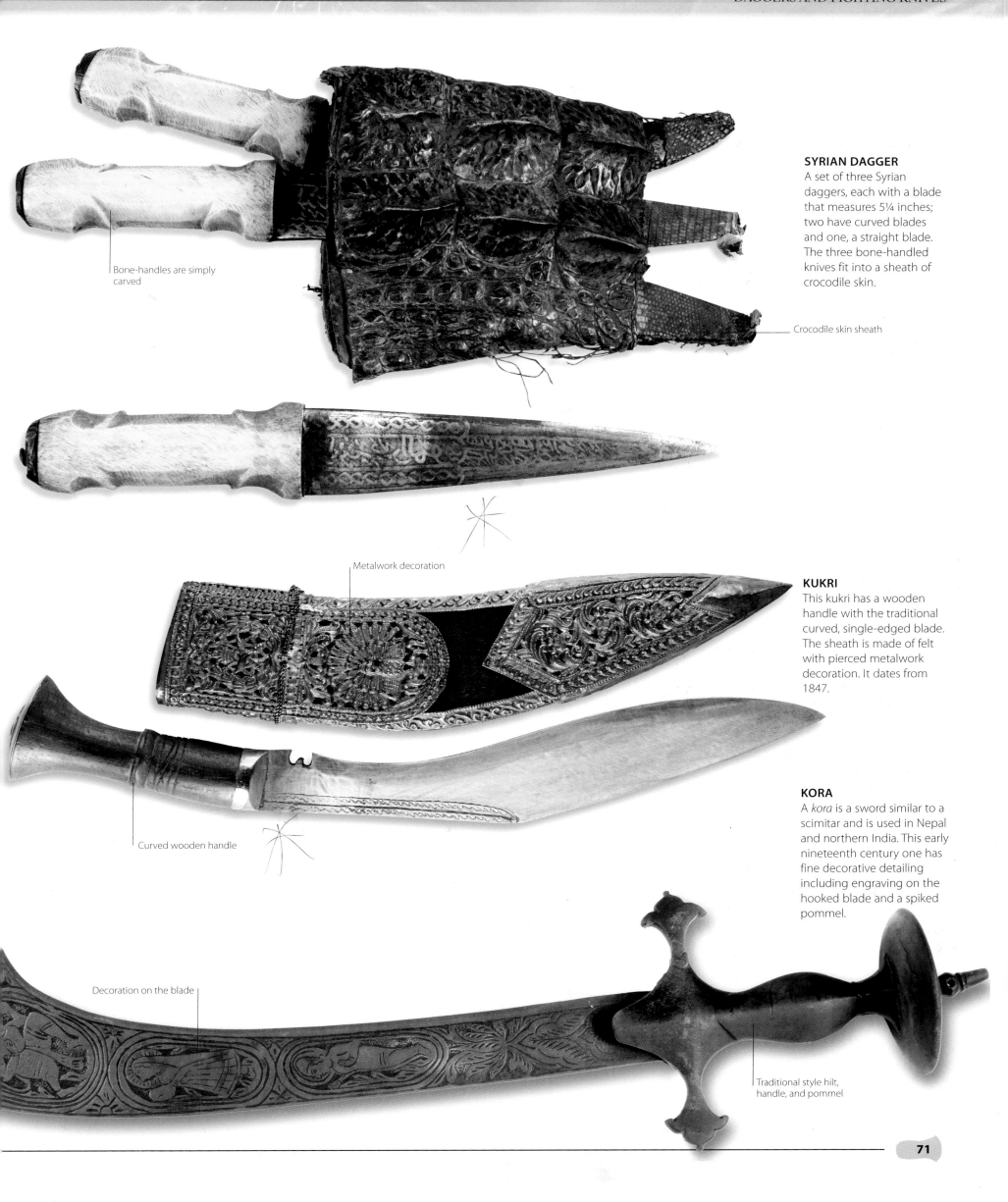

SYRIAN DAGGER

A set of three Syrian daggers, each with a blade that measures 5¼ inches; two have curved blades and one, a straight blade. The three bone-handled knives fit into a sheath of crocodile skin.

Bone-handles are simply carved

Crocodile skin sheath

Metalwork decoration

KUKRI

This kukri has a wooden handle with the traditional curved, single-edged blade. The sheath is made of felt with pierced metalwork decoration. It dates from 1847.

KORA

A *kora* is a sword similar to a scimitar and is used in Nepal and northern India. This early nineteenth century one has fine decorative detailing including engraving on the hooked blade and a spiked pommel.

Curved wooden handle

Decoration on the blade

Traditional style hilt, handle, and pommel

KATARA

Also known as the suwaiya, the katara is a kind of southern Asian push-dagger. The weapon originated in Tamil Nadu, southern India, and was first used by troops of the Deccan states in the medieval period. Instead of a conventional hilt it has an H-shaped, horizontal hand-grip, enabling the user to strike as though with a fist, but with the deadly extension of a blade. Usually aimed at the head or torso, the katara was a formidable attack weapon but, unlike conventional swords, was unsuited to parrying and defense. Fighters armed with the katara had to be nimble, darting in to inflict a lethal blow, then away to avoid retaliation. Some warriors fought with a katara in each hand, and the most courageous would even hunt animals such as tigers with the weapon.

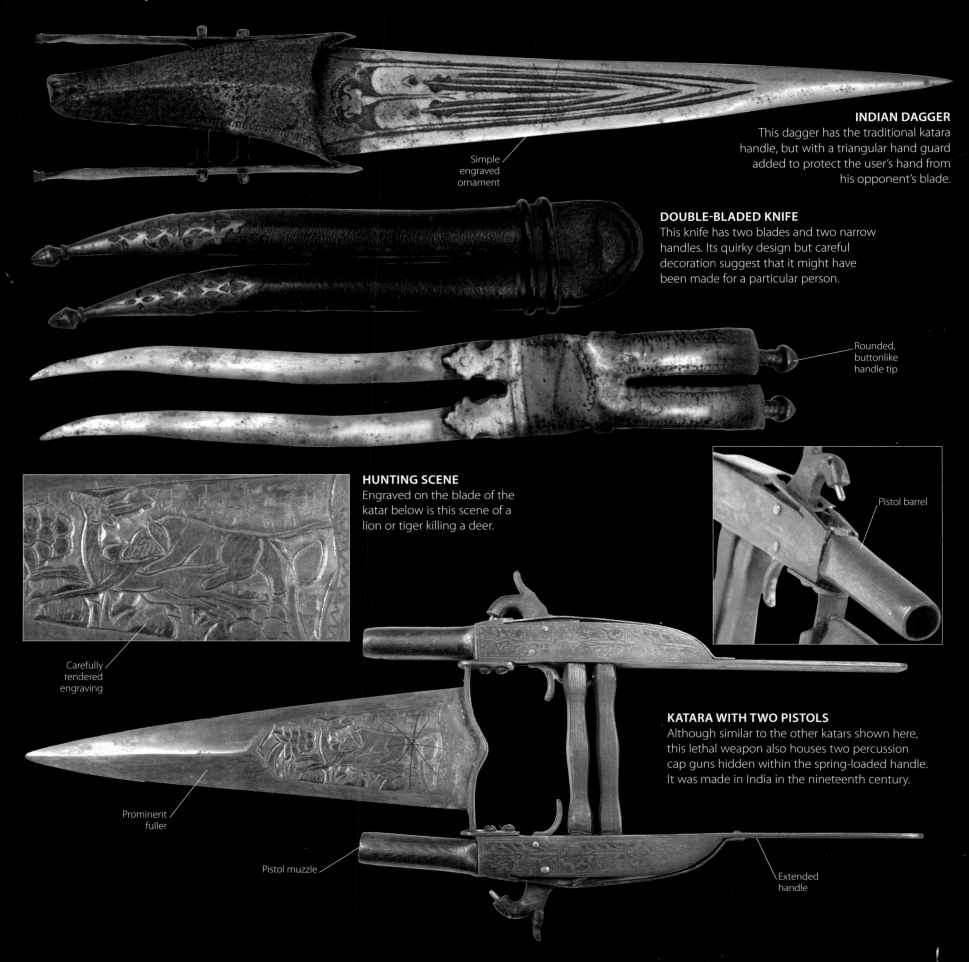

Simple engraved ornament

INDIAN DAGGER
This dagger has the traditional katara handle, but with a triangular hand guard added to protect the user's hand from his opponent's blade.

DOUBLE-BLADED KNIFE
This knife has two blades and two narrow handles. Its quirky design but careful decoration suggest that it might have been made for a particular person.

Rounded, buttonlike handle tip

HUNTING SCENE
Engraved on the blade of the katar below is this scene of a lion or tiger killing a deer.

Carefully rendered engraving

Pistol barrel

KATARA WITH TWO PISTOLS
Although similar to the other katars shown here, this lethal weapon also houses two percussion cap guns hidden within the spring-loaded handle. It was made in India in the nineteenth century.

Prominent fuller

Pistol muzzle

Extended handle

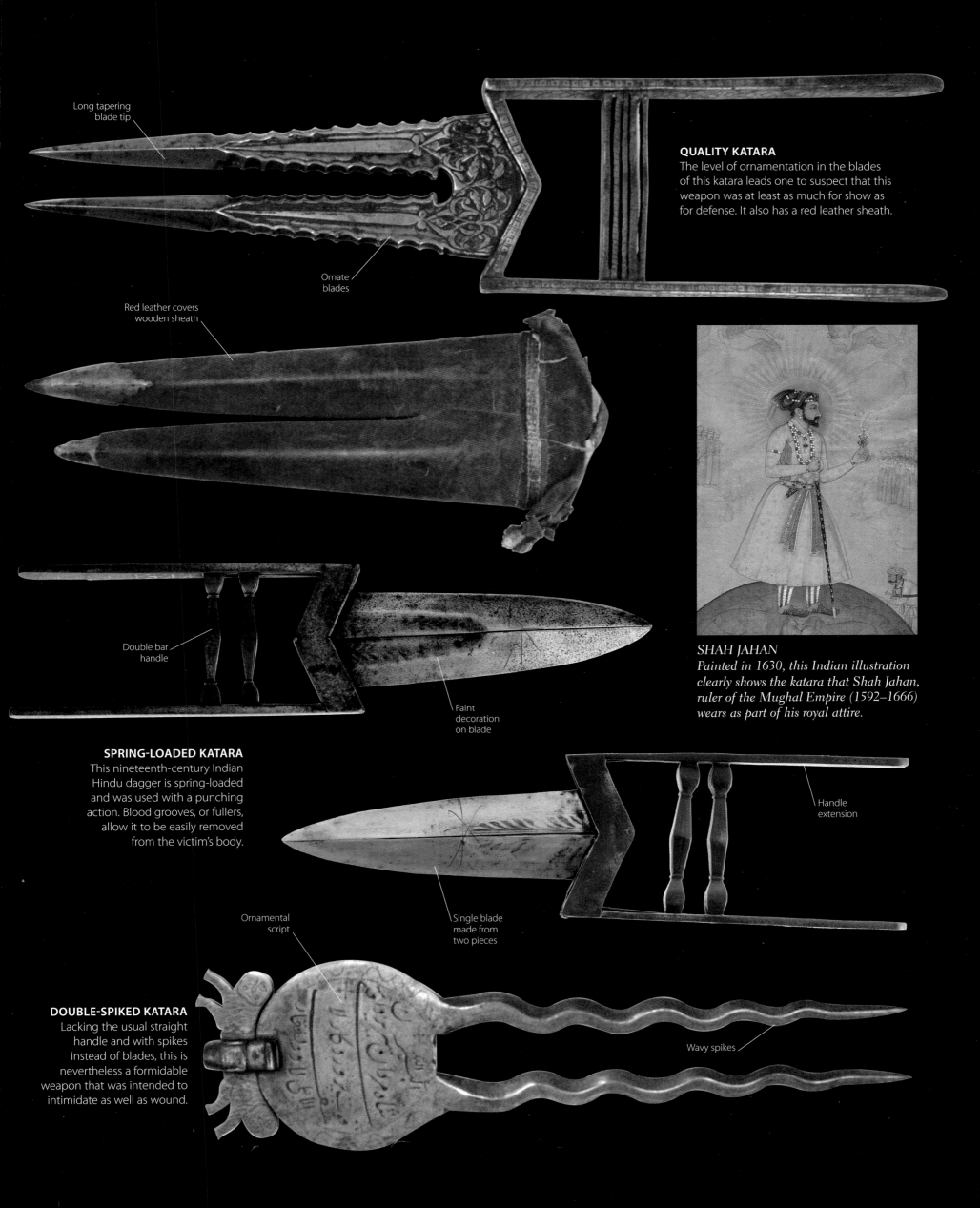

Long tapering
blade tip

QUALITY KATARA
The level of ornamentation in the blades
of this katara leads one to suspect that this
weapon was at least as much for show as
for defense. It also has a red leather sheath.

Ornate
blades

Red leather covers
wooden sheath

SHAH JAHAN
Painted in 1630, this Indian illustration
clearly shows the katara that Shah Jahan,
ruler of the Mughal Empire (1592–1666)
wears as part of his royal attire.

Double bar
handle

Faint
decoration
on blade

Handle
extension

SPRING-LOADED KATARA
This nineteenth-century Indian
Hindu dagger is spring-loaded
and was used with a punching
action. Blood grooves, or fullers,
allow it to be easily removed
from the victim's body.

Ornamental
script

Single blade
made from
two pieces

DOUBLE-SPIKED KATARA
Lacking the usual straight
handle and with spikes
instead of blades, this is
nevertheless a formidable
weapon that was intended to
intimidate as well as wound.

Wavy spikes

ASIA MINOR

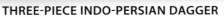

Trigger to release blade

THREE-PIECE INDO-PERSIAN DAGGER
This rare and unusual Indo-Persian knife has a three-piece blade. While it appeared to be an ordinary knife to a sword-wielding attacker, the user separated the blades by means of a spring-loaded hinge in the hope of catching the attacker's sword blade between the main blade and one of the auxiliary blades. Twisting the knife would then immobilize (or, even better, break) the sword blade, allowing the defender to use his own sword on his opponent.

Elegant, tapering blade

ARABIAN DAGGER
Another Arabian dagger, this one made in Tunis (capital of the modern nation of Tunis) in the nineteenth century.

PIHA KAETTA
The traditional knife of Sri Lanka (now Ceylon), the *piha kaetta* (from the Sinhalese for "resplendent") was mainly a ceremonial weapon; as such, these weapons were often elaborately decorated, with carved hilts of bone or even coral, as in this example.

Lion's head carved into handle

SMALL DAGGER WITH IVORY HANDLE
This lion-headed Indo-Persian dagger dates from the early nineteenth century.

Curved quillon

Carved pommel

Clip to attach sheath to knife handle

INDO-PERSIAN DAGGER
The fan-shaped hilt of this dagger is not unlike that of a khanjarli, but the shape of the blade is that of a traditional jambiya.

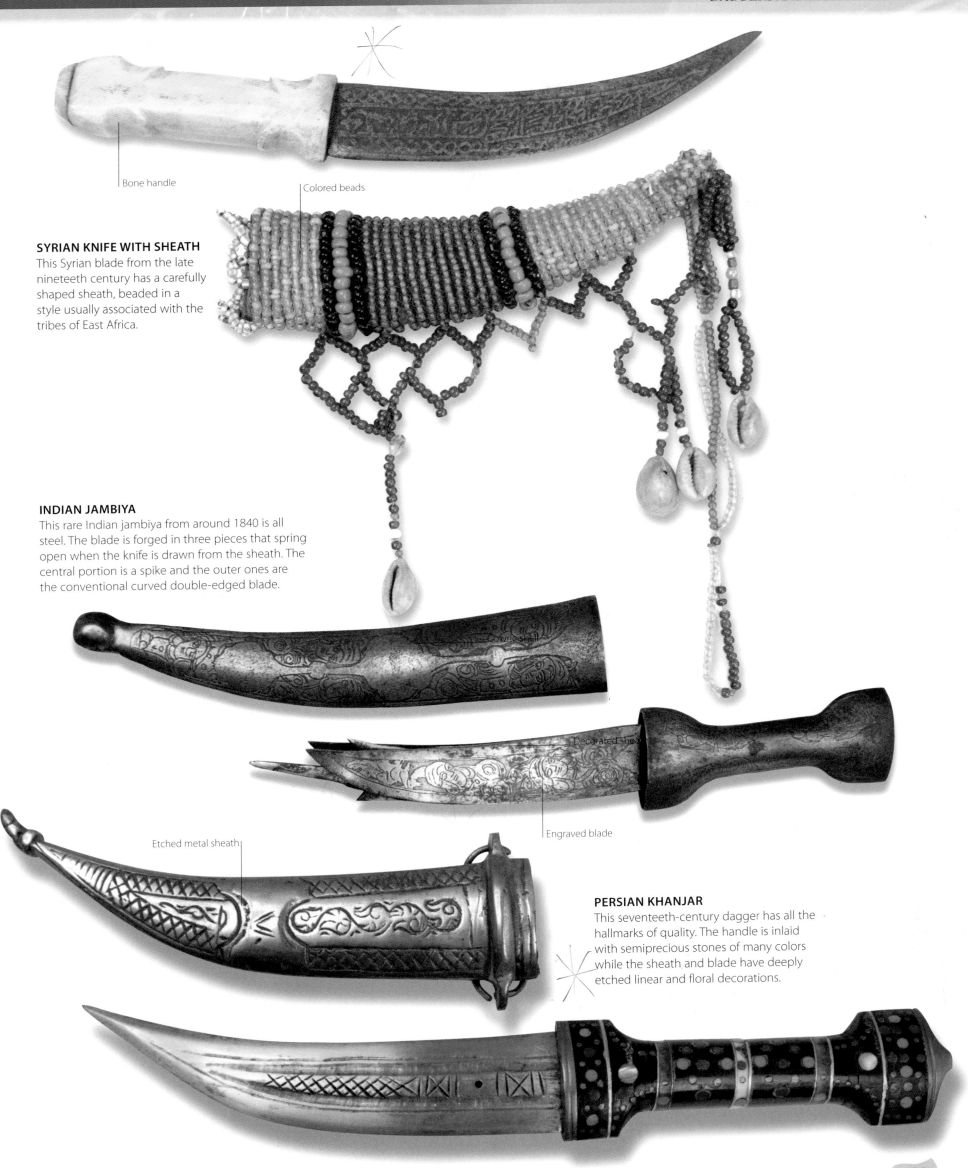

Bone handle

Colored beads

SYRIAN KNIFE WITH SHEATH
This Syrian blade from the late nineteeth century has a carefully shaped sheath, beaded in a style usually associated with the tribes of East Africa.

INDIAN JAMBIYA
This rare Indian jambiya from around 1840 is all steel. The blade is forged in three pieces that spring open when the knife is drawn from the sheath. The central portion is a spike and the outer ones are the conventional curved double-edged blade.

Cowrie shell

Decorated Shea

Engraved blade

Etched metal sheath

PERSIAN KHANJAR
This seventeeth-century dagger has all the hallmarks of quality. The handle is inlaid with semiprecious stones of many colors while the sheath and blade have deeply etched linear and floral decorations.

ASIA MINOR CONTINUED

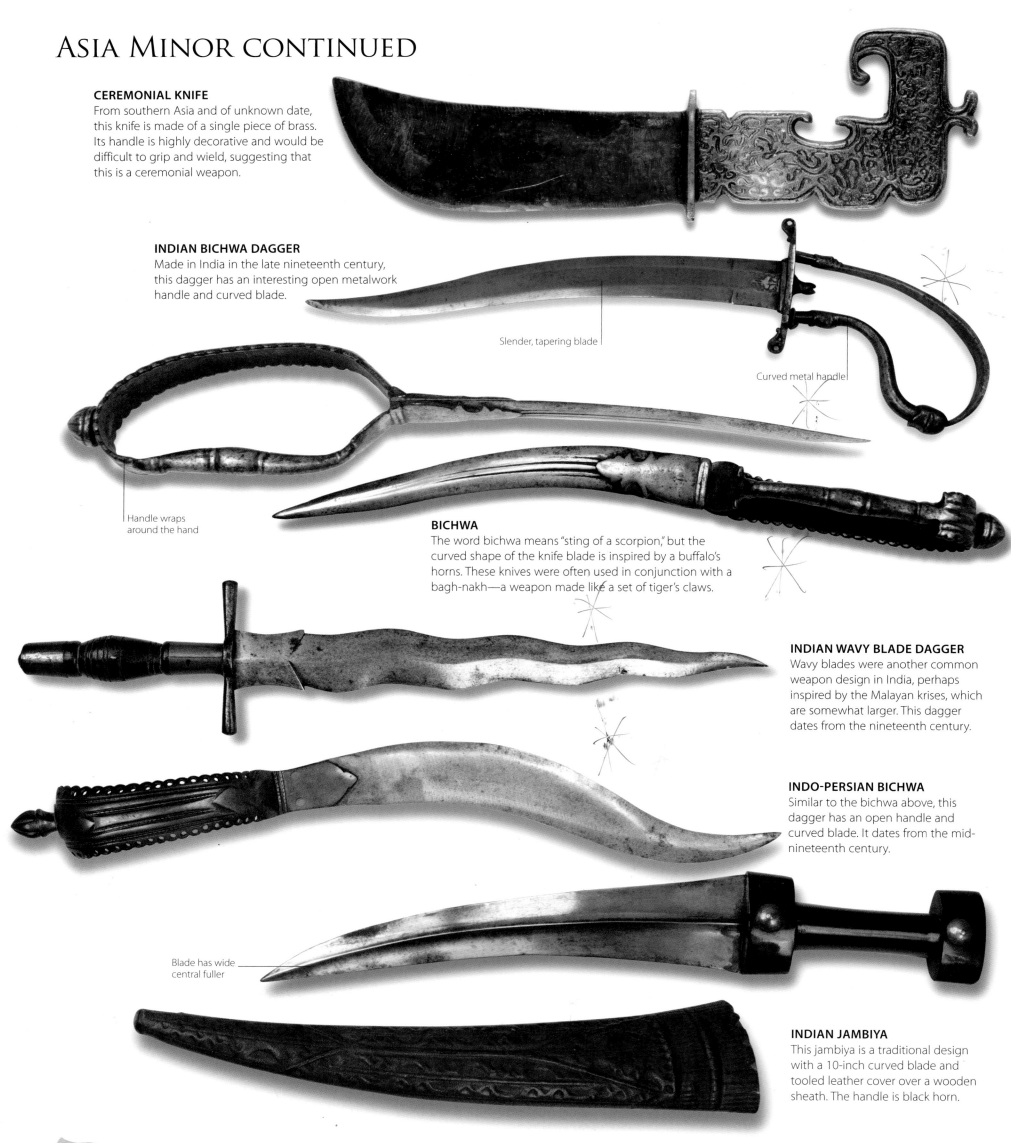

CEREMONIAL KNIFE
From southern Asia and of unknown date, this knife is made of a single piece of brass. Its handle is highly decorative and would be difficult to grip and wield, suggesting that this is a ceremonial weapon.

INDIAN BICHWA DAGGER
Made in India in the late nineteenth century, this dagger has an interesting open metalwork handle and curved blade.

Slender, tapering blade

Curved metal handle

Handle wraps around the hand

BICHWA
The word bichwa means "sting of a scorpion," but the curved shape of the knife blade is inspired by a buffalo's horns. These knives were often used in conjunction with a bagh-nakh—a weapon made like a set of tiger's claws.

INDIAN WAVY BLADE DAGGER
Wavy blades were another common weapon design in India, perhaps inspired by the Malayan krises, which are somewhat larger. This dagger dates from the nineteenth century.

INDO-PERSIAN BICHWA
Similar to the bichwa above, this dagger has an open handle and curved blade. It dates from the mid-nineteenth century.

Blade has wide central fuller

INDIAN JAMBIYA
This jambiya is a traditional design with a 10-inch curved blade and tooled leather cover over a wooden sheath. The handle is black horn.

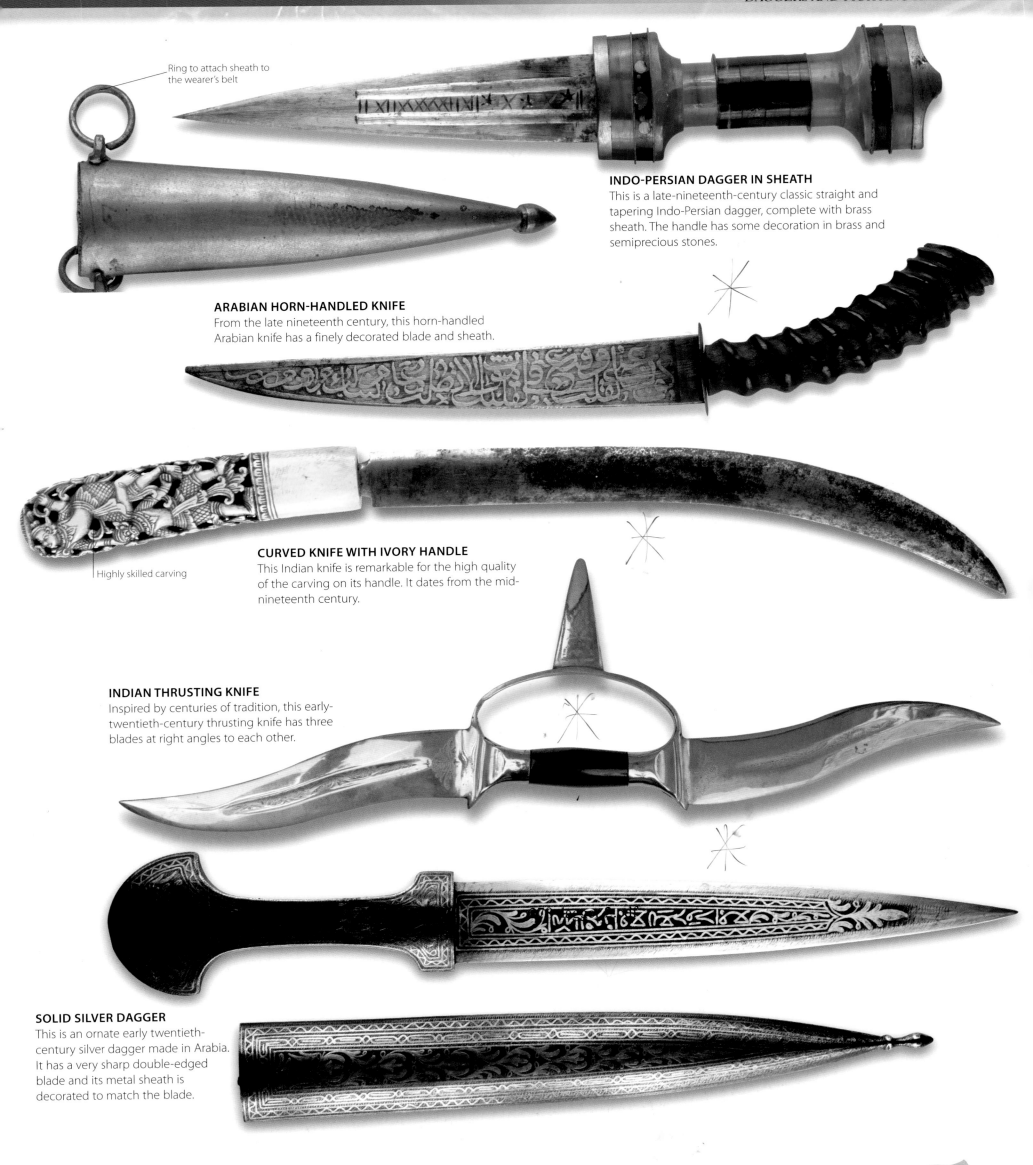

Ring to attach sheath to the wearer's belt

INDO-PERSIAN DAGGER IN SHEATH
This is a late-nineteenth-century classic straight and tapering Indo-Persian dagger, complete with brass sheath. The handle has some decoration in brass and semiprecious stones.

ARABIAN HORN-HANDLED KNIFE
From the late nineteenth century, this horn-handled Arabian knife has a finely decorated blade and sheath.

CURVED KNIFE WITH IVORY HANDLE
This Indian knife is remarkable for the high quality of the carving on its handle. It dates from the mid-nineteenth century.

Highly skilled carving

INDIAN THRUSTING KNIFE
Inspired by centuries of tradition, this early-twentieth-century thrusting knife has three blades at right angles to each other.

SOLID SILVER DAGGER
This is an ornate early twentieth-century silver dagger made in Arabia. It has a very sharp double-edged blade and its metal sheath is decorated to match the blade.

Fighting Implements

Ingenious though Western armorers were in devising close-combat weapons for cutting and piercing the enemy, the metalworkers of Asia and Africa found other ways of providing their warriors with an unexpected edge in battle. Grappling with their enemies, the warlike Turkana people of Kenya would use wrist knives and finger knives for slashing and cutting, as well as finger hooks for gouging out eyes. In India, the claw dagger combined a dagger blade with a form of "knuckleduster" grip armed with curved blades that was used in a raking motion. In India, an alternative to the conventional throwing knifes was a spiked circular one that was spun at the enemy. Deployed skillfully and unexpectedly, all these weapons could turn a fight to the user's advantage.

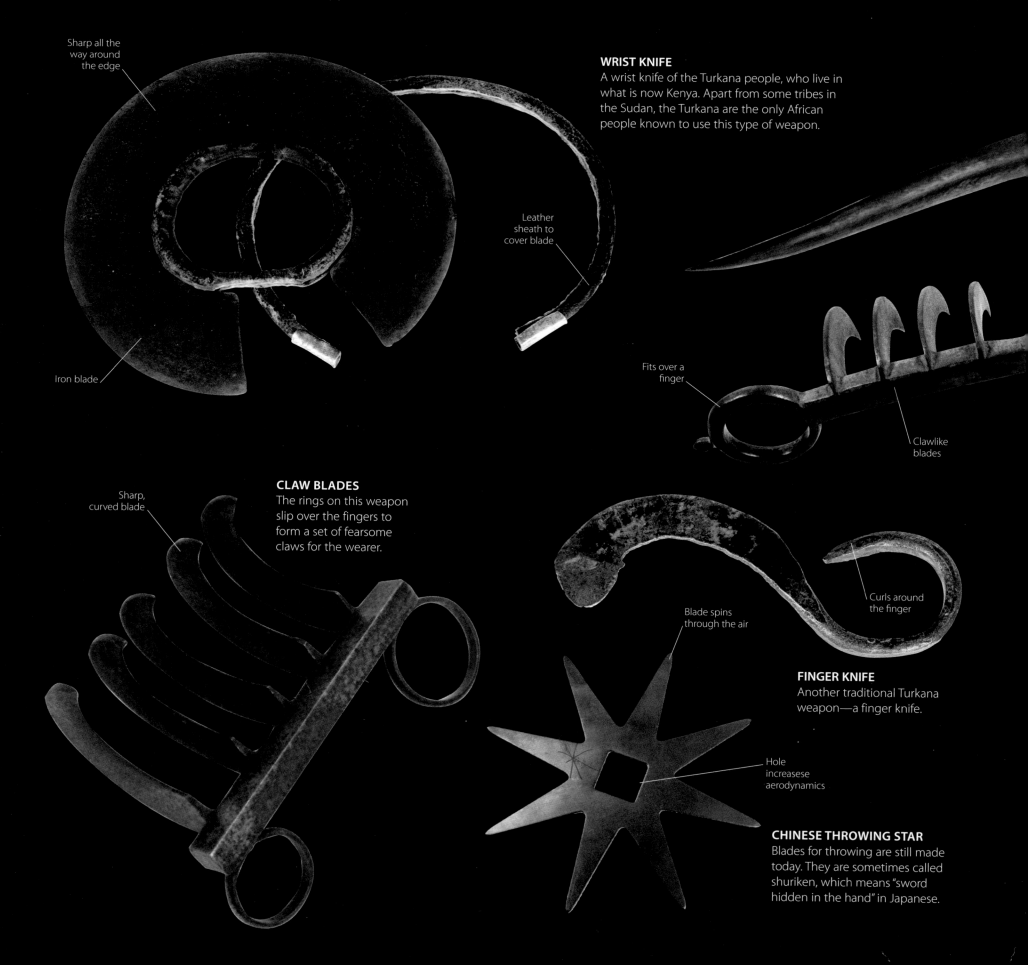

Sharp all the way around the edge

Iron blade

Leather sheath to cover blade

WRIST KNIFE
A wrist knife of the Turkana people, who live in what is now Kenya. Apart from some tribes in the Sudan, the Turkana are the only African people known to use this type of weapon.

Fits over a finger

Clawlike blades

CLAW BLADES
The rings on this weapon slip over the fingers to form a set of fearsome claws for the wearer.

Sharp, curved blade

Blade spins through the air

Curls around the finger

FINGER KNIFE
Another traditional Turkana weapon—a finger knife.

Hole increasese aerodynamics

CHINESE THROWING STAR
Blades for throwing are still made today. They are sometimes called shuriken, which means "sword hidden in the hand" in Japanese.

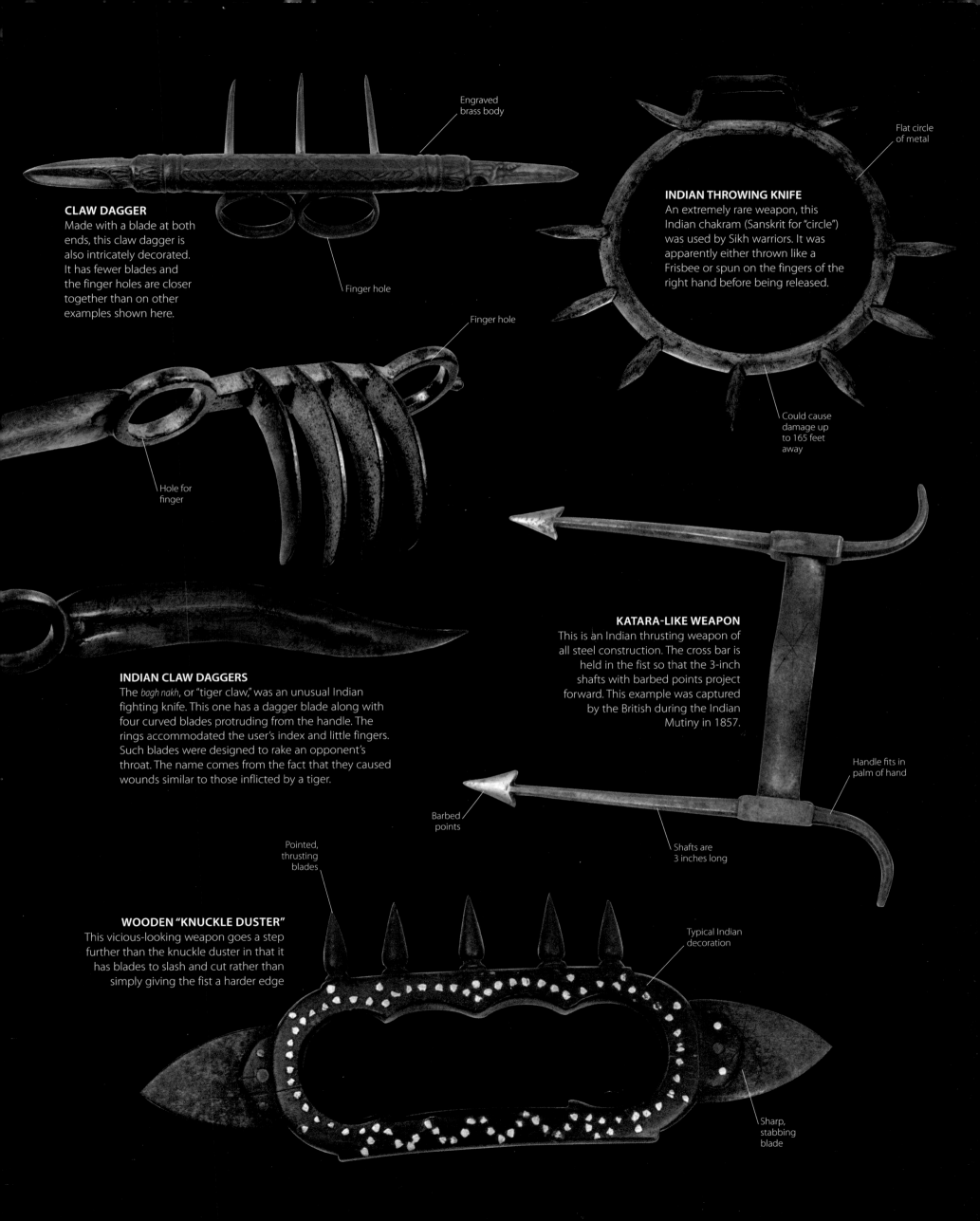

CLAW DAGGER
Made with a blade at both ends, this claw dagger is also intricately decorated. It has fewer blades and the finger holes are closer together than on other examples shown here.

Engraved brass body

Finger hole

INDIAN THROWING KNIFE
An extremely rare weapon, this Indian chakram (Sanskrit for "circle") was used by Sikh warriors. It was apparently either thrown like a Frisbee or spun on the fingers of the right hand before being released.

Flat circle of metal

Could cause damage up to 165 feet away

Finger hole

Hole for finger

KATARA-LIKE WEAPON
This is an Indian thrusting weapon of all steel construction. The cross bar is held in the fist so that the 3-inch shafts with barbed points project forward. This example was captured by the British during the Indian Mutiny in 1857.

Handle fits in palm of hand

INDIAN CLAW DAGGERS
The *bagh nakh*, or "tiger claw," was an unusual Indian fighting knife. This one has a dagger blade along with four curved blades protruding from the handle. The rings accommodated the user's index and little fingers. Such blades were designed to rake an opponent's throat. The name comes from the fact that they caused wounds similar to those inflicted by a tiger.

Barbed points

Shafts are 3 inches long

Pointed, thrusting blades

WOODEN "KNUCKLE DUSTER"
This vicious-looking weapon goes a step further than the knuckle duster in that it has blades to slash and cut rather than simply giving the fist a harder edge

Typical Indian decoration

Sharp, stabbing blade

DAGGERS AND FIGHTING KNIVES CONTINUED . . .

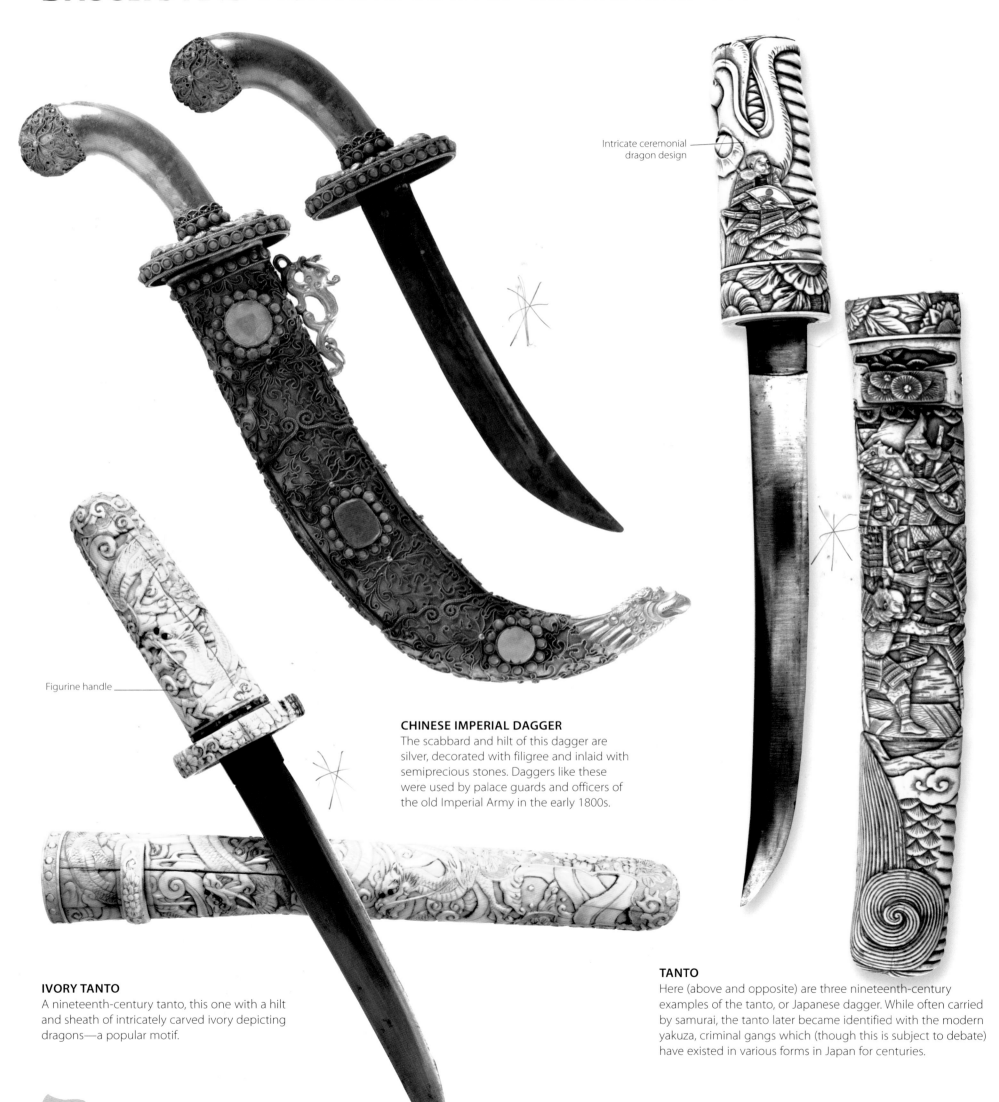

Intricate ceremonial dragon design

Figurine handle

CHINESE IMPERIAL DAGGER
The scabbard and hilt of this dagger are silver, decorated with filigree and inlaid with semiprecious stones. Daggers like these were used by palace guards and officers of the old Imperial Army in the early 1800s.

IVORY TANTO
A nineteenth-century tanto, this one with a hilt and sheath of intricately carved ivory depicting dragons—a popular motif.

TANTO
Here (above and opposite) are three nineteenth-century examples of the tanto, or Japanese dagger. While often carried by samurai, the tanto later became identified with the modern yakuza, criminal gangs which (though this is subject to debate) have existed in various forms in Japan for centuries.

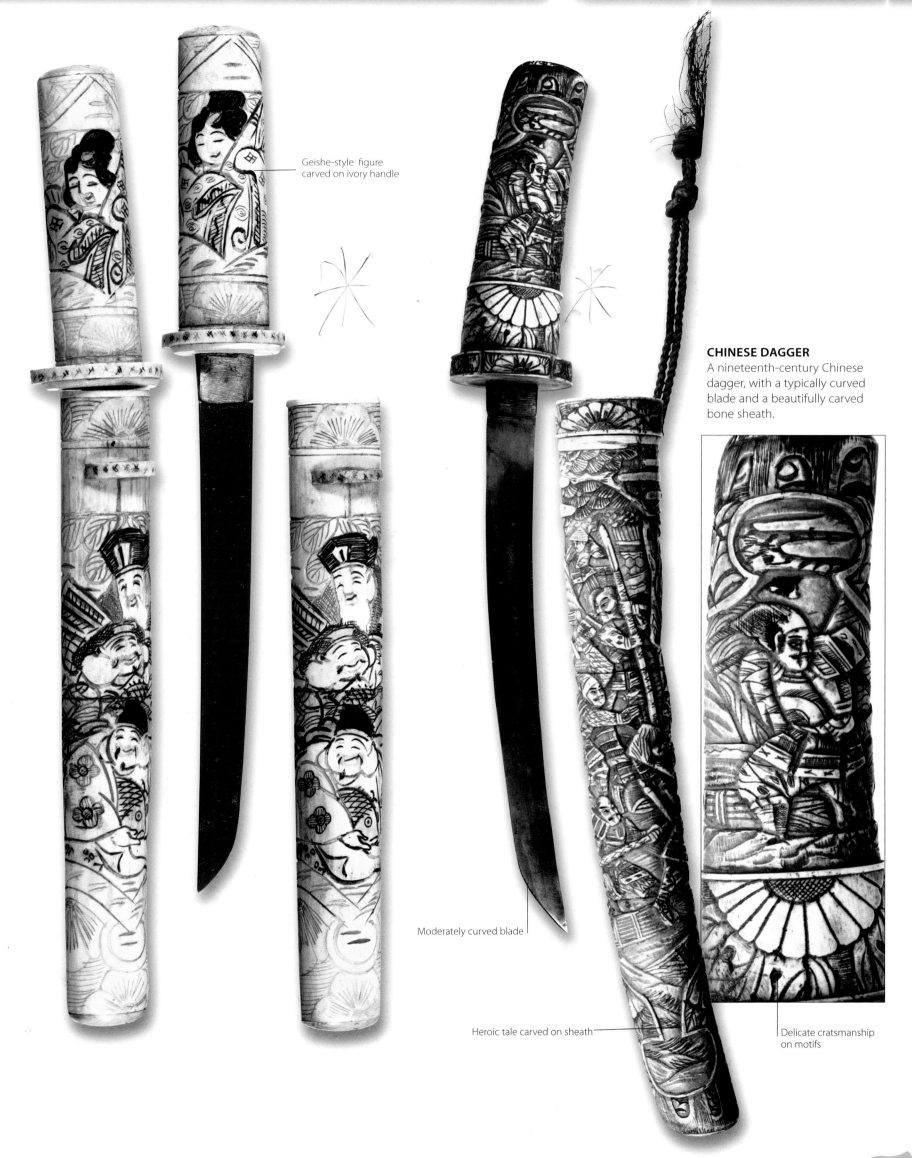

Geishe-style figure
carved on ivory handle

CHINESE DAGGER
A nineteenth-century Chinese
dagger, with a typically curved
blade and a beautifully carved
bone sheath.

Moderately curved blade

Heroic tale carved on sheath

Delicate cratsmanship
on motifs

DAGGERS AND FIGHTING KNIVES CONTINUED . . .

Dragon-shaped handle
made of ivory

Gently curved
cutting edge

ORNATE-HANDLED CHINESE KNIFE This
seventeenth-century Chinese knife has an
exquisitely carved and shaped ceremonial dragon.

CHINESE BRONZE DAGGER
Made in China at an unknown date this dagger consists of a
single piece of cast bronze. The handle is beautifully
decorated and the curved blade is 10 inches long.

Ten-inch-long forward
cureving blade

Bold geometric designs

ORIENTAL KNIFE
The handle and scabbard of this nineteenth-century Japanese knife are made
from beautifully carved wood. They make a beautiful composite 'whole' when
the blade is sealed. The blade narrows to a forward-pointing tip.

Curved shape when
sheath is in place

HORN HANDLED KUKRI
This simple kukri has a 12-inch blade and a horn handle. The simple leather sheath has a silver plaque inscribed with the words "From the Officers 2nd Battalion 5th Gurkha Rifles."

Sturdy leather scabbard

NEPALESE PRESENTATION KUKRI
This ornate kukri dates back to 1819. It has a horn hilt and a heavily decorated scabbard. The engraved panel reveals that the kukri was also given as a token of appreciation in more recent times.

Forward curved blade

REGIMENTAL KUKRI
This large curved knife dating from the early twentieth century has a simply decorated bone handle. The dark leather sheath bears the emblem of the British 5th Ghurka Rifles, an infantry regiment that is now part of the Indian Army. The sheath usually also contains a smaller knife, as here, for sharpening the kukri blade.

CLOISONNÉ

Named for the French cloisons meaning "partitions," cloisonné is the technique of creating designs on metal vessels—on these pages sword and dagger fittings—using colored-glass paste placed within the enclosed partitions that are made of copper or bronze wires. It is not a simple process: The partitions are bent or hammered into the desired pattern and are then pasted or soldered onto the metal body. The glass paste (or enamel) is colored with metallic oxide and painted before the object is fired at about 1475°F. As enamels shrink after firing, the process is repeated several times to fill in the designs. China and Japan excel at these techniques.

Cloisonné eggs showing the step-by-step enamelling process

BOX OF EGGS
Early Chinese cloisonné designs date back to the Ming Dynasty and were predominantl;y objects for a lady's boudoir. How they transformed into ceremonial amd actual weapons of war appears not to be recorded. Once this firing process is complete, the surface of the vessel is rubbed until the edges of the cloisons are visible. They are then gilded, often on the edges, in the interior, and on the base.

CLOISONNÉ TANTO
A very dark background highlight the pale pink and white flowers that decorate this tanto.

Sheath with delicate
cloisonné

Finely carved
jade handle

Chinese cloisonné dagger

Brass ring forms end of
ornate handle

CHINESE EXPORT DAGGERS

During the nineteenth and early twentieth centuries, skilled Chinese craftsmen produced vast numbers of knives for export to the West; most were put to no more lethal use than opening letters. The top example shown here has a cloisonné sheath and a jade hilt. Thew other examples have cloisonné hilts and sheaths.

Brass ring mark edge
of partitions

Cloisonné handle

CHINESE CLOISONNÉ SWORD

Blades like this one on an eighteenth-century sword were worn with a military uniform for formal occasions. This knife dates from about 1870 and its sheath is an extremely skilled work of cloisonné. This blade was probably owned by an affluent Chinese army officer.

BLUE-BASED CHINESE CLOISONNÉ SWORD

This turquoise dominated dagger and sheath features prominent forward facing brass quillions with large knops. The style for Chinese and Japaneses daggers was generally more restrained when it came to handle guards. A European influence is clearly evident. The two brass suspension rings for fixing to a uniform or belt also suggest a ceremonial function.

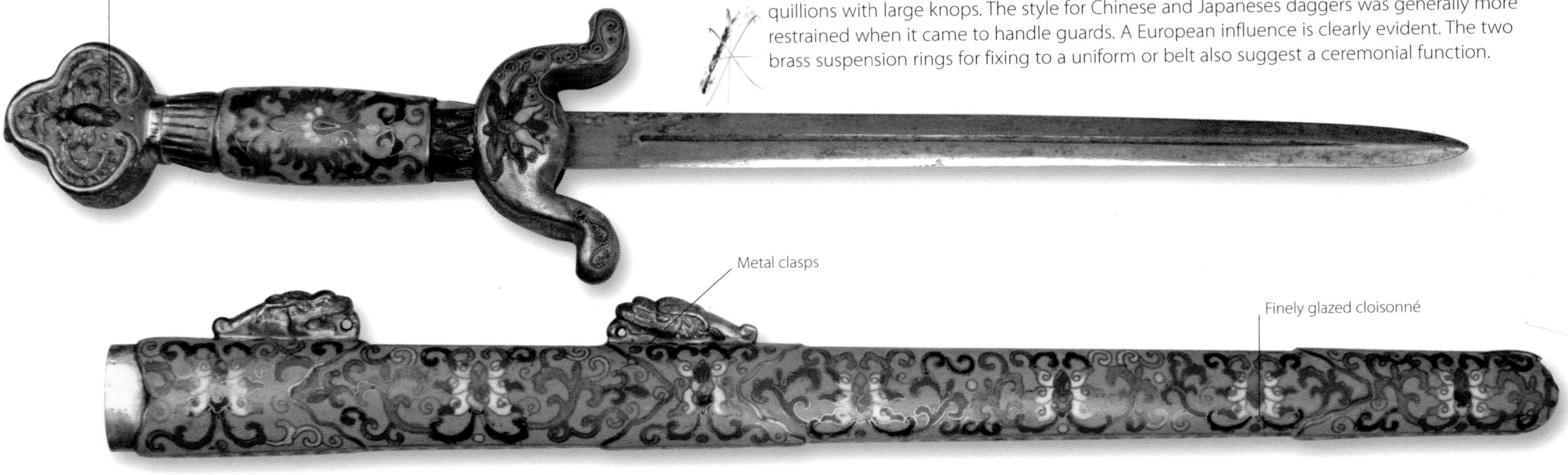

Finial

Metal clasps

Finely glazed cloisonné

CLOISONNÉ CONTINUED . . .

CHINESE CLOISONNÉ DAGGER.
A short straight-bladed dagger again with
beautiifully crafted cloisonné.

Attachment for blade to hang
from silk or leather sash

CLOISONNÉ DAGGERS AND SHEATHS
Two examples of highly decorated knives and sheathes dating from the nineteenth century. Cloisonné enamel has been used on both the hilt and sheath.

CHINESE CLOISONNÉ SWORD
This is a selection of swords that would have been worn with a military uniform for formal occasions. This greens and blues were popular colors. The detail in the cloisonné reveals the true skill of the craftsmen. These items would have taken many hours of work to produce.

Small ring pommel

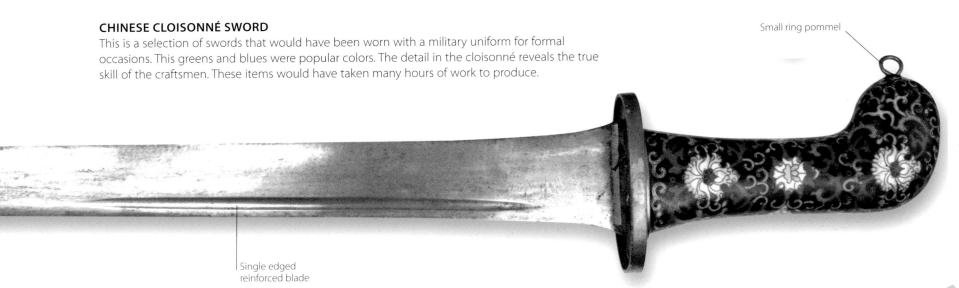

Single edged
reinforced blade

CLOISONNÉ CONTINUED . . .

CURVED CLOISONNÉ DAGGER
Another variaition on an intricately decorated Chinese dagger
with cloisonné enamel on both the hilt and sheath.

Brass hilt

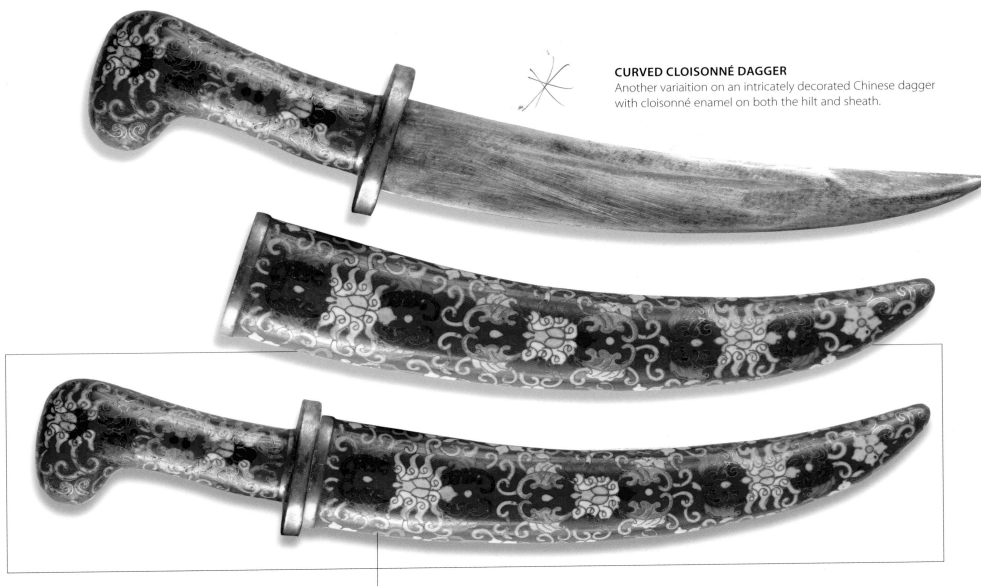

CURVED CLOISONNÉ DAGGER
Another variaition on an intricately decorated Chinese dagger with cloisonné enamel on both the hilt and sheath.

Cloisonné overlay on sheath

CURVED CLOISONNÉ DAGGER
Another Chinese curved dagger with an elaborate cloisonné enameled handle and sheath. It dates from the nineteenth century.

Curved blade

Cloisonné continued . . .

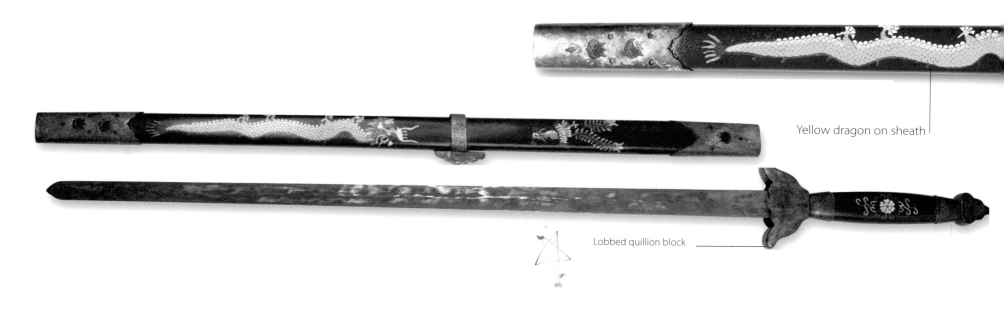

Yellow dragon on sheath

Lobbed quillion block

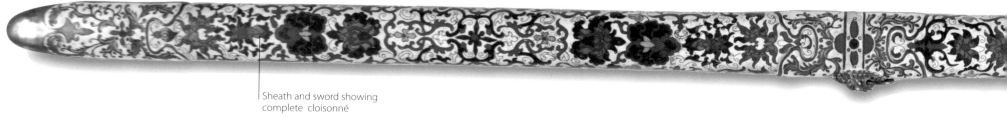

Sheath and sword showing
complete cloisonné

LONG CHINESE SWORD

A beautiful Chinese sword from the nineteenth century, with
detailed cloisonné enamel decoration on both the hilt and
scabbard. The long double-edged blade measures 31½ inches.

CHINESE DRAGON DESIGN SWORD WITH CLOISONNÉ
Intricate cloisonné work is a Chinese specialty and this sword is a finely-crafted example with a yellow dragon on a rich blue ground. The sword dates from the late nineteenth century and measures 39 inches long.

Forward facing quillions

Guard with cloisonné

JIAN
The practitioners of Chinese martial arts know the straight-edged jian as "the Gentleman of All Weapons." This nineteenth-century model features cloisonné decoration on the hilt and on the scabbard.

THE KRIS

This distinctive dagger has a long-standing and honored place in Malay culture. It is believed to have originated in Java in the fourteenth century, developed by Inakto Pali, king of Janggolo. From there it spread across Malaysia, with each island having its own variation on the original design. However, all krises are instantly recognizable with their usually wavy blades and wide gangas (top end of the blade next to the hilt). The hilts vary according to the skill of the craftsman, who often use this part of the kris as a way of showing off their artistic prowess.

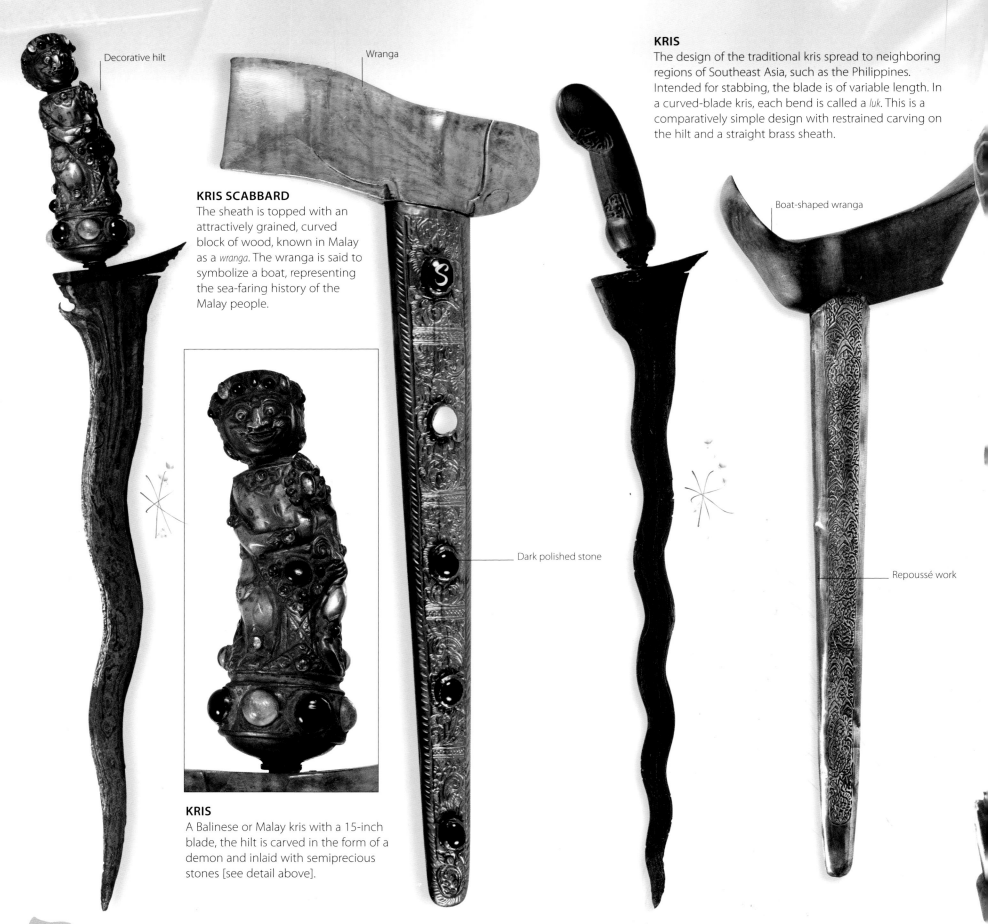

Decorative hilt

Wranga

KRIS SCABBARD
The sheath is topped with an attractively grained, curved block of wood, known in Malay as a *wranga*. The wranga is said to symbolize a boat, representing the sea-faring history of the Malay people.

KRIS
A Balinese or Malay kris with a 15-inch blade, the hilt is carved in the form of a demon and inlaid with semiprecious stones [see detail above].

Dark polished stone

KRIS
The design of the traditional kris spread to neighboring regions of Southeast Asia, such as the Philippines. Intended for stabbing, the blade is of variable length. In a curved-blade kris, each bend is called a *luk*. This is a comparatively simple design with restrained carving on the hilt and a straight brass sheath.

Boat-shaped wranga

Repoussé work

KRIS STAND
A Balinese kris in its stand, which is carved in the figure of a dancer. In Malay and other cultures, the kris was considered to be a living thing, with the power to bring good or bad luck, or even to operate on its own.

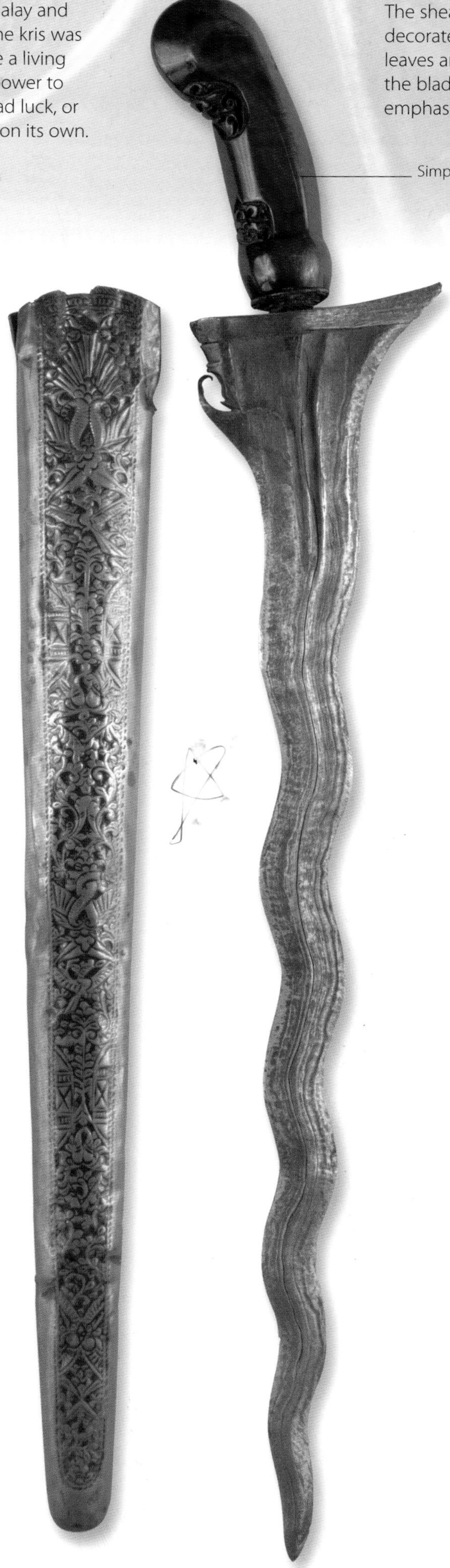

TRADITIONAL KRIS
While simple in design, this kris has some fascinating details. The sheath is beautifully decorated with finely wrought leaves and floral designs and the blade is scoured with lines, emphasizing each curve.

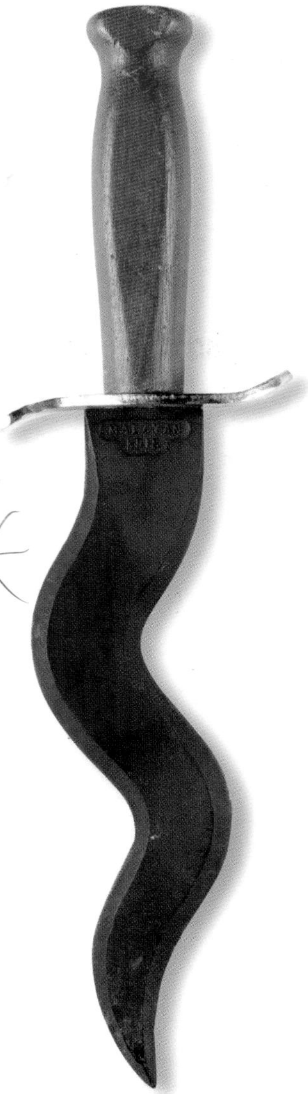

Simple carved wood hilt

MODERN KRIS
Made in Malaysia in the twentieth century, this dagger has the basic kris features but lacks the romance of the traditional design details.

THE 100 YEARS' WAR

The Hundred Years' War between France and England was a series of conflicts that lasted 116 years, from 1337 to 1453. Starting with Edward III (r. 1327–1377), English kings asserted their right to the throne of France on the basis of their descent from the Normans who had conquered England in 1066, and they also sought direct rule of the French province of Aquitaine. Historians view the long struggle as marking the end of the medieval way of war. It saw the use of devastating weapons like the longbow, and it was the first European conflict in which firearms, in the form of artillery, played a role. Also, by fueling nationalist sentiment and contributing to the rise of the centralized state in both countries, it led to the development of professional armies, replacing the earlier ad hoc mix of noble "men at arms" and peasant recruits and conscripts.

ARCHERS AT CRECY
In a French engraving of the Battle of Crécy in 1346, English and French archers face each other. Longbows proved more lethal than crossbows, which were slow to load.

CRÉCY AND POITIERS

In 1337 France had a population of 14 million, against England's 2 million, and enjoyed the reputation of being among Europe's best warriors. But the French still organized their forces in the old fashion, around heavily armored mounted knights. The English had greater tactical flexibility, less chivalrous notions of warfare—and the longbow.

In the first decisive battle of the war, fought at Crécy on August 26, 1346, French knights on horseback repeatedly charged Edward III's army, only to be cut down by volleys of arrows from English and Welsh longbowmen and hammered by English knights fighting on foot. Casualty figures for medieval battles are notoriously unreliable, but the French probably lost at least 10,000 men at Crécy, including many nobles. Then, in 1356, Edward III's son, Edward, "the Black Prince," ravaged much of northern France. His forces, were surrounded by a much larger French army near Poitiers and were attacked on September 19, 1356. Poitiers was a replay of the earlier battle, ending in a huge defeat for the French, with the French King John II (r. 1350–1364) captured. A later treaty yielded a third of French territory to the English.

AGINCOURT TO CASTILLON

Despite the English victory, French fortunes revived. King Henry V (r. 1413–1422) crossed the channel in 1415 and, although his force was outnumbered, beset by sickness, and low on supplies, it defeated a French army at Agincourt on October 24. But the English threat united the often-fractious French nobility to resist the invaders. In the last major battle of the war (Castillon, July 17, 1453) the French used about 300 cannon to defeat an English force—the first battle in which artillery was the deciding factor. English-held Calais ultimately fell to France in 1588.

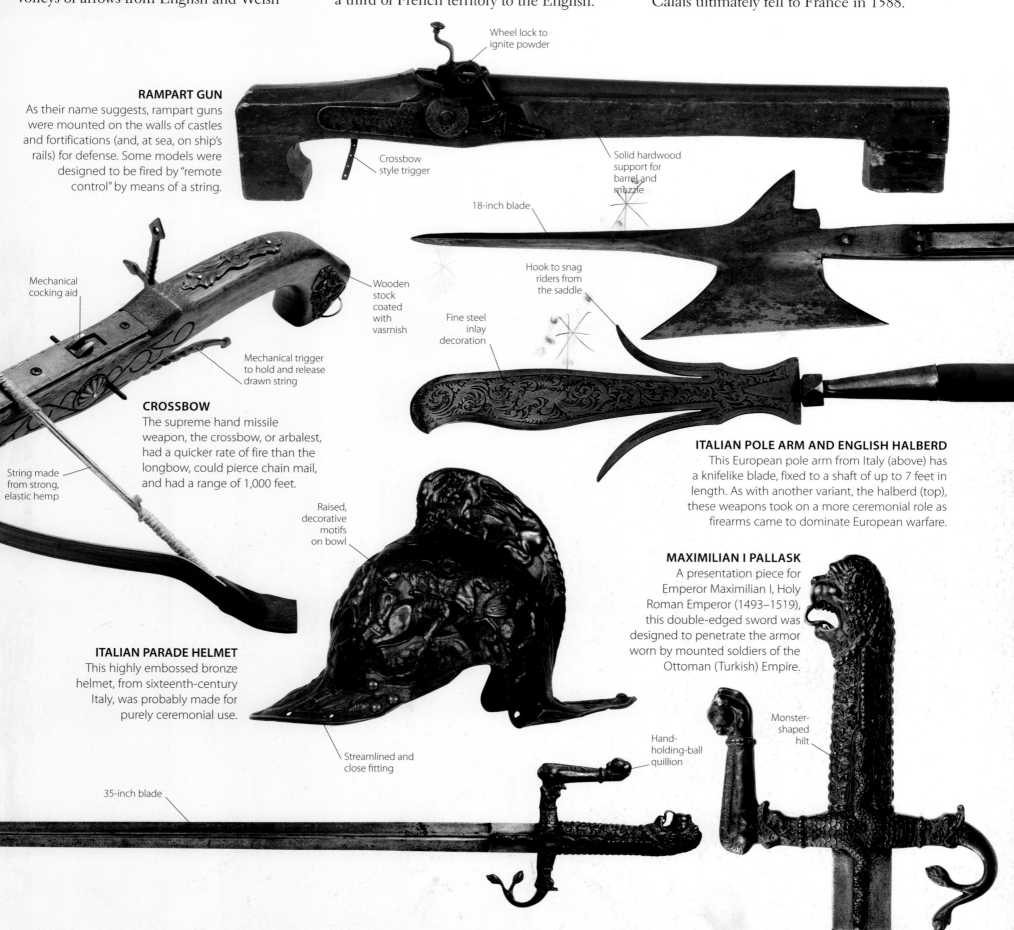

RAMPART GUN
As their name suggests, rampart guns were mounted on the walls of castles and fortifications (and, at sea, on ship's rails) for defense. Some models were designed to be fired by "remote control" by means of a string.

Wheel lock to ignite powder

Crossbow style trigger

Solid hardwood support for barrel and muzzle

18-inch blade

Mechanical cocking aid

Wooden stock coated with vasrnish

Hook to snag riders from the saddle

Fine steel inlay decoration

Mechanical trigger to hold and release drawn string

String made from strong, elastic hemp

CROSSBOW
The supreme hand missile weapon, the crossbow, or arbalest, had a quicker rate of fire than the longbow, could pierce chain mail, and had a range of 1,000 feet.

Raised, decorative motifs on bowl

ITALIAN POLE ARM AND ENGLISH HALBERD
This European pole arm from Italy (above) has a knifelike blade, fixed to a shaft of up to 7 feet in length. As with another variant, the halberd (top), these weapons took on a more ceremonial role as firearms came to dominate European warfare.

MAXIMILIAN I PALLASK
A presentation piece for Emperor Maximilian I, Holy Roman Emperor (1493–1519), this double-edged sword was designed to penetrate the armor worn by mounted soldiers of the Ottoman (Turkish) Empire.

ITALIAN PARADE HELMET
This highly embossed bronze helmet, from sixteenth-century Italy, was probably made for purely ceremonial use.

Streamlined and close fitting

35-inch blade

Hand-holding-ball quillion

Monster-shaped hilt

SWORDS

Until the advent of firearms, swords had played a vital part in warfare for many centuries. Even then, the transformation to firearms didn't happen overnight, and the sword remained part of the warrior's arsenal, especially among mounted knights and mercenary infantry. By the late seventeenth century, however, firearms reliability, technology, and tactics had advanced to a point at which the sword's battlefield usefulness was limited—but swords continued to enjoy a vogue among European men, both for dueling and as a status symbol.

A PROUD HERITAGE

Even before the end of the Napoleonic Wars in 1815, the sword's role as a true fighting weapon was in decline in the Western world. Swords, especially sabers, continued to be used by mounted troops, but as the nineteenth century went on, the development of revolvers and repeating carbines largely replaced swords in actual cavalry combat. Still, in all military branches, the sword retained its longstanding role as a symbol of authority for officers—but with the pistol now the officer's battlefield weapon, swords were increasingly worn only with full-dress uniforms on ceremonial occasions. In the civilian world, dueling with swords continued in Europe into the nineteenth century, evolving into the modern sport of fencing, while the growth of fraternal organizations in Europe and America created a demand for purely decorative swords to be carried in parades or used in ceremonies.

AMERICAN SWORDS

SHORT SWORD
With a design not much different from the short swords of antiquity, this weapon is patterned after the Model 1832 U.S. Army sword issued to foot-artillery soldiers. Some sources say it was intended not as a weapon, but as a tool—mainly for chopping brush to clear fields of fire for large artillery pieces to be able to come through.

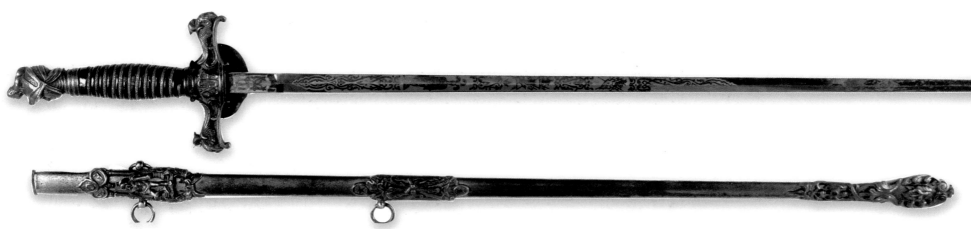

MASON'S SWORD
Belonging to Charles Comstock, who attained the 33rd degree in the Masons—the highest ranking—this nineteenth-century, American ceremonial sword is intricately decorated. The knight's head surmounted by a lion is particularly fine.

EUROPEAN SHORT SWORDS

DANISH SHORT SWORD
A Danish short sword from the eighteenth century, with a D-shaped guard and a grip of wire-wrapped leather. This weapon appears to be a Model 1788 Hirshfänger.

NAPOLEONIC SHORT SWORD
This is a French Sabre Briquet (model: AN IX 1800–01). It is the type of sword that would have been used by French infantry and artillery during the Battle of Waterloo 1815.

ARTILLERY SHORT SWORD
This neoclassical-style sword dating from 1816 was issued to a French foot soldier for used as a sidearm and a tool for clearing undergrowth.

ROYAL COMPANY OF ARCHERS SHORT SWORD
Originally founded in the 1670s, the Scots Royal Company of Archers was designated the "King's Body Guard for Scotland" in the early nineteenth century. Members carried this short sword, with a 16¾-inch blade etched with both the Royal Arms of Great Britain and the thistle, a traditional symbol of Scotland. The beautifully decorated hilt is cast bronze.

EUROPEAN SWORD
This mid-nineteenth century sword has the head of an eagle as its hilt. Eagle iconography and gladiator-style swords were very popular in Europe at this time.

SWORD BAYONET
This sword-style bayonet was designed to fit onto a rifle muzzle, but its hilt meant it could also be used as a short sword. It is French and dates from 1867.

EUROPEAN LONG SWORDS

BIGGER AND LONGER

Sword design closely followed changes in armor during the period between 1500–1800. By the turn of the sixteenth century, heavy plate armor had largely replaced the chain-mail armor formerly worn by knights and other warriors. This led to a movement away from shorter, easy to wield, cutting swords, which could penetrate mail, to much longer and heavier swords—generically known as longswords—with enlarged grips to permit two-handed use. The ultimate example of this

type is probably the *zweihänder*, which could be up to six feet in length.

While the longsword was devastating, it still lacked the ability to actually pierce plate armor, so swordsmiths developed the weapon variously known as the *estoc* (in France), the tuck (in England), and the *panzerstecher* (in German-speaking Europe). These swords had blades of varying lengths, but all ended in a cutting point. While they might not pierce plate armor, they could be thrust into the joints between plates with deadly effect.

LANDSKNECHT

The longest of all European swords of the Renaissance were those used by the *landsknechts*— mercenary soldiers recruited mostly from the Holy Roman Empire, which comprised much of modern-day Germany. Their swords, which could be as long as six feet, were known as *zweihänder*—"two-handers"—and they were used not only as antipersonnel weapons, but also to strike aside enemy pikes and halberds to break up infantry formations. This German example dates from the sixteenth century.

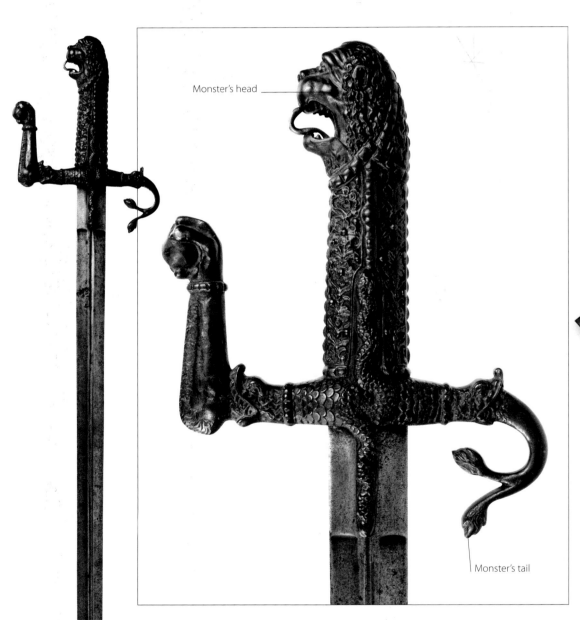

Monster's head

Monster's tail

Long, narrow blade

MAXIMILIAN I PALLASK

Known variously as the *pallasch* (in Austria), the *pallos* (in Hungary), and the *palasz* (in Poland), the pallask was a double-edged sword designed to penetrate the chain-mail armor worn by mounted soldiers of the Ottoman (Turkish) empire, which menaced the frontiers of Central Europe into the seventeenth century. This magnificent example was a presentation piece for Emperor Maximilian I (1459–1519) of the Hapsburg Dynasty, who became Holy Roman Emperor in 1493. The 35-inch blade is topped with a hilt in the form of a monster; the quillions take the form of a hand holding a ball and a monster's tail.

KNIGHT'S LONG SWORD

A knight's longsword from the fifteenth century. A slashing weapon wielded with both hands, these swords were known as langes *schwert* ("long swords") in German and *spadone* ("big sword") in Italian.

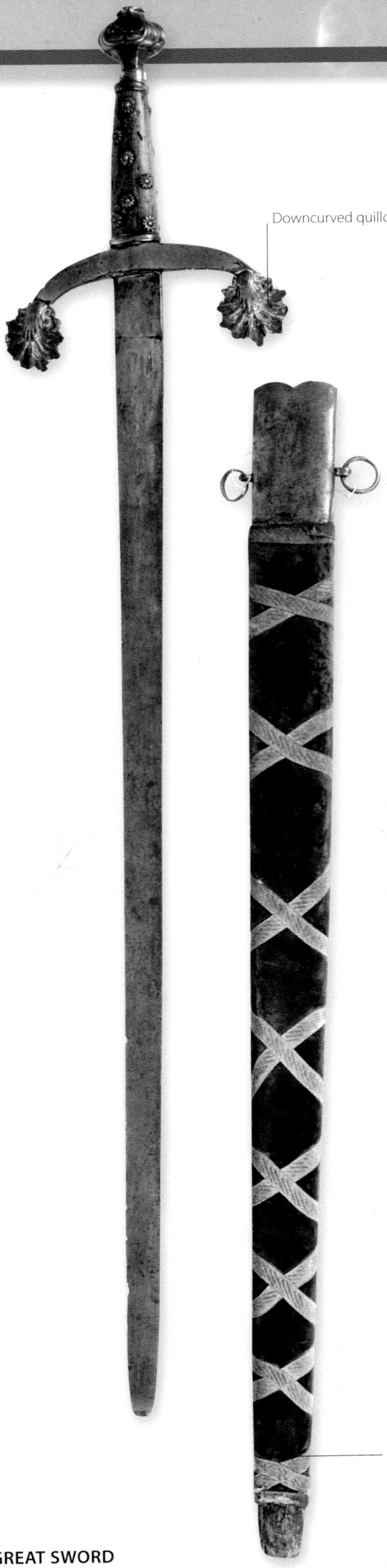

Downcurved quillons

Chiseled gold
crosspieces

Stirrup style hilt guard

Blade is 16
inches long

Simple sheath
decoration

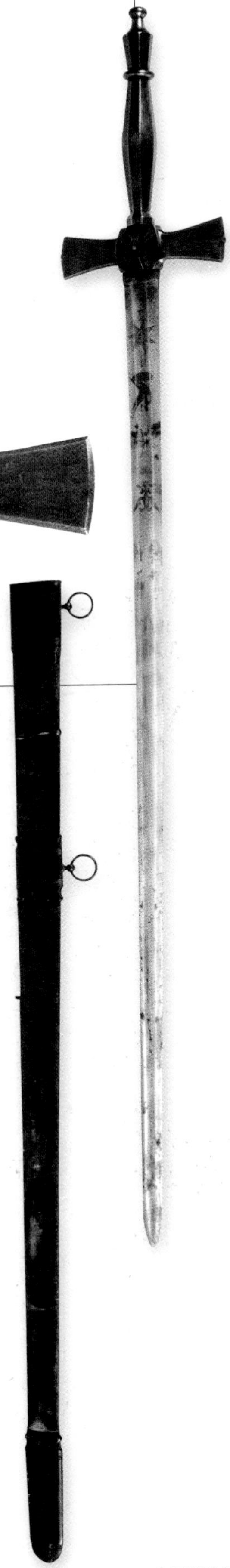

KNIGHTS OF MALTA

Also known as the Knights Hospitaller
and the Order of St John of Jerusalem,
the Knights of Malta was one of the
orders of "warrior monks" founded to
protect Christian pilgrims to the Holy
Land during the Crusades. A member
of the order carried this sword, with a
cruciform hilt that echoes the Maltese
cross, in the seventeenth century. By
this time the order had been driven
from the Holy Land to the
Mediterranean island of Malta. The
25.5in/65cm blade is etched with a
variety of religious symbols.

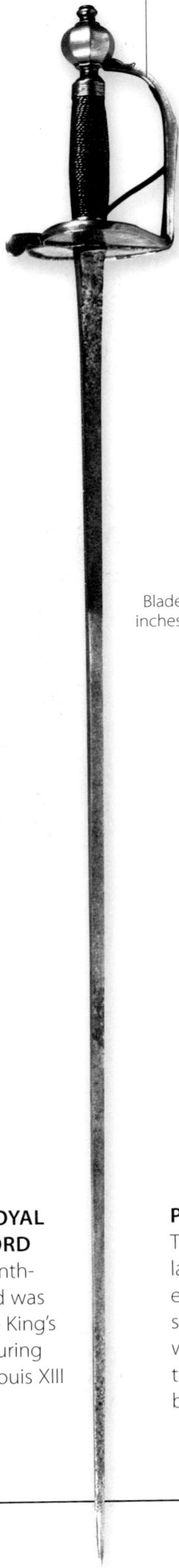

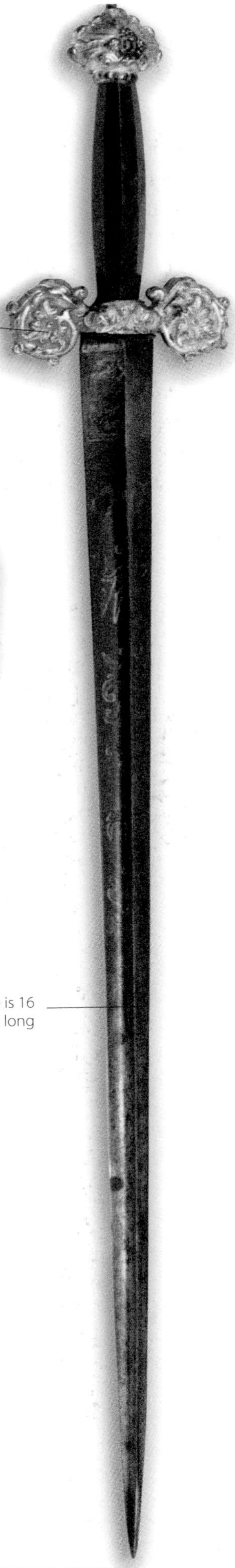

GREAT SWORD

In the late Middle Ages and early Renaissance eras, the term "great sword" was applied
to any very long sword designed to be used with two hands, like the *zweihänder* shown
opposite, and the sixteenth-century example shown here with its scabbard. While
they were relatively light in relation to their length, these formidable weapons
required skill and strength: In the armies of German-speaking states, soldiers who
carried them were called Doppelsöldners and received double pay.

LOUIS XIII ROYAL
GUARD SWORD

This seventeenth-
century sword was
carried by the King's
royal guard during
the reign of Louis XIII
(1601–1642)

PILLOW SWORD

This fine sword from the
late seventeenth century is
etched with trophies and
scroll devices. Pillow swords
were so named because
they were supposedly hung
by the bed at night.

EUROPEAN LONG SWORDS

SCOTTISH BROADSWORD

From the middle ages into the eighteenth century, Scots clansmen went into battle (both inter-clan, and against the encroaching English) armed with the fearsome claymore, a double-handed slashing weapon up to 55 inches long. (The name derives from the Gaelic word for sword, claidheamh.) The claymore name was later applied to basket-hilted swords like the one shown here, which were carried by officers in Highland Scots regiments of the British Army.

FRENCH GUNNER SABER

This French Model 1829 saber was carried by mounted artillerymen. Its design influenced the U.S. Army sabers introduced around 1840.

Brass hilt

Ribbed hilt

1886 CHASSEPOT BAYONET SWORD

The chassepot bayonet sword was crafted in the Manufactory of Châtellerault, and the initial model of the bayonet was created for the bolt-action rifle of the same name. The blade of this sword is hand-forged, as chassepot blades continued to be until 1916. The ribbed brass hilt has a curved quillion.

Long slender blade

Extra long blade

GERMAN LONG SWORD

Despite the progress of democracy in Europe in the 18th and 19th centuries, army officers still tended to be drawn from the aristocracy, and swords became family heirlooms. This Bavarian sword bears an aristocratic coat-of-arms and a family motto—"In firm faith."

THE BLADES OF TOLEDO

The city of Toledo in central Spain has long been famous for its high-quality swords and other edged weapons—a tradition that dates back at least to the fifth century BC, when local swordsmiths produced a type of sword that would later be called the falcata. The first reference to Toledan weapons comes from the first century BC, in a work by the Roman writer Grattius. The swordsmiths of Toledo used an excellent form of steel that was arguably better quality even than Damascus steel; the resulting swords were prized by warriors across Europe, and according to some sources at least, some Japanese samurai may have used Toledo blades. In *Guns, Germs,* *and Steel*, historian Jared Diamond contends that weapons of Toledo steel were instrumental in the Spanish conquest of the Americas—the steel swords and other weapons of the sixteenth-century Spanish conquistadores were far superior to those wielded by the soldiers of the Aztec and Inca empires.

A Spanish small sword with Fabrica de Toledo ("Made in Toledo") etched on the blade.

EUROPEAN DRESS SWORDS

THE SWORD AS STATUS SYMBOL

With firearms replacing edged weapons on the battlefield, the sword increasingly became a civilian weapon, used for self-defense, or for dueling. The narrow-bladed rapier, which evolved from the sixteenth-century Spanish *espada ropera*, became an especially popular dueling sword, and in turn evolved into the épée used in the modern sport of fencing.

By the eighteenth century, a sword was an essential fashion accessory for all European gentlemen—or those who wanted to look like a gentleman. The most common type of sword for everyday wear was the small sword, a lightweight thrusting weapon that first appeared in France late in the seventeenth century. Clearly there were clearly practical reasons for its popularity.

The ubiquity of the sword in the eighteenth century is evidenced by a newspaper advertisement for the first performance of G. W. Handel's oratorio *Messiah* in Dublin, Ireland, in 1742; the notice politely requested gentlemen to not wear their swords to the concert in order to increase seating space in the hall. (Handel, by the way, had fought a bloodless sword duel with a fellow composer some years earlier.)

By the turn of the nineteenth century, however, swords had fallen out of fashion, largely replaced by dueling pistols. These pages display a scintillating selection of blades.

Face on each side of pommel

Stylized quillon

FRENCH SMALL SWORD
This late eighteenth-century sword with a sun emblem honored the memory of the Sun King Louis XIV (1638–1715). Though Louis was long gone, the sun design was still popular until the time that Napoleon came to power.

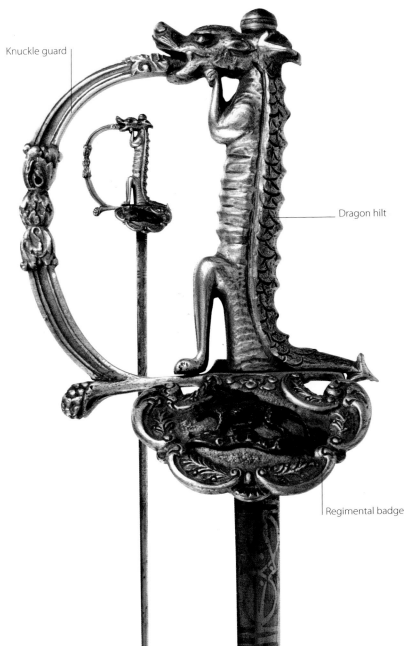

Knuckle guard

Dragon hilt

Regimental badge

BORDER REGIMENT
This sword was carried by an officer of the King's Own Royal Border Regiment, a regiment in the British Army that traces its ancestry back to 1680; it is so-called because it recruited from the counties of Lancashire and Cumbria on the border between Scotland and England. The hilt, of gilded brass, is modeled in the form of a dragon.

DRESS SWORDS CONTINUED. . .

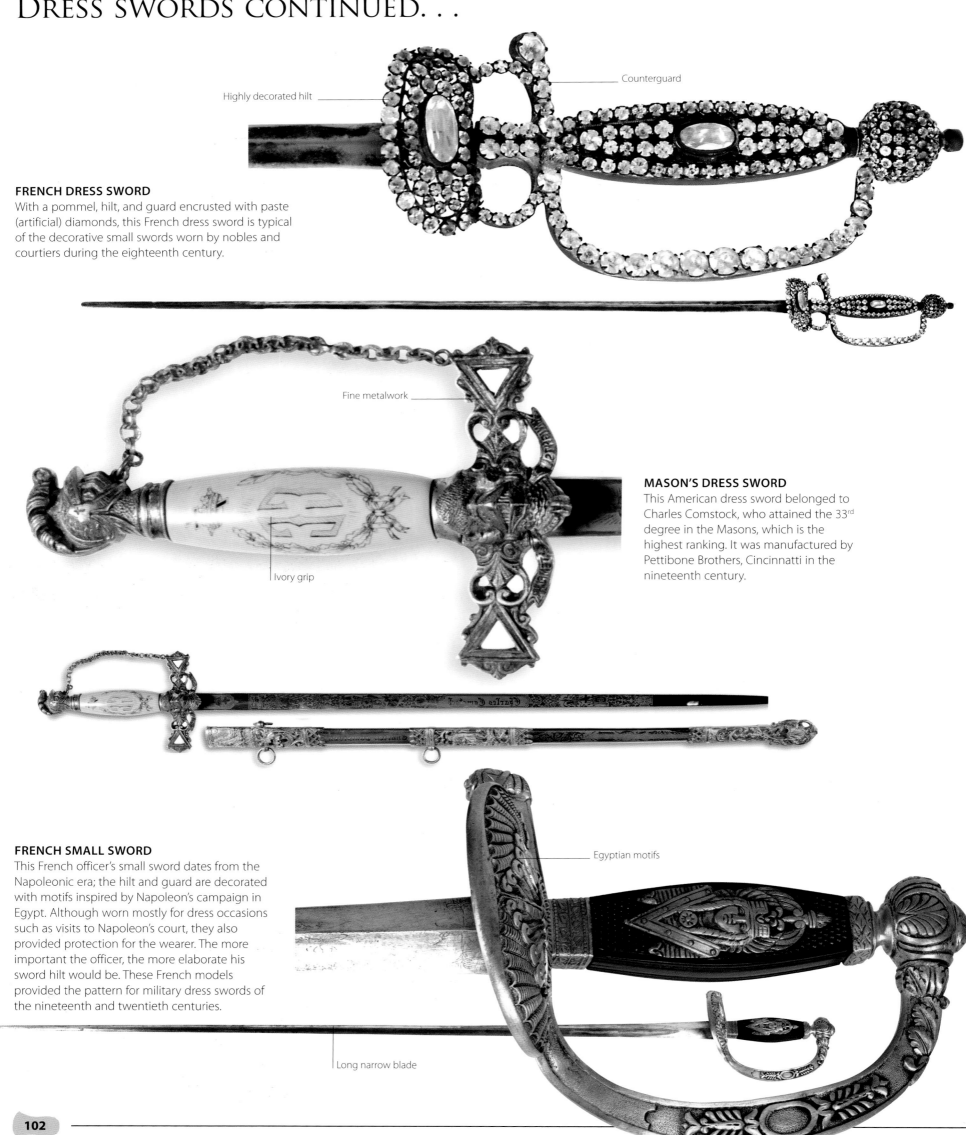

Highly decorated hilt

Counterguard

FRENCH DRESS SWORD
With a pommel, hilt, and guard encrusted with paste (artificial) diamonds, this French dress sword is typical of the decorative small swords worn by nobles and courtiers during the eighteenth century.

Fine metalwork

MASON'S DRESS SWORD
This American dress sword belonged to Charles Comstock, who attained the 33rd degree in the Masons, which is the highest ranking. It was manufactured by Pettibone Brothers, Cincinnatti in the nineteenth century.

Ivory grip

FRENCH SMALL SWORD
This French officer's small sword dates from the Napoleonic era; the hilt and guard are decorated with motifs inspired by Napoleon's campaign in Egypt. Although worn mostly for dress occasions such as visits to Napoleon's court, they also provided protection for the wearer. The more important the officer, the more elaborate his sword hilt would be. These French models provided the pattern for military dress swords of the nineteenth and twentieth centuries.

Egyptian motifs

Long narrow blade

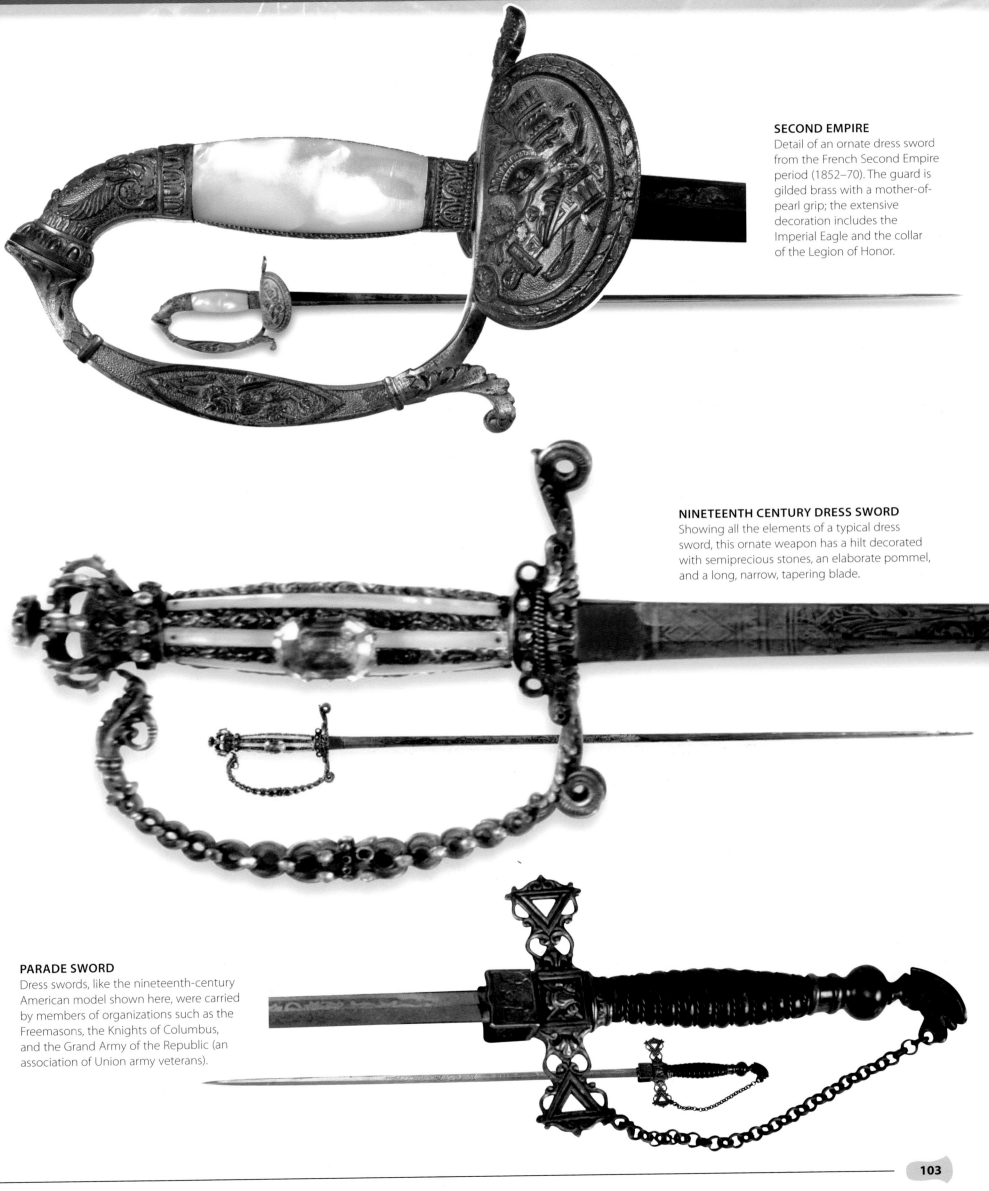

SECOND EMPIRE
Detail of an ornate dress sword from the French Second Empire period (1852–70). The guard is gilded brass with a mother-of-pearl grip; the extensive decoration includes the Imperial Eagle and the collar of the Legion of Honor.

NINETEENTH CENTURY DRESS SWORD
Showing all the elements of a typical dress sword, this ornate weapon has a hilt decorated with semiprecious stones, an elaborate pommel, and a long, narrow, tapering blade.

PARADE SWORD
Dress swords, like the nineteenth-century American model shown here, were carried by members of organizations such as the Freemasons, the Knights of Columbus, and the Grand Army of the Republic (an association of Union army veterans).

DRESS SWORDS CONTINUED . . .

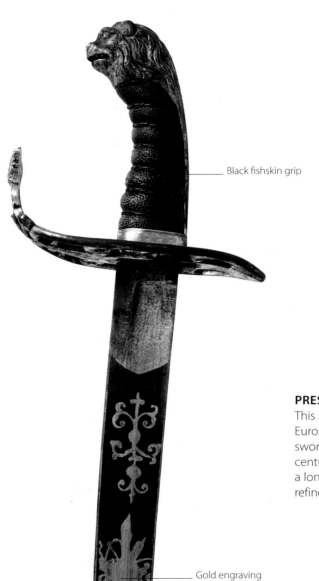

Black fishskin grip

Gold engraving

Stirrup hilt

Long sword

PRESENTATION SWORD

This simple sword is a European court presentation sword from the nineteenth century. It is very stylish with a long narrow blade and neat refined hilt.

ROYAL HORSE GUARD

A cavalry sword carried by a member of the British Army's elite Horse Guards regiment. The 33-inch, straight, single-edged blade is engraved with the regiment's battle honors, ranging from Dettingen (Germany, 1743) to Tel-El-Kebir (Egypt, 1882).

DRAGOON

A British dragoon officer's sword with a black fishskin grip and a straight-single-edged, spear-pointed blade (not shown). The sheath is engraved with gold battle honors commemorating Sevastopol (Crimean War, 1854–55) and Delhi (Indian "Mutiny", 1857).

BRITISH PRESENTATION

A finely wrought British presentation sword; the hilt is made of gold-plated brass with mother-of-pearl inlay.

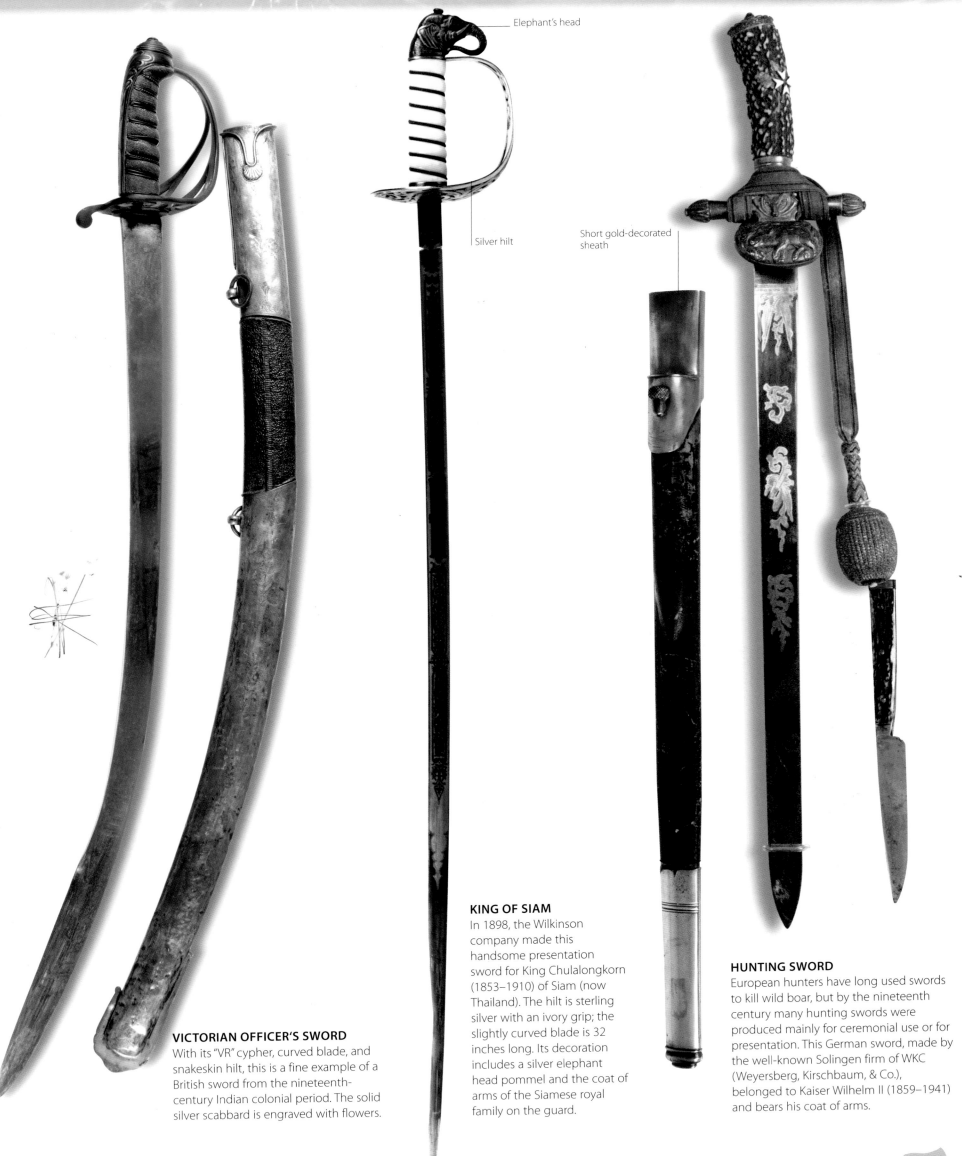

Elephant's head

Silver hilt

Short gold-decorated
sheath

KING OF SIAM
In 1898, the Wilkinson
company made this
handsome presentation
sword for King Chulalongkorn
(1853–1910) of Siam (now
Thailand). The hilt is sterling
silver with an ivory grip; the
slightly curved blade is 32
inches long. Its decoration
includes a silver elephant
head pommel and the coat of
arms of the Siamese royal
family on the guard.

VICTORIAN OFFICER'S SWORD
With its "VR" cypher, curved blade, and
snakeskin hilt, this is a fine example of a
British sword from the nineteenth-
century Indian colonial period. The solid
silver scabbard is engraved with flowers.

HUNTING SWORD
European hunters have long used swords
to kill wild boar, but by the nineteenth
century many hunting swords were
produced mainly for ceremonial use or for
presentation. This German sword, made by
the well-known Solingen firm of WKC
(Weyersberg, Kirschbaum, & Co.),
belonged to Kaiser Wilhelm II (1859–1941)
and bears his coat of arms.

OFFICER'S SWORDS

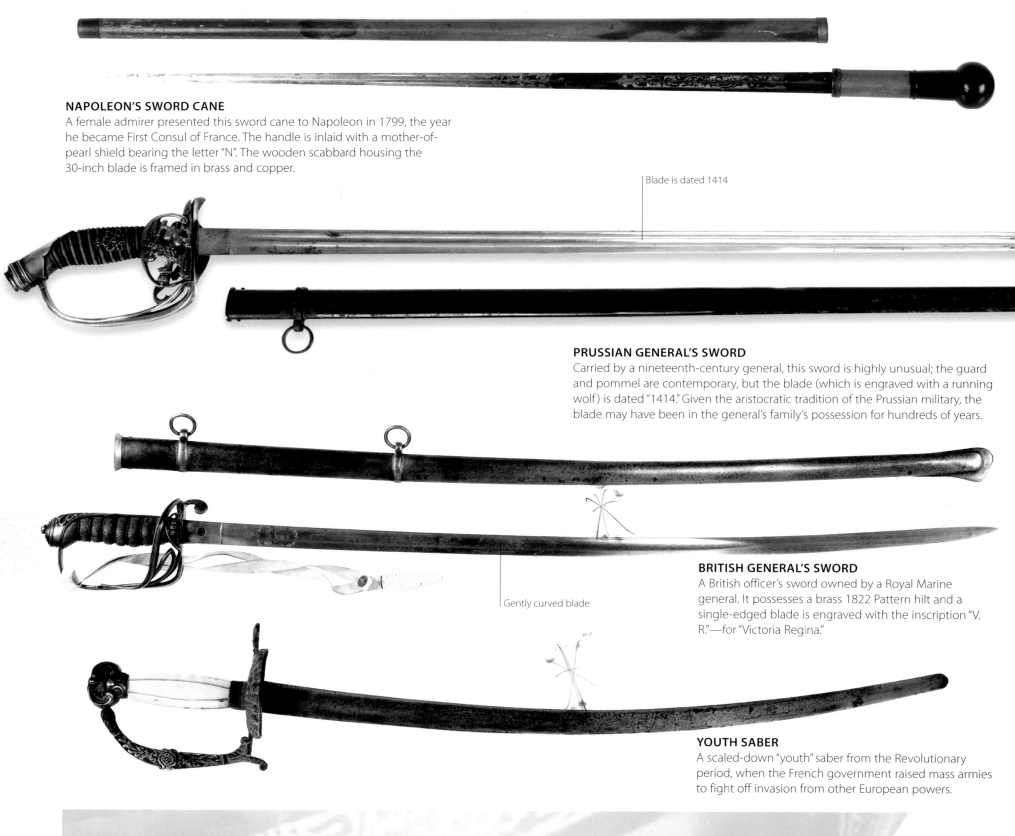

NAPOLEON'S SWORD CANE

A female admirer presented this sword cane to Napoleon in 1799, the year he became First Consul of France. The handle is inlaid with a mother-of-pearl shield bearing the letter "N". The wooden scabbard housing the 30-inch blade is framed in brass and copper.

Blade is dated 1414

PRUSSIAN GENERAL'S SWORD

Carried by a nineteenth-century general, this sword is highly unusual; the guard and pommel are contemporary, but the blade (which is engraved with a running wolf) is dated "1414." Given the aristocratic tradition of the Prussian military, the blade may have been in the general's family's possession for hundreds of years.

Gently curved blade

BRITISH GENERAL'S SWORD

A British officer's sword owned by a Royal Marine general. It possesses a brass 1822 Pattern hilt and a single-edged blade is engraved with the inscription "V. R."—for "Victoria Regina."

YOUTH SABER

A scaled-down "youth" saber from the Revolutionary period, when the French government raised mass armies to fight off invasion from other European powers.

THE WILKINSON SWORD COMPANY

Although the Wilkinson name has long been associated with sword-making, the company began when gunsmith Henry Nock set up shop in Ludgate Street, London, in 1772. Nock became one of the most celebrated gunmakers of the time, later (1804) receiving a Royal Appointment as gunmaker to King George III. The company also made bayonets for its long arms, and following Nock's death in 1805, his son-in-law, Henry Wilkinson, diversified the product line to include swords. Wilkinson moved the company's production facilities to Pall Mall, and the Wilkinson Sword Company soon gained an international reputation for its high-quality swords and other edged weapons.

Later in the nineteenth century, the company began making other metal products, from typewriters to garden tools. Wilkinson Sword also became a leading manufacturer of razors after introducing one of the first "safety" razors in 1898—a position it retains today.

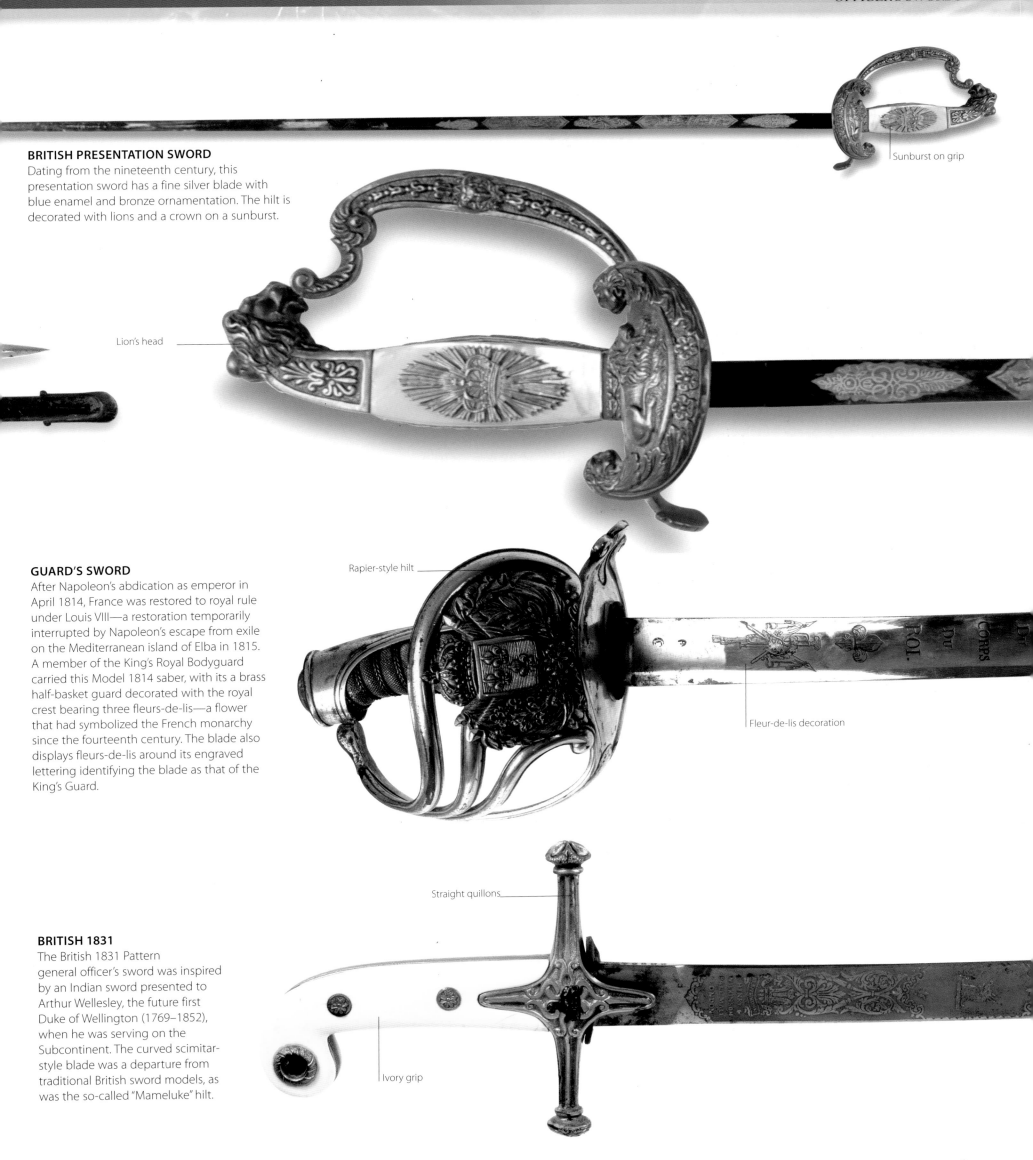

Sunburst on grip

BRITISH PRESENTATION SWORD
Dating from the nineteenth century, this presentation sword has a fine silver blade with blue enamel and bronze ornamentation. The hilt is decorated with lions and a crown on a sunburst.

Lion's head

GUARD'S SWORD
After Napoleon's abdication as emperor in April 1814, France was restored to royal rule under Louis VIII—a restoration temporarily interrupted by Napoleon's escape from exile on the Mediterranean island of Elba in 1815. A member of the King's Royal Bodyguard carried this Model 1814 saber, with its a brass half-basket guard decorated with the royal crest bearing three fleurs-de-lis—a flower that had symbolized the French monarchy since the fourteenth century. The blade also displays fleurs-de-lis around its engraved lettering identifying the blade as that of the King's Guard.

Rapier-style hilt

Fleur-de-lis decoration

Straight quillons

BRITISH 1831
The British 1831 Pattern general officer's sword was inspired by an Indian sword presented to Arthur Wellesley, the future first Duke of Wellington (1769–1852), when he was serving on the Subcontinent. The curved scimitar-style blade was a departure from traditional British sword models, as was the so-called "Mameluke" hilt.

Ivory grip

ROYAL PERSIAN SCIMITAR

This scimitar was commissioned by Abbas the Great, Shah of Persia (modern-day Iran) from 1588 to 1629. Abbas, who was born in Heras in what is now Afghanistan, came to the throne at the age of 16. The country was in a chaotic state, not least because of the poor leadership of Abbas's father. Even though Abbas had been put on the throne to be a figurehead under the direction of the Qizilbash—a disaffected faction within the country—he soon proved himself an able leader. He avenged the death of his mother, who had been killed by the Qizilbash, then he set about reducing their power in goverment and the army. Although he also had to accept the loss of some territories to neighboring powers, Abbas managed to regain land that had been lost in the time of his grandfather. Abbas was deeply interested in the arts and set about creating a new capital city, Isfahan, with mosques, colleges, baths, and caravansarais (roadside inns). Isfahan is still a major art center.

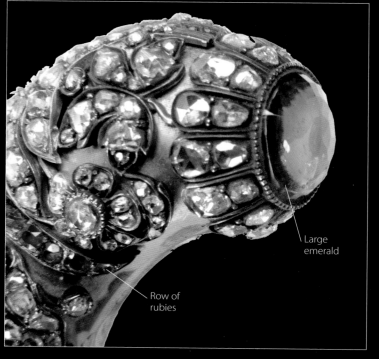

EMERALD IN THE POMMEL
An 11-karat emerald is set into the very top of the hilt. It is surrounded by diamonds and rubies, all set in finely made filigree gold.

Large emerald

Row of rubies

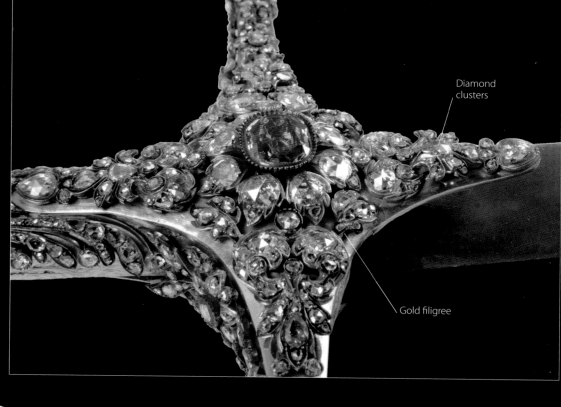

RUBY QUILLON BLOCK
The gold quillons and quillon block form a cross with a huge ruby at its center. Clusters of dimonds in leaf and floral gold settings surround the main jewel.

Diamond clusters

Gold filigree

Gem-encrusted quillon

Curved pommel

Curved blade

SCIMITAR AND SCABBARD
The decoration on the hilt and scabbard is incredibly finely detailed, with lines of rubies and clusters of diamonds. The scimitar is in remarkable condition considering what it has experienced over the last four centuries.

Rubies in top of scabbard

AN ARTISTIC LEGACY

Abbas became a patron of the arts and supported the establishment of a school of painting in Isfahan. He also encouraged the development of ceramics by inviting Chinese potters to come to the city. Although less is known about his love of jewelry, precious stones, and metalwork, it is likely that he appreciated these as much as he did the other arts, especially because such fine arts are a very good outward display an individual's wealth, social standing, and power.

It is known that Abbas commissioned this beautiful royal Persian Court sword and it is clear that no expense was spared in its making. It is decorated with 1,295 rose-cut diamonds, 50 karats of rubies, and an 11-karat emerald set in the hilt—all set in three pounds of gold. The sword's history is no less fascinating than its appearance. After the fall of the Safavid Dynasty in the eighteenth century, the sword fell into the hands of the Ottoman Turkish government, which then presented it to Empress Catherine the Great (1729–96) of Russia. It resided in the Czarist Treasury until it disappeared in the chaos of the Russian Revolution of 1917.

The sword resurfaced in Europe after World War II and spent some years in a private museum before being purchased by Colonel Farley Berman in 1962. It is now one of the "crown jewels" of the Berman Collection.

GOLD REPOUSSE
The back of the scabbard is decorated with intricate repoussé work featuring floral motifs and repeated geometric patterns.

EMPRESS CATHERINE THE GREAT
Catherine was passionate about the arts. Her personal collection formed the basis for the Hermitage Museum in St. Petersburg. This scimitar would have been among her most cherished items.

SCABBARD
When they were making a ceremonial sword, or one for presentation, artists used the scabbard to show off their skills. This scabbard is richly decorated at top and bottom to match the scimitar, but still has the classic sheath to protect the blade.

Fine gold repoussé decoration

The blade tapers to a fine point

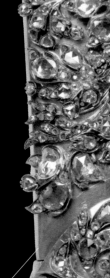

Gems in a floral decoration

Diamond and ruby medallion

AFRICAN SWORDS

INDIGENOUS SWORDS

Although often thought of as a European weapon, swords and swordmaking has flourished in Africa and Asia for many centuries. In Africa examples include the tabouka of the Tuareg, a nomadic North African people, and the Sudanese kaskara. Some of the finest swords of sub-Saharan Africa were the work of the Kuban culture, a coalition of Bantu-speaking peoples living in what is now Congo.

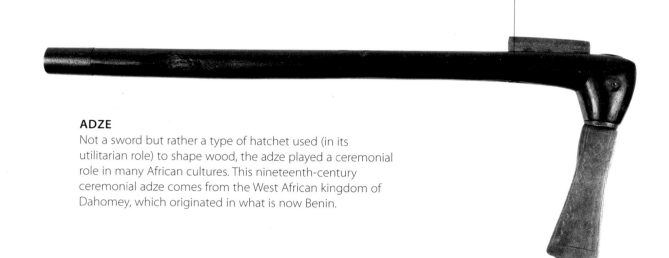

Decorative blade

ADZE

Not a sword but rather a type of hatchet used (in its utilitarian role) to shape wood, the adze played a ceremonial role in many African cultures. This nineteenth-century ceremonial adze comes from the West African kingdom of Dahomey, which originated in what is now Benin.

KUBAN SWORD

The name of the Kuba people of West Africa translates to "People of Lightning"—an apt description; they were one of the most warlike cultures of the region, and even sent women warriors into battle. They carried beautifully made but deadly weapons like the metal-bladed hardwood-handled sword shown here. The larger the blade, the greater the bearer's social status.

Short grip

AFRICAN SWORDS

A rare pair of African swords, these weapons—with 27-inch double-edged blades—have hand-carved hilts with male and female figures as pommels.

Pierced metal knuckle guard

Sickle-shaped blade

VICTORIAN PATTERN SWORD

This 1897 pattern infantry officers' sword has a sickle-shaped blade, based on the Ethiopian shotel. It is designed to strike around or over an enemy's shield. The blade also has the royal cypher ("VR") etched in the fullers.

AFRICAN MANDINGO SWORD
Mandingo swords come in various designs, but most have highly decorative leather hilts and scabbards. Most are west African; this one dates from the early twentieth century.

Elaborate decoration on sheath

Slightly curved blade

No protection for hand on grip

Man's head

NORTH AFRICAN SWORD
A nineteenth-century North African ceremonial sword with a carved wooden hilt ending in a pommel shaped like a man's head. The guard is unusual in that it includes a thumb-rest.

Simple hand guard

ASIAN SWORDS

THE MONGOL INFLUENCE

From in the early thirteenth century, the mounted armies of the Mongols came out of Central Asia to conquer much of China, India, and what is now known as the Middle East. The Mongol horseman's primary weapon was the bow, but he also carried a curved-bladed, single-edge sword designed for one-handed slashing from horseback. This weapon, referred to by historians as the Turko-Mongol saber, had a huge influence on the development of the sword throughout much of the world. The offspring of this "parent sword" includes the Arab saif, the Indian tulwar (and its Afghani counterpart, the pulwar), the Persian shamshir, the Turkish kilic, and eventually the European saber. In the West, curved swords of this type became generally known as "scimitars"—a designation that may derive from the Persian shamshir—although this catch-all term doesn't do justice to the wide variety of local adaptations to the original Turko-Mongol saber.

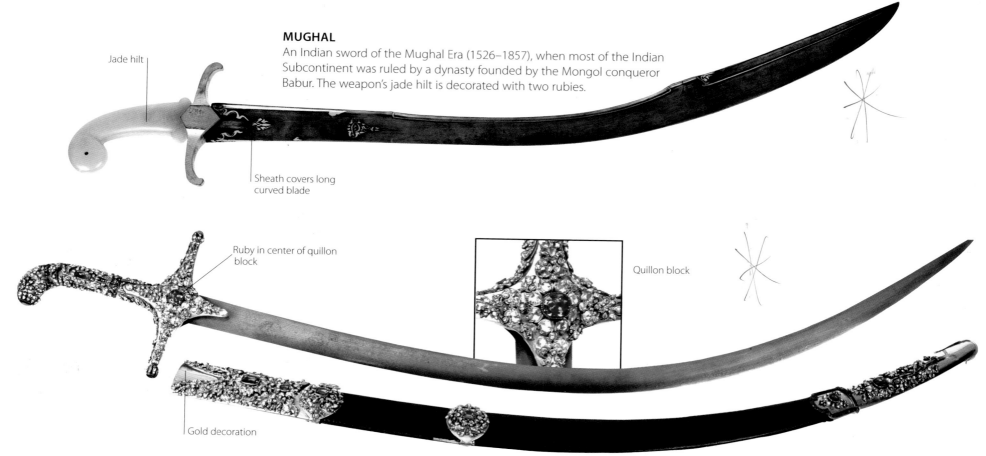

MUGHAL
An Indian sword of the Mughal Era (1526–1857), when most of the Indian Subcontinent was ruled by a dynasty founded by the Mongol conqueror Babur. The weapon's jade hilt is decorated with two rubies.

Jade hilt

Sheath covers long curved blade

Ruby in center of quillon block

Quillon block

Gold decoration

ROYAL PERSIAN SCIMITAR
Certainly one of the most beautiful weapons in existence, this royal Persian court sword was commissioned by Abbas the Great, Shah of Persia (modern-day Iran) from 1588 to 1629. It is decorated with 1,295 rose-cut diamonds, 50 karats worth of rubies, and an 11-karat emerald set in the hilt—all set in three pounds of gold.

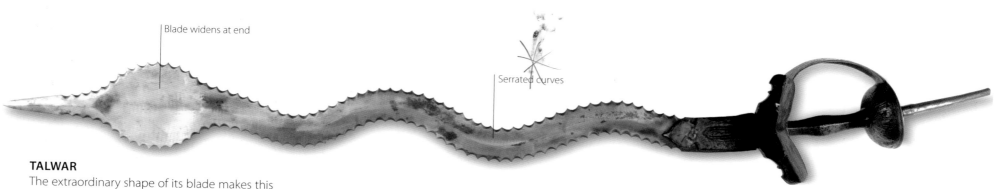

Blade widens at end

Serrated curves

TALWAR
The extraordinary shape of its blade makes this *talwar* (curved sword) stand out. From India and made around 1650, the hilt is iron and still has some of the original silver finish.

THE MAMELUKE SWORD

The Turko-Mongol saber also influenced the design of swords used by the Mamluks, or Mamelukes—slave-soldiers who formed a major part of Islamic armies from the ninth century on, and who set up dynasties of their own in Egypt and Syria from the thirteenth to sixteenth centuries. The Mamelukes were succeeded by the Ottoman Turks in Egypt. In 1804, an Ottoman official presented a Mameluke-style sword to U.S. Marine Corps Lieutenant Presley O'Bannon in recognition of his leadership of a mixed force of marines and mercenaries in an expedition to the city of Derne (in what is now Libya). There, he and his troops defeated the "Barbary pirates" of the North African coast, who were attacking American and European shipping and enslaving captured crew and passengers. The Commandant of the Marine Corps decreed the adoption of the "Mameluke sword" for marine officers, and marines still proudly wear the sword in the twenty-first century.

Curved grip and pommel

Basket pattern

PERSIAN SWORD

A Persian sword—this one with a straight blade and dating from the eighteenth century. The hilt features strips of gold in a basket pattern, and the Damascus steel blade is inlaid with gold.

TULWAR

This Indian tulwar from the late eighteenth or early nineteenth century, is of all-steel construction. The weapon typically had a curved blade of up to 30 inches; one of its distinctive features is the disk-shaped pommel. Like the Japanese katana, the tulwar was designed to be effective as both a slashing and thrusting weapon.

Disk-shaped pommel

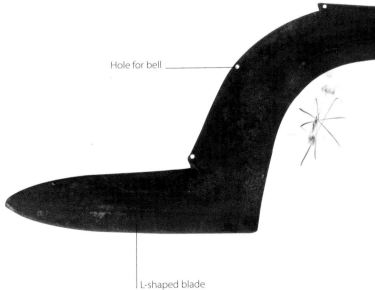

Hole for bell

INDIAN RITUAL SWORD

This rare ceremonial temple sword originated in Southern India in the early eighteenth century. The steel blade is double edged and peculiarly bent. It's upper edge possesses seven minute holes used for hanging small enclosed bells that would jangle with any movement of the blade.

L-shaped blade

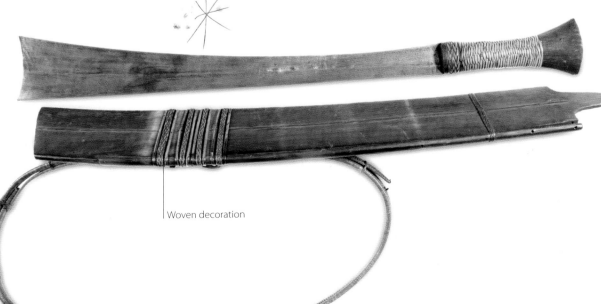

Woven decoration

DAO SWORD

In a wooden scabbard with a woven shoulder strap and hilt, this dao sword is Indo-Asian and dates from the late nineteenth century.

ASIAN SWORDS CONTINUED . . .

JAPANESE BLADES

In Japan, the sword played a unique and important cultural role. For centuries, sword ownership was restricted to the samurai—members of the warrior class, who had pledged to follow the code of bushido and bound to serve a lord, or daimyo. Samurai typically carried a katana, a curved single-edged weapon often wielded with both hands, and the wakizashi, a shorter sword; together, the two weapons were known as daisho, which translates to "big and little."

Although samurai fought primarily with bows and spears in actual battle, the sword was considered "the soul of the warrior," and countless hours were spent mastering it. Swordsmanship was an integral part of Japanese martial arts traditions that survive today.

Swordsmiths were the most highly respected craftsmen in medieval Japan; because of the sword's cultural significance, their work was considered as much spiritual as artisanal. The making of a katana was a long and intricate process, involving multiple hammerings and forgings of layers of steel to create blades whose sharpness and strength became legendary.

SAMURAI SWORD
The wearing of a katana, such as the eighteenth-century one shown here, was restricted to the samurai. It is traditionally worn with its blade edge-up. With the fall of the feudal system, the warrior aristocracy was outlawed in 1868, and sword makers set to work creating their goods for export.

Blade narrows to point

Square-ended scabbard

EIGHTEENTH-CENTURY SWORD
This photo shows the *tsuka* (handle) and *kashira* (pommel) of an eighteenth-century katana.

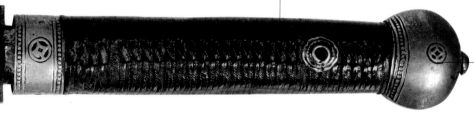

Plaited and woven grip

Pommel

MŌKO SHŪRAI EKOTOBA
This is the name of a pictorial scroll painted in 1293 showing the exploits of Takezaki Suenaga. He fought in the Battles of Bun'ei and Kōan, both against the Mongols, who were invading Japan. The scroll shows swords being used among other weapons, including bows and arrows and spears.

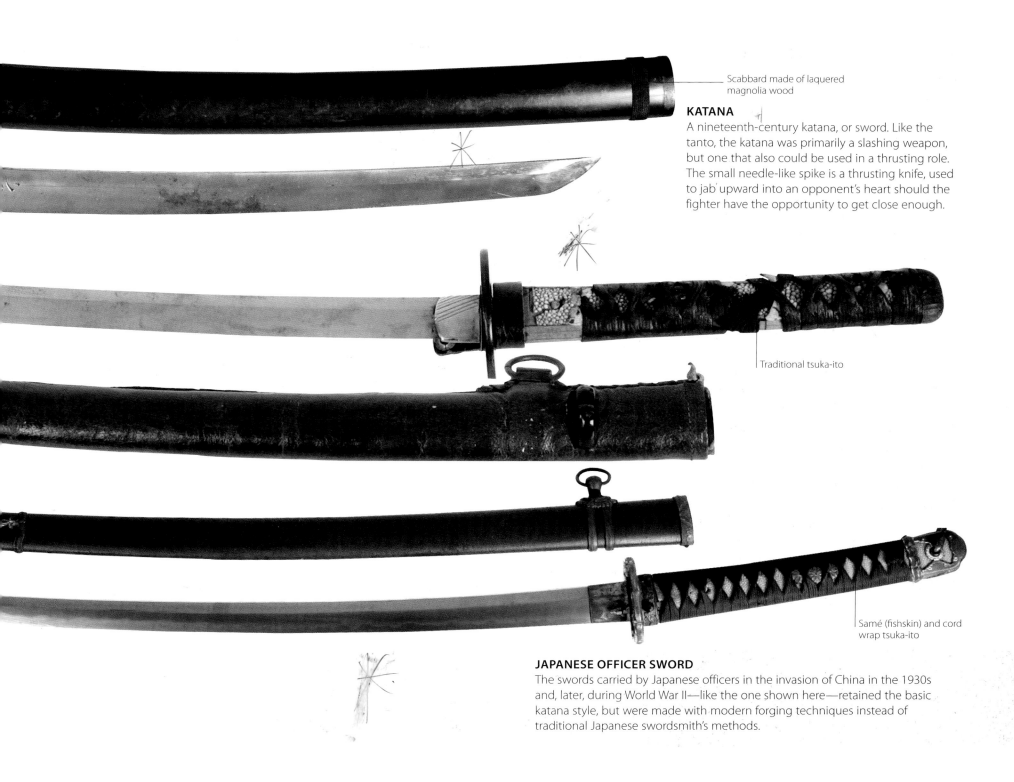

Scabbard made of laquered magnolia wood

KATANA
A nineteenth-century katana, or sword. Like the tanto, the katana was primarily a slashing weapon, but one that also could be used in a thrusting role. The small needle-like spike is a thrusting knife, used to jab upward into an opponent's heart should the fighter have the opportunity to get close enough.

Traditional tsuka-ito

Samé (fishskin) and cord wrap tsuka-ito

JAPANESE OFFICER SWORD
The swords carried by Japanese officers in the invasion of China in the 1930s and, later, during World War II—like the one shown here—retained the basic katana style, but were made with modern forging techniques instead of traditional Japanese swordsmith's methods.

ASIAN SWORDS CONTINUED . . .

THE CRAFT IN CHINA

Chinese swordmaking has a long and distinguished history, beginning with the bronze swords of the Chou Dynasty (1122–770 BC). Through the centuries, Chinese swordsmiths progressed from bronze to iron and eventually to steel, and developed techniques—like repeated forging and folding and differential hardening of edges—that influenced swordmaking throughout South and Southeast Asia, particularly in Japan. Some Chinese swordsmiths would leave blades exposed to the open air for years, subjecting them to all kinds of weather and extremes of temperature, as a form of "stress test"; only after blades survived this ordeal were they deemed worthy of completion.

As in Japan, swords had a cultural significance in China that went beyond mere weaponry: In the words of one historian, "Swords went on to assume multiple roles such as decoration, symbols of honor, power, and rank, and articles used in ceremonial or religious rites."

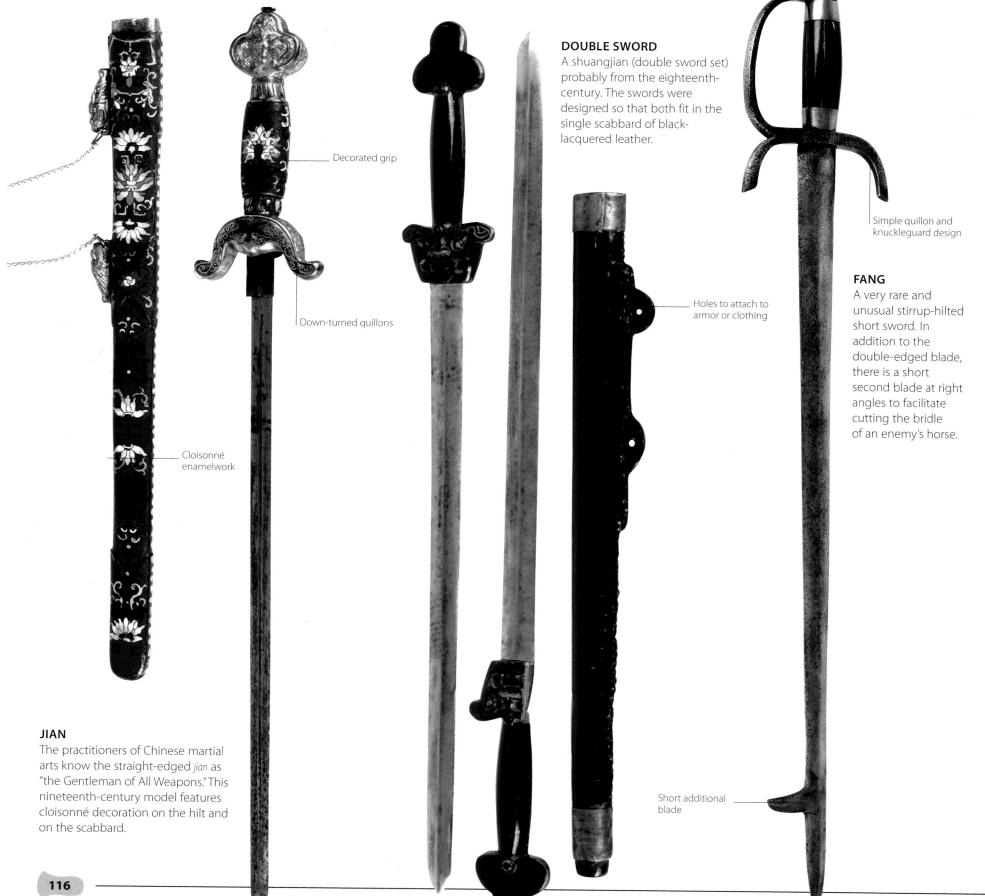

Decorated grip

Down-turned quillons

Cloisonné enamelwork

DOUBLE SWORD
A shuangjian (double sword set) probably from the eighteenth-century. The swords were designed so that both fit in the single scabbard of black-lacquered leather.

Holes to attach to armor or clothing

Simple quillon and knuckleguard design

FANG
A very rare and unusual stirrup-hilted short sword. In addition to the double-edged blade, there is a short second blade at right angles to facilitate cutting the bridle of an enemy's horse.

JIAN
The practitioners of Chinese martial arts know the straight-edged *jian* as "the Gentleman of All Weapons." This nineteenth-century model features cloisonné decoration on the hilt and on the scabbard.

Short additional blade

HELMET BREAKER
This Chinese helmet breaker was used like a club. Made of solid brass, this implement could knock out an opponent in battle even if he wore protective head gear.

Dragon mouth

Individual scenes from a legend

Close up detail

Intricate carving

SHORT SWORD
A richly decorated short sword with a hilt and scabbard of carved ivory. The carving on the latter depicts a monkey-hunting expedition.

117

ASIAN SWORDS CONTINUED . . .

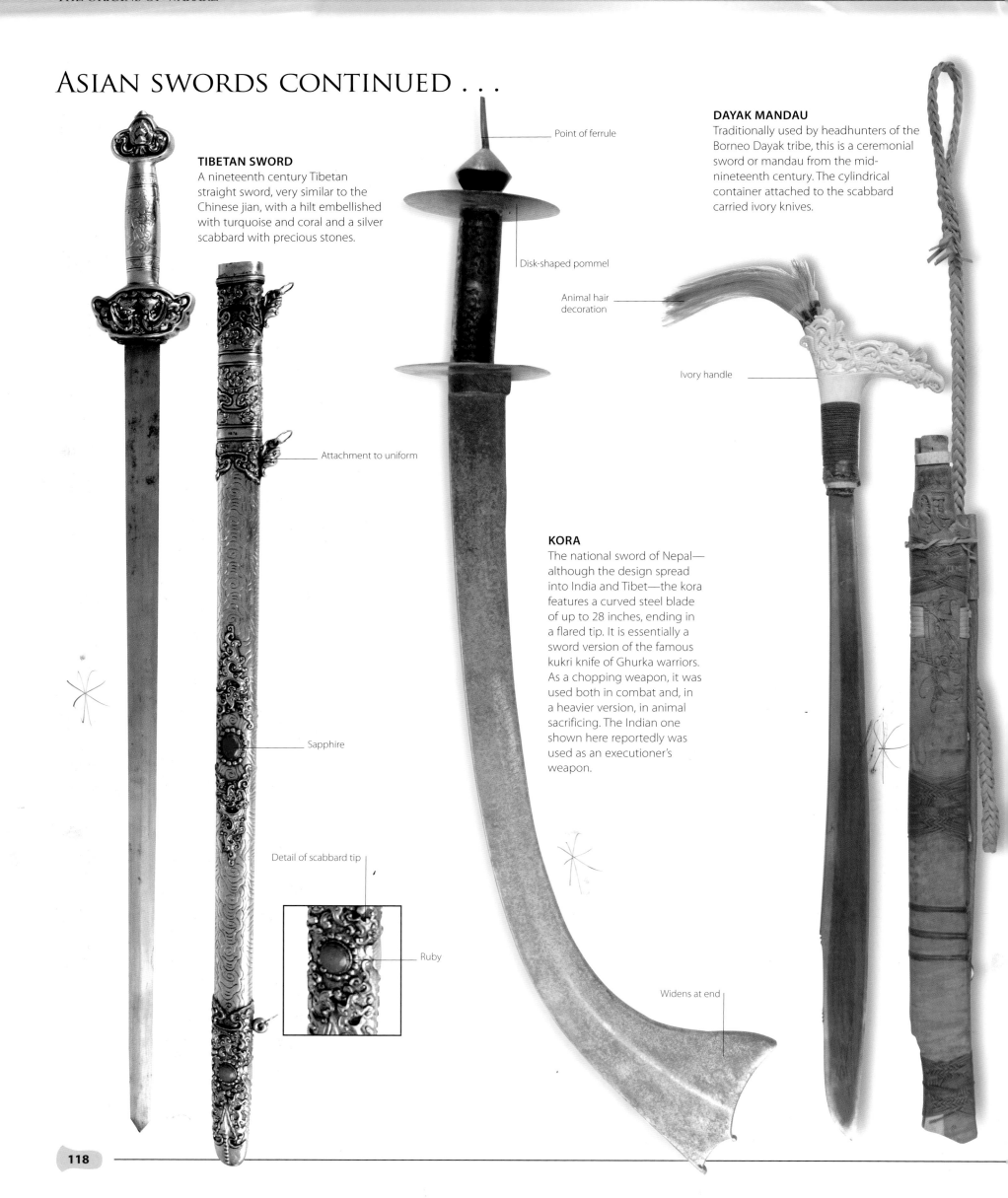

TIBETAN SWORD

A nineteenth century Tibetan straight sword, very similar to the Chinese jian, with a hilt embellished with turquoise and coral and a silver scabbard with precious stones.

Point of ferrule

Disk-shaped pommel

Attachment to uniform

Sapphire

Detail of scabbard tip

Ruby

DAYAK MANDAU

Traditionally used by headhunters of the Borneo Dayak tribe, this is a ceremonial sword or mandau from the mid-nineteenth century. The cylindrical container attached to the scabbard carried ivory knives.

Animal hair decoration

Ivory handle

KORA

The national sword of Nepal—although the design spread into India and Tibet—the kora features a curved steel blade of up to 28 inches, ending in a flared tip. It is essentially a sword version of the famous kukri knife of Ghurka warriors. As a chopping weapon, it was used both in combat and, in a heavier version, in animal sacrificing. The Indian one shown here reportedly was used as an executioner's weapon.

Widens at end

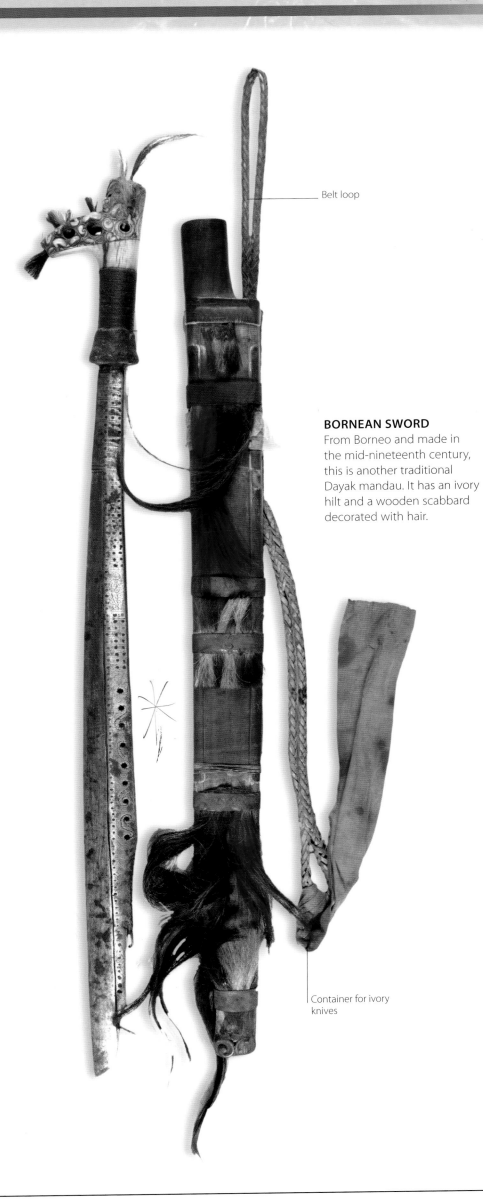

Belt loop

BORNEAN SWORD

From Borneo and made in the mid-nineteenth century, this is another traditional Dayak mandau. It has an ivory hilt and a wooden scabbard decorated with hair.

Container for ivory knives

MANDUA

A nineteenth-century mandau—a sword used by the headhunting Dayak people who lived in the interior of Borneo (part of the modern nation of Malaysia). Despite its relatively small size and light weight, it proved a deadly weapon in the hands of an experienced user, and also functioned as an all-purpose blade in addition to its role in combat. The small knife shown beside the sheath was used to clean heads taken from the enemy.

Ivory handle

Beaded ornamentation

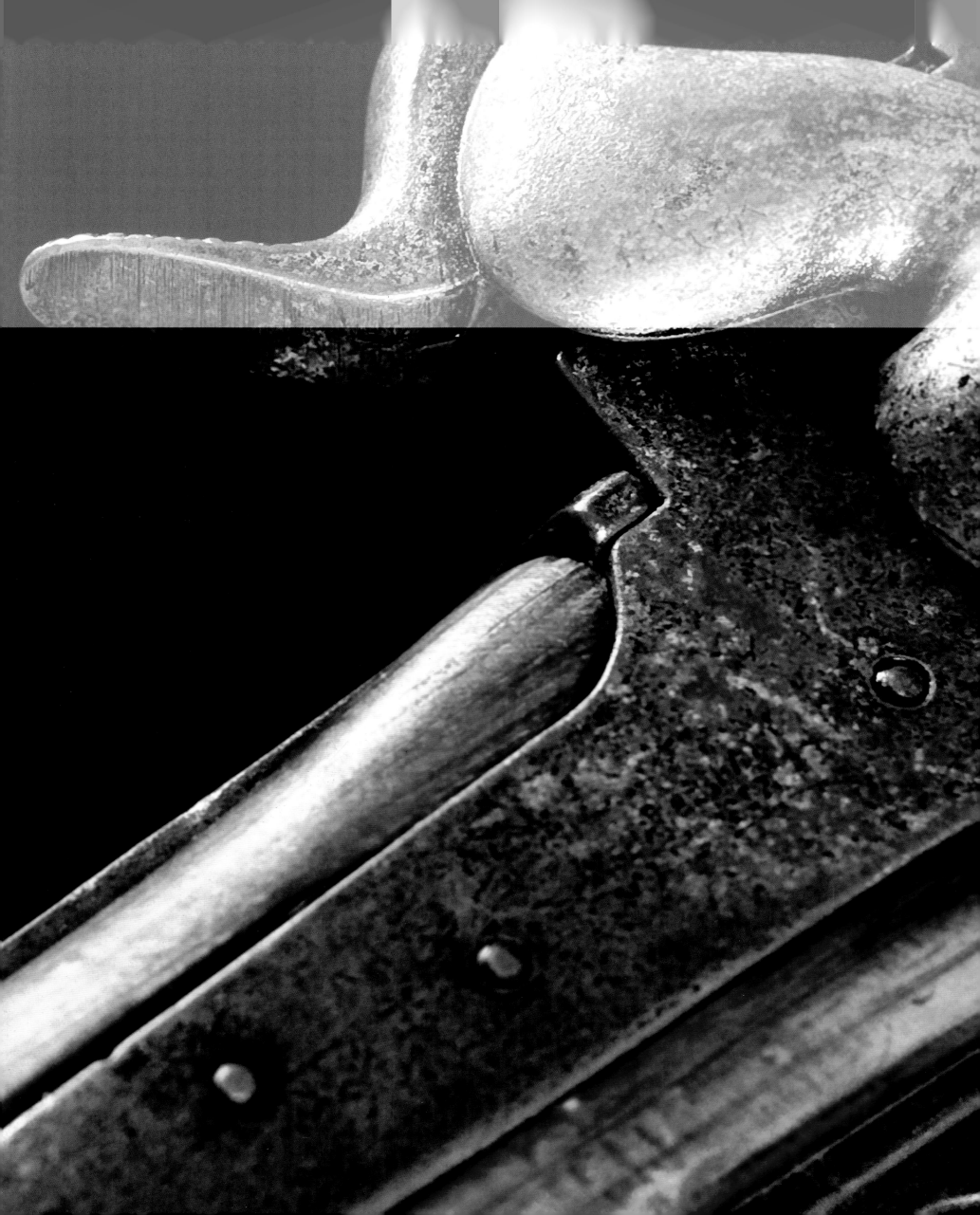

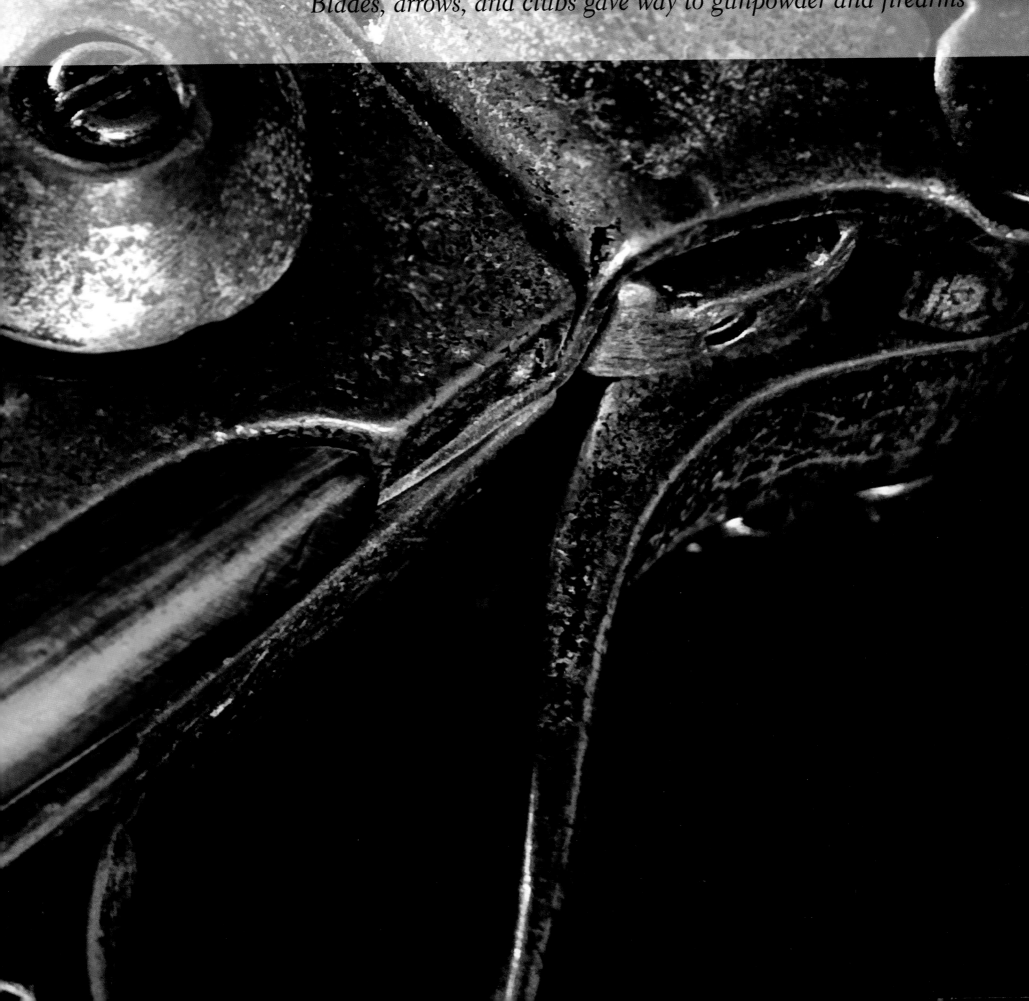

EARLY MODERN WARFARE

1150–1850

Blades, arrows, and clubs gave way to gunpowder and firearms

EARLY FIREARMS

Early firearms timeline
The ability of firearms to shoot accurately and kill from a distance was offset by the gunman's vulnerability while reloading his single-shot weapon. The evolution of firearms led inevitably to the multi-shot weapon.

1364
First recorded firearm

1440
Matchlock gun
(arquebus)

Gunpowder was probably introduced into European warfare in the fourteenth century, but cannon and bombs may have been used in Chinese warfare as early as the twelfth century. Although the so-called "Gunpowder Revolution" heralded a period of great change in weapon technology, this didn't happen overnight. Early cannon were crude and dangerous to operate—often firing balls of carved stone—but they were effective against fortifications and their use on battlefields must have had a powerful psychological effect. The subsequent development of handheld firearms had profound consequences, giving infantry the upper hand in battle and ultimately ending the era of the mounted knight. By the eighteenth century, firearms technology had advanced from the matchlock arquebus to the flintlock musket, which—in the hands of drilled, disciplined, professional armies— came to dominate the battlefield. The use of a range of firearms also gave European soldiers an advantage over indigenous peoples as Western powers began to build empires in what they called "the New World."

The Boston Massacre
Based on Henry Pelham's depiction of the Boston Massacre (March 5, 1770), this image vividly shows the devastating power of gunpowder.

1509
Wheellock gun

1540
Rifling appears in firearms

1570
Snaphaunce two-piece
flintlock mechanism

1612
One-piece
flintlock
mechanism

1750
Kentucky rifle

1825
Percussion-cap gun

1835
First Colt revolver

1840
Pin-fire cartridge

HAND-HELD GUNPOWDER WEAPONS

Handheld gunpowder weapons—usually called hand cannons or hand gonnes—developed in parallel with artillery. They first appeared in Europe during the midfifteenth century and were basically just miniature cannons, held under a soldier's arm or braced against his shoulder—and often supported by a stake—with a second soldier firing the weapon by means of a slow match (see below). The introduction of the matchlock firing system led to the development of lighter, less awkward handheld guns that could be loaded and fired by one man, including the arquebus and its successor, the musket. In the next century, infantry equipped with matchlock-equipped guns would become a major component of armies in both Europe and Asia.

THE MATCHLOCK MECHANISM

The "match" was a length of cord soaked in a chemical compound (usually potassium nitrate, a.k.a. saltpeter) to make it burn slowly. The match was held in an S-shaped lever (the serpentine) over a pan of priming powder. Pulling the trigger lowered the match, igniting the priming powder, which then (by means of a touch-hole) ignited the main powder charge in the barrel and fired the projectile. A later, spring-loaded variation, the snap lock, "snapped" the serpentine down into the pan. Below are examples of matchlock (top) and flintlock (bottom) mechanisms.

FRENCH HAND GONNE
An early French hand cannon, with a one-inch barrel attached to a rough wooden stock with iron bands. This weapon eventually wound up in Morocco, North Africa.

CHINESE SIGNAL GUN
While the Chinese probably made the first use of gunpowder as early as the tenth century, just when they applied gunpowder to weaponry is debated. They certainly made use of gunpowder for ceremonial purposes, for firecrackers, and for signaling purposes early on. This Chinese hand cannon from the eighteenth century was probably used for signaling. It is made of bronze and decorated with a dragon stretching from breech to muzzle.

SPANISH HAND CANNON

While hand cannons were usually braced against the chest or shoulder or held under the arm, this sixteenth-century Spanish weapon, just 5 inches in overall length, was fired literally from the hand—making it an early pistol. It is made of bronze, and has a handle in the form of a seated lion.

BATTLE OF MORAT GUN

This hand cannon—which hints at the form of the later pistol—was captured by Swiss troops after the Battle of Morat, fought near Bern on June 22, 1476. The battle saw the outnumbered Swiss defeat the forces of Charles the Bold, the Duke of Burgundy. The battle was notable in being one of the first in which large numbers of handheld firearms were used; as many as 10,000 on both sides combined, according to some sources.

"WHAT GUNPOWDER DID FOR WAR THE PRINTING PRESS HAS DONE FOR THE MIND."

Wendell Phillips

KEY PISTOL

Shown here is a highly unusual adaptation of the matchlock mechanism: a combination gate key and matchlock pistol from eighteenth-century Scotland.

Key bow

HAND-HELD GUNPOWDER WEAPONS CONTINUED . . .

MATCHLOCK FIREARMS

Shoulder-fired matchlock guns—variously known as arquebuses, hackbuts, calivers, culverins, and eventually muskets—had many drawbacks, most notably their unreliability in wet weather and the fact that the smoldering match could betray the firer's position to the enemy. Despite these deficiencies, they proved remarkably enduring—largely because they were inexpensive to manufacture and simple to use. However, gunsmiths continued to experiment with better firing systems.

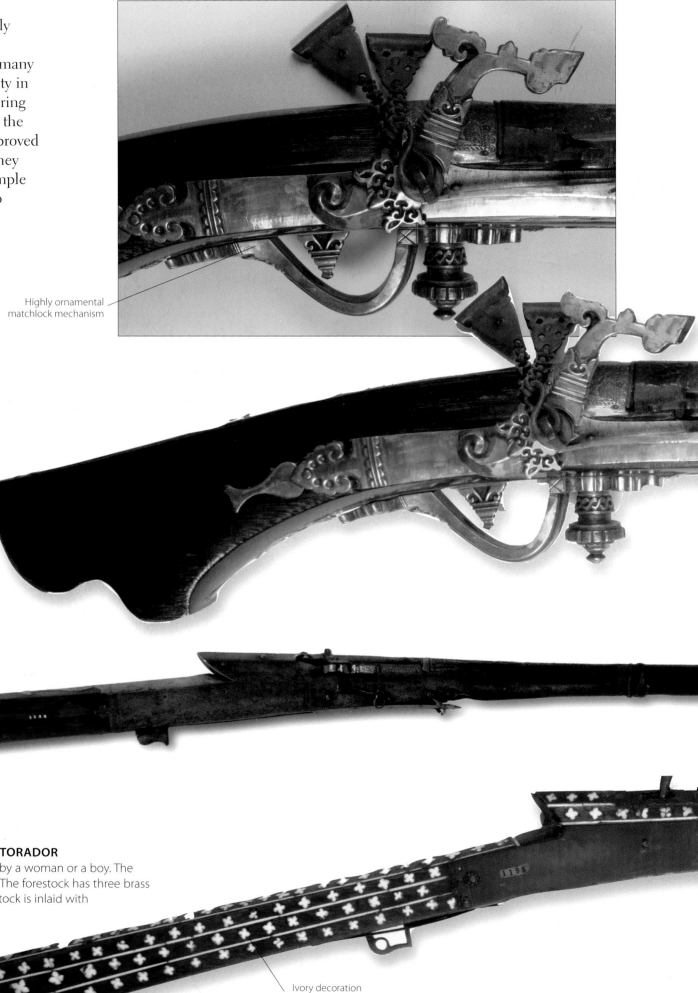

Highly ornamental
matchlock mechanism

INDIAN MATCHLOCK RIFLE

Along with its wooden body and cast-iron barrel, this rifle has a highly ornamental silver and brass mechanism and barrel decoration. It was made in the early seventeenth century.

INDIAN EIGHTEENTH-CENTURY MATCHLOCK TORADOR

This small rifle would have been intended for use by a woman or a boy. The barrel is 17½ inches long and has a flared muzzle. The forestock has three brass bands, brass sideplates, and a match holder. The stock is inlaid with ivory lines and stars and has an ivory butt.

Ivory decoration

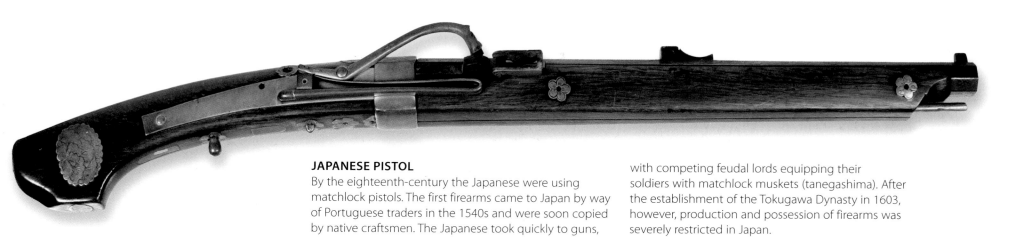

JAPANESE PISTOL

By the eighteenth-century the Japanese were using matchlock pistols. The first firearms came to Japan by way of Portuguese traders in the 1540s and were soon copied by native craftsmen. The Japanese took quickly to guns, with competing feudal lords equipping their soldiers with matchlock muskets (tanegashima). After the establishment of the Tokugawa Dynasty in 1603, however, production and possession of firearms was severely restricted in Japan.

INDIAN TORADOR

The torador was a type of matchlock gun used in India for hundreds of years. This model, from the eighteenth or early nineteenth century, has a 46-inch barrel ending in a muzzle chiseled in the form of a leopard's head; the breach and muzzle feature koftgari decoration—a form of inlaying gold and steel.

Muzzle is chiseled in the form of a leopard's head and decorated with gold koftgari.

RIFLING

As early as the fifteenth century, European gunsmiths began boring grooves on the inside of gun barrels—a process that would become known as rifling. The initial purpose was probably to reduce the buildup of gunpowder residue in the barrel, but it was discovered that a barrel with spiral grooves gave stability to a bullet in flight, greatly increasing its accuracy. Rifling, however, was a difficult process until improvements in technology brought by the Industrial Revolution. Although rifles were used in hunting and carried by specialized military units, most firearms remained smoothbore (i.e., nonrifled) until well into the nineteenth century.

HAND-HELD GUNPOWDER WEAPONS CONTINUED . . .

THE WHEEL LOCK

The wheel lock, the next major advance after the matchlock, combined a spring-loaded, serrated metal wheel and a dog, or cock—a pair of metal jaws that held a piece of iron pyrite. The wheel was wound up (usually with a key) to put tension on the spring. When the trigger was pulled, the cock struck against the rotating wheel, striking sparks to fire the weapon. The wheel lock gun was likely inspired by the handheld tinder-lighters in use at the time.

The introduction of the wheel lock spurred the development of the pistol. (The term "pistol" may derive from the arms-producing city of Pistoia in Italy, although there are other theories; early pistols were often called dags, which probably derives from an old French word for "dagger.") Pistols put firepower into the hands of mounted troops; as concealable weapons, criminals and assassins also quickly adopted them. In 1584, a wheel lock pistol was employed to murder the Dutch leader William the Silent in the world's first political assassination by pistol.

GERMAN WHEEL LOCK PISTOLS

This rare and magnificent pair of wheel lock pistols was made in Saxony, Germany, around 1590. They are shown with a matching box designed to carry five cartridges—which at the time consisted of powder and ball wrapped in paper or leather—and the key required to wind the wheel lock mechanism.

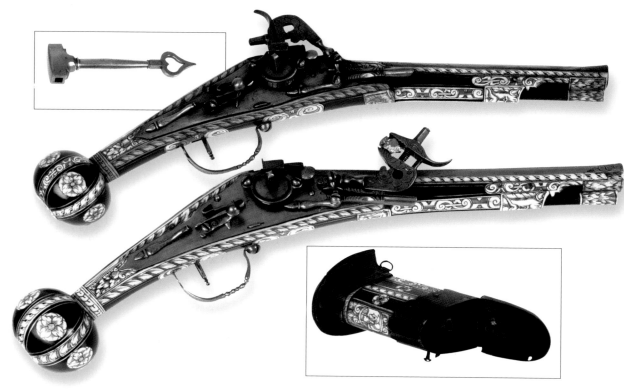

RAMPART GUN

A wheel lock European rampart gun from about 1600. Rampart guns were mounted on the walls of castles and fortifications (and, at sea, on ship's rails) for defense; this .76 model was designed so that it could be fired by "remote control" by means of a string.

GERMAN WHEEL LOCK RIFLE

This German wheel lock rifle was probably made in Nuremberg in 1597. The stock is inlaid with ivory carvings of deer and fowl. Wheel lock muskets and rifles were expensive, so they enjoyed much popularity as hunting weapons for the aristocracy and the rich.

GERMAN WHEEL LOCK MUSKET

Another finely made example of a wheel lock weapon.

WHEEL LOCK PISTOL
This sixteenth-century wheel lock pistol was made in Britain. It has two triggers, which are fired by two separate mechanisms, giving the pistol its unusual appearance.

THE FLINTLOCK

The wheel lock's heyday was brief. By the mid- to late sixteenth century, Northern Europe saw the development of the snaphance, or snaphaunce, lock. (The term came from a Dutch word for "pecking bird.") In the snaphance, the cock held a piece of flint, which sprang forward on the trigger-pull to strike a piece of steel (the frizzen), sending sparks into the priming pan. A similar type of lock, the miquelet, appeared around the same time in southern Europe. Technical refinements to both eventually led to the introduction of the true flintlock early in the seventeenth century.

CANNON IGNITER
Flintlock mechanisms were not only used on handheld guns but were also fitted to artillery, particularly naval guns. Shown here is a British flintlock cannon igniter from the early nineteenth century. The 22-inch weapon's lock was placed against the touch-hole of a cannon; pulling the trigger pulled back an external link that fired it and ignited the powder charge .

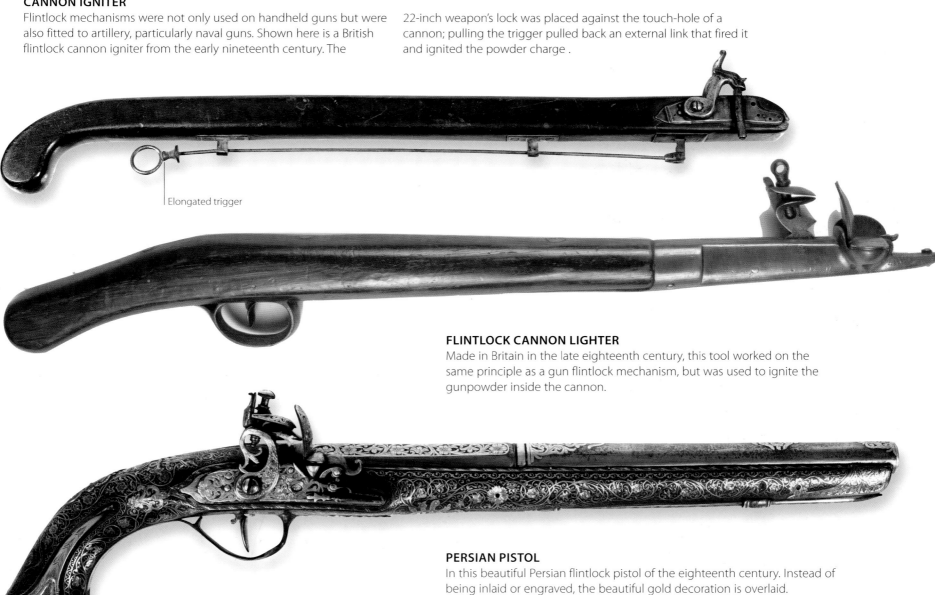

Elongated trigger

FLINTLOCK CANNON LIGHTER
Made in Britain in the late eighteenth century, this tool worked on the same principle as a gun flintlock mechanism, but was used to ignite the gunpowder inside the cannon.

PERSIAN PISTOL
In this beautiful Persian flintlock pistol of the eighteenth century. Instead of being inlaid or engraved, the beautiful gold decoration is overlaid.

Key Guns

The task of guarding a door can be fraught with danger. Would-be intruders might try to trick or force their way in, and prisoners naturally do the same to get out of their cells. Often, the doorman is at his most vulnerable when he is close to the door and lifting its bars or, in more recent times, actually turning the key in its lock. The key gun was an ingenious device invented in the seventeenth century to protect the doorman in the act of locking a door if he was under threat from the other side. Fired while in the lock, it could send a small projectile into the body of a person pressing against the door, perhaps gaining precious moments to turn the key and secure the door. However, key guns are rare enough to suggest that were made more for collectors than jailors.

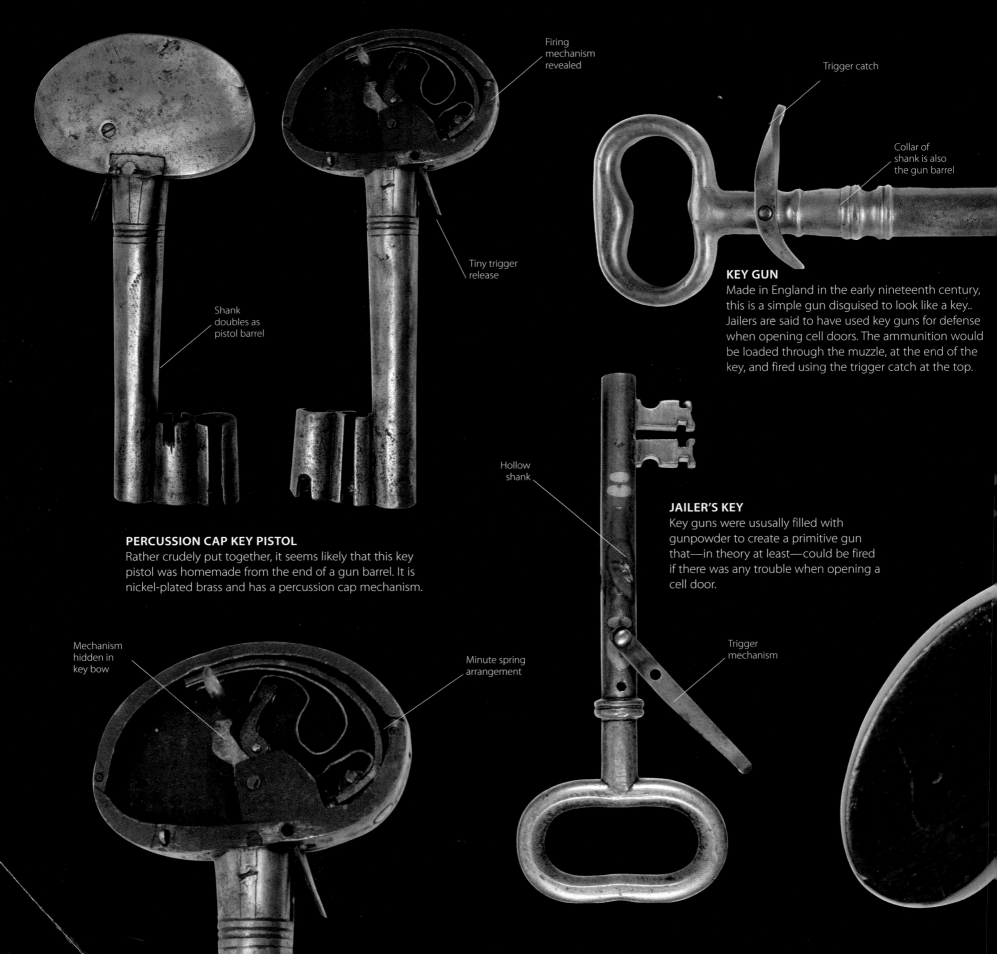

Firing mechanism revealed

Tiny trigger release

Shank doubles as pistol barrel

Trigger catch

Collar of shank is also the gun barrel

KEY GUN
Made in England in the early nineteenth century, this is a simple gun disguised to look like a key.. Jailers are said to have used key guns for defense when opening cell doors. The ammunition would be loaded through the muzzle, at the end of the key, and fired using the trigger catch at the top.

PERCUSSION CAP KEY PISTOL
Rather crudely put together, it seems likely that this key pistol was homemade from the end of a gun barrel. It is nickel-plated brass and has a percussion cap mechanism.

Hollow shank

JAILER'S KEY
Key guns were ususally filled with gunpowder to create a primitive gun that—in theory at least—could be fired if there was any trouble when opening a cell door.

Mechanism hidden in key bow

Minute spring arrangement

Trigger mechanism

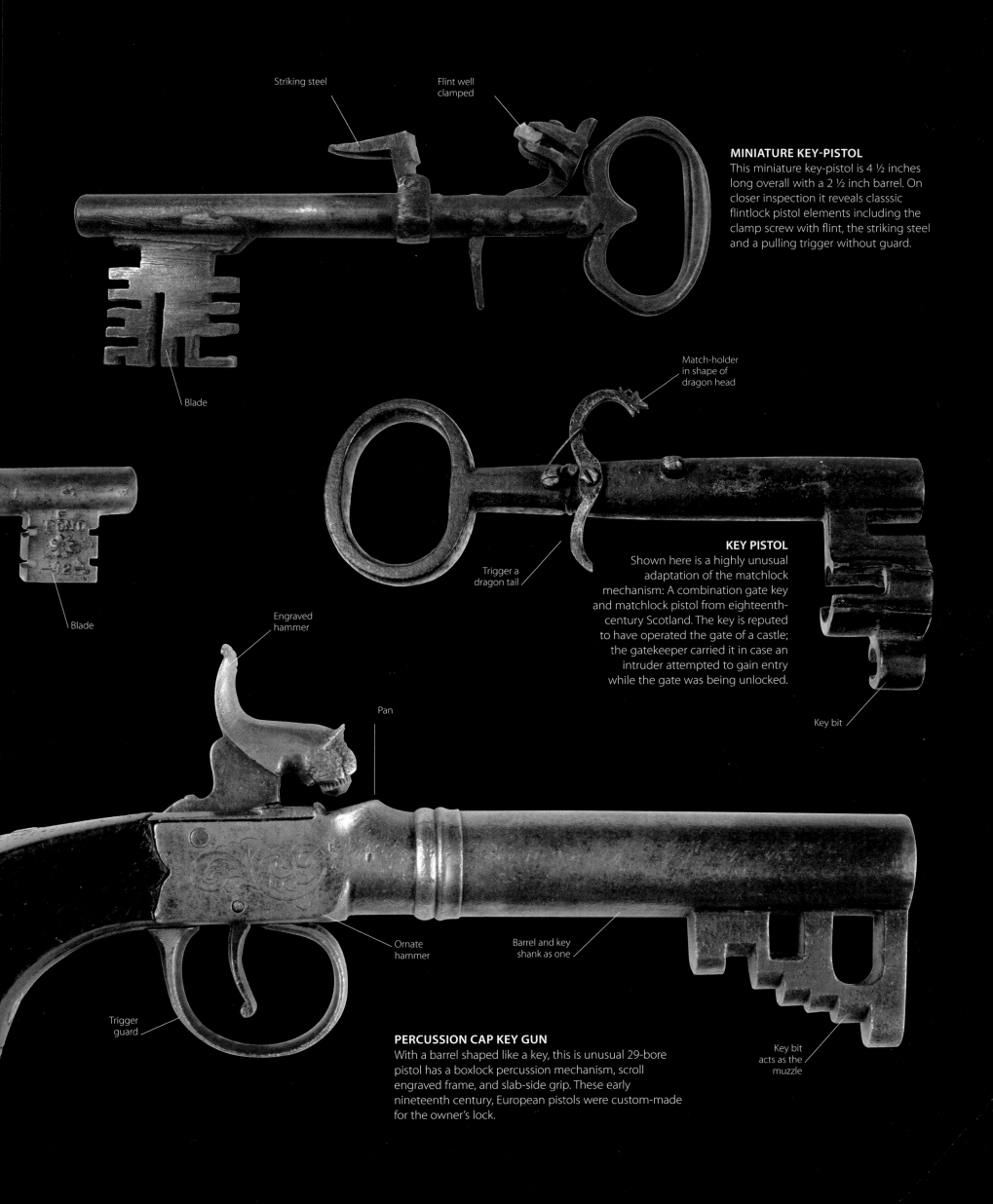

Striking steel

Flint well clamped

MINIATURE KEY-PISTOL
This miniature key-pistol is 4 ½ inches long overall with a 2 ½ inch barrel. On closer inspection it reveals classsic flintlock pistol elements including the clamp screw with flint, the striking steel and a pulling trigger without guard.

Blade

Match-holder in shape of dragon head

Blade

Trigger a dragon tail

KEY PISTOL
Shown here is a highly unusual adaptation of the matchlock mechanism: A combination gate key and matchlock pistol from eighteenth-century Scotland. The key is reputed to have operated the gate of a castle; the gatekeeper carried it in case an intruder attempted to gain entry while the gate was being unlocked.

Key bit

Engraved hammer

Pan

Ornate hammer

Barrel and key shank as one

Trigger guard

PERCUSSION CAP KEY GUN
With a barrel shaped like a key, this is unusual 29-bore pistol has a boxlock percussion mechanism, scroll engraved frame, and slab-side grip. These early nineteenth century, European pistols were custom-made for the owner's lock.

Key bit acts as the muzzle

THE FLINTLOCK

The adoption of the flintlock firing mechanism led to a proliferation of pistols. Despite their considerable drawbacks—ineffectiveness at any but close ranges, slow loading by the muzzle, vulnerability to inclement weather—these guns gave individuals a potent weapon for self-defense, which was no small thing in an era without the benefit of any organized police forces, and in which robbers lurked after dark on the streets of towns and cities and highwaymen haunted rural roads.

COAT, HOLSTER, AND BELT PISTOLS

Generally, pistols of the flintlock era fall into three types:

The first were coat pistols, also known as traveler's pistols. As the name implies, these were personal-defense weapons compact enough to be carried in the pockets of the overcoats worn by men of the time; very short-barreled versions could also be carried in a waistcoat pocket or elsewhere on one's person.

The second type were holster, or horse pistols—weapons with relatively long barrels that were intended to be worn in a holster attached to a horse's saddle.

The third type were belt pistols. Of an intermediate size and caliber between coat and holster pistols, they were usually fitted with a hook, which could be attached to the belt.

CLERMONT PISTOL
A very finely made .48 pistol, probably French in origin

COAT PISTOL
A short-barreled coat pistol, probably made in France around the turn of the nineteenth century

DUBLIN CASTLE PISTOL

This walnut-stocked, brass-finished .65 pistol was made in Dublin, Ireland, and bears the royal cipher of King George III (1738–1820). Ireland was a British colony at the time, and the armory at Dublin Castle was—together with the armories at Birmingham and at the Tower of London in England—a principal supplier of arms to the British Army and Navy.

Square-shaped bullet

SQUARE BARREL

This early nineteenth century British pistol is unusual in having a square barrel designed to fire matching bullets. The bullets produced more ragged—and thus more fatal—entry and exit wounds.

FLINTLOCK TRAP GUN

The stock on this gun has a rectangular hole in it, which suggests it would be mounted on a support or rest. A string or wire would have been tied to the trigger mechanism and then to a door. When the door was opened, it pulled the trigger, firing the gun—hence the name "trap." It was made by Heinrich Kappell, one of the most famous Danish gunsmiths during the period of 1674–1718. He was based in Copenhagen.

THE FLINTLOCK CONTINUED . . .

TURN-OFFS AND TURN-OVERS

While a majority of flintlock pistols were muzzle-loaders, like their long-arm counterparts, the so-called turn-off, or screw-off pistol appeared in the mid-seventeenth century. These weapons had a cannon-shaped barrel that could be unscrewed, loaded with a bullet, and replaced; the powder charge went into a compartment in the breech. In contrast to the mostly smoothbore pistols of the time, turn-offs often had rifled barrels, greatly increasing accuracy. During the English Civil Wars (1642–51), Prince Rupert, commander of the Royalist cavalry, is said to have used such a weapon to hit the weathervane on top of a church at a distance of about 300 feet; he then repeated the shot to prove that the first was not a fluke.

There were also multiple-barreled pistols. One type had two side-by-side barrels, each fired by a separate lock; another, the turn-over pistol, had two or more barrels that were loaded individually and rotated into place to be fired by a single lock. Gunsmiths also experimented with producing flintlock pepperboxes and even revolvers; however, most multiple-shot flintlock pistols tended to be unreliable and prone to accidental firing. An exception was the duckfoot pistol, which had several barrels in a horizontal configuration that were designed for simultaneous firing.

This fascinating selection of flintlocks features both rare and significant items from the fifteenth through nineteenth centuries.

CANNON BARREL PISTOL
A .52 cannon-barreled pistol made by Patrick of Liverpool around 1805. This type of pistol got its name from the resemblance of their barrels to those of artillery pieces; they were also known as "Queen Anne pistols," although according to firearms historian David Miller, most were produced well after that British queen's death in 1714. The pistol also uses a boxlock action, in which the firing mechanism is located on top of the breech rather than on the side of the weapon.

Cannon shaped barrel

Engraved brass trimmings

SNAPHANCE FLINTLOCK PISTOL
Along with a comparatively short-barrel, this pistol has a snaphance mechanism—technically a less complicated development of the wheel lock firing mechanism and designed before the even simpler "true" flintlock. It fires from a flint struck against a striker plate above a steel pan to ignite the priming powder, which then fires the gun. This handsome model is Spanish and dates from the early eighteenth century.

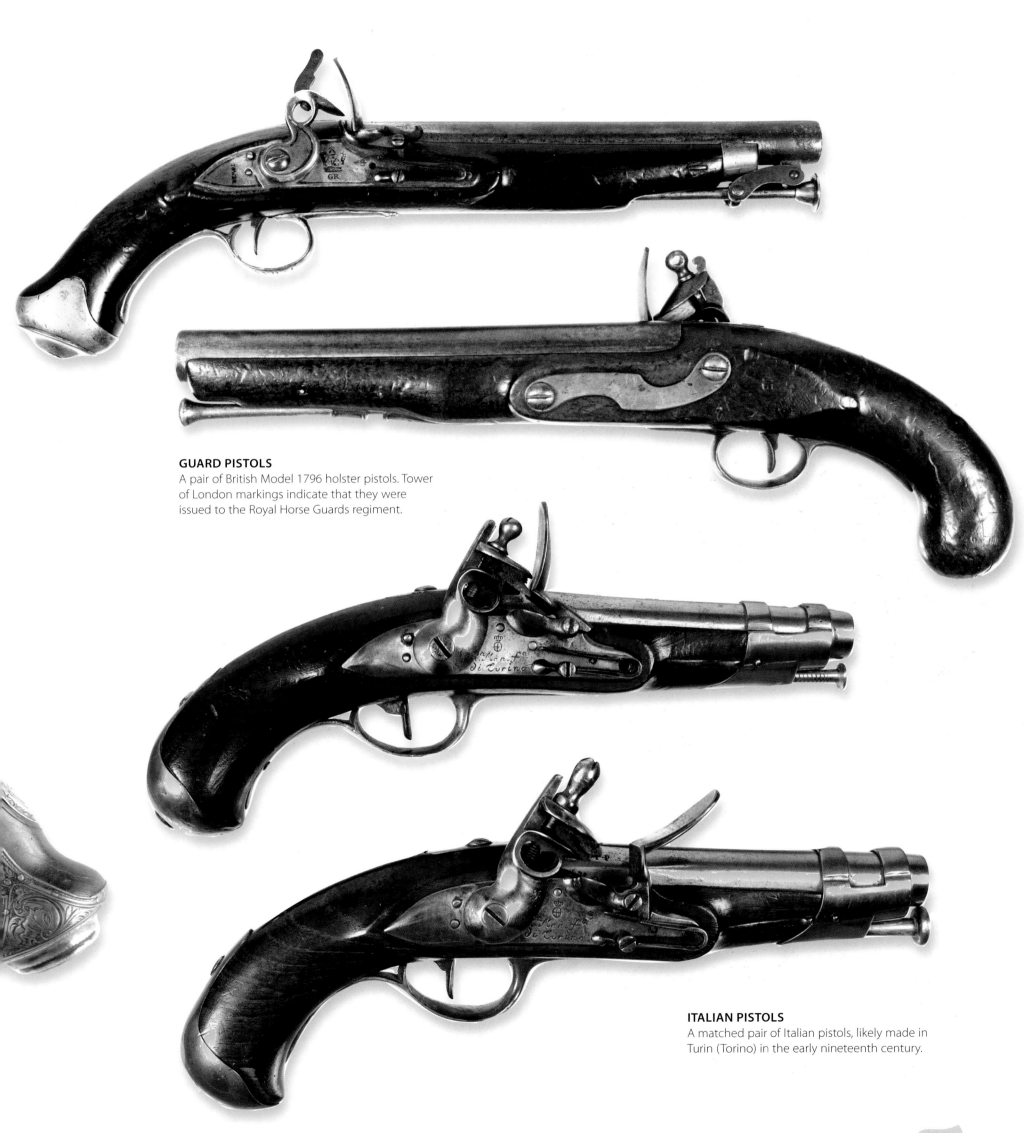

GUARD PISTOLS
A pair of British Model 1796 holster pistols. Tower of London markings indicate that they were issued to the Royal Horse Guards regiment.

ITALIAN PISTOLS
A matched pair of Italian pistols, likely made in Turin (Torino) in the early nineteenth century.

THE FLINTLOCK CONTINUED . . .

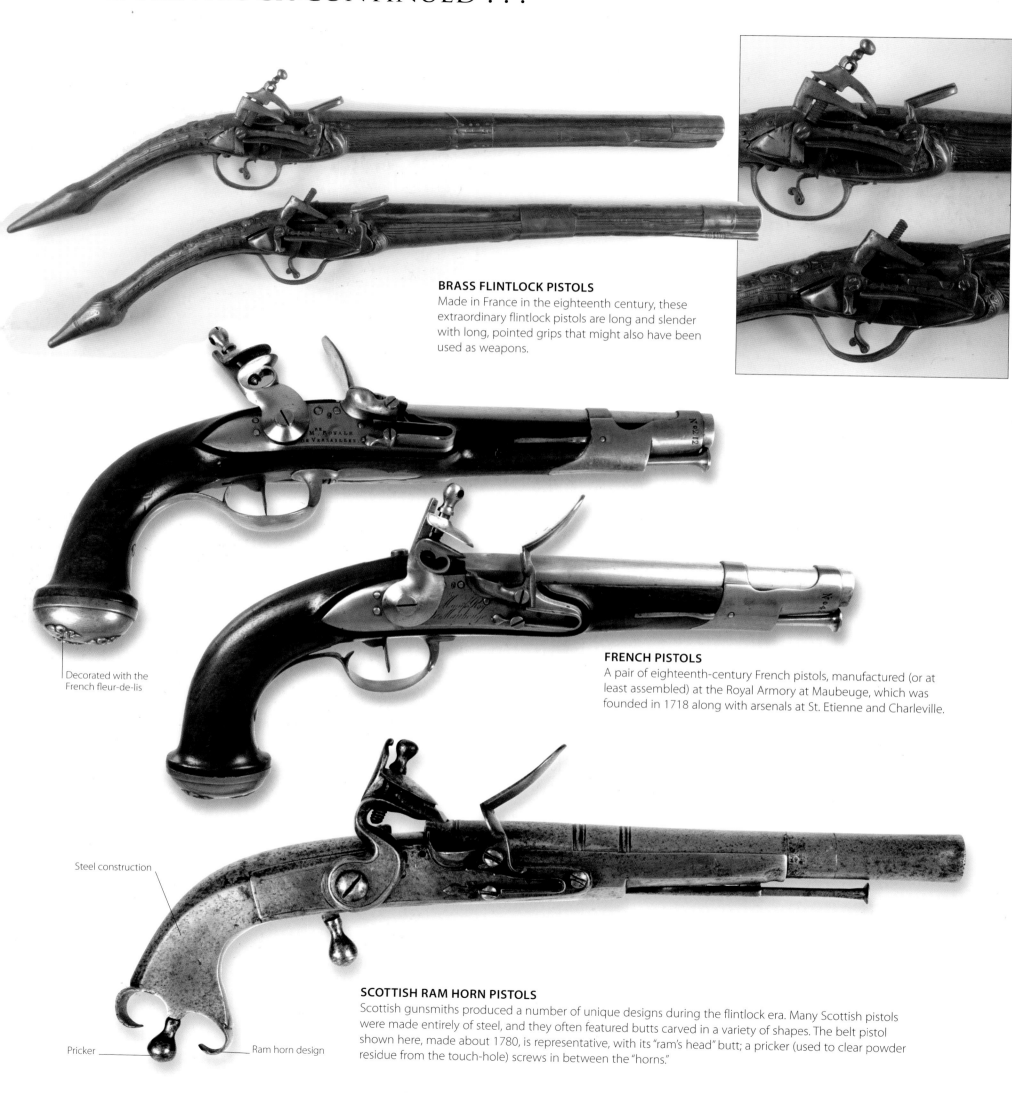

BRASS FLINTLOCK PISTOLS
Made in France in the eighteenth century, these extraordinary flintlock pistols are long and slender with long, pointed grips that might also have been used as weapons.

Decorated with the
French fleur-de-lis

FRENCH PISTOLS
A pair of eighteenth-century French pistols, manufactured (or at least assembled) at the Royal Armory at Maubeuge, which was founded in 1718 along with arsenals at St. Etienne and Charleville.

Steel construction

Pricker   Ram horn design

SCOTTISH RAM HORN PISTOLS
Scottish gunsmiths produced a number of unique designs during the flintlock era. Many Scottish pistols were made entirely of steel, and they often featured butts carved in a variety of shapes. The belt pistol shown here, made about 1780, is representative, with its "ram's head" butt; a pricker (used to clear powder residue from the touch-hole) screws in between the "horns."

DUCKFOOT PISTOL

"Duckfoot" pistols were multiple-barreled weapons, and named after the angled barrels that resembled a duck's web. This four-barreled version was made by the London shop of Goodwin & Co. In popular legend, at least, "Duckfoot" pistols were favorites of sea captains and prison warders, because they could be used to keep a mutinous crew or rioting prisoners at bay.

BALKAN DRESS PISTOL

This interesting pistol is not a weapon at all. Although it might resemble a locally made pistol, right down to its elaborate decoration and "rat-tail" butt, it lacks a functioning lock. Balkan nobles of the sixteenth and seventeenth centuries were required by custom to carry pistols, but this led to a spate of assassinations. As a compromise, nonfunctioning pistols like the one shown here were worn at meetings and on ceremonial occasions.

PISTOL-SWORD

A rare sword-pistol combination from the mid-eighteenth century. Weapons like these were apparently used mainly by marines and naval officers in boarding engagements at sea.

GERMAN AX-PISTOL

Made in the central European region of Silesia in the seventeenth century, this weapon combines a flintlock pistol with a battle ax. Its decorative elements include an elephant stamped into the lock and a stock inlaid with bone.

BALKAN AX-PISTOL

Another ax-pistol combination, this one made in the Balkans in the 18th century. The stock is inlaid with silver wire in traditional Balkan designs.

TINDER LIGHTER

Although not a gun, this tinder lighter's design was based on the flintlock mechanism and was used to start fires with wood shavings or chips. The sparks were created by the friction of the flint against metal. Made around 1820, this item predates the match.

UNUSUAL FIREARMS

The "Gunpowder Revolution" brought a huge variety of single-shot weapons—short-barreled pistols or long-barreled guns—onto the battlefield. Those made in regions other than Europe and North America were often distinct in appearance, their decoration reflecting regional skills and preferences. The revolution also saw a range of firearms built with single, specific functions in mind. One such was the Coehorn mortar, small enough to be carried by two men; six of these weapons were used by the Hanoverian army at the Battle of Culloden in 1746. Multi-barrel weapons were also introduced to produce concentrated firepower in a defensive capacity. But perhaps the most ingenious use of gunpowder was a sundial gun caused by the sun to fire at a specific time.

COEHORN MORTAR

Mortar like this were ideal for siege warfare because they could lob explosives over the walls of a castle or fort. Early mortars were often massive and crude weapons, but in the late seventeenth century the Dutch military engineer Menno van Coehorn (1641–1704) invented a compact, lightweight mortar that could be carried close to the target by a crew of two to four men. It is the ancestor of the mortars used for infantry support in all contemporary armies.

Short barrel angled for "plunging fire"

Lobs exploding shell (hollow projectile filled with gunpowder and fitted with a fuse before firing)

Eighteenth-century English model

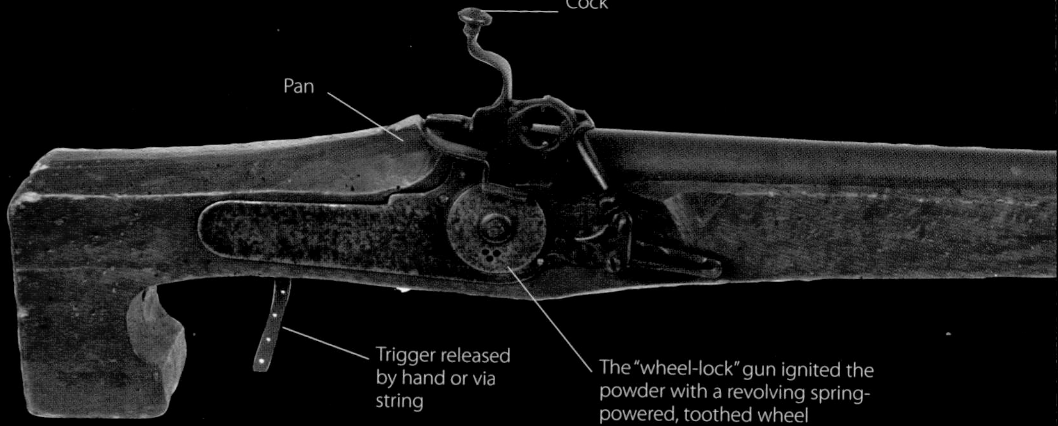

Cock

Pan

Trigger released by hand or via string

The "wheel-lock" gun ignited the powder with a revolving spring-powered, toothed wheel

RAMPART GUN

A wheel-lock European rampart gun from about 1600. Rampart guns were mounted on the walls of castles and fortifications (and, at sea, on ship's rails) for defense. They epitomized the age of gunpowder weapons in early modern European warfare.

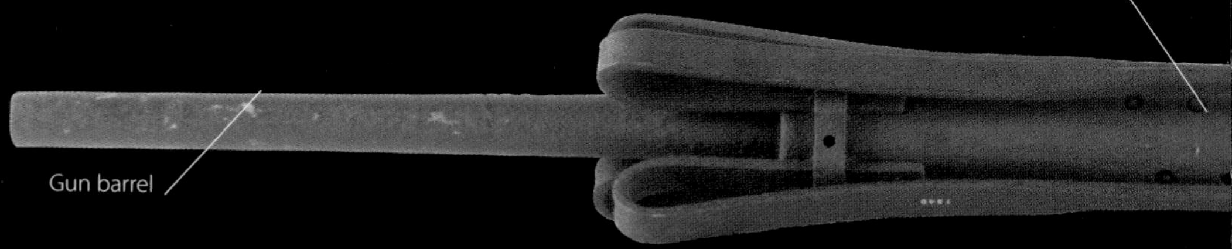

Rows of 4 and 5 percusssion caps

Gun barrel

Fifteen barrels, each 17½ inches long, fixed to a wooden base

DEATH BATTERY

Known as "death organs" or "organ guns," because their rows of barrels resemble a rack of organ pipes, weapons like the one shown here—which dates from the seventeenth century—were an early form of multishot firearm. Organ guns evolved into battery guns, which were used to defend bridges and other vulnerable locations in conflicts up until the time of the American Civil War.

DA VINCI THE DEATH MERCHANT

Along with his amazing skills as a painter, illustrator, and sculptor, renaissance artist Leonardo Da Vinci also had an incredible imagination that enabled him to envisage mechanical innovations long before it was possible to manufacture them. For example, he drew a detailed illustration of what he called an ornithopter to show how man could fly. Some experts say that the modern day helicopter was inspired by this design.

Da Vinci's inventions included an arsenal of formidable weapons. Among his lethal weaponry was a design for an multibarreled organ or volley gun, otherwise known as a ribauldequin—effectively an early machine gun (see below). By fanning out the field of fire, it had potential to be effective against a line of advancing troops. It was also wheel-based, making it easy to move around on the battlefield. He also envisaged a range of other ideas that included the cluster bomb (round shells fitted around iron spacers and stitched inside a pliable casing), the parachute, and a mechanical knight or armored robot. On a more gruesome note, he conceived horse-drawn carriages covered with sharp, rotating blades that would move through the thick of a battle slashing and severing as it went.

Among his other ideas were a giant crossbow that was so big that it was carried by six wheels and fired heavy balls rather than arrows. There was also a machine for storming walls (1480), a metal-prowed armored boat with cannon, and an automatic igniting device for firearms. Not content with this, he made a drawing for a massive bombardment machine consisting of sixteen cannons facing outward in a circle and run by a pair of mechanical paddles and gear wheels .

Perhaps one of his most famous weapons was his precursor to the modern tank—a tortoise-shaped vehicle, reinforced with metal plates, and ringed with cannons. "I can make armored cars, safe and unassailable," he declared". . . and behind these the infantry will be able to follow quite unharmed and without any opposition."

Round barrel

SUPERIMPOSED CHARGE GUN

This unusual gun is designed to take many charges, each stacked on the last—powder and ball, powder and ball and so on—there are four sets of percussion cap firing mechanisms—two of five and two four, but it is not clear how they would have been ignited.

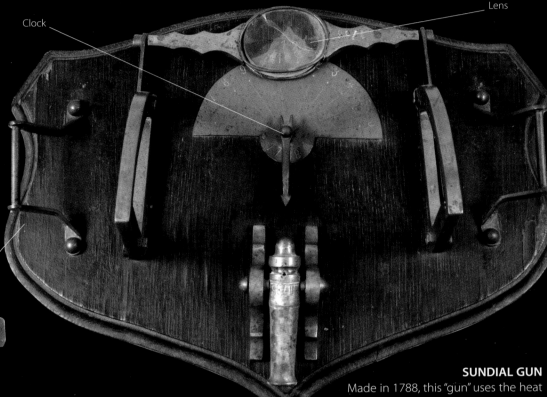

Lens

Clock

Brass handles

SUNDIAL GUN

Made in 1788, this "gun" uses the heat of the sun's rays, rather than any type of lock, to fire. Aligned on a north-south axis, a lens was adjusted, according to the season, to focus the sun's rays on a powder charge, which discharged a small gun. The gun was designed to fire when the sun was directly overhead.

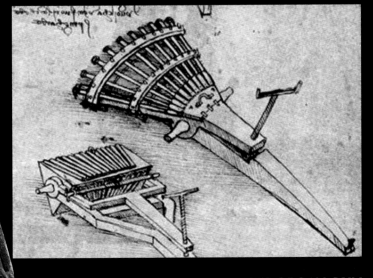

RIBAULDEQUIN

This sixteenth-century, Germany reconstruction of Da Vinci's organ gun is a mobile weapon consisting of 12 barrels each 2 feet long, which can shoot lead balls.

LEONARDO DA VINCI'S ORGAN GUN
Among the great genius's drawings is this design
for a ribauldequin, or organ gun. It has many
small-caliber iron barrels set up in a fan-shape on
a platform. They would be fired in a volley,
creating a shower of iron shot over a wide area.

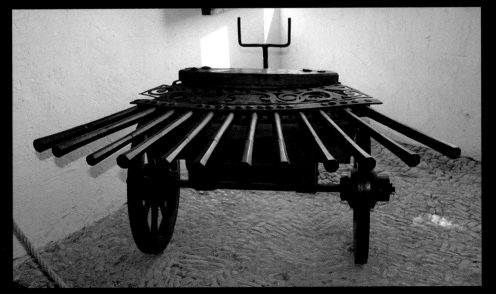

THE FLINTLOCK CONTINUED . . .

BELGIAN PISTOL
A .74 Belgian naval pistol, manufactured around 1810 according to the proof marks on the barrel.

EUROPEAN FLINTLOCK PISTOL
Intended for personal defense, this is a pocket-sized flintlock pistol with an extremely short barrel and minimal brass ornamentation.

Walnut and brass dog
head design

DOG HEAD PISTOL
Another French coat pistol, this one with a butt
carved in the form of a fierce dog's head.

Grenade or mortar barrel

GRENADE LAUNCHER
This late eighteenth-century grenade launcher was made in
Britain. It has a flintlock mechanism. The "grenade" was placed the
barrel and the launcher was fired in the same way as a shotgun.
It weighed between seven to nine pounds and released a one to
two pound grenade. Two men were needed to fire the weapon:
one to light, and one to pull the trigger.

THE FLINTLOCK CONTINUED . . .

CAUCASIAN MOUNTAINEER'S BLUNDERBUSS
Made in Russia in the eighteenth century, this beautiful flintlock blunderbuss was a close-range weapon. The bell-mouthed barrel made it easier load and disperse the shot.

Shortened striker _____ Cock

FLINTLOCK PISTOL
This Spanish pistol dating from the eighteenth century uses the distinctive miquelet lock (a form of flintlock), common in guns from Spain and neighboring countries during this period. Miquelet guns were reputed to be less efficient than conventional flintlocks.

WOODEN FLINTLOCK PISTOL
Carefully fashioned with a great deal of craftsmanship, this pistol has ornamental brass work on the grip and barrel. It was made in Europe in the seventeenth century.

Detail of ornamental brass work

EUROPEAN FLINTLOCK PISTOL
Intended for personal defense, this is a pocket-sized flintlock pistol with a brass blunderbuss barrel design set in a mostly walnut frame.

Steel plate

Ramrod

Steel tip to butt

"THE NEXT THING I LAID HOLD OF WAS A BRACE OF PISTOLS, ... A POWDER-HORN AND BULLETS, I FELT MYSELF WELL SUPPLIED WITH ARMS."

Jim Hawkins prepares for trouble in Robert Louis Stevenson's *Treasure Island*

Naval Warfare

Until the sixteenth century, sea warfare in the Western world was often simply an extension of land fighting. Sea battles were fought close to shore by oar-propelled galleys. The object was to ram the enemy with the galley's fortified bow or to get close enough to grapple with the enemy vessel. Then soldiers armed with infantry weapons—spears, swords, and bows—would board the opposing galley to fight on deck. In the fourteenth century heavy guns were mounted on European ships, but they were put in "castles" on the main decks, which limited their number and usefulness. By the mid-seventeenth century, however, ships were stable enough to carry heavy cannon on their lower decks. This transformed naval battles, which now consisted of lines (columns) of warships battering each other with cannon at ranges of 300 feet or less.

"SOMETHING MUST BE LEFT TO CHANCE; NOTHING IS CERTAIN IN A SEA FIGHT"

Admiral Horatio Nelson 22 June 1801

BROADSIDE
Firing all the guns on one side of a ship was called a broadside. Being first to fire a broadside in a battle gave a ship an immediate advantage but to be successful the ship had to sail very close to its opponent.

THE BROADSIDE

It was during the reign of King Henry VIII (from 1509 to 1547) that English warships began mounting cannon on lower decks, firing through gunports that could be closed when not in action. This eventually led to the massive "ships of the line" of the Napoleonic Wars—vessels that carried as many as 136 guns on two to four decks. These guns were muzzle-loading with brass or iron barrels. They were rated by the weight of the shot they fired, with 24- and 32-pounders being the most common sizes. Round shot made of iron was the usual projectile, but specialized ammunition such as chain shot (two small round shot joined by a length of chain, intended to tear the enemy's sails and rigging) were also used. In addition to these "long guns," warships carried carronades, or "smashers"—shorter guns that fired the same weight of shot, for use at close range. The weight of a broadside (the combined weight of shot fired by all the guns on one side of a ship in a single volley) was devastating. The broadside weight of the Royal Navy's HMS *Victory* (flagship of Admiral Horatio Nelson at the Battle of Trafalgar in 1805) was 1150 pounds.

BOARDERS AWAY!

Warships usually also had a contingent of marines; in battle, these "sea soldiers" would take to the fighting tops (platforms on the masts) to fire at enemy sailors with muskets and—if the range was close enough—to throw grenades onto the enemy vessel's deck. If the ship came alongside its opponent, both marines and sailors would make up a boarding party, armed with a wide variety of weapons that could include pikes, cutlasses, pistols, blunderbusses, and musketoons (short-barreled muskets).

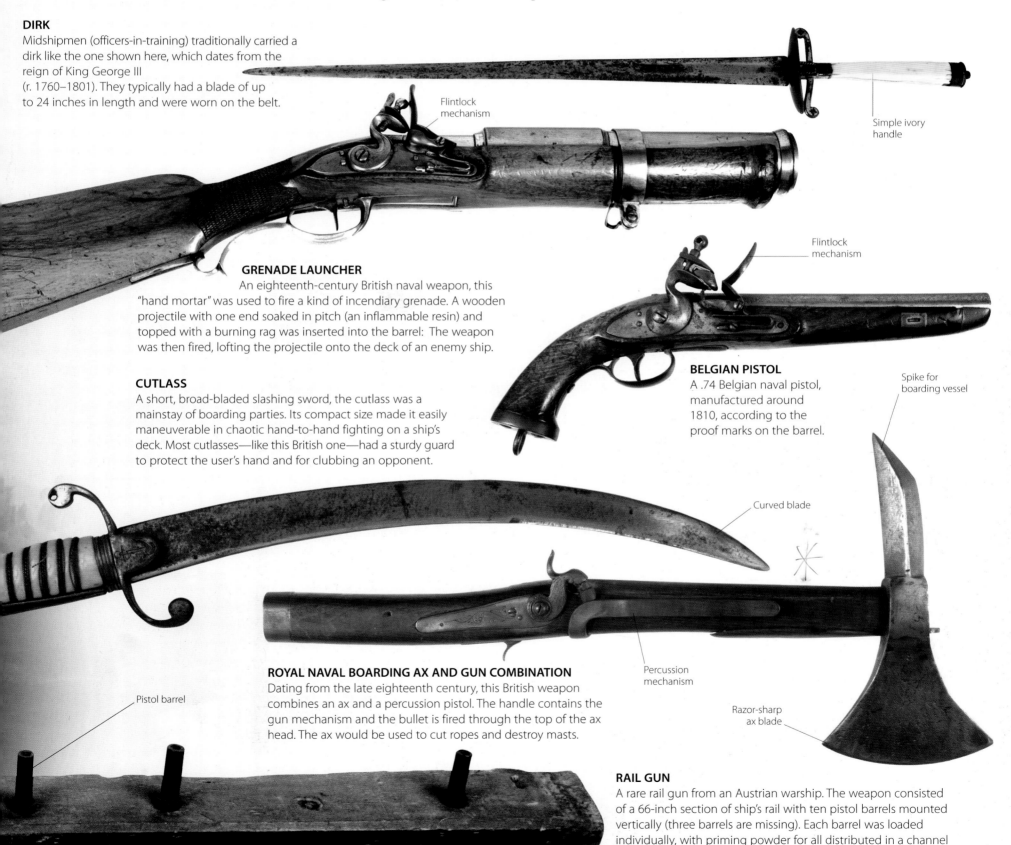

DIRK
Midshipmen (officers-in-training) traditionally carried a dirk like the one shown here, which dates from the reign of King George III (r. 1760–1801). They typically had a blade of up to 24 inches in length and were worn on the belt.

Flintlock mechanism

Simple ivory handle

GRENADE LAUNCHER
An eighteenth-century British naval weapon, this "hand mortar" was used to fire a kind of incendiary grenade. A wooden projectile with one end soaked in pitch (an inflammable resin) and topped with a burning rag was inserted into the barrel. The weapon was then fired, lofting the projectile onto the deck of an enemy ship.

Flintlock mechanism

CUTLASS
A short, broad-bladed slashing sword, the cutlass was a mainstay of boarding parties. Its compact size made it easily maneuverable in chaotic hand-to-hand fighting on a ship's deck. Most cutlasses—like this British one—had a sturdy guard to protect the user's hand and for clubbing an opponent.

BELGIAN PISTOL
A .74 Belgian naval pistol, manufactured around 1810, according to the proof marks on the barrel.

Spike for boarding vessel

Curved blade

ROYAL NAVAL BOARDING AX AND GUN COMBINATION
Dating from the late eighteenth century, this British weapon combines an ax and a percussion pistol. The handle contains the gun mechanism and the bullet is fired through the top of the ax head. The ax would be used to cut ropes and destroy masts.

Percussion mechanism

Razor-sharp ax blade

Pistol barrel

RAIL GUN
A rare rail gun from an Austrian warship. The weapon consisted of a 66-inch section of ship's rail with ten pistol barrels mounted vertically (three barrels are missing). Each barrel was loaded individually, with priming powder for all distributed in a channel inside the rail. The idea was to ignite the charge and fire all the barrels at the moment an enemy boarding party tried to board.

THE FLINTLOCK CONTINUED . . .

Taps for each vertical pair

Four barrels mounted side by side in vertical pairs

FOUR-BARREL PEPPERBOX PISTOL
Made in Europe in the early 1800s, this flintlock repeater pistol has two triggers and four flip barrels. Such guns would eventually be superceded by the cylinder revolver.

INDIAN COMBINATION RIFLE
Made in the late eighteenth century, this rare Indian rifle combines flintlock and percussion cap firing mechanisms. There is a revolving powder pan/nipple block and the percussion hammer is the lower jaw of the flint cock.

Cock holds flint between metal jaws below which lower jaw acts as percussion hammer against pan

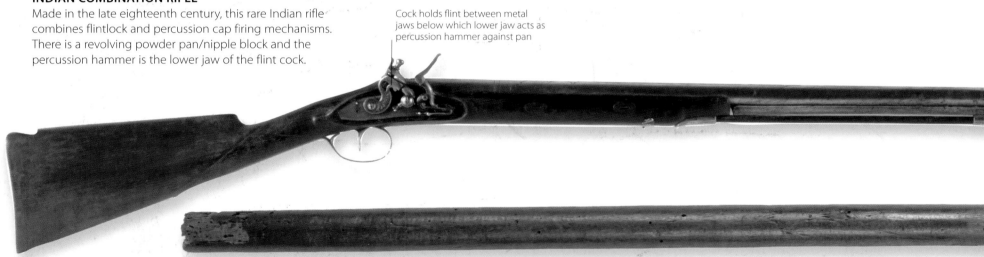

AFRICAN TRADE RIFLE
This red flintlock rifle is a .72 caliber lightweight gun, manufactured by Lazarino in Italy in the seventeenth century. It is likely the color was added at a later date.

DOUBLE-BARRELED PISTOL
Made in Europe in the nineteenth century, this double-barreled flintlock pistol fires both barrels at the same time.

Box lock tap action

RIFLE AND BOARDING AX COMBINATION
This flintlock rifle also has a boarding ax as part of the buttstock, a construction that must have made it rather awkward to fire. It also has a very long barrel and a small trigger with no safety guard.

Muzzle

Ramrod

THE FLINTLOCK CONTINUED . . .

ARAB MIQUELET

An Arab flintlock gun using a snaphance-style mechanism. The stock is inlaid with silver wire and, as with many guns from North Africa and the Middle East, the buttstock is of finely carved ivory.

NOCK VOLLEY GUN

Volley guns—weapons with multiple barrels, all of which discharged simultaneously—were used in close-in naval fighting to repel boarders. The most famous of these guns is probably the Nock volley gun. (While the famous British gunsmith Henry Nock made the weapon, he was apparently not the designer.) First appearing around 1780, the flintlock gun had seven 20-inch, .50 rifled barrels. Some 600 were produced for the Royal Navy. While obviously a formidable weapon, it had its downside: the recoil was said to be severe enough to break the firer's shoulder, and the muzzle blast sometimes set sails and rigging on fire.

ARABIAN RIFLE

This ancient Arabian flintlock rifle with its unusual trigger dates from the late 1700s. Used by mounted Arabian sheiks, it has a very heavy, thick, and sturdy barrel, inlaid with bone decoration.

FRENCH MUSKET

This French military musket made in 1813 and shown with its bayonet, is typical of the last generation of smoothbore flintlock long arms. Within a couple of decades they would be replaced by rifled weapons using the percussion-cap firing system.

THE KENTUCKY RIFLE

A weapon steeped in American history and folklore, the Kentucky rifle (or long rifle) was first produced by immigrant German gunsmiths in Pennsylvania, Virginia, and other colonies in the mid-eighteenth century. (The designation "Kentucky rifle" was popularized in a song, "The Hunters of Kentucky," which celebrated the marksmanship of volunteers from that state in the Battle of New Orleans on January 8, 1815.) German gunsmiths had long produced rifled weapons, but the traditional German hunting rifle was relatively short, with a barrel of about 30 inches.

In America, gunsmiths began lengthening the barrel to between 40 inches and 46 inches, greatly increasing its accuracy. The resulting weapon, typically .50, proved ideal for hunting in the North American wilderness. They were handsome weapons as well, usually with stocks made of curly maple and often beautifully decorated with individual touches added by their owners.

Formations of riflemen recruited from the frontier fought against the British in the Revolutionary War and in the War of 1812. Although capable of dealing death at long distances (during the Revolutionary War, an astonished British officer reported that a rifleman hit his bugler's horse at a range of 400 yards), the long rifle was even slower to reload than the smoothbore musket, a fact that limited its effectiveness in conventional battle.

Originally flintlock, many long rifles were later converted to percussion, including the two examples shown here; the lower one was made by the Lemans of Lancaster County, Pennsylvania, a family of prominent gunsmiths active from the mid-1700s to around 1875.

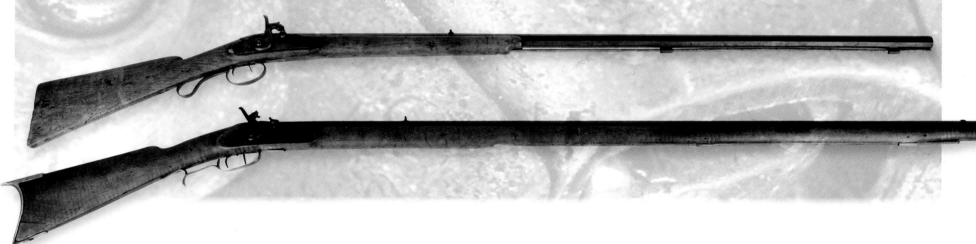

"FOR 'TIS NOT OFTEN HERE YOU SEE A HUNTER FROM KENTUCKY."

—lyrics from "The Hunters of Kentucky," 1824

AFRICAN TRADE GUNS

Guns were a major factor in the slave trade that brought some 10 million Africans to the Americas (with untold deaths along the way) from the fifteenth through the nineteenth centuries. European slavers exchanged guns, and other goods, with West African tribal leaders; these guns were then used in intertribal warfare to capture more slaves to sell. The .72 musket shown here was made for African export in the eighteenth century, although the barrel was apparently manufactured in Italy much earlier.

NAPOLEONIC WARFARE

On July 14, 1789, a Parisian mob stormed the Bastille prison—an infamous symbol of royal power—sparking the French Revolution and setting off a series of events that plunged Europe, and eventually much of the world, into war. Out of France's revolutionary chaos emerged a leader, Napoleon Bonaparte, whose astonishing success as a military commander formed the foundation of his political power. The Napoleonic Wars—which lasted from 1799 until the Emperor's final defeat at Waterloo in 1815—did not see any extraordinary technological leaps in weaponry, but Napoleon masterfully exploited the existing weapons of the day to conquer much of Europe. He also appropriated the Bourbon innovation of conscription to his own dictatorial ends, drafting about 2.5 million Frenchmen into military service between 1804 and 1813 and squandering many of their lives.

SHOULDER TO SHOULDER
The Napoleonic Wars were fought by tight formations of infantry who could support each other if wounded but had little defense against firearms. Horse-mounted officers directed operations and rallied faltering troops.

"A SOLDIER WILL FIGHT LONG AND HARD FOR A BIT OF COLORED RIBBON"

Napoleon Bonaparte, April 6, 1801

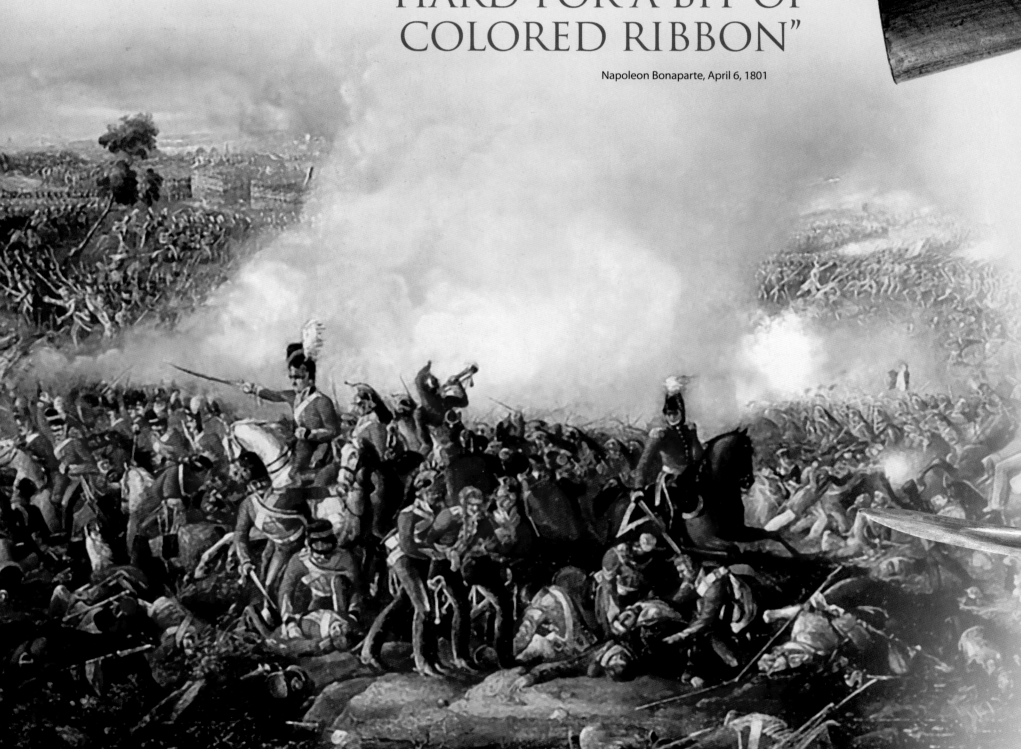

TECHNOLOGY AND TACTICS

The standard infantry weapon of the Napoleonic Wars was the smoothbore, muzzle-loading flintlock musket, an inherently inaccurate weapon with an effective range of no more than 300 feet. Accuracy was not essential, however, because the tactics of the time relied on massed formations of infantry firing in volleys to send, in effect, a "wall of lead" at the opposing line. If the enemy broke ranks in the face of this intense fire, a bayonet charge usually followed, but the bayonet's effect was mostly psychological. All armies had units that carried the much more accurate rifle, but because rifles were even slower to load than muskets, their use was largely limited to specialized troops.

CAVALRY WEAPONS

Mounted forces of Napoleonic-era armies were divided between light and heavy cavalry. Both carried swords, usually sabers designed for slashing, although the French retained a preference for "running through" their opponents with the point of their swords. Light cavalry often dismounted and fought with carbines or pistols. Heavy cavalry, like the French Army's cuirassiers, usually fought from the saddle and were armed with heavy, straight-bladed swords. The French Army also made use of mounted troops armed with lances, as did its opponents in the Russian, Prussian, and Austrian forces. Lancers were often pitted against infantry formations because their lances could outdistance a bayonet thrust. Naturally, the use of edged weapons was not limited to mounted troops. Officers of all military branches continued to carry swords, while noncommissioned officers in several armies carried pikes, which also outdistanced a bayonet thrust.

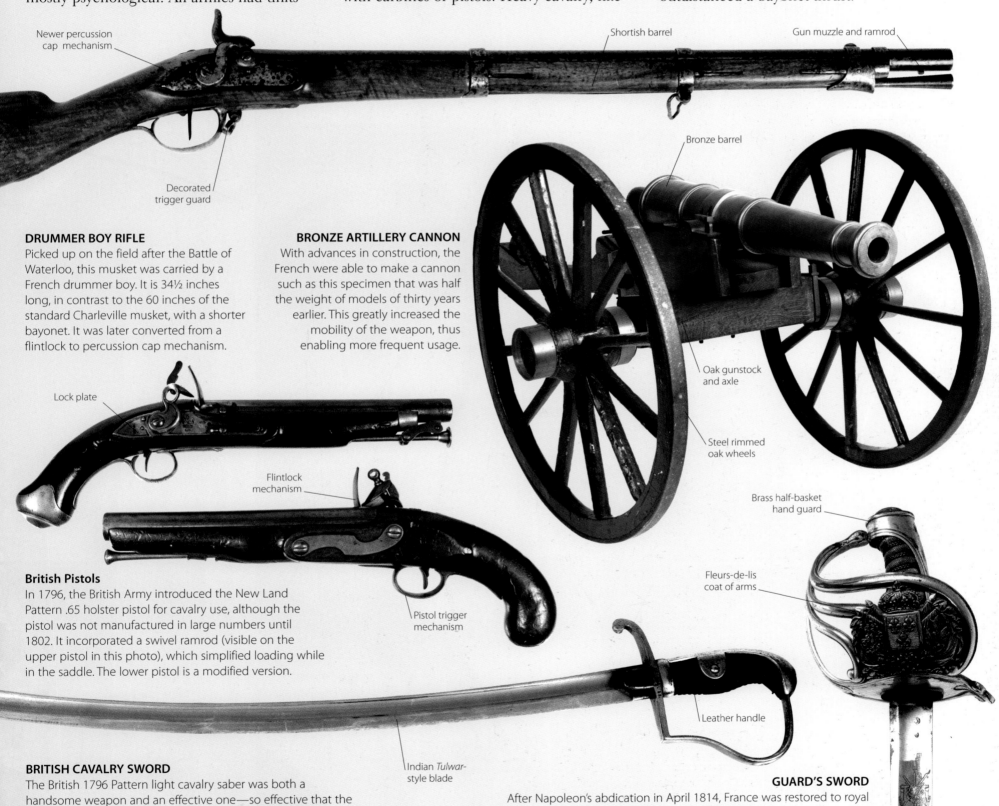

Newer percussion cap mechanism

Shortish barrel

Gun muzzle and ramrod

Decorated trigger guard

Bronze barrel

DRUMMER BOY RIFLE

Picked up on the field after the Battle of Waterloo, this musket was carried by a French drummer boy. It is 34½ inches long, in contrast to the 60 inches of the standard Charleville musket, with a shorter bayonet. It was later converted from a flintlock to percussion cap mechanism.

BRONZE ARTILLERY CANNON

With advances in construction, the French were able to make a cannon such as this specimen that was half the weight of models of thirty years earlier. This greatly increased the mobility of the weapon, thus enabling more frequent usage.

Oak gunstock and axle

Steel rimmed oak wheels

Lock plate

Flintlock mechanism

Brass half-basket hand guard

Fleurs-de-lis coat of arms

British Pistols

In 1796, the British Army introduced the New Land Pattern .65 holster pistol for cavalry use, although the pistol was not manufactured in large numbers until 1802. It incorporated a swivel ramrod (visible on the upper pistol in this photo), which simplified loading while in the saddle. The lower pistol is a modified version.

Pistol trigger mechanism

Leather handle

Indian *Tulwar*-style blade

BRITISH CAVALRY SWORD

The British 1796 Pattern light cavalry saber was both a handsome weapon and an effective one—so effective that the Prussian Army, Britain's ally in the struggle against Napoleon, adopted it as well. Its design was likely inspired by the Indian *tulwar*. Intended for use as a slashing weapon, the saber's 33-inch blade inflicted such terrible wounds that, according to some sources, French officers protested its use.

GUARD'S SWORD

After Napoleon's abdication in April 1814, France was restored to royal rule under Louis VIII—a restoration temporarily interrupted by Napoleon's escape from the Mediterranean island of Elba in 1815. One of the King's bodyguards carried this Model 1814 saber. Its guard and blade are decorated with the royal crest of three fleurs-de-lis—a flower that had symbolized the French monarchy since the fourteenth century.

DUELING PISTOLS

Combat between individuals to settle disputes over personal honor is as old as history, but the practice of dueling that is familiar to us today developed in Southern Europe during the Renaissance and began to flourish—largely among the upper classes—in Europe and North America in the eighteenth century. Although widely outlawed and denounced (George Washington forbade his officers to fight duels, calling it a "murderous practice"), dueling continued in Britain and America into the early nineteenth century, and somewhat later in Continental Europe. Until the mid-1700s, duelists fought mainly with swords, but then it became fashionable to use firearms and this created a new class of weapon—the dueling pistol.

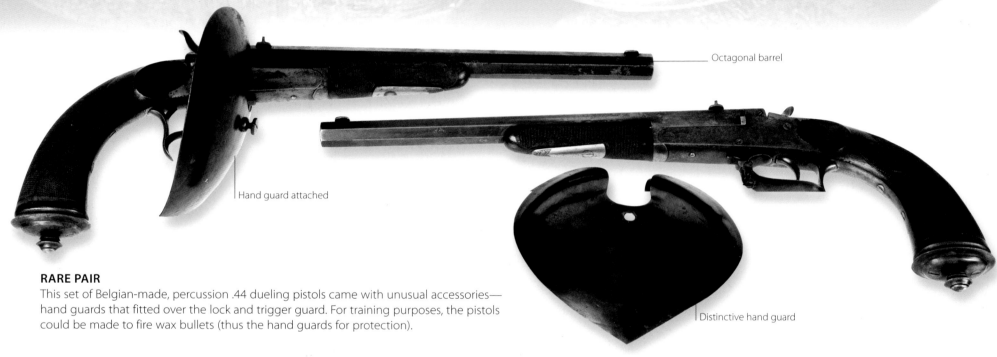

Octagonal barrel

Hand guard attached

Distinctive hand guard

RARE PAIR
This set of Belgian-made, percussion .44 dueling pistols came with unusual accessories—hand guards that fitted over the lock and trigger guard. For training purposes, the pistols could be made to fire wax bullets (thus the hand guards for protection).

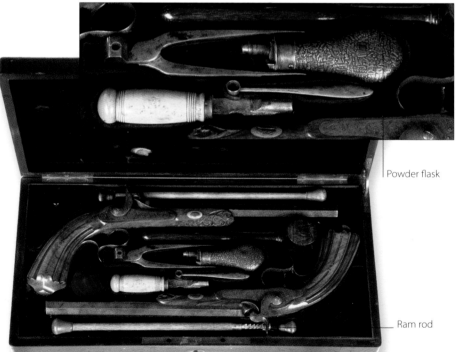

Powder flask

Ram rod

CARON'S CASE
France's royal gunmaker, Alphonse Caron of Paris, made this cased set of pistols in the late 1840s. The case contains the standard accessories—powder flask, bullet mold, ramrods, cleaning rods, and boxes for percussion caps. The powder flask is decorated with Egyptian hieroglyphs—a reflection of the popularity of ancient Egyptian motifs in nineteenth-century France.

BELGIAN PISTOLS
Flintlock dueling pistols had all the disadvantages of the flintlock system—they misfired frequently, were unreliable in damp conditions, and the relative slowness of the firing mechanism hampered accuracy even with the use of set triggers (see main text). After 1815 (just as dueling was on the wane), makers of dueling pistols—like the Belgian gunsmith who produced the handsome pair below—increasingly switched to the more robust and reliable percussion-cap system.

Finely carved grip

THE GREAT GUNSMITHS

Originally, duelists used ordinary pistols, but around 1770, gunsmiths—chiefly in England and France—began producing purpose-made dueling pistols. These were usually made as "cased pairs"—two identical pistols in a box with powder flasks, bullet molds, and other accessories. With dueling mainly an upper-class custom (in Europe at least), owning a costly cased set of dueling pistols was a status symbol—like driving a high-powered sports car today. The pistols produced by the most famous (and expensive) London gunsmiths—like Robert Wogdon and the rival brothers John and Joseph Manton— were, in this sense, the Ferraris and Porsches of their time.

ACCURACY AND RELIABILITY

Most dueling pistols were approximately 15 inches long with 10-inch barrels; the usual caliber was between .40 and .50. They were extremely accurate at about 20 yards—the usual distance at which duelists fired— although the commonly accepted rules of dueling stipulated smoothbore barrels and only the simplest sights. (Some duelists cheated by rifling all but the last couple of inches of the barrel—a practice known as "blind rifling.")

For maximum accuracy, many dueling pistols featured a "set" or "hair" trigger. The set trigger utilized a mechanism that kept tension on the trigger so that only a slight pressure would fire the weapon.

(Conventional triggers required a heavy pull that tended to distort the firer's aim.)

Besides accuracy, reliability was the duelist's paramount concern in a pistol, so all components were finely tooled and fitted. In contrast to many firearms of the era, most dueling pistols had only minimal ornamentation, so that sunlight gleaming off gold or silver inlay wouldn't distract the duelist. Continental gunsmiths, however, did make some richly ornamented dueling pistols, and elaborately inlaid and engraved cased pairs were often produced as presentation pieces not intended for actual use on the "field of honor."

WOGDON PISTOL
This pistol could be fitted with a shoulder stock for non-dueling use. Originally a flintlock, it was converted to percussion action. Robert Wogdon also made the pistols used in the famous 1804 duel in which Vice President Aaron Burr mortally wounded his personal and political enemy Alexander Hamilton.

Neatly fitted ramrod

Wooden shoulder stock

Spurred trigger guard

FRENCH DUELING PISTOLS
These dueling pistols have discrete decorative features, a pinfire mechanism, spurs on the trigger guard, and double barrels. They were made in the nineteenth century.

THE BLUNDERBUSS

The blunderbuss was a short smoothbore musket with a barrel that ended in a flared muzzle. It was usually fired with a flintlock mechanism. The weapon was developed in Europe, probably in Germany at first, early in the seventeenth century, although it didn't come into widespread use until about a hundred years later. (The weapon got its name from the Anglicization of the Dutch term donderbuse, meaning "thunder-box" or "thunder-gun.") Firing lead shot, the blunderbuss was deadly at short range and was generally used as a defensive weapon—by coachmen against highwaymen, by merchants and homeowners against burglars, and by innkeepers against robbers. It was also used at sea because it was an ideal weapon in a boarding attack.

THE "THUNDER-BOX"

There are a couple of popular misconceptions about the blunderbuss. The first is that its flared muzzle (often described as bell-shaped or trumpet-shaped) served to scatter its load of shot in the manner of a modern shotgun. In fact, the dispersal pattern for the shot was little different from that of a nonflared barrel. The muzzle's wide mouth, however, facilitated quick reloading. It also had a psychological effect. In the words of firearms historian Richard Akehurst, "[T]he great bell mouth was most intimidating: those at whom it was aimed were convinced that there was no escaping the dreadful blast."

Akehurst also notes that some English blunderbuss owners took pleasure in upping the intimidation factor by having the chilling inscription "Happy is he that escapeth me" engraved on the barrel.

The second misconception is that a blunderbuss was often loaded not with conventional shot but with scrap metal, nails, stones, gravel, or even broken glass for a particularly devastating effect. This may have happened on occasion, but such loads would quickly ruin the weapon's barrel.

Flintlock mechanism with manton-type roller and a frizzen spring

Elliptical brass barrel with flared end

Fixing to hold weapon in place

FRENCH BLUNDERBUSS
While most blunderbusses had musket-type shoulder stocks, eighteenth- and nineteenth-century gunsmiths also produced blunderbuss pistols, like this French weapon. They were often carried by French naval officers, and were also used widely in the street fighting that accompanied the French Revolution.

TRAP GUN
Made for hunting rather than for use against human targets, this nineteenth-century European percussion-cap trap gun utilizes a blunderbuss-style barrel. Trap guns were connected by string or wire to a baited trap; when the animal took the bait, the string or wire tripped the trigger.

Chain for connecting wire or string to bait

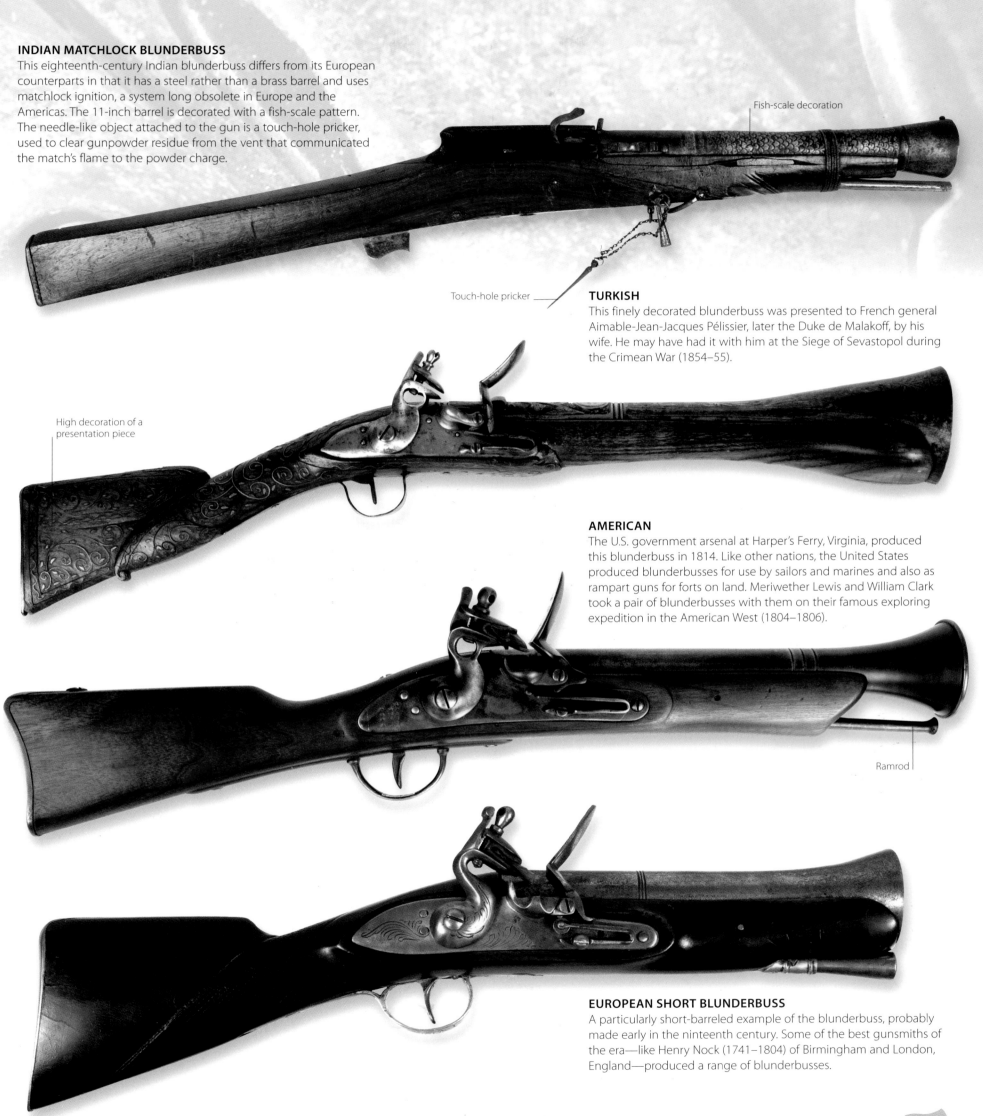

INDIAN MATCHLOCK BLUNDERBUSS

This eighteenth-century Indian blunderbuss differs from its European counterparts in that it has a steel rather than a brass barrel and uses matchlock ignition, a system long obsolete in Europe and the Americas. The 11-inch barrel is decorated with a fish-scale pattern. The needle-like object attached to the gun is a touch-hole pricker, used to clear gunpowder residue from the vent that communicated the match's flame to the powder charge.

Fish-scale decoration

Touch-hole pricker

TURKISH

This finely decorated blunderbuss was presented to French general Aimable-Jean-Jacques Pélissier, later the Duke de Malakoff, by his wife. He may have had it with him at the Siege of Sevastopol during the Crimean War (1854–55).

High decoration of a presentation piece

AMERICAN

The U.S. government arsenal at Harper's Ferry, Virginia, produced this blunderbuss in 1814. Like other nations, the United States produced blunderbusses for use by sailors and marines and also as rampart guns for forts on land. Meriwether Lewis and William Clark took a pair of blunderbusses with them on their famous exploring expedition in the American West (1804–1806).

Ramrod

EUROPEAN SHORT BLUNDERBUSS

A particularly short-barreled example of the blunderbuss, probably made early in the nineteenth century. Some of the best gunsmiths of the era—like Henry Nock (1741–1804) of Birmingham and London, England—produced a range of blunderbusses.

The Blunderbuss continued . . .

Bayonet folded against barrel

BLUNDERBUSS WITH BAYONET
This English blunderbuss with its beautiful brass barrel has a hinged bayonet. It dates from the early nineteenth century.

Carved wood detailing

CAUCASIAN MOUNTAINEER'S BLUNDERBUSS
Made in Russia in the eighteenth century, this flintlock blunderbuss is decorated with engraved silver plate and carving. Such weapons were greatly prized by bandit chiefs, who often received them in return for safe passage through the Caucasian mountains.

BRITISH BLUNDERBUSS
Made by Patrick, who was gunmaker to the Duke of Gloucester, Liverpool, England, this flintlock blunderbuss has a folded bayonet and is similar to that at the top of the page. It dates from around 1806.

ON THE ROAD AND OFF

The blunderbuss's height of popularity was in the eighteenth century, when more and more people were traveling the primitive roads of Europe, and the danger of being waylaid by pistol-wielding highwaymen was almost a certainty. The blunderbuss's barrel was usually made of nonrusting brass—a necessity because they were often carried ready to use by coach drivers and guards who sat on the outside of the carriage, exposed to the weather.

In addition to its use at sea—by both the regular naval forces and by pirates and privateers—the blunderbuss saw some military service on land. The Austrian, British, and Prussian armies of the eighteenth century all fielded units armed with the weapon, and according to some sources, the American Continental Army considered adopting the blunderbuss in preference to the carbine for its mounted troops during the Revolutionary War. However, the blunderbuss's very short range limited its effectiveness in a conventional combat role. The blunderbuss remained popular into the early nineteenth century, when the shotgun replaced it as the preferred short-range defensive firearm.

INDIAN BLUNDERBUSS
An eighteenth-century Indian flintlock blunderbuss pistol with silver damascening on the barrel. This gun has the typical "swamped" barrel, which tapers to a flared muzzle.

Engraved brass plate

FLINTLOCK BLUNDERBUSS
Made in India in the late 1700s, this blunderbuss is wooden with a cast-iron barrel. The wood is carved and decorated in a traditional Indian style.

Stylized floral decoration on butt

PERCUSSION WEAPONS

By the turn of the nineteenth century, the flintlock had been the standard firing mechanism for guns for more than a century. The flintlock's deficiencies—its vulnerability to inclement weather, and the delay between the ignition of the powder in the priming pan and the main charge—led several inventors to develop firing systems that used the strike of a hammer on chemical compounds, like fulminate of mercury, as the means of ignition. First implemented mainly on sporting guns, the percussion system (sometimes called the caplock) came into widespread military use in the mid-nineteenth century.

EARLY PERCUSSION WEAPONS

The percussion system was inspired by a sportsman's frustration. A Scottish clergyman, the Rev. Alexander Forsyth, realized that the interval between the trigger pull and the actual firing of his fowling piece gave birds enough of a warning to fly away. Around 1805, Forsyth developed a new lock in which a hammer struck a firing pin inserted into a small bottle containing a special detonating charge, which in turn fired the powder charge in the barrel. Forsyth's "scent bottle" lock, as it was called from its shape, was a major advance, although weapons based on the system had their drawbacks, like the possibility of the entire "bottle" exploding. But it inspired several gunsmiths—including notables like Joseph Manton—to work on alternative systems, especially after Forsyth's British patent expired in 1821. In the words of firearms historian Richard Akehurst, a variety of percussion-fired "pills, tapes, tubes, and caps" containing several different types of detonating compounds came into use.

SPANISH
The incompatibility of percussion systems introduced in the early nineteenth century led to the development of "dual ignition" weapons. This rare brass-barreled pistol had a firing mechanism that could use both a Forsyth-type priming system and the later percussion cap.

Hammer rather than cock-and-flint

Brass barrel

Cap fits over nipple

PERCUSSION BREECHLOCK PISTOL
A rare example of a percussion pistol with a breechlock mechanism, this gun is made of steel and has a wooden handle. It dates from the nineteenth century and was made in Europe.

THE PERCUSSION CAP

The percussion design that ultimately won widespread adoption was a metallic cap (first made of steel, later of copper) filled with a compound based around fulminate of mercury. The cap was placed on a nipple in the lock and was struck by a hammer when the firer pulled the trigger.

There is some debate about how and when the metallic percussion cap was developed, but it's generally credited to a British-born American artist and inventor, Joshua Shaw (1776–1860), who developed it around 1814 but did not patent it until several years later. While some other percussion systems came into use—like the tape-primer system introduced in the 1840s by American inventor Edward Maynard (1813–91), which operated much like a contemporary toy cap pistol—the stand-alone metallic cap became standard from the 1820s onward. The percussion system's popularity was helped by the relative ease with which flintlock weapons could be converted to the new mechanism.

The percussion system's advantages over the flintlock were considerable. It was reliable in all weathers and far less prone to misfire. The system also facilitated the introduction of reliable repeating weapons, especially the revolver. It took several decades, however, for the percussion system to win acceptance in military circles. (Napoleon Bonaparte was reportedly interested in developing weapons based on the Forsyth system, but the patriotic reverend rebuffed the French dictator's overtures.) It was not until the early 1840s, when the British Army began retrofitting its muskets with percussion locks,

that percussion weapons became standard in the armies of the day.

The heyday of the percussion cap was relatively brief. Percussion firearms still had the drawbacks of muzzle-loading weapons, and following the introduction of self-contained metallic cartridges starting in the 1850s, they rapidly gave way to cartridge-firing weapons.

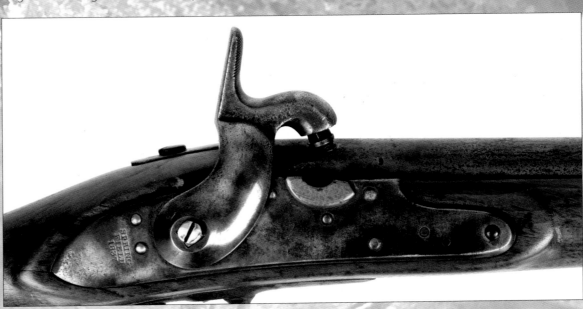

PERCUSSION PISTOL
A fine example of an early nineteenth-century American percussion cap pistol, designed as a single-shot, small-bore pocket pistol. It includes a carved wooden handle and plain metal barrel.

Percussion cap

FLINTLOCK TO PERCUSSION CONVERSIONS

The "true" or "French" flintlock was developed in the early seventeenth century by French gunsmith Marin le Bourgeoys and was characterized by a combined steel and pan cover (they were separate in the snaphance mechanism) and a gooseneck-shaped cock that engaged in two notches as half-cock (the safety position) and full cock (ready to fire). The French flintlock rifle was much more reliable and faster-firing than its antecedents, but its appearance on the battlefield was delayed by the outbreak of English civil wars in 1642 and the Thirty Years' War in Germany (1618–48). In France, however, the new guns were widely made, and by 1670 the French monarch, Louis XIV, had equipped five full regiments with crude rifles featuring the improved mechanism.

AMERICAN CARBINE
Made in Americc in 1760, this is a rare example of a percussion carbine that has been converted from a flintlock mechanism. It has a 24-inch barrel and a spring-loaded trap containing a small bayonet, 6 inches long.

Percussion hammer

Lock plate

Trigger guard

Frizen or steel

Cock for the flint

Buttstock

Trigger

Matchlock mechanism

Trigger without guard

Long, narrow barrel

Converted mechanism

Spring-out dagger

CONVERTED MATCHLOCK
A Chinese gunsmith converted what was originally a matchlock gun, probably made in the eighteenth century, into a percussion gun. In this weapon, however, the original matchlock mechanism was modified instead of being totally replaced. The firer had to engage a hook around the back of the hammer, which fell forward to strike the percussion cap when the trigger was squeezed.

SPANISH BLUNDERBUSS
This Spanish blunderbuss was converted from flintlock to percussion; it also has a spring-out dagger mounted above the barrel.

THE PERCUSSION CAP

The percussion system was first developed by Rev. Alexander Forsyth around 1805. He made a new lock with a hammer that struck a firing pin in a small bottle containing a detonating charge, which in turn fired the powder charge in the barrel. Forsyth's "scent bottle" lock was a major advance and it inspired several gunsmiths—including notables like Joseph Manton—to work on alternate systems. The variety that ultimately won widespread adoption was a metallic cap—first made of steel, later of copper—filled with a compound based around fulminate of mercury. The cap was placed on a nipple in the lock and was struck by a hammer when the firer pulled the trigger. The metallic percussion cap is generally credited to a British-born American artist and inventor, Joshua Shaw (1776–1860), who developed it around 1814 but did not patent it until several years later. While some other percussion systems came into use, the stand-alone metallic cap was most widely used from the 1820s onward. The percussion system's popularity was helped by the relative ease with which flintlock weapons could be converted to the new mechanism.

The percussion system's advantages over the flintlock were considerable. It was reliable in all weathers and far less prone to misfire. The system also facilitated the introduction of reliable repeating weapons, especially the revolver. Still, it took several decades for the percussion system to win acceptance in military circles. It was not until the early 1840s, when the British Army began retrofitting its muskets with percussion locks, that percussion weapons became standard in the armies of the day.

THE METAL CARTRIDGE

The heyday of the percussion cap was relatively brief. Percussion firearms still had the drawbacks of muzzle-loading weapons, and after the introduction of self-contained metallic cartridges starting in the 1850s, they rapidly gave way to cartridge-firing weapons.

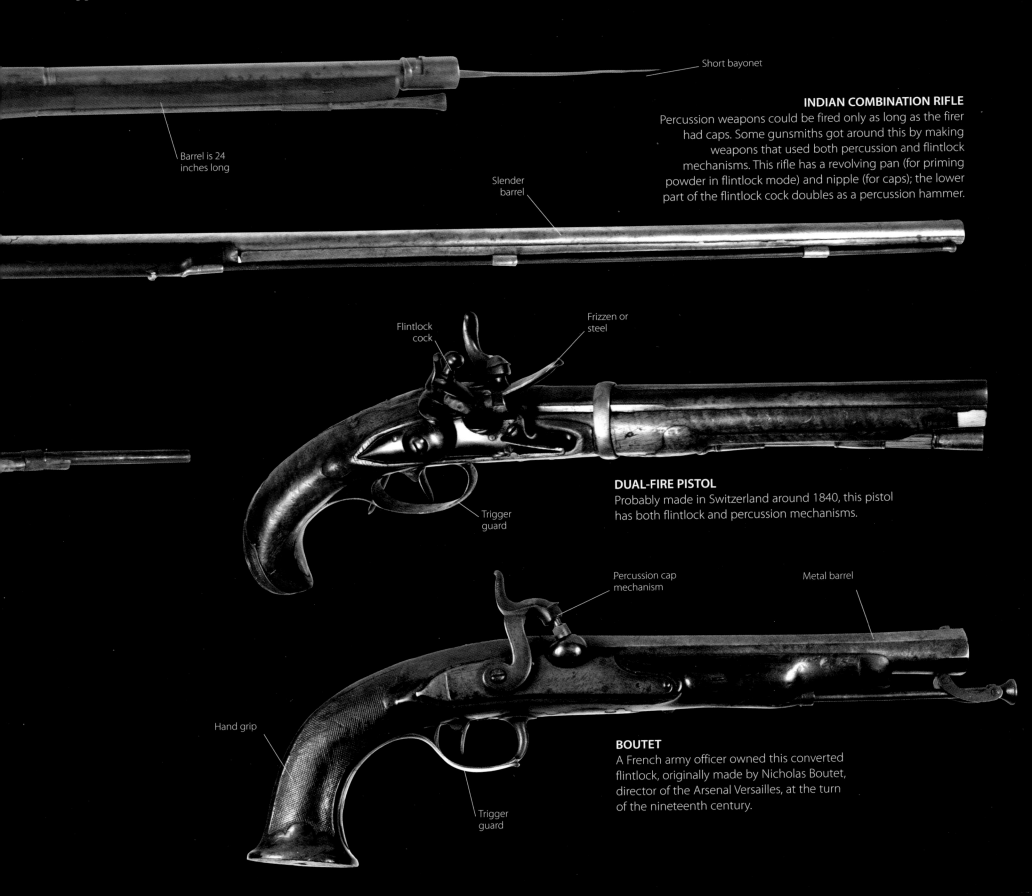

Short bayonet

Barrel is 24 inches long

Slender barrel

INDIAN COMBINATION RIFLE
Percussion weapons could be fired only as long as the firer had caps. Some gunsmiths got around this by making weapons that used both percussion and flintlock mechanisms. This rifle has a revolving pan (for priming powder in flintlock mode) and nipple (for caps); the lower part of the flintlock cock doubles as a percussion hammer.

Flintlock cock

Frizzen or steel

Trigger guard

DUAL-FIRE PISTOL
Probably made in Switzerland around 1840, this pistol has both flintlock and percussion mechanisms.

Percussion cap mechanism

Metal barrel

Hand grip

BOUTET
A French army officer owned this converted flintlock, originally made by Nicholas Boutet, director of the Arsenal Versailles, at the turn of the nineteenth century.

Trigger guard

PERCUSSION WEAPONS CONTINUED . . .

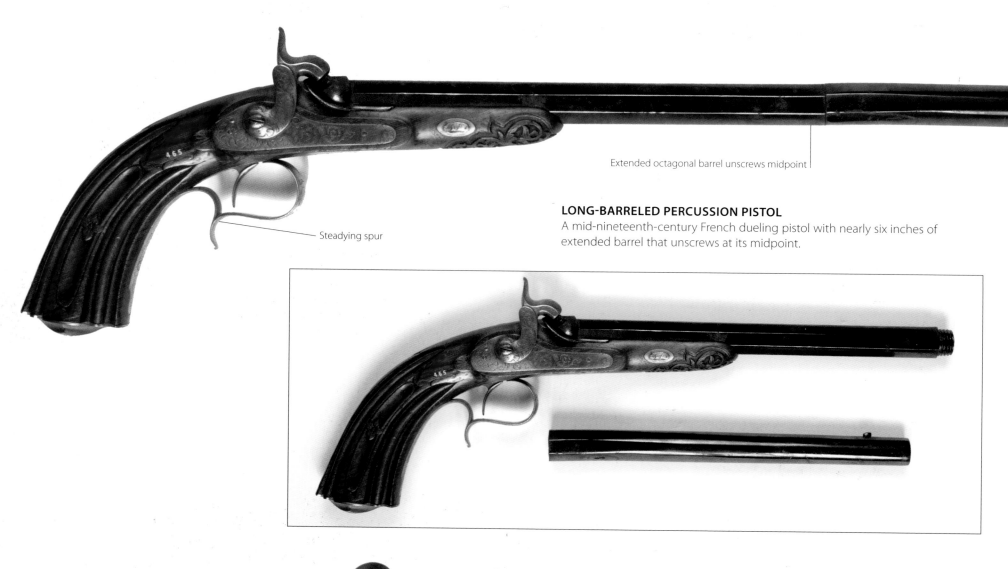

Extended octagonal barrel unscrews midpoint

Steadying spur

LONG-BARRELED PERCUSSION PISTOL
A mid-nineteenth-century French dueling pistol with nearly six inches of extended barrel that unscrews at its midpoint.

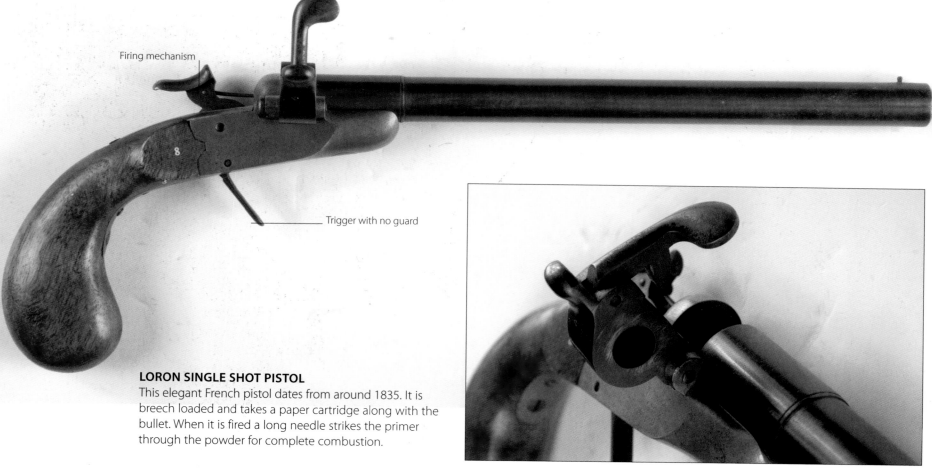

Firing mechanism

Trigger with no guard

LORON SINGLE SHOT PISTOL
This elegant French pistol dates from around 1835. It is breech loaded and takes a paper cartridge along with the bullet. When it is fired a long needle strikes the primer through the powder for complete combustion.

Cocking the hammer reveals the trigger

SILVER-PLATED SINGLE SHOT PISTOL
This late nineteenth-century American .22-caliber pistol has a blued, silver-plated barrel and target sights with stud trigger. It was made by J. Stevens Arms & Bicycle Co., a company best-known for making rifles and target pistols.

PERCUSSION REVOLVER
Made of solid brass with a wooden grip, this mid-nineteenth-century British flare pistol takes a single round, and is loaded by unscrewing the barrel.

FLARE GUN
This British flare gun dates from the nineteenth century.

TEMPLE COX HUMANE ANIMAL KILLER
This is a Mark V version of the humane killer, which kills by lethal concussion using a captive .22 caliber bolt.

PERCUSSION WEAPONS CONTINUED . . .

ENGLISH LANCASTER PISTOL
This is a four-barrel, centerfire, .455 pistol that can also be used with buckshot thanks to its oval rifling. It is breechloaded with a hinged frame and the barrels fire in succession by double action as the trigger is pulled.

FOUR-BARRELED DERRINGER-STYLE PISTOL
Neither a single action four-barreled gun nor a "pepperbox" pistol, this gun has four underside hammers and caps located in front of the trigger guard to fire one round from each barrel.

One hammer hits the underside cap

DARRA PISTOL

Since the late nineteenth century, the town of Darra Adam Khel (then part of India, now part of Pakistan) has been renowned for its gunsmiths, who are legendary for their ability to produce meticulous copies of the most complex firearms. The gunsmiths of Darra have also made some highly original weapons, like this nineteenth-century pistol chambered to fire 12-gauge shotgun shells.

Incised checkering on butt

Octagonal barrel

PAIR OF DUELING PISTOLS

Made in London by the renowned gunsmith John Twigg, this pair of rifle-barrel percussion pistols dates from the late eighteenth century. They are also mounted with spring-loaded side-bayonets.

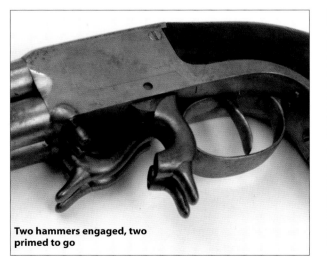

Two hammers engaged, two primed to go

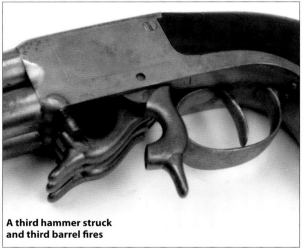

A third hammer struck and third barrel fires

All barrels emptied with all hammers engaged

PERCUSSION WEAPONS CONTINUED . . .

BELGIAN DOUBLE-BARREL PISTOL
This nineteenth-century pistol loads like a double-barrel shotgun—a forward pull on the trigger guard cocks the gun and allows the barrels to swing up for loading. It takes a .38-caliber centerfire cartridge and has two triggers.

SNEIDER-ENFIELD RIFLE
This British Sneider-Enfield Model 1870 rifle has a hinged breechblock design and takes a .577 cartridge. By the mid-1870s the British army was using Henry-Martini rifles instead, but this rifle was still popular in the British colonies, such as India and Africa.

DOUBLE-BARREL PISTOL WITH FIRING PINS

Made in Belgium in the nineteenth century, this .38-caliber pistol is broken open to load in the same way as a modern shotgun. It has a centerfire mechanism, with exposed double firing pins, and two triggers.

AMERICAN LONG-BARRELED PISTOL

Made in the late nineteenth century by J. Stevens Arms & Bicycle Co., this elegant percussion-cap pistol requires a 410 guage shot.

MUTZIG FRENCH CAVALRY RIFLE

This 1822 rifle is named after the French town where these weapons were manufactured. It originally had a flintlock mechanism, but this was changed to a percussion cap in 1835. Much of the appeal of percussion-cap pistols and rifles came from the ease with which they could be upgraded from flintlock-based weapons.

Percussion weapons continued . . .

HARPER'S FERRY

In 1841 one of the major U.S. arsenals—at Harper's Ferry, Virginia—began producing a new smoothbore percussion musket to be used in the Civil War. The Springfield and Harper's Ferry arsenals together turned out about 175,000 Model 1842 muskets (like the one shown here) before 1855, when a rifled version was introduced. Many Model 1842s were returned to the arsenals to have their barrels rifled to take the new Minié ball ammunition.

GERMAN RIFLE

The butt of this mid-nineteenth-century percussion-cap gun is beautifully engraved. It has two barrels—one is a shotgun, the other is a rifle—and two triggers.

BRUNSWICK RIFLE

Made in Europe in the early nineteenth century, this muzzle-loading percussion rifle has a "patch box" compartment for ammunition with a grease-pot for greasing the musket balls.

TARGET RIFLE
This percussion-cap target rifle has some fancy detailing. It was made in the early twentieth century by Emil Pachmayr of Traunstein in Bavaria, now part of Germany.

REMINGTON RIFLE
Dating from 1941, this model 24 semi-automatic .22 sporting rifle is based on a John Browning design. It is very similar to the Browning 22, which is still made today. It is a takedown design making it easy to take apart for transportation..

WAR, DEFENSE, AND A CHANGING WORLD

18TH CENTURY & 19TH CENTURY

Wars in the United States and Europe increased the demand for reliable firearms

REPEATING WEAPONS

Repeating weapons timeline
Soldiers armed with single-shot firearms were particularly vulnerable while reloading their weapons. Repeating firearms greatly reduced the risk of facing the enemy "unarmed."

1835
First Colt revolver

1836
Pin-fire cartridge

The period from the Battle of Waterloo in 1815 to the outbreak of World War I saw rapid advances in weapons technology. By the mid-nineteenth century, the old smoothbore musket had given way to the rifle, a weapon of much greater range and accuracy. The flintlock firing mechanism was replaced, first by the percussion cap system, and later by weapons firing fully enclosed metallic cartridges. Such cartridges made the development of repeating weapons—which could fire multiple shots without reloading—a practical proposition, and by the end of the nineteenth century, most armies would be equipped with bolt-action, magazine-fed rifles. The revolver, popularized by Samuel Colt at mid-century, gave individuals a potent pistol, and, by the end of the century, automatic handguns had become widespread and reliable. With firearms now dominating the battlefield, edged weapons like swords came to be increasingly relegated to purely ceremonial roles.

ASSAULT ON FORT SAUNDERS
During this ill-planned and short-lived battle in 1863, the Confederates failed to break the well-defended Union lines and suffered many casualties.

1837
Ethan Allen pepperbox pistol

1851
Robert Adams
double-action revolver

1860
Spencer repeating carbine

1869
Center-fire cartridge

1873
Winchester rifle

1879
Lee box magazine

1892
Schönberger-Laumann
semiautomatic pistol

PEPPERBOXES AND DERRINGERS

Before Samuel Colt's revolvers gained a widespread following in the 1850s, the most popular multiple-shot handgun was the pepperbox pistol. Unlike the revolver, which loads from a cylinder rotating around a single barrel, the pepperbox had multiple rotating barrels—usually four to six. Around the same time, the compact but powerful handguns known as derringers also became popular, while gunsmiths around the world developed handguns suited to local requirements, like the "howdah" pistols used in British-ruled India, and the weapons made by indigenous gunsmiths in Darra on what was, in the nineteenth century, the frontier between India and Afghanistan.

THE PEPPERBOX

The pepperbox was the brainchild of Massachusetts gunsmith Ethan Allen (1806–71; apparently no relation to the Revolutionary War hero of the same name), who patented the weapon in 1837 (some sources say 1834) and manufactured it first in Grafton, Massachusetts, then in Norwich, Connecticut, and finally in Worcester, Massachusetts, most of that time in partnership with his brother-in-law under the company name of Allen & Thurber. The weapon is said to have got its name from the fact that the percussion-cap firing system sometimes accidentally discharged all the barrels at once, "peppering" anything (or anyone) in front of it.

The pepperbox was capable of rapid fire because of its double-action firing system—one long pull of the trigger rotated the barrel into position and fired the weapon, and it was immediately ready to fire again with the next trigger pull. Pepperboxes, however, were never renowned for their accuracy. In *Roughing It*, Mark Twain's best-selling account of his Western adventures, the author quotes a stagecoach driver's experience with the weapon: "'If she [the gun] didn't get what she went after, she would fetch something else.' And so she did. She went after a deuce of spades nailed against a tree, once, and fetched a mule standing about thirty yards to the left of it."

The pepperbox fell victim to the growing popularity of the revolver, and Allen & Thurber ceased production of the weapon in the mid-1860s.

MARIETTE
A very finely made Belgian Mariette .38 pepperbox, with a ring trigger, four Damascus-steel barrels, and an ebonized grip. The Mariette system used a key to disengage all four barrels from the frame for loading.

HOWDAH

One unusual category of nineteenth-century handguns are the "howdah" pistols used by British officers and colonial officials in India. Howdahs are the passenger-carrying platforms mounted on the backs of elephants, which were a common form of transportation on hunting trips or administrative rounds in rural areas of the Subcontinent. Riders needed a hard-hitting weapon to fend off attacks by tigers, so British gunsmiths produced heavy-caliber pistols (usually .50—like the one shown here—or .60), which were often double-barreled, to give the firer a second shot if the first one missed.

MARIETTE BREVETÉ D26

This attractive pistol is a 5-shot pepperbox with a hand-rotated cylinder. It was made by Guillaume Mariette, an armorer in Liège, Belgium, in the nineteenth century. Mariette introduced several improvements in the pepperbox design.

PEPPERBOXES CONTINUED . . .

TURRET PISTOL

This very rare and interesting American revolver design appeared around the same time as Samuel Colt's first pistol. Patented by J. W. Cochran of New York City and made by C. B. Allen of Springfield, Massachusetts, the "turret" or "monitor" pistol had a .40, seven-shot, horizontally oriented cylinder. The percussion-cap weapon was fired by a sideways-mounted hammer. Only five or so were made.

NORTH & COUCH GAMESHOOTER

This American percussion cap pistol has six barrels that fire almost simultaneously. Patented in 1959, it was used to shoot game or as a hand gun.

ALLEN & THURBER

A classic Allen & Thurber pepperbox. This six-shot, .36 model was made sometime after 1857. Allen & Thurber guns were famed for their excellent construction; for example, the barrel assembly was machined from a single piece of steel.

FRENCH PEPPERBOX
A French pepperbox from around 1840; like the Mariette (see previous page), it is finely made, and also richly finished with gold and silver inlay.

Four individual barrels

TURNOVER
A predecessor to the derringer was the turnover pistol, which had two muzzle-loaded barrels which (as the name implies) could be unscrewed and flipped over, allowing the firer to get off two shots in (relatively) quick succession. The percussion-cap model shown here, made in Britain, features a concealed trigger.

TURNOVER
This is a rare turnover percussion pistol with four very short barrels, made by London gunsmith Thomas Lloyd.

THREE-SHOT PISTOL
This volley pistol bears similarities with a duckfoot pistol and shoots all three of its rounds at the same time. It has a percussion cap mechanism and was made in Europe in the nineteenth century.

PEPPERBOXES CONTINUED . . .

THE DERRINGER

"Derringer" is a catch-all term for the small, short-barreled, easily concealable pistols introduced in the 1830s. The name derives from a Philadelphia gunsmith, Henry Deringer (1786–1878). (Generally, firearms historians refer to the weapons made by Deringer himself as "deringers" and those made by his imitators as "derringers.") The original deringers were single-shot, muzzle-loading, percussion-cap weapons, usually .41, and with barrel lengths as short as 1½ inches. Actor John Wilkes Booth used such a weapon to assassinate President Abraham Lincoln at Ford's Theater in Washington, D.C., on the Saturday evening of April 15, 1865.

Later weapons of the type were made by a number of manufacturers, including Colt and Remington; they typically fired cartridges and often had two barrels in an over-and-under configuration. Derringers had widespread appeal as personal-defense weapons because they provided considerable "stopping power"—at least at close range—in a weapon that could be stowed inconspicuously in a coat pocket, or a boot, or tucked into a "lady's" garter belt.

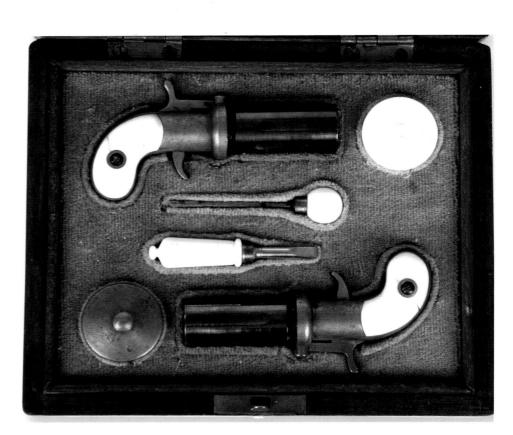

MUFF PISTOL
This Belgian-made, ivory-handled .36 single-shot percussion "muff pistol" was designed to be carried in a woman's hand muff. It has a concealed trigger and was made in the nineteenth century.

Lady's vanity case

Hidden drawer

LADIES' CASE WITH PISTOL COMPARTMENT
The derringer's compact size made it a popular personal-defense gun for women—whether "respectable," by nineteenth-century standards, or otherwise. This traveling case, made by Halstaffe of Regent Street, London, has a tray for cosmetics, a hidden compartment for money—and a concealed drawer fitted for two .44, single-shot Colt Model No. 3 derringers. The Model No. 3 was manufactured between 1875 and 1912.

ENGLISH MINIATURES
British gunsmith John Maycock produced this cased set of miniature pepperboxes. The six-shot, 2mm pistols feature 1-inch blued steel barrels, ivory butts, and brass frames; the mahogany case also holds an ivory cartridge box, ivory-handled screwdriver and cleaning rod, and a brass flask for lubricating oil. These tiny pistols are single-action—i.e., each barrel had to be manually rotated into place—because a double-action mechanism would have been impossible to incorporate into weapons of this diminutive size.

PIN-FIRE REVOLVER

Made in France in the midnineteenth century, this revolver has an unusual wrist-loop trigger and uses .30-caliber ammunition. It is cast iron with a wooden grip.

PERCUSSION CAP PISTOL

Although not a pepperbox, this pistol is a good example of the typically small size of guns that found favor as weapons of self-defense in the nineteenth century.

Mouth of powder flask

BOXLOCK PISTOL

This tiny boxlock pistol is three inches long with an octagonal brass barrel measuring just one inch. It also has a pear-shaped copper powder flask and originally came in a small case.

Round steel barrel

POCKET PISTOL

This .22-caliber pocket-sized pistol was made in Europe in the nineteenth century. The trigger is a crude stud-style design without trigger guard.

REMINGTON

While perhaps not strictly a derringer, the Remington-Rider magazine pistol, manufactured between 1871 and 1888, meets the derringer criteria of compact size (it had a barrel of 3 inches), but it fired a special short .32 cartridge. Also, it used an unusual repeating mechanism, with five rounds in a tubular magazine below the barrel. The firer pressed downward on a projection to depress the breechblock, ejecting the spent cartridge and chambering a new one.

COLT'S REVOLVERS

While Samuel Colt didn't invent the revolver, his name is now synonymous with the weapon—and for good reason. First, while the mechanical advances that Colt patented in 1835–36 were not a huge leap forward in innovation, they collectively made the revolver a practical weapon for both military and civilian use. Second, although it took years for Colt to win widespread acceptance for his revolvers, his skill in marketing the weapon ultimately established the Colt revolver as the standard by which all similar pistols were judged. Finally, Colt's significance to weapon history extends beyond his designs. His armory in Hartford, Connecticut, was the first to harness the technological advances of the Industrial Revolution—mass-production using interchangeable parts—and by 1861 had more than 1,000 employees and annual earnings of about $250,000.

THE REVOLVER'S EVOLUTION

The idea of a repeating firearm that fired successive shots from a cylinder rotating around a single barrel (the opposite of the pepperbox system) was not new in the early nineteenth century. Flintlock revolvers were made in England as early as the mid-1600s. The problem with these early revolvers was that each chamber of the cylinder needed its own pan of priming powder, and firing one round sometimes ignited the powder in the rest of the pans, leading to all the cylinders discharging at once.

At the turn of the nineteenth century, an American inventor, Elisha Collier, designed a much improved flintlock revolver that used a single priming pan. A number of these were manufactured in Britain after 1810. However, it would take the introduction of the percussion cap—and Samuel Colt's basic design, which linked the cylinder to the firing mechanism, eliminating the need for manual rotation of the cylinder—to make a truly safe and practical revolver.

Colt's revolvers earned their good reputation because they were powerful, well made, and reliable. That reliability stemmed in large part from their relative mechanical simplicity. Until the mid-1870s, all Colt models were single-action. To fire, the user pulled back the hammer, which rotated the cylinder and lined up the chamber with the barrel. Then the user had only to pull the trigger to discharge the weapon. This required a mechanism with fewer moving parts than the double-action revolvers developed in the early 1850s. For the same reason, Colts were also more accurate than their double-action counterparts, if slower to fire. (An experienced user could, however, discharge his Colt quickly by "fanning" the hammer with the palm of his nonshooting hand—a technique that is very familiar to viewers of countless Western movies and cowboy TV shows.)

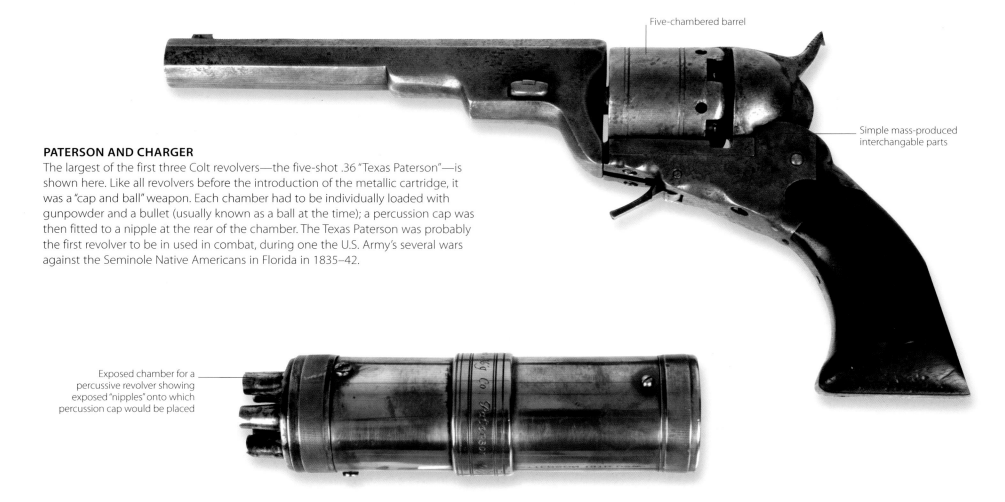

Five-chambered barrel

Simple mass-produced interchangable parts

PATERSON AND CHARGER
The largest of the first three Colt revolvers—the five-shot .36 "Texas Paterson"—is shown here. Like all revolvers before the introduction of the metallic cartridge, it was a "cap and ball" weapon. Each chamber had to be individually loaded with gunpowder and a bullet (usually known as a ball at the time); a percussion cap was then fitted to a nipple at the rear of the chamber. The Texas Paterson was probably the first revolver to be in used in combat, during one the U.S. Army's several wars against the Seminole Native Americans in Florida in 1835–42.

Exposed chamber for a percussive revolver showing exposed "nipples" onto which percussion cap would be placed

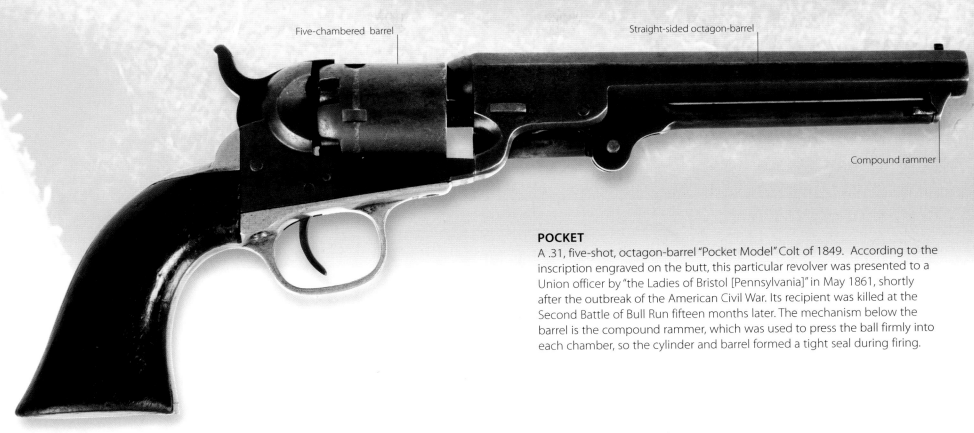

Five-chambered barrel

Straight-sided octagon-barrel

Compound rammer

POCKET

A .31, five-shot, octagon-barrel "Pocket Model" Colt of 1849. According to the inscription engraved on the butt, this particular revolver was presented to a Union officer by "the Ladies of Bristol [Pennsylvania]" in May 1861, shortly after the outbreak of the American Civil War. Its recipient was killed at the Second Battle of Bull Run fifteen months later. The mechanism below the barrel is the compound rammer, which was used to press the ball firmly into each chamber, so the cylinder and barrel formed a tight seal during firing.

NAVY

One of Colt's most successful revolvers was the six-shot .44 "Navy" series, the first model of which appeared in 1851. (Navy Colts weren't specifically made for use at sea; they got their name from the naval scene engraved on their barrels.) As with several other designs, Colt produced a smaller "pocket model," in this case .36.

The "Pocket Navy Revolver" shown here was converted from its original percussion-cap firing system to fire .38 centerfire cartridges. (Owners of cap-and-ball Colts could send their pistols back to the Hartford factory for conversion after Colt began making cartridge pistols in the early 1870s.)

Converted hammer mechanism

Compound rammer

Muzzle pivot

Brass trigger guard

"ABE LINCOLN MAY HAVE FREED ALL MEN, BUT SAM COLT MADE THEM EQUAL."

Post-Civil War slogan

SAMUEL COLT

Born in Hartford, Connecticut, in 1814, Samuel L. Colt was—like most of the great gunmakers—something of a mechanical prodigy. As a boy, he liked to disassemble and reassemble clocks, firearms, and other devices. Bored with working in his father's textile mill, he went to sea at age fifteen as an apprentice seaman. It was on this voyage that he conceived his initial design. The origin of Colt's inspiration is shrouded in legend, variously attributed to his observation of the ship's wheel; or the capstan used to raise the anchor; or a steamboat's paddlewheel—or, more prosaically, he may have seen Collier flintlock revolvers in India, where they were used by British troops. In any event, by the time he returned to the United States, he had carved a working model out of wood.

To get his gun built, Colt needed money. Billing himself as "Dr. S. Coult," he became a traveling "lecturer" whose specialty was demonstrating the effects of nitrous oxide—laughing gas—on curious locals. With the proceeds of this work, he had two gunsmiths, Anton Chase and John Pearson, make experimental models. After receiving his U.S. Patent in 1836, Colt set up the Patent Arms Manufacturing Company in Paterson, New Jersey, to make the new weapon. The three "Paterson" revolver models that appeared that year, however, found few takers. In 1842, Colt went bankrupt. That experience—and the years of litigation that followed—might have driven a lesser personality into despairing retirement. As determined as he was ambitious, Colt made an astonishing comeback a few years later.

Some early Colts had found their way into the hands of soldiers and frontiersmen, including Captain Samuel Walker of the Texas Rangers. In 1844, Walker and fifteen rangers, armed with Colts, fought off a war party of about eighty Comanche Native Americans. When the Mexican-American War broke out in 1846, Walker (now an army officer) and Colt collaborated on a design for a new revolver. The result was the huge (4.9-pound), powerful (.41), "Walker Colt." A government order for a thousand put Colt back in business; because he no longer had his own plant, Colt contracted with Eli Whitney Jr. (son of the famous cotton gin inventor) to make them in Whitneyville, Connecticut. The success of Colt revolvers in the Mexican-American War greatly raised the weapons' profile. They began to attract international orders when Colt exhibited his guns at the Great Exhibition in London in 1851, and also when they proved their worth in the Crimean War (1854–55). By 1855, Colt was so successful that he was able to build a huge and highly advanced factory in Hartford, Connecticut—soon to become the world's largest nongovernment armory.

Colt died in 1862, eleven years before his company's most successful revolver—the single-action Army Model, and its civilian variants—came into being. Made in several calibers (including 44. and .45), this was the legendary "Peacemaker" and "Six-Shooter" of the American West.

Factory in Hartford, Connecticut
The original Colt Armory was built in 1855 in the district of Hartford known as Coltsville. It was destroyed by fire in 1864, and rebuilt with its most dramatic feature of the original structure, the blue onion dome with gold stars, topped by a gold orb and a rampant colt, the original symbol of the Colt Manufacturing Company.

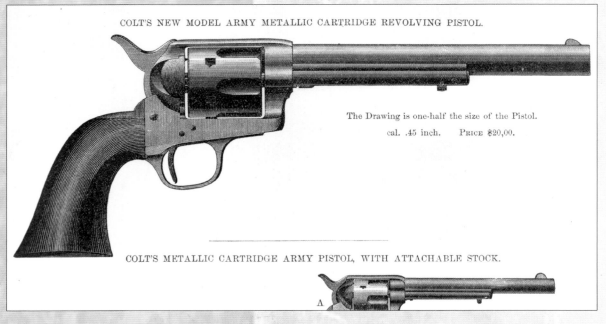

COLT'S NEW MODEL ARMY METALLIC CARTRIDGE REVOLVING PISTOL.

The Drawing is one-half the size of the Pistol.

cal. .45 inch.   PRICE $20,00.

COLT'S METALLIC CARTRIDGE ARMY PISTOL, WITH ATTACHABLE STOCK.

A

NEW NAVY
Introduced in 1892 and produced through 1908, the double-action Colt "New Navy" revolver was typical of the revolvers made by Colt from the late 1880s through the 1910s. (These guns, unlike the earlier "Navy Colts," were actually bought by the U.S. Navy and were the standard side-arm during the Spanish-American War.) Colt revolvers of this era were available in several different barrel lengths and chambered for a range of calibers. The New Navy series was made in .38 and .41—the latter version is shown here.

Lanyard ring

Recessed hammer spur

Trigger guard

FAMOUS COLT CUSTOMER
Billy the Kid (1859–81) was a notorious gunfighter who started rustling horses and cattle at a very young age. His real name was Henry McCarty but after shooting a man in an argument in 1873, he changed his name to William Bonney. He joined a group of gunmen fighting a frontier feud in Lincoln County, killing yet more men, including a sheriff. His gun of choice was the Colt Single Action Army revolver and the double-action Colt Thunderer. The feud ended but Billy, unlike his fellow gunmen, was not offered a pardon. In 1880 local ranchers elected Pat Garrett sherriff to stop his continued cattle rustling. Garret trapped and shot him dead in 1881, by which time Bill had killed at least 21 men.

NEW DOUBLE-ACTION REVOLVER
In the mid-1870s Colt finally began to make double-action pistols, starting with the "Lightning" model. The pistol shown here—which makes use of a slide-rod ejector to push spent cartridges from the cylinder chambers—is a model .38 made for export to Britain.

COLT'S REVOLVERS CONTINUED . . .

COLT IMITATION
Many different firearms companies have made Colt imitations in an attempt to benefit from that company's success. This is a .38 long, double action revolver made in Eibar, Spain. Most of these replicas were made in the 1920s. This one has some custom work on the grips—some small gems have been added around the edges.

Shortened barrel, originally longer

RIFLE
From its beginnings in Paterson, New Jersey, Colt manufactured carbines, rifles, and even shotguns as well as pistols. Most early Colt long arms (such as the Model 1855, .56 carbine shown here) used a revolving cylinder, but later the company made lever- and slide-action guns as well. While Colt's nineteenth-century long arms enjoyed some success in both military and civilian hands, their popularity never reached the level achieved by the company's pistols. At some point in this particular rifle's history, the barrel has been shortened.

"Colt DA 41" etched on barrel

The famous rampant colt logo of the company

COLT DA 41REVOLVER

This model, dating from 1903, is another typical Colt revolver. It has a trigger cocking, double-action allowing it to be fired with a simple pull of the trigger.

Revolving cylinder axis rod

Iron carbine butt plate

Sling swivel mounted on lower butt

COLT'S COMPETITORS

Colt's revolvers dominated the field thanks to a combination of patents, marketing, and general excellence, but gunmakers on both sides of the Atlantic started to introduce a number of competing revolver designs, many of which would be combat-tested in battlefields from the Crimea (1854–55) to India (the "mutiny" of 1857), and the United States itself, in the Civil War of 1861–65, in which an amazing variety of revolvers were used by Union and Confederate troops. This period also saw a sort of civil war among gunmakers themselves over real and perceived patent infringement. However, by the 1870s, it was clear that the overall victor (whether double- or single-action) was the cartridge-firing revolver.

DOUBLE VERSUS SINGLE ACTION

At the 1851 Great Exhibition in London—the same "world's fair" at which Samuel Colt proudly displayed his revolvers—British gunsmith Robert Adams (1809–70) exhibited a new type of revolver. Instead of requiring the separate step of cocking the hammer before pulling the trigger, Adams's "double-action" revolver could be cocked and fired with one pull of the trigger. This made it faster to fire than Colt's single-action revolvers, but somewhat less accurate because of the heavy pressure the firer had to exert on the trigger. Early Adams revolvers suffered from various technical problems, but based on combat experience during the Crimean War, an improved version, the Beaumont-Adams, was introduced in 1855.

Revolvers of this type—which could be fired using either single- or double-action—soon became the standard British Army sidearm, effectively shutting Colt out of the British market. Although Adams revolvers were purchased for use by both the Union and Confederate armies during the Civil War, Colt retained its dominance in both camps during this conflict, no doubt partly due to being mass-produced and therefore cheaper than the hand-crafted Adams revolvers. The simpler Colt revolvers were also better suited to conditions in the rugged American West.

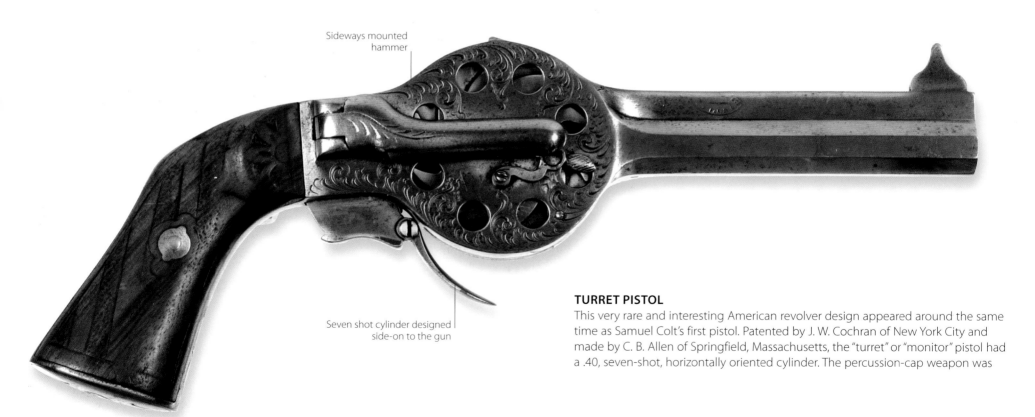

Sideways mounted hammer

Seven shot cylinder designed side-on to the gun

TURRET PISTOL

This very rare and interesting American revolver design appeared around the same time as Samuel Colt's first pistol. Patented by J. W. Cochran of New York City and made by C. B. Allen of Springfield, Massachusetts, the "turret" or "monitor" pistol had a .40, seven-shot, horizontally oriented cylinder. The percussion-cap weapon was

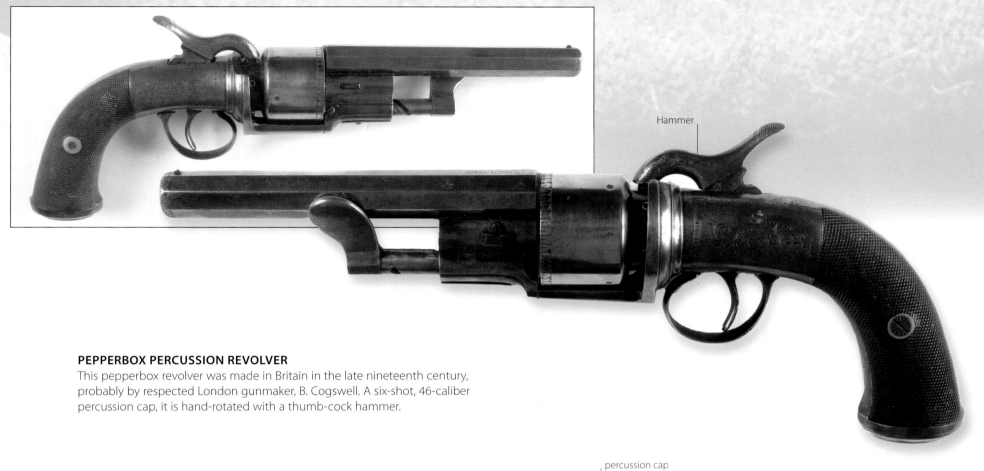

PEPPERBOX PERCUSSION REVOLVER

This pepperbox revolver was made in Britain in the late nineteenth century, probably by respected London gunmaker, B. Cogswell. A six-shot, 46-caliber percussion cap, it is hand-rotated with a thumb-cock hammer.

COGSWELL TRANSITION GUN

A major maker of pepperbox pistols, the London gunmakers Cogswell & Harrison also produced this revolver—known to firearms historians as a "transition gun"—in the early 1850s. The single-action weapon had a six-shot cylinder firing .44 rounds.

COLT'S COMPETITORS CONTINUED . . .

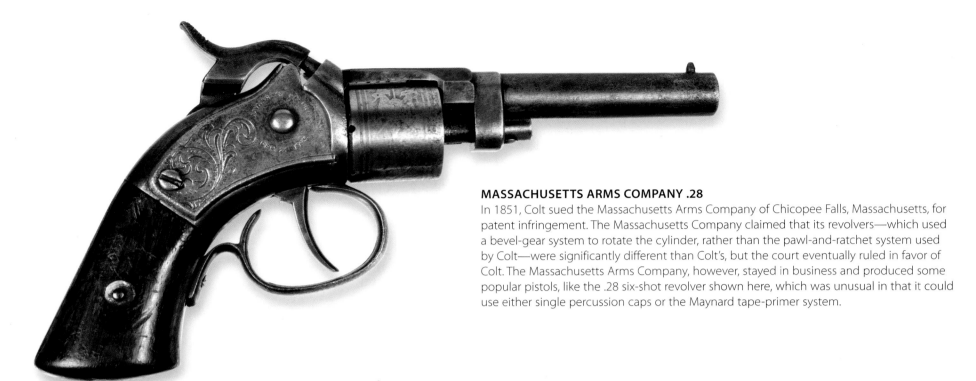

MASSACHUSETTS ARMS COMPANY .28
In 1851, Colt sued the Massachusetts Arms Company of Chicopee Falls, Massachusetts, for patent infringement. The Massachusetts Company claimed that its revolvers—which used a bevel-gear system to rotate the cylinder, rather than the pawl-and-ratchet system used by Colt—were significantly different than Colt's, but the court eventually ruled in favor of Colt. The Massachusetts Arms Company, however, stayed in business and produced some popular pistols, like the .28 six-shot revolver shown here, which was unusual in that it could use either single percussion caps or the Maynard tape-primer system.

MASSACHUSETTS ARMS CASED SET
Between about 1849 and 1851, Massachusetts Arms also made Wesson & Leavitt revolvers, like the .31, six-shot model one shown here cased with its accessories.

A few later guns of this model had a loading lever

Brass rammer

Bullet mold

Powder flask

Caps

THE CARTRIDGE PISTOL

Another potential challenge to Colt came from the introduction of fully enclosed metallic cartridges. In the mid-1850s, Americans Horace Smith and Daniel Wesson, who had pioneered both the metallic cartridge and the repeating rifle, developed a revolver firing rimfire cartridges that was based on a cylinder design purchased from a former Colt employee, Rollin White. (According to some sources, White first offered his innovative design to Samuel Colt, but with an uncharacteristic failure of foresight, Colt didn't think metallic cartridges had any potential.) Smith & Wesson put their pistol, in a .22 model, on the market in 1857, after Colt's patents had expired.

The combat advantages of a revolver that could load cartridges quickly—as opposed to the slow-loading cap-and-ball system used by Colt and others—were obvious, and a .32 version proved popular with Union forces during the Civil War. But again, Colt's dominance was not seriously challenged, because S&W's production was not fast enough to keep up with demand, both in pistols and in ammunition. In the last years of the conflict, Colt revolvers did face a serious competitor in the form of the Remington Model 1863 Army revolver. While still a cap-and-ball weapon, many soldiers found it to be easier to load and fire than its Colt counterparts. When S&W's patent expired in 1872, Colt and a host of other gunmakers rushed to get their own cartridge revolvers on the market.

SLOCUM
In 1863, the Brooklyn Arms Company of New York introduced a .32 five-shot revolver, the "Slocum," named apparently for a New York-born Civil War general. The pistol loaded from the front; the chambers were actually sliding tubes that moved forward over a fixed ejecting mechanism. The Slocum was another attempt to circumvent the patent controlled by Smith & Wesson.

Sliding sleeve moves forward

Varnished rosewood grips

Stud trigger

MOORE
In an effort to get around Smith & Wesson's patent on cartridge revolvers, Moore's Patent Firearms Company of Brooklyn made a number of revolvers based on a design by Daniel Moore and Daniel Wilson in the 1860s. Instead of loading from the rear of the cylinder, these revolvers loaded from the front; the cartridge's priming charge was contained in a "teat" in its base, and so these revolvers became known as "teat," or "tit," guns. On the patent issue the courts eventually found for Smith & Wesson.

REMINGTON NEW ARMY
The .44 six-shot "New Army" revolver was (after the Colt Model 1860) perhaps the second most widely issued revolver for Union troops during the American Civil War (1861–65). At least 130,000 were manufactured at Remington's Ilion, New York, factory.

Trigger guard

COLT'S COMPETITORS CONTINUED . . .

SMITH & WESSON

Horace Smith (b. Cheshire, Massachusetts; 1808–93) and Daniel Wesson (b. Worcester, Massachusetts; 1825–96) both entered the gunmaking trade in their youth: Smith as an employee of the federal armory at Springfield, Massachusetts, and Wesson as an apprentice to his elder brother Edwin, a leading New England gunsmith. The two first joined forces in Norwich, Connecticut, in the early 1850s, when they collaborated to produce a repeating rifle that could fire metallic cartridges. As with Samuel Colt, their technological innovation didn't meet with commercial success at first, and they had to sell out to Oliver Winchester. But also like Colt, they persevered, patenting a revolver firing a rimfire cartridge (1854) and reconstituting their company (1856). The success of their designs during the Civil War and in the years that followed—especially the Model 3 revolver, introduced in 1870—laid the foundations of a company that remains one of the foremost gunmakers in the twenty-first century.

While Smith & Wesson today manufactures automatics, revolvers continue to be the firm's signature product, and long after the death of its founders, their tradition of innovation continued in such weapons as the .38 Model 1910 "Military & Police" revolver (introduced in 1899 and still in production through numerous variations, and probably the most popular pistol ever made for law-enforcement use); the .357 (1935) and .44 (1956) magnums (beloved by Hollywood—Clint Eastwood's character "Dirty Harry" wielded the latter); and the Model 60 (1965), which ushered in the era of the stainless steel pistol.

Spike for pushing out spent cartidges

SMITH & WESSON

The six-shot, .32 Smith & Wesson No. 2 revolver, which saw much use in the Civil War and on the Western frontier, was—like other early Smith & Wessons—known as a "tip-up" revolver from the system it used for loading and extracting cartridges: Manipulating a catch released the barrel to swing upward, allowing the cylinder to be removed completely from the frame; the firer used the spike below the barrel to push out the spent cartridges; the cylinder was then reloaded, replaced, and the barrel swung downward into firing position. Later Smith & Wesson revolvers pioneered the "break-open" system, in which the barrel swung downward and an extractor mechanism in the cylinder (which remained attached to the frame) ejected all the spent cartridges at once.

Engraved lock plate

Stud trigger

ALLEN & WHEELOCK

Another interesting early cartridge pistol was the .32 "lipfire" revolver made by the Allen & Wheelock Company of Worcester, Massachusetts. First made in 1858, these pistols not only fired a unique cartridge, but also utilized a lever-operated, rack-and-pinion ejection system.

WILLIAMS AND POWELL REVOLVER
This is a five-shot double action revolver made by Williams & Powell of Liverpool, England in the late nineteeth century. It is similar to the Tranter.

BELGIAN REVOLVER
Made in Belgium in the mid-nineteenth century, this early six-shot revolver is .38-caliber with a

SNAKECHARMER
This is the popular Handy Gun made by Harrington & Richardson Arms Co. of Worcester, Massachusetts from 1921 until short-barreled shotguns were outlawed by the National Firearms Act in 1934.

COLT'S COMPETITORS CONTINUED . . .

Five-shot cylinder

Firing trigger

Cocking trigger

TRANTER

Based in Birmingham, England, British gunsmith William Tranter (1816–90) produced a variety of revolver designs in his long career. His pistols had a good reputation for quality, and large numbers were purchased by the Confederate government for issue to its forces in the American Civil War (1861–65), while others (like the five-shot .54 pistol shown here) were bought privately by British officers. This model used a double-trigger firing system; the lower trigger cocked the weapon, the upper one fired it. This is a cap-and-ball pistol, but after the Civil War, Tranter produced many cartridge-firing designs.

Ejector mechanism

WILLIAMS AND POWELL REVOLVER

This is a five-shot double-action revolver made by Williams & Powell of Liverpool, England, in the late nineteeth century. It is similar to the Tranter.

Staggered chambers

Folding trigger

LEFAUCHEUX REVOLVER

This is a double-barrel 20-shot revolver with staggered chambers, firing one at a time. It has a pinfire mechanism and was made in France in the nineteenth century.

BELGIAN DOUBLE-BARREL PISTOL
Made in Belgium in the nineteenth century, this
.38-caliber pistol is broken open to load in the same way
as a modern shotgun. It has a center-fire mechanism, with
exposed firing pins, and two triggers.

Decorative grip

Triggers

Trigger sits behind
hammer

MANUAL REVOLVER
Made in the early nineteenth century, the
chamber on this revolver is hand-cocked. It has
some fine decorative detailing, including a fox
chasing birds engraved on the chamber.

Ejector rod

BELGIAN REVOLVER
This interesting example of a percussion cap revolver with
six barrels was made in the early nineteenth century.

Colt's Competitors continued . . .

Octagonal barrel

BELGIAN REVOLVER
This Belgian copy of the French Chamelot-Delvigne Model 1872 revolver dates from the nineteenth century.

Six-shot cylinder

Front sight

BELGIAN REVOLVER
Made in Belgium in the mid-nineteenth century, this early six-shot revolver is .38-caliber with a pinfire mechanism.

EUROPEAN SIX-SHOT REVOLVER
Dating from 1887, this six-shot Reichsrevolver M1879 has classic styling. It was made by a consortium of three companies—Spanenburger & Sauer, V. C. Schilling, and C. G. Haenel in Suhl, Germany—who often made Reischsrevolvers together.

Latch for hinged frame

DANISH DOUBLE ACTION PISTOL
Made by J. B. Ronge & Fils of Liège, Belgium, this revolver has a half-round, half-octagonal barrel and takes a 9mm cartridge. It was issued to units in the Danish navy from 1891 to 1941.

Lever in off position

BELGIAN PISTOL
This percussion cap .32-caliber revolver dates from the early 1800s and takes six shots via an unusual side-loading lever; most other revolvers of the time have their levers on the underside of the barrel.

Side-loading lever

COLT'S COMPETITORS CONTINUED . . .

Cylinder

BLACK METAL REVOLVER
This is a large caliber cast-steel revolver with an octagonal barrel inscribed "John Clarke, Newton Abbot," which is a town in England. This is a "Thomas's Patent #158" design and these guns were made by Tipping & Lawden until around 1877.

Hammer spur

HUSQVARNA 1433 REVOLVER
Made in the late nineteenth century by the well-known Swedish firearms manufacturer Husqvarna Vapenfabriks Aktiebolag, this is a standard, high-quality, six-shot revolver.

Eight-shot cylinder

Ejector rod

L-shaped grip

RAST & GASSER REVOLVER

Made in Europe in the late nineteenth century, this is an eight-shot, 8mm, single- and double-action revolver. The Model 1898 has an ejector rod under the barrel and is loaded through a gate that has a safety device to prevent accidental firing. The L-shaped grip is a drawback, making accurate aim difficult.

Trigger guard

Front of trigger guard

Center pin

Hinge

Original position of barrel

CAST STEEL REVOLVER #9990

This is a Belgian .44-caliber revolver made for the British market in the 1870s. Its unusual feature is that the trigger guard moves to the side, allowing the gun to break open and backward in the middle. Further movement of the guard ejects the cartridges.

Release button

Release button

THE AMERICAN CIVIL WAR

The American Civil War (1861–65) is often described, with much justification, as the first modern war. The conflict saw the introduction (or at least the first widespread use) of innovations like photography, the telegraph, aircraft (balloons were used for observation of enemy forces), submarines, armored ships, breech-loading artillery, and infantry weapons, repeating rifles, and rapid-fire guns. Almost a century and a half later,

the American Civil War remains both the largest civil war fought in the Western Hemisphere and America's deadliest conflict, with a combined death toll estimated at 700,000—more than in all other American wars combined. While disease claimed twice as many men as combat, the high casualty rate owed much to technical advances in weaponry, including the first use in combat of the Gatling gun.

PITCHED BATTLE
On those occasions when Union and Confederate forces met at close quarters, a deadly combination of cannons, rifles, pistols, and swords was mercilessly deployed.

> ## "A RICH MAN'S WAR AND A POOR MAN'S FIGHT ..."
>
> Southern opposition slogan, in *The Civil War* by Shelby Foote

TECHNOLOGY AND TACTICS

The years before the Civil War had seen a revolution in infantry weapons. The old smoothbore musket had given way to the rifle, which was the standard infantryman's weapon on both sides. These fired a heavy lead bullet (usually .58 caliber) to an effective range of up to 500 yards. While still muzzle-loaders, these rifles used a new type of bullet, the Minié ball, which expanded upon firing to fit snugly the grooves of a rifled barrel. The introduction of the rifle shifted the advantage from the offensive to the defensive on the battlefield. Riflemen, "dug in" behind cover and, firing several shots a minute, could mow down several times their number attacking in the open.

EXPERIMENTS AND INNOVATION

The Civil War also saw the introduction of weapons that were "high-tech" for their time. Because it was virtually impossible to use a muzzle-loading weapon in the saddle, Union cavalry rode into battle armed with breech-loading weapons like the Burnside and Sharps carbines. Especially effective was the repeating Spencer carbine, which had a seven-shot magazine—Confederate soldiers called it "That damned Yankee gun that can be loaded on Sunday and fired all week." Both sides also raised units of marksmen, or "sharpshooters," to engage in what would later become known as sniping. Although the technology of the time was unable to develop machine guns in the modern sense, both sides experimented with manually operated rapid-fire weapons. The Confederacy used a crank-operated light cannon during the Peninsular Campaign, and the Union deployed a multiple-barreled bullet-firing weapon, the Requa-Billinghurst battery gun, mainly to defend bridges and other positions.

Barrel band retains barrel in stock

Barrel reduced from three to two bands

SPRINGFIELD MUSKET
Early in the war, many Union troops were issued with a version of the old .69 flintlock musket converted to the percussion-cap firing system, like the gun shown here, though this one has been cut down to two bands from the usual three. The Springfield rifled musket would largely replace these obsolete weapons, although many of the conversions stayed in use by state militias.

Triangular stabbing blade

AUSTRIAN STEEL
This socket bayonet fit the Model 1854 Austrian Infanteriegewehr, also known as the Lorenz rifled musket. Despite being purchased in large numbers by both sides, the Lorenz, according to one historian, was "universally loathed by many of the soldiers who used them." In fact, the Union government bought thousands of these guns simply to keep them from being bought by the Confederacy.

CSA (Confederate States of America) engraved on blad

Double trigger in guard

GATLING GUN
Circular magazine holder

The original Gatling gun of 1861 had six barrels and fed from a hopper containing paper cartridges; a later model took metallic cartridges, greatly increasing the rate of fire, and post–Civil War models—like the one shown here—had ten barrels and used a drum magazine. The Gatling is often cited as the world's first machine gun, but this is an inaccurate description: the weapon was manually operated, rather than functioning by means of recoil or gas energy. Still, Gatlings could achieve a rate of fire in excess of 1,000 rounds per minute.

SAVAGE-NORTH REVOLVER
Manufactured by the Savage Revolving Arms Co. of Middletown, Connecticut, the 1859 "Navy Model" revolver—a six-shot, .36 weapon—had an unusual firing system. The trigger guard enclosed not one but two triggers: The lower ring trigger rotated the cylinder and cocked the hammer, while the conventional upper trigger fired it. Despite its designation as a "Navy" revolver, the Union Navy apparently purchased only about a thousand, while the Union Army bought ten times that number.

HOMEMADE BLADES
Confederate privates carried these crude knives, which may well have been made from a saw or farm-implement blade. The design of this and similar Southern knives was inspired by the famous Bowie knife, the long-bladed weapon popularized by the frontiersmen Jim and Rezin Bowie in the 1830s.

Lever on hammer to select bullets or buckshot

Ten barrels

LEMAT PISTOL
A favorite sidearm of Confederate officers, the LeMat pistol had two barrels: The upper discharged .40 bullets via a nine-shot cylinder, the lower, a single charge of buckshot. This powerful hybrid of revolver and shotgun was first made in New Orleans in 1856 by a French-born doctor, Jean Alexander Francois LeMat, who later moved production to Europe when the war broke out.

Polished walnut grip

WEAPONS OF THE CIVIL WAR

In terms of weapons production, the Union was much more fortunate than the Confederacy during the Civil War. The northern states contained not only most of the government arsenals, but the region was also much more heavily industrialized than the South. Although the Union, like the Confederacy, had to scramble for weapons to equip its troops early in the war, by 1862 the Union had largely settled on a few standardized firearms whose manufacture could be contracted out to private firms. By 1864, the Union was self-sufficient in weapons production, while the Confederacy still relied on imports for many of its firearms.

UNION WEAPONS

The closest thing to a standard long arm for the Union infantry was the Springfield rifled musket. The weapon got its name from the federal government's arsenal at Springfield, Massachusetts, which had been founded in 1794. Many Springfields were actually manufactured here, but during the war, more than thirty companies produced Springfields under contract, making a total of about 1.5 million pieces.

The most common version of the weapon was the Model 1861. However, the first of the .58 Springfield series had appeared in the 1840s, when the U.S. Army began to replace .69 flintlock muskets with percussion-cap weapons. After 1855 these incorporated a rifled barrel as well. The greater accuracy of the rifle over its smoothbore predecessors led to the introduction of a ladder-style rear sight, and it also came with a spike bayonet. It was a heavy piece, weighing in at 9¼ pounds, with an overall length of about 58 inches—which meant that with bayonet fixed, the Springfield was about as tall as the average Civil War soldier. Springfields were also widely used by the Confederacy—some were seized when the federal arsenal at Harper's Ferry, Virginia, fell to Stonewall Jackson's troops during the campaign that culminated in the Battle of Antietam (September 1862), and many others were obtained through scavenging on the battlefield.

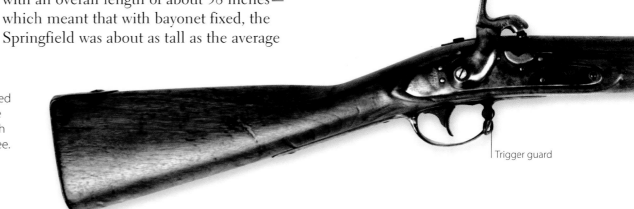

SPRINGFIELD MUSKET
In the first year or so of the war many Union troops were issued with a version of the old .69 flintlock musket converted to the percussion-cap firing system, like the gun shown here, though this one has been cut down to two bands from the usual three. The Springfield rifled musket would largely replace these obsolete weapons over time, although many of the conversions remained in service with state militias.

Trigger guard

RICHARD GATLING
Ironically, Richard Jordan Gatling (1818–1903), the inventor of the Gatling gun—which first saw action with the Union Army in the siege of Petersburg, Virginia, in 1864—was a North Carolinian by birth and (according to some historians) a Confederate sympathizer. In another irony, Gatling (a doctor by training) claimed that his inspiration in developing the weapon—considered to be the first successful rapid-fire gun—was the desire to lower the number of men needed to fight battles in order to reduce the spread of disease: "It occurred to me that if I could invent a machine—a gun— which could by its rapidity of fire, enable one man to do as much battle duty as a hundred, that it would, to a large extent supersede the necessity of large armies, and consequently, exposure to battle and disease [would] be greatly diminished." In 1861, Gatling designed a multiple-barreled, hand-cranked weapon, which he demonstrated to the U.S. Ordnance Bureau a year later. The weapon was rejected in 1862 as too complicated and heavy, and it was not officially adopted until 1866, after the war's end—but some commanders purchased Gatlings on their own initiative and these saw service toward the end of the conflict.

In later decades, Britain's Royal Navy adopted guns based on the Gatling design, and Gatlings were used to good effect by the U.S. Army in Cuba during the Spanish-American War (1898). After World War II, the multiple-barrel Gatling concept was revived by the U.S. military—in an electrically operated form—in aircraft weapons such as the M1961 Vulcan 20mm cannon and the 7.62mm "minigun" machine gun.

GATLING GUN
The original Gatling gun of 1861 had six barrels and fed from a hopper containing paper cartridges; a later model took metallic cartridges, greatly increasing the rate of fire, and post-Civil War models—like the one shown here—had ten barrels and utilized a drum magazine. The Gatling is often cited as the world's first machine gun, but this is an inaccurate description, as the weapon was manually operated, rather than functioning by means of recoil or gas energy. Still, Gatlings could achieve a rate of fire in excess of 1,000 rounds per minute.

Both "Johnny Reb" and "Billy Yank," the ordinary infantrymen of the American Civil War (1861–65), carried essentially the same weapon—a muzzle-loading rifled musket, usually .58 or .577 caliber. While the workshops and factories of the North kept the Union armies relatively well supplied with weapons (despite shortages early in the war), the South lacked industry and had to import most of its arms from Europe, something that became increasingly difficult as the war went on and the Union Navy's blockade of Southern ports cut the Confederacy off from its sources of supply.

CARBINES AND PISTOLS

The Union was also fortunate in being able to take advantage of the designs of gunmakers like Christian Sharps, Christopher Spencer, and Benjamin Tyler Henry, who produced innovative breech-loading (and, in the case of Spencer and Henry, repeating) rifles and carbines. However, these weapons were never issued in large numbers by the Union's Ordnance Department; many of them were purchased by state governments for issue to their regiments, or were personally bought by individual soldiers. In the opinion of some historians, the Union might have defeated the Confederacy more quickly had it been less conservative in adopting these kinds of weapons. As for the Union Army's pistols, these, too were a mix of government-issue and privately purchased weapons. The .44 Colt Model 1860 was probably the most popular single revolver among Union officers, but a wide variety of revolvers were used, including the Starr (also .44), British-made Adams revolvers, and the .36 Savage-North "Navy" model shown below.

Six-shot cylinder

Octagonal barrel

SAVAGE-NORTH REVOLVER
Manufactured by the Savage Revolving Arms Co. of Middletown, Connecticut, the 1859 "Navy Model" revolver—a six-shot, .36 weapon—had an unusual firing system. The trigger guard enclosed not one but two triggers: The lower ring trigger rotated the cylinder and cocked the hammer, while the conventional upper trigger fired it. Despite its designation as a "Navy" revolver, the Union Navy apparently purchased only about a thousand, while the Union Army bought ten times that number.

Falling-block breech

SPENCER CARBINE
The Spencer rifle, model 1860, has the distinction of being the first magazine-fed repeating rifle officially adopted by a major army. The gun, designed by Christopher Spencer (1833–1922), utilized a falling-block breech, operated by a lever that doubled as a trigger and was fed by a tubular magazine of seven .56 copper-jacketed cartridges located in the stock. After the war started, both the Union army and navy placed orders for the weapon. However, this gave Spencer's company impossible delivery deadlines, and unfortunate accidents in testing led the government to have second thoughts. Spencer personally called on President Abraham Lincoln in August 1863, and the president test-fired the weapon to his satisfaction. The Union ultimately bought more than 100,000 Spencers, including the carbine model shown here.

CONFEDERATE WEAPONS

Early in the war, the severe Southern arms shortage forced many Confederate soldiers to arm themselves with shotguns and hunting rifles brought from home.

Contemporary historian Andrew Leckie writes that "When the 27th Alabama [Regiment] marched off to war it was said the men carried a thousand double-barreled shotguns and a thousand homemade Bowie knives." The situation improved somewhat when arms began arriving from overseas, and when Confederate forces captured the federal arsenal at Harper's Ferry, Virginia, in 1861. Some of the machinery from Harper's Ferry was used to set up arms factories throughout the South, but these small manufacturers could produce only a fraction of the rifles, artillery pieces, and other weapons needed by the Confederacy.

IMPORTS AND IMITATIONS

The closest thing to a standard infantry weapon in the Confederate armies was the British-made .577 Enfield rifled musket. Despite the name, the Enfields used in the Civil War were not made at the Royal Arsenal located at Enfield in England, because Great Britain was officially neutral in the conflict; instead, private manufacturers produced rifles to the Enfield pattern and it was these that were exported. The Confederate government purchased about 400,000 Enfields over the course of the war, and the rifle was also widely used by the Union forces. Besides the Enfield, the Confederacy bought around 50,000 Model 1854 Infanteriegewehr (infantry rifles) from Austria.

Throughout the war, the Confederate cavalry lacked an effective breech-loading saddle weapon like the Sharps carbine used by Union horsemen. Confederate gunsmiths tried to copy the Sharps, but the result—the so-called "Richmond Sharps," named for the Confederate capital, where it was manufactured—performed so poorly that Confederate General Robert E. Lee described the gun as "so defective as to be demoralizing to our men." Only about 5,000 were made.

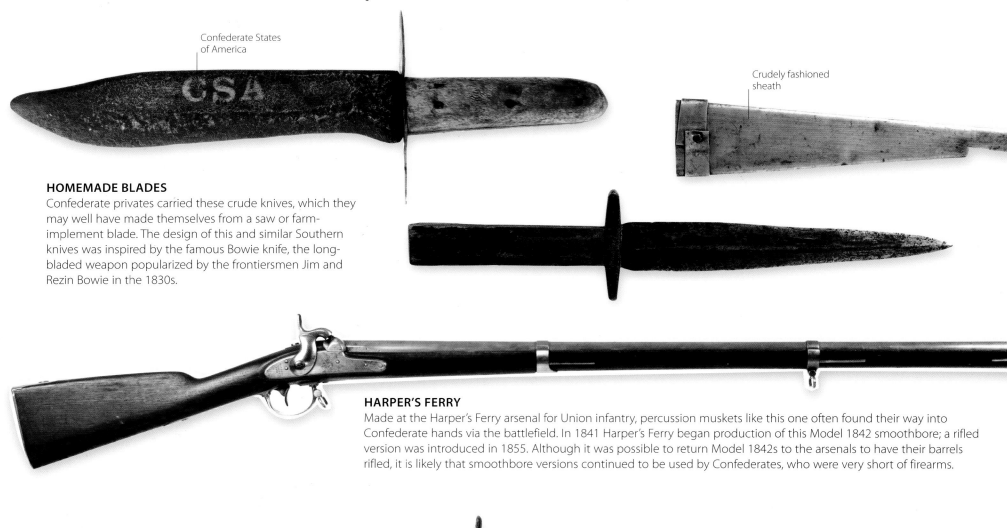

Confederate States of America

Crudely fashioned sheath

HOMEMADE BLADES
Confederate privates carried these crude knives, which they may well have made themselves from a saw or farm-implement blade. The design of this and similar Southern knives was inspired by the famous Bowie knife, the long-bladed weapon popularized by the frontiersmen Jim and Rezin Bowie in the 1830s.

HARPER'S FERRY
Made at the Harper's Ferry arsenal for Union infantry, percussion muskets like this one often found their way into Confederate hands via the battlefield. In 1841 Harper's Ferry began production of this Model 1842 smoothbore; a rifled version was introduced in 1855. Although it was possible to return Model 1842s to the arsenals to have their barrels rifled, it is likely that smoothbore versions continued to be used by Confederates, who were very short of firearms.

CONFEDERATE CONVERSION
Early in the war the Confederacy managed to obtain a small quantity of converted muzzle-loaders made by the Massachusetts Arms Company, like the one shown here. The carbine used the Maynard Percussion Tape Primer system, rather than the more common percussion cap.

JEFFERSON DAVIS

Unlike Abraham Lincoln—whose only military experience was a brief stint in the Illinois militia—Jefferson Davis spent many years as a professional soldier before assuming the presidency of the Confederate States of America in February 1861. Born in Kentucky in 1808, Davis graduated from West Point and saw service on the frontier before resigning his commission in 1835. He later fought with distinction—and was wounded—in the Mexican-American War (1846–48). Entering politics as Secretary of War in President Franklin Pierce's cabinet, he pushed through significant reforms like the adoption of the rifled musket. Davis was a U.S. Senator from Mississippi when the war broke out. He was imprisoned for two years after the Confederacy defeat in the spring of 1865 and died in Louisiana in 1889.

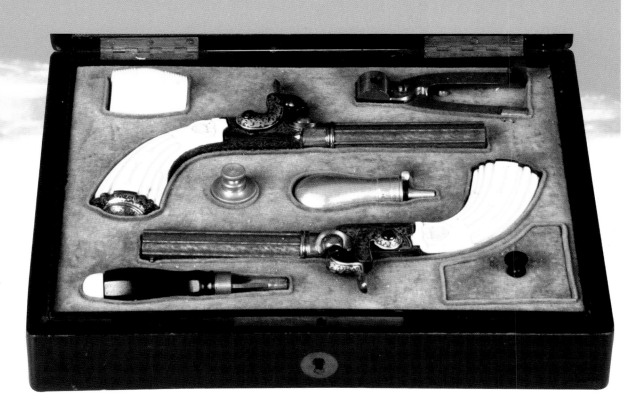

JEFFERSON DAVIS' PISTOLS

This magnificent set of cased pistols was made in Belgium in 1861 for presentation to the newly appointed president of the Confederate States of America. They feature Damascus steel barrels, grips of fluted, carved ivory, and gold inlay on the frames and other parts. Davis never got to enjoy this gift, however; the ship carrying them to the Confederacy was captured as it tried to run the Union blockade.

Hammer spur

LEMAT PISTOL

A favorite side-arm of Confederate officers, the LeMat pistol had two barrels: The upper discharged .40 bullets via a nine-shot cylinder, the lower a single charge of buckshot. This powerful hybrid of revolver and shotgun was first made in New Orleans in 1856 by a French-born doctor, Jean Alexander Francois LeMat, who later moved production to Europe when the war broke out.

Slender bayonet blade

AUSTRIAN STEEL

This socket bayonet fit the Model 1854 Austrian Infanteriegewehr, also known as the Lorenz rifled musket. According to one historian, the Lorenz was "loathed by many of the soldiers who used them." In fact, the Union government bought thousands of these guns simply to keep them from being bought by the Confederacy.

WEAPONS OF THE AMERICAN WEST

Few eras in history are more identified with the widespread use of firearms than the settling of western United States in the nineteenth century: The phrase "Wild West" instantly conjures up images of cowboys, outlaws, and lawmen wielding "six-shooters;" scouts and buffalo-hunters with their lever-action "repeaters" and high-powered single-shot rifles; Cavalrymen and Native Americans skirmishing with carbines and revolvers pitted against knives, tomahawks, and bows and arrows. Countless books and movies have established this romantic period in the popular imagination—not always accurately—but the fact is that on the frontier, having a reliable gun (or two, or three) to hand often meant the difference between life and death.

ACROSS THE MOUNTAINS

At the start of the nineteenth century, the frontier was just over the Appalachian Mountains; westward-moving pioneers from the states of the Eastern Seaboard brought with them their long Kentucky rifles both to bag game for the pot and to fight the Native Americans who resisted the tide of settlement. When the Louisiana Purchase (1803) pushed the frontier to the Rocky Mountains and the land beyond, the legendary "Mountain Men" went into the wilderness in search of furs, often armed with the heavy caliber rifles manufactured by the brothers Samuel and Jacob Hawken of St. Louis.

In the 1850s, during the run-up to the American Civil War, the western territory of Kansas became a battleground as antislavery settlers from the North clashed with proslavery settlers from the South, each side hoping to gain a majority when the time came for the territory to apply for statehood. Many of the Northern settlers were armed with a new and technically advanced weapon—the carbine designed by Christian Sharps (1811–74) in 1848. The breech-loading Sharps had a falling-block action; a lever (which doubled as the trigger guard) dropped the breechblock for loading. Rifles and carbines based on the Sharps design remained popular in the West for decades.

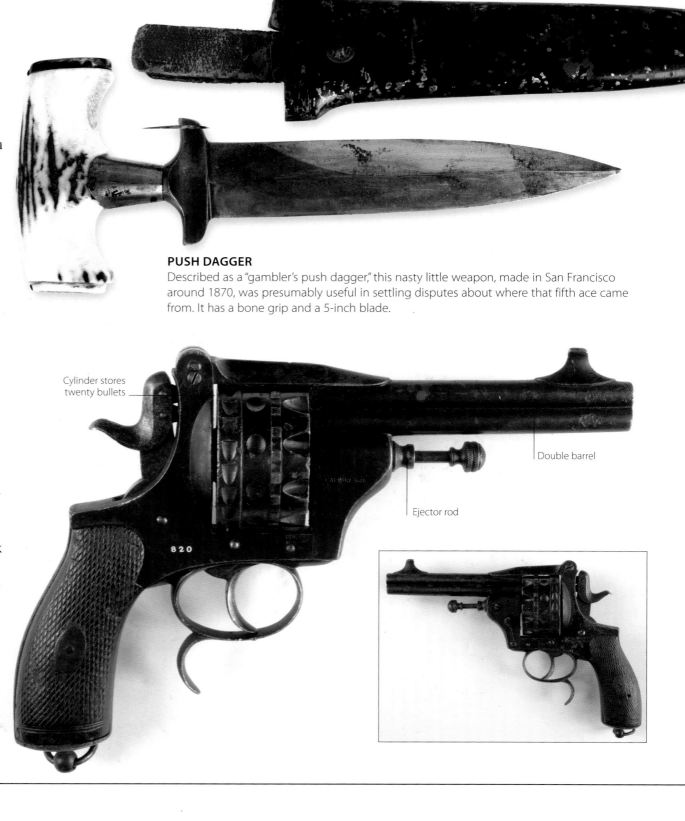

PUSH DAGGER
Described as a "gambler's push dagger," this nasty little weapon, made in San Francisco around 1870, was presumably useful in settling disputes about where that fifth ace came from. It has a bone grip and a 5-inch blade.

Cylinder stores twenty bullets

Double barrel

Ejector rod

"WILD WEST" REVOLVER
Gun manufacturers attempted to cash in on the romance of the West as late as the 1920s. This extraordinary revolver, made by Henrion, Dassy & Heuschen, has a 20-round cylinder. Other examples were called "Redoubtable" and "Terrible."

ON THE FRONTIER

The original Sharps was a single-shot weapon, but in 1860 Christopher Spencer (1833–1922) introduced a falling-block rifle with a tubular seven-round magazine under the barrel—a true "repeater"—which also saw widespread use in the West.

Around the same time, the Winchester Repeating Arms Co. was developing a lever-action magazine rifle, which went into production in 1866; its successor, the Model 1873, proved immensely popular and has often been called "the gun that won the West." The U.S. Army's main task from the end of the Civil War until the "end of the frontier" in 1890 was fighting the Native Americans. Although repeaters had proved their worth in the Civil War, the army had so many Springfield muzzle-loaders left over from that conflict that they fought the Indian Wars largely with "trap-door" Springfields—so-called because they'd been converted to single-shot breech-loaders. Another category of Western weapon was the high-powered (usually .50 caliber) rifles used by professional buffalo hunters. Killed for their hides, to keep them from blocking railroad construction, or just for sport, the buffalo—whose herds had once ranged across the Western plains in hundreds of thousands—had almost been hunted out of existence by the mid-1880s.

As for pistols, those on either side of the law used a wide variety, but Colts—especially the 1873 single-action Army model—were favorites.

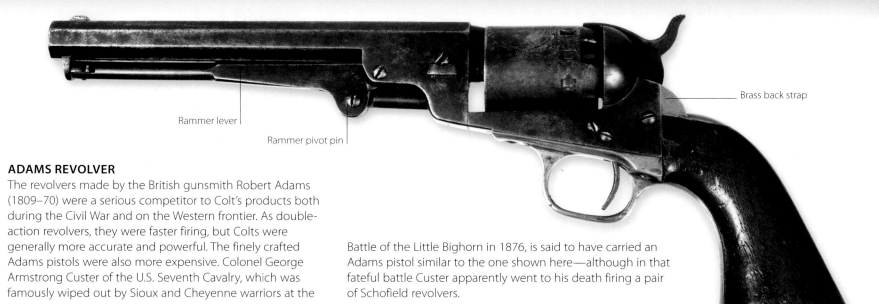

Rammer lever

Rammer pivot pin

Brass back strap

ADAMS REVOLVER

The revolvers made by the British gunsmith Robert Adams (1809–70) were a serious competitor to Colt's products both during the Civil War and on the Western frontier. As double-action revolvers, they were faster firing, but Colts were generally more accurate and powerful. The finely crafted Adams pistols were also more expensive. Colonel George Armstrong Custer of the U.S. Seventh Cavalry, which was famously wiped out by Sioux and Cheyenne warriors at the Battle of the Little Bighorn in 1876, is said to have carried an Adams pistol similar to the one shown here—although in that fateful battle Custer apparently went to his death firing a pair of Schofield revolvers.

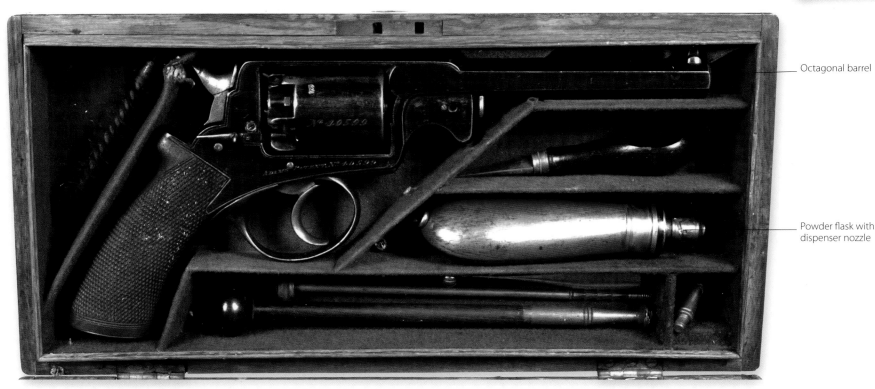

Octagonal barrel

Powder flask with dispenser nozzle

BELLE STAR REVOLVER

The famous female outlaw Belle Star (1848–89) carried this five-shot, .36, single-action "Navy Model" revolver, which was manufactured by the Manhattan Firearms Co. of Newark, New Jersey, between 1859 and 1868. Known in her time as "the female Jesse James," Starr is said to have liked to ride through the streets of Western towns firing her revolver in the air. After a career that included a stint in prison for horse theft (and the violent deaths of most of the men in her life) Starr herself was killed by a shotgun blast in Eufaula, Oklahoma.

THE AMERICAN WEST: RIFLES

OLIVER WINCHESTER

Born in Boston in 1810, Oliver Fisher Winchester made his first fortune as a manufacturer of men's shirts in Baltimore, New York City, and New Haven. As his clothing business prospered, he invested in the Volcanic Repeating Arms Company, taking control of that firm in 1856 and renaming it the New Haven Arms Co., and, later, the Winchester Repeating Arms Co. The Volcanic Company had produced a briefly popular repeating rifle, and Winchester hired gunsmith Benjamin Tyler Henry (1821–98) to refine the design. The result, in 1860, was the so-called Henry rifle, a lever-action repeater, which saw service in the American Civil War (1861–65), even though the Union Army never officially adopted it. After the war Winchester introduced the Model 1866, followed by the Model 1873, and their successors. Winchester was also a politician, serving as lieutenant governor of Connecticut (1866-67).

Oliver Winchester died in 1881 and control of the company passed to his son, William Winchester. William died the following year, but the company went on, and it remains one of the great American armsmakers, producing a wide range of rifles and shotguns for the sporting market. In a curious footnote to the Winchester story, William's widow, Sarah Pardee Winchester, was supposedly told by a Spiritualist medium that she had to build a home for the souls of those killed by Winchester weapons, or else the family would be forever cursed. Whether this incident and the ghostly tale is true or not is still debated, but in 1884 Sarah moved to San Jose, California, where she bought a modest house, which she proceeded to expand, at enormous cost, until her death in 1922. By that time the dwelling had 160 rooms and a host of bizarre features like staircases that went nowhere and doors that opened onto walls. The Winchester "mystery house" is now a major tourist attraction.

Rear sling swivel

Breech opening lever

MASSACHUSETTS ARMS COMPANY CARBINE

A breech-loading percussion .50 caliber carbine made by the Massachusetts Arms Company; this type of rifle, accurate up to 600 feet, was known as a Maynard Carbine because it used Maynard primer tape for igniting the powder. The carbine was popular with the military as well as sportsmen. It was patented in 1851 and later saw wide use in the Confederate Army during the American Civil War. However, this particular rifle, with its silver cartouche and the Napoleonic emblem, was actually owned by Napoleon III (1808–73; r. 1852–70), Napoleon Bonaparte's nephew.

Gold-plated lock plate

WINCHESTER M1866 MAXIMILIAN RIFLE

This Model 1866 rifle was created by the Winchester Arms Company as a gift to Spanish-appointed Mexican ruler Emperor Maximilian. Maximilian's weapon has a solid ivory stock, gold-plated lock mechanism, and is engraved with the Mexican eagle.

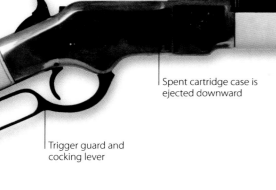

Spent cartridge case is ejected downward

Trigger guard and cocking lever

WINCHESTER 66

The Winchester Model 1866 was nicknamed "the Yellow Boy," because of the color of its receiver. A direct descendant of the Henry rifle, the gun fired the same .44 rimfire cartridge, but its tubular magazine more than doubled the Henry's capacity, from seven to fifteen rounds. This model (converted to centerfire) was owned by Czar Alexander II of Russia (1818–81) and is engraved with the czar's royal cipher and other symbols of the Russian monarchy.

Rear sight above forestock

Exposed hammer showing if rifle cocked

WINCHESTER 73

In 1873 Winchester produced an improved version of the Model 1866 chambered for a new, centerfire version of the .44 round. The "Winchester '73" became the most famous of the Winchester rifles and one of the most celebrated guns of the West, period. The gun shown here was owned by Albert Edward, Prince of Wales, later King Edward VII (1841–1910); the silver medallion inset into the stock is engraved with imperial symbols including the Star of India. The rifle received a special blued vision by the gunsmith James Kerr at the London Armoury Co.

THE AMERICAN WEST: RIFLES

ELIPHALET REMINGTON

Born in Connecticut in 1793, Eliphalet Remington moved—like many New Englanders of the time—to upstate New York, where he worked as a blacksmith alongside his father. In his early twenties, he decided that he could make a better gun than those available for commercial purchase. The resulting weapon impressed local users so much that he entered into gunmaking full-time, establishing what would become E. Remington & Sons (later the Remington Arms Co.) in Ilion, New York. By the time Remington died in 1861, the small firm was on its way to becoming one of the nation's leading gunmakers—a status that, like Winchester, it retains today. Although Remington diversified to produce products ranging from typewriters to bicycles, it's said that the Remington Arms Co. is the oldest American company still making its original product.

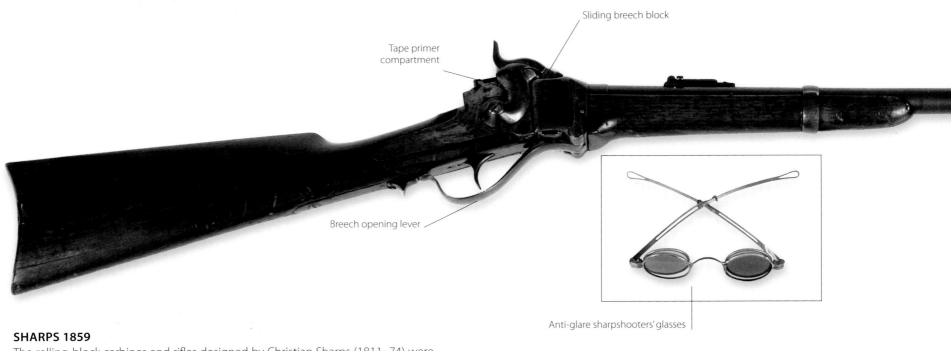

Tape primer compartment

Sliding breech block

Breech opening lever

Anti-glare sharpshooters' glasses

SHARPS 1859

The rolling-block carbines and rifles designed by Christian Sharps (1811–74) were popular with hunters, scouts, and other Western outdoorsmen. Shown here is the 1859 Sharps New Model carbine, with a pair of colored "sharpshooter's glasses" used to cut down on glare. Perhaps the most famous Sharps model was the .50 rifle—known as the "Big Fifty"—which was widely used by buffalo hunters. The weapon could reportedly drop a buffalo at 200 yards with a single shot.

Long, lightweight barrel
Graceful buttstock

KENTUCKY RIFLE

For more than 100 years, the Kentucky, or American long rifle, played a key role in the push West from the Eastern seaboard of the U.S. Initially developed by German gunsmiths in Pennsylvania, probably in the 1730, it continued to be upgraded until the mid-nineteenth century, when it fell from fashion. However, these rifles could be made by hand, making them popular among frontiersmen and they were still common in small rural communities well into the twentieth century.

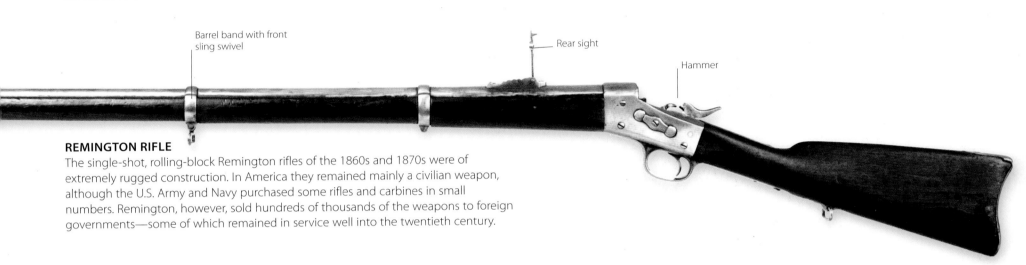

Barrel band with front
sling swivel

Rear sight

Hammer

REMINGTON RIFLE

The single-shot, rolling-block Remington rifles of the 1860s and 1870s were of extremely rugged construction. In America they remained mainly a civilian weapon, although the U.S. Army and Navy purchased some rifles and carbines in small numbers. Remington, however, sold hundreds of thousands of the weapons to foreign governments—some of which remained in service well into the twentieth century.

> "MAN GETS SHOT THAT'S GOT A GUN,
> THERE'S ROOM FOR REASONABLE DOUBT.
> MAN GETS SHOT THAT HASN'T GOT A
> GUN, WHAT WOULD YOU CALL IT?"
>
> Sherrif John T. Chance (John Wayne)—*Rio Bravo*, 1959

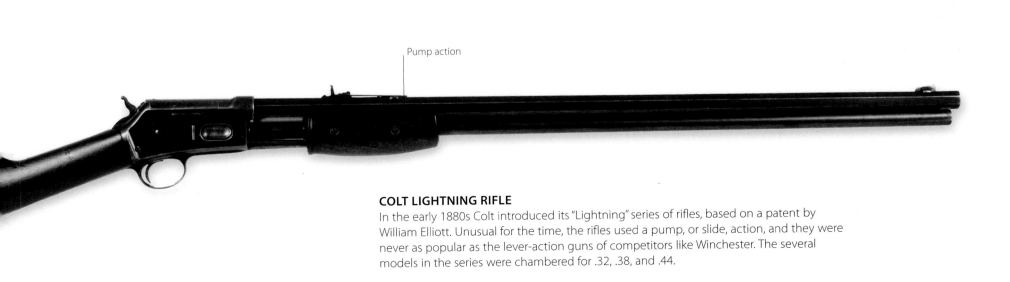

Pump action

COLT LIGHTNING RIFLE

In the early 1880s Colt introduced its "Lightning" series of rifles, based on a patent by William Elliott. Unusual for the time, the rifles used a pump, or slide, action, and they were never as popular as the lever-action guns of competitors like Winchester. The several models in the series were chambered for .32, .38, and .44.

MAUSERS

In the late nineteenth century and into the twentieth, the high quality of the German Mauser company's bolt-action rifles led to scores of nations adopting Mauser designs for their armed forces. According to company figures, some 100 million Mauser rifles were made in factories worldwide, from the single-shot M1871 through to the Karabiner 98k, which was still in production at the end of World War II. Many of the countries that ordered large quantities of rifles from the German company did so to their own specifications. Some required calibers to accommodate the ammunition they manufactured, others opted for specific magazines or ammunition-feed arrangements. Shown here are just a few of the many early Mauser variants.

CZECHOSLOVAKIAN VZ24 MAUSER
This high-quality Mauser was a version designed and made in Czechoslovakia soon after the end of World War I. When Germany occupied Czechoslovakia in World War II, its army adopted the Mauser, which was similar to the KAR 98K, already used by German forces and firing the same 7.92mm ammunition.

PERSIAN MAUSER
An 8mm Persian (later Iranian) Army Mauser with bayonet. Many of these were manufactured at the Brno Arms Works in Czechoslovakia.

ARGENTINE MAUSER
In 1891, Argentina's army replaced its antiquated .43 Remington rolling-block action rifle with the 7.55mm Mauser shown here, together with its bayonet and scabbard.

SWEDISH MAUSER
Sweden adopted the Mauser in 1893—although chambered for 6.65mm, a small round by the standards of military rifles of the era. The Swedes also insisted that while made in Germany, their Mausers be manufactured using Swedish steel.

Straight bolt pull

Receiver

Buttstock

Trigger guard

Magazine

THE MAUSERS

Wilhelm (1834–1882) and Paul Mauser (1838–1914) followed in their father's footsteps as gunsmiths at the royal armory in the German kingdom of Württemberg. When the government of the newly unified Germany sought an improved rifle in response to the performance of the French chassepot in the Franco-Prussian War, the brothers developed a single-shot bolt-action weapon, the Gewehr (rifle) Model 1871, which Germany adopted that same year. After Wilhelm's death, Paul came up with a new 7mm design based on the newly developed box magazine. In Models 1893, 1894, and 1895, the rifle proved hugely successful and orders poured in from around the world. While the Mauser's straight-pull bolt didn't allow for as rapid a rate of fire as, say, the British SMLE, it was strong, safe, and effective. In 1898 Mauser introduced the 7.92mm Gewehr 98—the finest bolt-action rifle ever made, in the opinion of many weapons historians. The G98 remained in service with the Germany Army until the mid-1930s, when it was replaced by a shorter version, the Karabiner (KAR) 98. The three principal Mauser factories were destroyed during World War II; today, the company—now owned by Rheinmetall—makes mostly hunting rifles. Several former Mauser engineers, however, were instrumental in founding Heckler & Koch, Germany's greatest weapons-maker of the post-World War II era.

AFRICAN STRUGGLES
Mausers played a part in the many bitter wars fought in South Africa in the late nineteenth century. Here Afrikaner Commandos are armed with Mausers and Martini-Henry rifles.

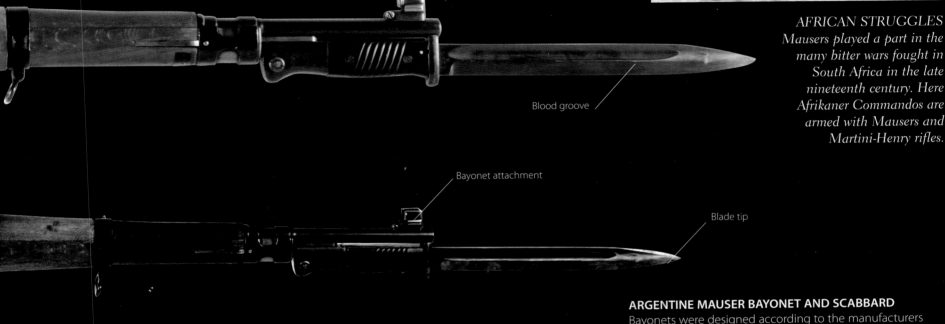

Blood groove

Bayonet attachment

Blade tip

ARGENTINE MAUSER BAYONET AND SCABBARD
Bayonets were designed according to the manufacturers wishes and varied from country to country.

Stocky medium-length blade

Tapering barrel

Clip to attach to leather sheath

Leather sling

Box magazine

BROOMHANDLE MAUSER
Mauser's first foray into automatic-pistol production came in 1896, with the introduction of a 7.63mm model which (along with its improved successor, the Model 1898) was popularly known as the "Broomhandle Mauser" from the distinctive design of its grip.

BOLT-ACTION MAGAZINE RIFLES

The bolt-action, magazine-fed rifle, firing a completely enclosed metallic cartridge of substantial caliber and firepower, was the principal infantry weapon of modern armies for about seventy-five years, from the 1860s until the era of the World War II, when it was largely replaced, first by self-loading rifles, and later by selective-fire assault rifles. However, it continues to have a strong following among civilians for hunting and target shooting, thanks in the main to its reliability and the robust simplicity of its straightforward mechanism.

Short, carbine-style barrel

BELGIAN CARBINE
Firing a .45 centerfire cartridge, this single-shot, breech-loading Belgian carbine is typical of the cavalry weapons developed in the 1860s and 1870s. Following the introduction of bolt-action magazine rifles, weapons designers sought to "split the difference" between carbines and infantry rifles with general purpose weapons like the British SMLE (Short Magazine Lee Enfield) and the U.S. Springfield Model 1903.

BRITISH MARTINI-HENRY RIFLE
This Mark II, model 1876 rifle is a single-shot, breech-loading, lever-action rifle. The lever-action mechanism was developed around the same time as the bolt-action, the intention of both being to produce a repeating shotgun. Lever-action rifles are still popular with sportshooters today, but were never as popular as the bolt-action with the military because they were difficult to shoot from a prone position.

NEEDLE-GUN

Although the gun battles of the American Civil War (1861–65) demonstrated the effectiveness of rapid-fire, breech-loading rifles and carbines, the powerful German state of Prussia had already adopted such a weapon for its army in 1848. Their version was the so-called "needle gun" developed by Nikolaus von Dreyse (1787–1867).

This 15.4mm gun got its name because it used a needlelike firing pin to explode a primer cap that was embedded in a paper cartridge which also comprised the main powder charge and bullet. The needle gun's great innovation, besides the incorporation of a self-contained cartridge, was the introduction of a bolt-handle firing mechanism. Together, these advances made it faster to load and fire than the muzzle-loading, percussion-cap muskets and rifles in use at the time. The weapon had two chief disadvantages: The explosion of the primer cap tended to weaken and eventually corrode the needle firing pin, and the design of the breech was poor and allowed much propellant gas to escape in firing.

The needle gun first saw action against revolutionary mobs in 1848–49 and then in Prussia's wars against Denmark (1864), Austria (1866), and France (1870–71).

CHASSEPOT

In the Franco-Prussian War, Prussian troops with needle guns faced French infantry armed with a similar weapon, the chassepot, named for its inventor, Antoine Chassepot (1833–1905), which the French army had adopted in 1866. The 11mm chassepot was technically superior to the needle gun in several respects and had a longer range, but Prussian superiority in artillery and tactics countered its advantages.

BEAUMONT "MOUSQUETON"
In the early 1870s, a Dutch engineer named Beaumont developed a turnbolt-action, single-shot rifle based on the French chassepot. The rifle was unusual in that its action used a V-spring placed inside a hollow, two-piece bolt handle, rather than the coil mainspring found in other bolt-action rifles. This particular model, an experimental carbine for use by artilleryman, was made at the French arsenal at St. Etienne in 1874.

BELGIAN POLICE CARBINE
This Belgian police carbine is a percussion-cap weapon manufactured in 1858.

BOLT-ACTION MAGAZINE RIFLES CONTINUED . . .

GEWEHR 1888
Afraid of falling behind the French in rifle development, the German army set up a commission in 1888 to spur innovation. One result was the Gewehr Model 1888, aka the 7.92mm "commission rifle," which incorporated elements from both Mauser and Austrian Mannlicher designs. One unusual feature was that a metal sleeve, rather than the usual wooden forestock, surrounded the barrel—it was thought that this would be a more effective means of keeping the barrel from overheating during rapid fire.

GERMAN ARMY RIFLE
This model 71/84 army rifle was developed by Mauser during World War I and manufactured at Spandau, Germany. It has an eight-round, tubular magazine.

ITALIAN MODEL 1871 VETTERLI
Made in Switzerland in the late nineteenth century, probably around 1880, this model 1871 Vetterli is a single-shot, bolt-action short artillery rifle, modified for the Italian army. The maker's mark is Giisenti Brescia.

TORINO RIFLE WITH BAYONET
This is a model 1871 Vetterli cavalry saddle gun carbine. It has the mark "Torino" and year 1882 on it. This indicates that it was made in the arms factory at Turin, presumably for the Italian army. The P.P. mark just behind the sight stands for "parti permutabili," and refers to the fact that the parts were all changeable.

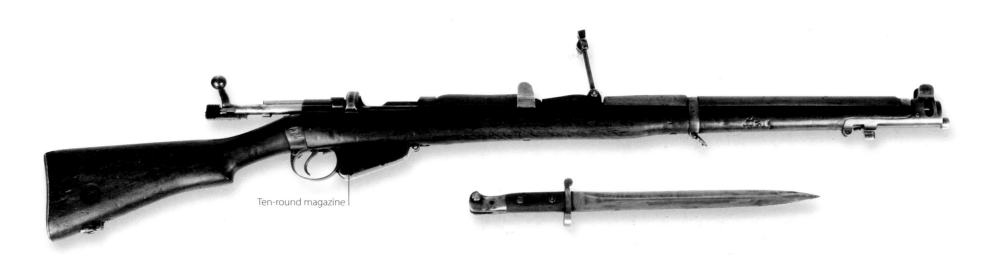

SMLE

During the Boer War (1899–1902) the British army decided that modern combat conditions demanded a shorter infantry rifle that could double as a carbine, greatly reducing the logistical hassles of

Ten-round magazine

supplying two types of parts and ammunition. The result, introduced in 1907, was the .303 SMLE (Short Magazine Lee Enfield), which would remain in service, in various models, for more almost a half-century. Shown here is the Mark III model, with its 18

ENTER THE MAGAZINE

The success of the needle gun and the chassepot led to the adoption of the bolt-action rifles by other Western armies. The needle gun and chassepot, however, were single-shot weapons; the next step forward was the development of multiple-shot magazine weapons utilizing the new firing system. In 1868, for example, the Swiss Army adopted a rifle developed by Freidrich Vetterli (1822–82), which was fed from a tubular magazine located under the barrel.

Most of this new generation of rifles, however, used a fixed or detachable box magazine holding five or more cartridges, charged either with individual rounds or by means of a stripper clip, which held several cartridges in a metal frame and which was inserted into the magazine from either the top or bottom.

The British army adopted its first magazine bolt-action rifle, the Lee-Metford, in 1877. In 1889, Denmark started to use the Krag-Jorgensen, which was later also taken on by Norway and the United States. The most successful of the new-style rifles, however, were the designs produced by the German brothers Wilhelm and Paul Mauser.

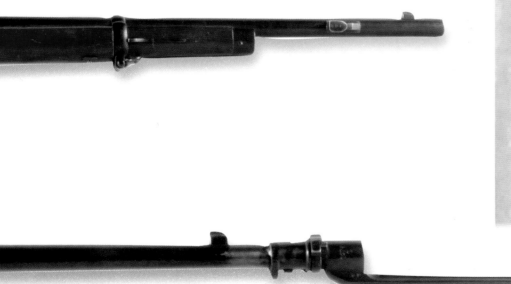

Magazine receiver

VETTERLI MODEL 1878

Preceding the more famous Mauser by several years, Switzerland's .41 Model 1869 Vetterli infantry rifle was the first multiple-shot, bolt-action rifle adopted by a major army—although it fed from a twelve-round tubular magazine, in a manner similar to the Winchester and Henry rifles, rather than from a box magazine. The model 1878 had a few minor improvements, but was basically the same rifle as the M1869.

BOLT-ACTION MAGAZINE RIFLES CONTINUED . . .

FRENCH VOLLEY GUN
Called a "Buffalo" mitraille (grapeshot), this is a bolt-action, .22 caliber rifle with three barrels that fire simultaneously. It is a sporting gun that was manufactured in France in the 1930s.

STEYR MANNLICHER M1895 RIFLE
This bolt-action rifle has a straight-pull bolt rather than the rotating bolt-handle of other rifles. This allowed for very rapid firing, but it had to be used with care, because this same feature was easy to damage. It had a 5-round en-bloc clip system with a fixed magazine and was made in Austria between 1895 and 1921.

Custom decoration

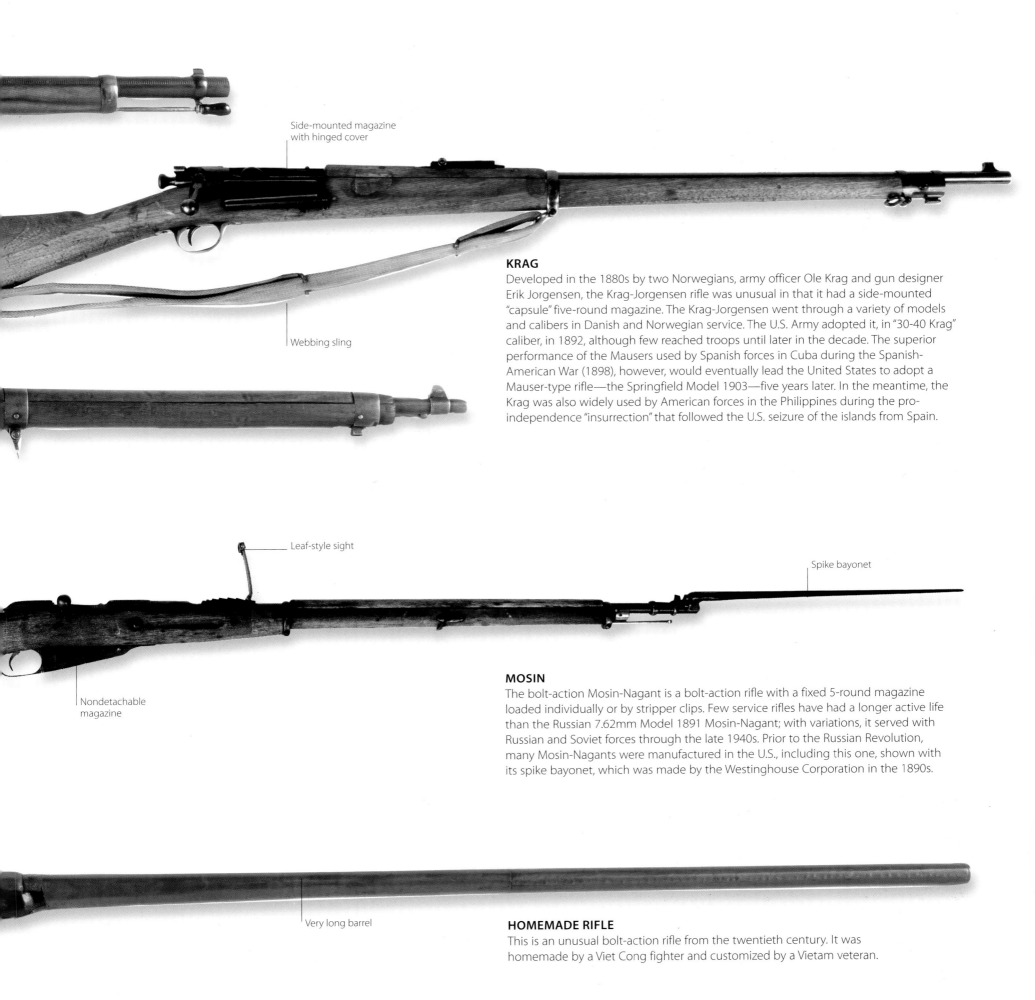

Side-mounted magazine
with hinged cover

Webbing sling

KRAG

Developed in the 1880s by two Norwegians, army officer Ole Krag and gun designer Erik Jorgensen, the Krag-Jorgensen rifle was unusual in that it had a side-mounted "capsule" five-round magazine. The Krag-Jorgensen went through a variety of models and calibers in Danish and Norwegian service. The U.S. Army adopted it, in "30-40 Krag" caliber, in 1892, although few reached troops until later in the decade. The superior performance of the Mausers used by Spanish forces in Cuba during the Spanish-American War (1898), however, would eventually lead the United States to adopt a Mauser-type rifle—the Springfield Model 1903—five years later. In the meantime, the Krag was also widely used by American forces in the Philippines during the pro-independence "insurrection" that followed the U.S. seizure of the islands from Spain.

Leaf-style sight

Spike bayonet

MOSIN

The bolt-action Mosin-Nagant is a bolt-action rifle with a fixed 5-round magazine loaded individually or by stripper clips. Few service rifles have had a longer active life than the Russian 7.62mm Model 1891 Mosin-Nagant; with variations, it served with Russian and Soviet forces through the late 1940s. Prior to the Russian Revolution, many Mosin-Nagants were manufactured in the U.S., including this one, shown with its spike bayonet, which was made by the Westinghouse Corporation in the 1890s.

Nondetachable
magazine

Very long barrel

HOMEMADE RIFLE

This is an unusual bolt-action rifle from the twentieth century. It was homemade by a Viet Cong fighter and customized by a Vietam veteran.

THE AUTOMATIC PISTOL

Automatic pistols are, strictly speaking, semiautomatic weapons because they fire once with every trigger pull, rather than continuously, like a machine gun (although fully automatic pistols have been developed). Nevertheless, automatic pistols are self-loading and are considered related to the machine gun. After Hiram Maxim figured out how to use a weapon's recoil to load, fire, eject, and reload a cartridge in the 1880s, weapons designers in several countries worked to scale down the system to the handgun level. Early automatics had technical problems such as with cartridge size, but designers like John Browning made the weapon viable.

BORCHARDT, BERGMANN, AND LUGER

The first successful automatic pistol was the brainchild of a German-born American inventor, Hugo Borchardt (1844–1924), who worked for several U.S. arms manufacturers, including Colt and Winchester. In 1893 Borchardt designed a pistol that used the Maxim recoil principle to send a toggle backward and upward to eject the spent cartridge and chamber a new one, fed from a magazine in the grip. (Reportedly, Borchardt's design was inspired by the movement of the human knee.)

Borchardt found no takers for his pistol in America, so he moved to Germany, where the firm of Ludwig Loewe & Company brought the pioneering pistol to the market.

Also in Germany, Austrian-born entrepreneur Theodor Bergmann (1850–1931) and German weapons designer Louis Schmeisser (1848–1917) began developing a series of blowback-operated automatics, although these fed from a magazine in front of a trigger guard instead of from the grip—as did the "Broomhandle" Mauser developed around the same time.

Deutsch Waffen & Munitions Fabriken (DWM), the successor to Ludwig Loewe & Co., failed to sell the Borchardt pistol to the U.S. Army in the 1890s, but one of its employees, Georg Luger, improved on its design and eventually developed the first version of the famous pistol that would bear his name.

The Swiss Army's adoption of the Luger in 1900 marked a major step forward in military acceptance of the automatic pistol. The German Army, however, still considered the original Luger's 7.65mm round too weak. Luger then developed a new 9mm round (the parabellum, from the Latin "for war"). Germany adopted the 9mm version in 1908.

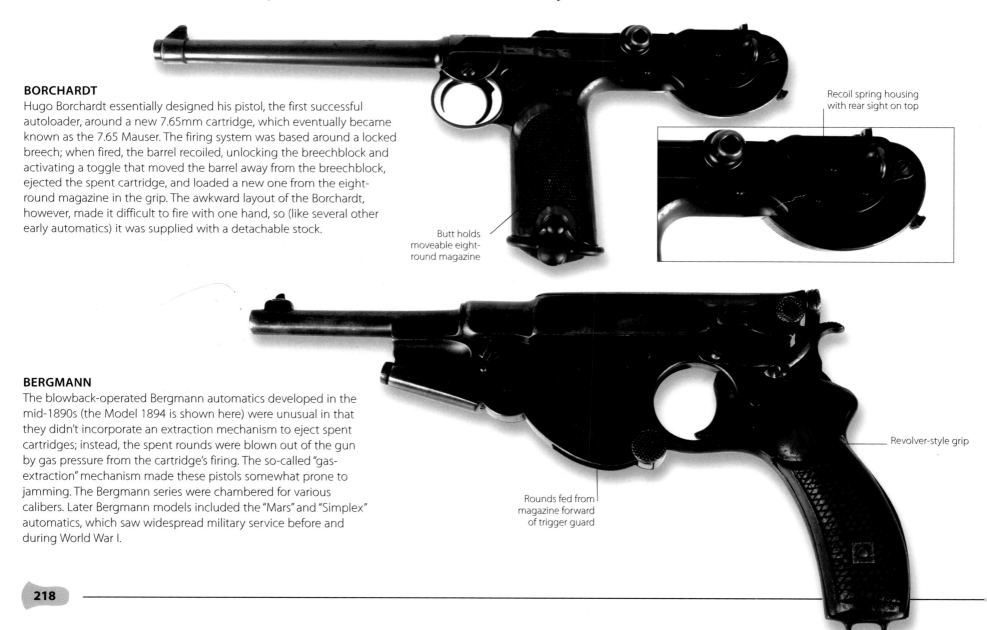

BORCHARDT
Hugo Borchardt essentially designed his pistol, the first successful autoloader, around a new 7.65mm cartridge, which eventually became known as the 7.65 Mauser. The firing system was based around a locked breech; when fired, the barrel recoiled, unlocking the breechblock and activating a toggle that moved the barrel away from the breechblock, ejected the spent cartridge, and loaded a new one from the eight-round magazine in the grip. The awkward layout of the Borchardt, however, made it difficult to fire with one hand, so (like several other early automatics) it was supplied with a detachable stock.

Recoil spring housing with rear sight on top

Butt holds moveable eight-round magazine

BERGMANN
The blowback-operated Bergmann automatics developed in the mid-1890s (the Model 1894 is shown here) were unusual in that they didn't incorporate an extraction mechanism to eject spent cartridges; instead, the spent rounds were blown out of the gun by gas pressure from the cartridge's firing. The so-called "gas-extraction" mechanism made these pistols somewhat prone to jamming. The Bergmann series were chambered for various calibers. Later Bergmann models included the "Mars" and "Simplex" automatics, which saw widespread military service before and during World War I.

Rounds fed from magazine forward of trigger guard

Revolver-style grip

Eight-inch barrel

ARTILLERY LUGER

Toward the end of World War I, the German Army introduced an interesting Luger variant—the so-called Artillery Model. The Artillery Luger had an eight-inch barrel instead of the standard model's four-inch barrel, and was intended for use as a carbine with a wooden shoulder stock and a 32-round drum magazine. As the name implies, it was originally issued to gun crews as a defensive weapon, but it proved useful in the hands of trench-raiding infantry units.

4inch barrel

Toggle doubles as cocking grip

Safety catch

Magazine catch

Ten-round removable magazine

LUGER

The Luger model adopted by the Swiss Army (like the one shown here) fired 7.65mm ammunition; the German P08 model, adopted in 1908, fired the 9mm parabellum round, which remains, almost a century later, the most popular caliber for automatic pistols and submachine guns. Designer Georg Luger adopted several features of Borchardt's gun but placed a leaf recoil spring inside the butt. While the Luger was undoubtedly an excellent weapon, its legendary status—it was a coveted souvenir among Allied troops in both world wars—exaggerates its overall performance.

Tangent (sliding) rear sight

Hammer

Blade fore sight

Ten rounds held in box magazine

Distinctive "broomhandle" design of grip

BROOMHANDLE MAUSER

Mauser's first foray into automatic-pistol production came in 1896, with the introduction of a 7.63mm model that (along with its improved successor, the Model 1898), was known as the "Broomhandle Mauser" from the distinctive design of its grip. Like the Borchardt and the Artillery Luger, the Broomhandle doubled as a carbine and came with a wooden stock that also served as a holster. One of the weapon's innovations was that the bolt remained open after the last of the ten rounds held in the box magazine was fired, facilitating reloading from a stripper clip. Broomhandles were a popular choice for private purchase by officers in several armies—among them a young British Army cavalryman named Winston Churchill, who used one in action at the Battle of Omdurman in the Sudan in 1898.

THE AUTOMATIC PISTOL CONTINUED . . .

ENTER JOHN BROWNING

The main objection military customers had to the early automatics was the perceived lack of "stopping power" of their cartridges. (Automatic mechanisms couldn't function using the heavy revolver cartridges of the era.)

In the early 1900s, the U.S. Army, however, found that even its .38 revolver was insufficient when used against determined Muslim insurgents in the Philippines (then an American colony). John Browning met the challenge with a pistol that, while automatic,

fired an extremely powerful .45 round; the cartridge was called .45 ACP (Automatic Colt Pistol). Officially adopted by the U.S. Army in 1911, the Colt M1911 automatic went on to become one of the world's most successful and long-serving handguns.

JOHN M. BROWNING

Browning was certainly the most influential and versatile gunmaker of all time. His work encompassed both civilian and military weapons and included shotguns, machine guns, automatic rifles, and automatic pistols. Indeed, many of his designs are still in production today. John Moses Browning was born in Ogden, Utah, in 1855. Browning's father, a gunsmith, was among the Mormon pioneers who had trekked westward to Utah, and it was in his father's shop that he built his first gun at the age of thirteen. In 1883 Browning went to work for Winchester, where he designed several legendary shotguns and rifles in the 1890s and early 1900s. His interest in automatic weapons led to the development of a machine gun in 1895 and several automatic pistols, which ultimately included the .45 M1911A1 Colt. His .30 and .50 machine guns became standard throughout the U.S. military, as did the Browning Automatic Rifle (BAR). He died in Belgium in 1926 while working on the handgun that would eventually be produced as the Browning Hi-Power (see below) and would be used by the armed services of 50 countries.

BROWNING PATENT PISTOL

Browning left Winchester gun-makers, where he had produced the first pump-and self-loading shotguns, to begin an alliance in 1895 with Fabrique Nationale d'Armes de Guerre, (FN) Herstal (near Liège in Belgium). Here he produced designs for self-loading pistols, including the model shown here, which were to develop into the world-class Colts.

BROWNING HI-POWER

This is another handgun Browning started designing in 1914 while working with Fabrique Nationale d'Armes de Guerre (although Browning died in 1926, several years before the design was finalized). It is a single-action 9mm semiautomatic and one of the most widely-used military pistols of all time. The Hi-Power comes from the 13-round magazine which at the time was nearly double that of competitors like the Luger or Mauser.

"TOUGH, RELIABLE, AND PACKING A PUNCH, [COLT .45'S] HAVE ENDEARED THEMSELVES TO SOLDIERS OF ALL NATIONS."

Firearms historian Craig Philip

COLT .45

At least 3 million of these pistols have been produced in the United States, and an unknown number made under license (or simply copied) worldwide since its introduction in 1911. The original "government" model was slightly modified, based on combat experience in World War I, to become the M1911A1, which remained in U.S. military service until the mid-1980s. The weapon's main drawbacks were its heavy weight (2½ pounds) and that, as a double-action weapon, it had to be carried with the slide pulled back to be ready to fire the first round quickly—something that could lead to accidental discharge in the hands of an inexperienced user.

GLISENTI

First produced in 1910, the 9mm Glisenti (so-called by its manufacturer, Real Fabbrica d'Armi Glisenti) was the standard sidearm of the Italian Army in World War I. An overly complex firing system, combined with an unusual trigger mechanism, undercut its effectiveness.

SCHWARZLOSE

Named for its designer, German Andreas Schwarzlose, the 9mm Schwarzlose Model 1908 automatic is virtually unique in that it uses a blow-forward operating system, with the slide moving forward rather than backward to load and eject each round. It was an effective system, but the novel experience of a pistol that recoiled away from, and not toward the firer surely took some getting used to. Schwarzlose also designed a well-regarded water-cooled machine gun, which was used by the Austro-Hungarian Army in World War II.

PERSONAL DEFENSE WEAPONS

Despite advances in public safety, including the introduction of organized police forces, crime remained a major problem in Europe and the Americas in the nineteenth century. As a result, wealthy people armed themselves with small, easily concealable firearms for defense against robbers and villains—although the same types of weapons were frequently used by criminals themselves. Short-barreled pistols became the gentlemen's preferred weapon of self-defense, replacing the sword, while the use of dueling pistols was well established to settle affairs of honor. Women also used small pistols for defense. Dueling, pocket, and blunderbuss pistols were readily available to anyone—on either side of the law—who could afford them.

THE PERSONAL PISTOL

The most famous were the derringers (named after their inventor Henry Deringer—where the extra 'r' came from, nobody is sure), which were "pocket pistols." As that name implies, they were meant to be carried clandestinely on the owner's person. Typically, these were short-barreled revolvers firing very small caliber rounds, often specially manufactured for a particular model of pistol. In order to be as compact as possible, many of these pistols had folding triggers and/or a completely enclosed hammer to reduce the danger of accidental discharge. The pocket-pistol concept continued into the twentieth century with the introduction of compact small-caliber automatics.

A subset of these weapons were "lady's pistols" or "muff pistols." These were extremely small guns intended for use by women, which could be concealed in a handbag or in the thick fur muffs many women of the era wore as hand-warmers.

An unusual weapon was the "palm" or "squeezer" pistol, introduced in the late nineteenth century. They were horizontally oriented and could be concealed in the user's palm, with a "squeeze" firing mechanism replacing the standard trigger. The best-known models were the Belgian/French Le Merveilleux and Gauloise series and the American "Chicago Protector."

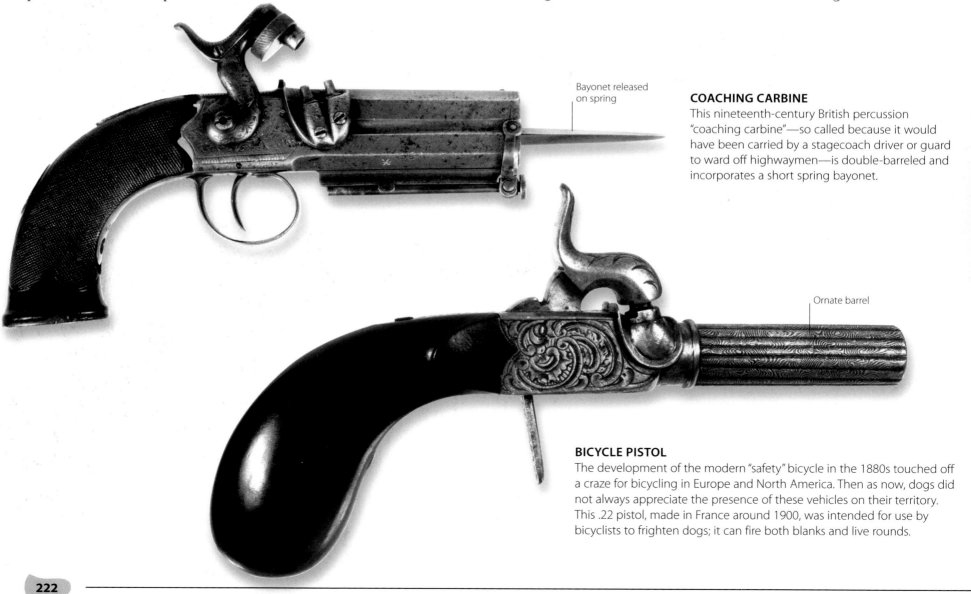

Bayonet released on spring

COACHING CARBINE
This nineteenth-century British percussion "coaching carbine"—so called because it would have been carried by a stagecoach driver or guard to ward off highwaymen—is double-barreled and incorporates a short spring bayonet.

Ornate barrel

BICYCLE PISTOL
The development of the modern "safety" bicycle in the 1880s touched off a craze for bicycling in Europe and North America. Then as now, dogs did not always appreciate the presence of these vehicles on their territory. This .22 pistol, made in France around 1900, was intended for use by bicyclists to frighten dogs; it can fire both blanks and live rounds.

PAIR OF MUFF PISTOLS

These Belgian-made, ivory-handled .36 single-shot percussion "muff pistols" were designed to be carried in a woman's hand muff, so were often also called muff pistols. They have concealed triggers and were made in the nineteenth century.

Ivory handle

Trigger extended

Trigger folded away

MUFF GUN

This small weapon was made in France in the nineteenth century. It is a simply designed percussion cap pistol (see inset) with a decorative ivory grip.

POCKET PISTOL

This small-bore pocket pistol was made in France in the nineteenth century. It has some interesting engraving on the frame and is notable for the lack of trigger guard.

Stud trigger

PERSONAL DEFENSE WEAPONS CONTINUED . . .

POCKET PISTOL
This .22-caliber pocket-sized pistol was made in Europe in the nineteenth century. The trigger is a crude stud-style design without trigger guard.

Round steel barrel

PATTI PINFIRE REVOLVER
This single-shot, .30 pin-fire pistol with a folding trigger was owned by Adelina Patti (1843–1919). Born in Spain to Italian parents, Patti was one of the great operatic sopranos of her era.

Compartments for ammunition

Hammer

SINGLE SHOT POCKET PISTOL
This tiny percussion cap pistol was designed for easy concealment. It was made in the late nineteenth century in France.

Trigger

Rotatable double barrel

DOUBLE-BARREL POCKET PISTOL
Probably American and dating from the late nineteenth
century, this small percussion pistol works by twisting
the barrel through 180 degrees after firing the first shot.

Hammer

LADY'S PISTOL
Another example of the so-called "lady's pistol," this .22
revolver has a folding trigger and pearl grips. Such compact
pistols were usually no more than four to five inches in
length, fitting snugly inside a hand for concealment.

Folding trigger

Pearl grips

BABY REVOLVER
Starting in the late 1800s, Philadelphia gunmaker
Henry Kolb produced a series of ultra-compact,
hammerless "Baby" revolvers. This .22 folding-
trigger model is nickel-plated with pearl grips.

PERSONAL DEFENSE WEAPONS CONTINUED . . .

"Harmonica"-style barrels

Safety catch

FOUR-BARREL POCKET PISTOL
This nineteenth-century French repeating pocket pistol is sometimes called a harmonica pistol after the arrangement of the barrels. The barrel rises into firing position after each shot until all four barrels are empty.

Short 1¼-inch barrels

BREVETE REFORM PISTOLE
Consisting of four stacked barrels, this tiny .25 caliber repeater pistol was made in France in the nineteenth century.

COLT POCKET PISTOL
This neat little automatic pistol is known as the Vest Pocket Hammerless. It takes .25 caliber ammunition and was made in the United States in 1908–48.

BELGIAN PALM PISTOL
This rare Belgian five-shot revolver has a grip designed to fit between the thumb and index finger like a wedge. In addition to the eccentric design, the pistol's folding trigger and double-action hammer are made of gold.

GAULOIS GUN
Manufactured in 1894–1912, this French pistol was made to fit into the palm of the hand. Squeezing the sliding handle moves a cartridge from the magazine in the handle into the barrel and fires it.

FRENCH PALM PISTOL
In the mid-1880s French gunmaker Jacques Rouchouse developed a palm pistol called Le Merveilleux. The design was triggerless; to fire, the user squeezed the frame, which activated the side-mounted hammer and discharged a specially made 6mm round. The same system was later used in pistols such as the Gaulois guns.

PROTECTOR PALM PISTOL
In 1882, French gunsmith Jacques Turbiaux patented a pistol designed to fit snugly in the palm; the cartridges (either ten 6mm rounds or seven 8mm) were contained in a horizontal radial cylinder. The design was licensed in the U.S. (firing a special short .32 round) by the Minneapolis Arms Company, and, later, by the Chicago Firearms Company, which marketed it as the "Chicago Protector."

TRIBUZIO PISTOL
Invented in 1890 by Catello Tribuzio of Turin, Italy, this is a highly collectable squeeze pistol. Cartridges are loaded through the top of the gun into a vertical magazine. It has a ring trigger and is as flat as a notebook.

1¾-inch half octagonal barrel

WEAPONS OF DECEPTION

While canes and walking sticks concealing daggers or sword blades were commonplace by the nineteenth century, the introduction of the percussion-cap firing system in the 1810s and 1820s made the idea of a "cane gun" a practical proposition. In 1823, British gunsmith John Day patented a mechanism in which a downward pull on a hammer, concealed in the cane, dropped a trigger; thereafter, "Day's Patent" cane guns

SWAGGER-STICK GUN
A .22 wood-covered swagger-stick gun.

HIKING-STICK GUN
This British gentleman's nineteenth-century hiking stick does double duty with its detachable percussion-cap single shot.

Gun muzzle

AMERICAN MACHINE GUN SHELL
Carefully hidden inside this .50-caliber machine gun shell is a minute, spring-loaded .22-caliber gun dating from the mid-twentieth century.

WALKING-STICK GUN
A nineteenth-century English walking-stick that contains a single-shot percussion-cap gun—the system devised by British gunsmith John Day.

Hammer

UMBRELLA GUN
A nineteenth-century percussion-cap gun disguised as an umbrella. A modern version of the umbrella gun—in this case, firing a projectile coated with Ricin—was used to assassinate a Bulgarian dissident in London in 1978.

Percussion cap mechanism

became the industry standard. According to firearms historian Charles Edward Chapel, nineteenth-century cane guns were "made in large quantities for naturalists, gamekeepers, and poachers." Later in the century, cane guns firing the new fully enclosed metallic cartridge came into use. Most cane guns were single-shot no matter which firing system they used, but apparently some cane revolvers were manufactured.

Trigger

LANE CANE GUN

One of the rarest examples of this type of weapon is the nineteeth-century percussion-cap British Lane Cane Gun. The upper part of the cane, which contained the gun, was detached from the lower part and could be fired from the shoulder.

Muzzle

WEAPONS OF DECEPTION CONTINUED . . .

INDIAN WALKING STICK GUN
This fine walking stick gun has a ferrule that is unscrewed to reveal a 2-inch lance blade, which in turn unscrews to expose the gun muzzle. The jointed ramrod hides another blade. Signed "Molabuks," it dates from the nineteeth-century.

INDIAN WALKING STICK GUN
Made of steel with a gold koftgari monster's head on the top, this nineteenth-century three-piece walking stick conceals a gun. It has a screw-in ramrod that loads to a central internal nipple operated by a spring plunger.

SHOTGUN CANE
This European-style cane contains a centerfire shotgun, triggered by a tiny knot in the handle. It dates from the nineteenth century.

Mechanism hidden in handle

DAY'S CANE GUN
Patented by John Day in 1823, this is an underhammer percussion cap gun. A British poacher's rifle, it comes apart quickly and easily and the stock can be concealed, while the barrel is carried openly as a walking stick.

WALKING STICK BLOWPIPE
Despite its neat brass top and wooden cane, this walking stick is a well-disguised and very rare, twentieth-century blowpipe from southeast Asia.

Trigger and firing mechanism

ZIP GUNS

These zip guns are improvized weapons made with a piece of steel tubing and a small spring to propel the hammer against the firing pin. They date from the Cold War era just after World War II.

Dragon's head hand grip

Ferule is removed to fire gun

Brass top converts to a blowpipe

KEY PISTOL

Shaped like a key, this is an early nineteenth-century, 29-bore pistol with a boxlock percussion mechanism. It was made in Europe.

WEAPONS OF DECEPTION CONTINUED . . .

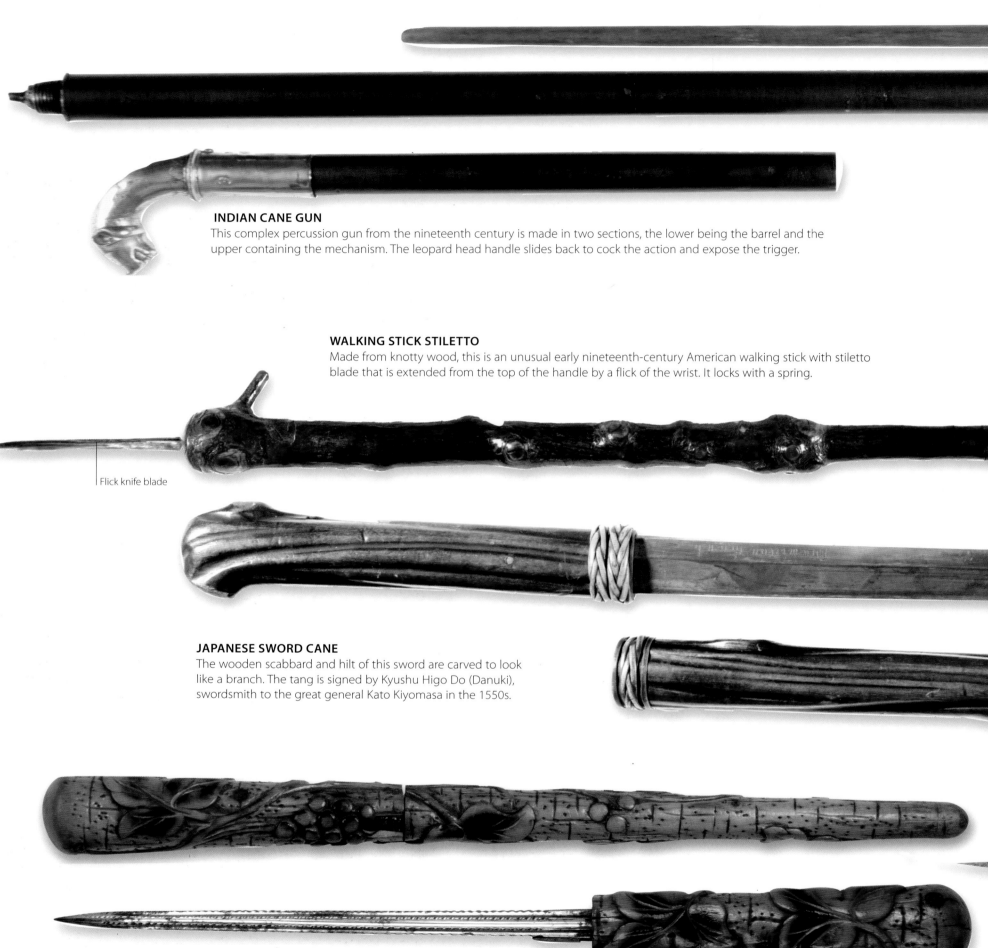

INDIAN CANE GUN
This complex percussion gun from the nineteenth century is made in two sections, the lower being the barrel and the upper containing the mechanism. The leopard head handle slides back to cock the action and expose the trigger.

WALKING STICK STILETTO
Made from knotty wood, this is an unusual early nineteenth-century American walking stick with stiletto blade that is extended from the top of the handle by a flick of the wrist. It locks with a spring.

Flick knife blade

JAPANESE SWORD CANE
The wooden scabbard and hilt of this sword are carved to look like a branch. The tang is signed by Kyushu Higo Do (Danuki), swordsmith to the great general Kato Kiyomasa in the 1550s.

DAGGER IN WOODEN SHEATH
An intricately carved wooden baton contains a narrow blade. Thought to be from the western Pacific and made in the twentieth century, this weapon is reputed to have been used by a priest to free a wrongly convicted man.

Tiny revolver

Wallet and coin storage

POCKET BOOK REVOLVER

This petite revolver is concealed in a case intended to look like a pocket book. Made in France, it was used by women for self-defense and dates from the mid-nineteenth century.

TOURIST DAGGER

This twentieth-century flick knife is cased in an innocuous-looking piece of wood to allow for easier concealment.

Bark-covered branch

ALARM AND TRAP WEAPONS

Not all guns are made to kill. From the introduction of gunpowder, various firearms have been used for purposes like signaling, timekeeping, and sounding alarms. The number of these special-purpose guns grew after the introduction of the percussion cap in the first half of the nineteenth century. These pages present some interesting examples from the era.

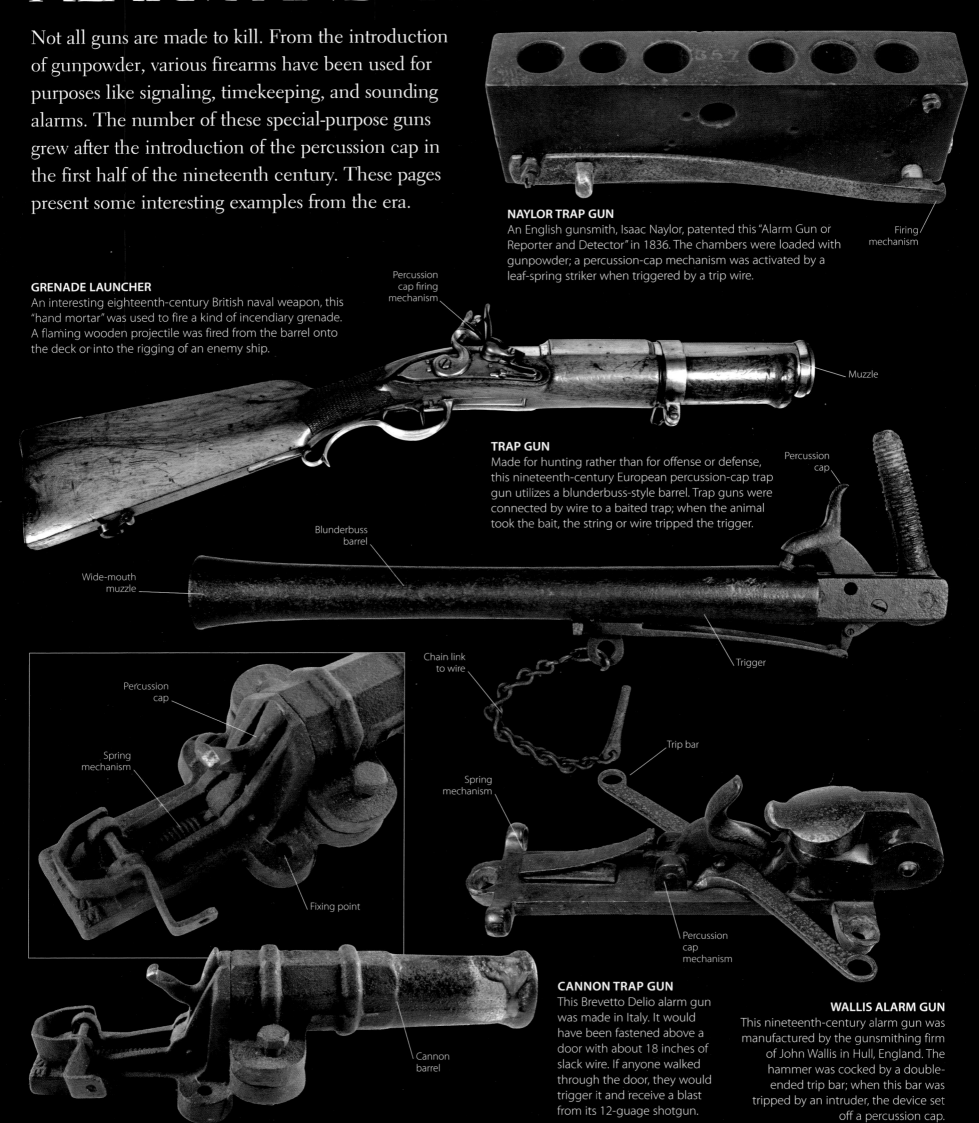

NAYLOR TRAP GUN
An English gunsmith, Isaac Naylor, patented this "Alarm Gun or Reporter and Detector" in 1836. The chambers were loaded with gunpowder; a percussion-cap mechanism was activated by a leaf-spring striker when triggered by a trip wire.

Firing mechanism

GRENADE LAUNCHER
An interesting eighteenth-century British naval weapon, this "hand mortar" was used to fire a kind of incendiary grenade. A flaming wooden projectile was fired from the barrel onto the deck or into the rigging of an enemy ship.

Percussion cap firing mechanism

Muzzle

TRAP GUN
Made for hunting rather than for offense or defense, this nineteenth-century European percussion-cap trap gun utilizes a blunderbuss-style barrel. Trap guns were connected by wire to a baited trap; when the animal took the bait, the string or wire tripped the trigger.

Percussion cap

Blunderbuss barrel

Wide-mouth muzzle

Trigger

Chain link to wire

Percussion cap

Spring mechanism

Fixing point

Trip bar

Spring mechanism

Percussion cap mechanism

Cannon barrel

CANNON TRAP GUN
This Brevetto Delio alarm gun was made in Italy. It would have been fastened above a door with about 18 inches of slack wire. If anyone walked through the door, they would trigger it and receive a blast from its 12-guage shotgun.

WALLIS ALARM GUN
This nineteenth-century alarm gun was manufactured by the gunsmithing firm of John Wallis in Hull, England. The hammer was cocked by a double-ended trip bar; when this bar was tripped by an intruder, the device set off a percussion cap.

ALARM AND TRAP GUNS

The alarm gun developed to give homeowners a means of warding off burglars. Usually they were attached to windows or doors. If someone tried to open these, a trip wire would activate a percussion cap and fire a powder charge, alerting the homeowner and, presumably, sending the intruder fleeing. Later versions fired a blank cartridge. Another variation consisted of a small-caliber, blank-firing pistol attached via a screw to a door or window frame, which would discharge when the door or window was opened.

Trap guns—also known as spring guns—were most commonly deployed in rural areas against poachers. Like many alarm guns, they were activated by trip wires, but unlike alarm guns, some of them were intended to fire bullets or shot instead of powder charges or blanks.

LINE-THROWING AND SIGNAL GUNS

At sea it was often necessary for one ship to get a line onto the deck of another, whether to take a damaged vessel in tow or to send across messages or supplies. This led to the development of line-throwing guns, like the pistol version shown below. Coast Guards and lifeboatmen also used line-throwing cannon—like the famous U.S. Lyle Gun, used from the late nineteenth century until the 1950s—to fire lines onto wrecked ships in order to be able to bring passengers and crew safely ashore.

Before the introduction of radio, it was customary for both merchant vessels and warships to announce their arrival in port by firing a signal gun, and it was also often necessary for ships to signal to one another with guns when fog and other weather conditions made visual signaling with flags impossible. Because firing a ship's "big guns" for such purposes was impractical, many ships carried small signal cannons to be used instead.

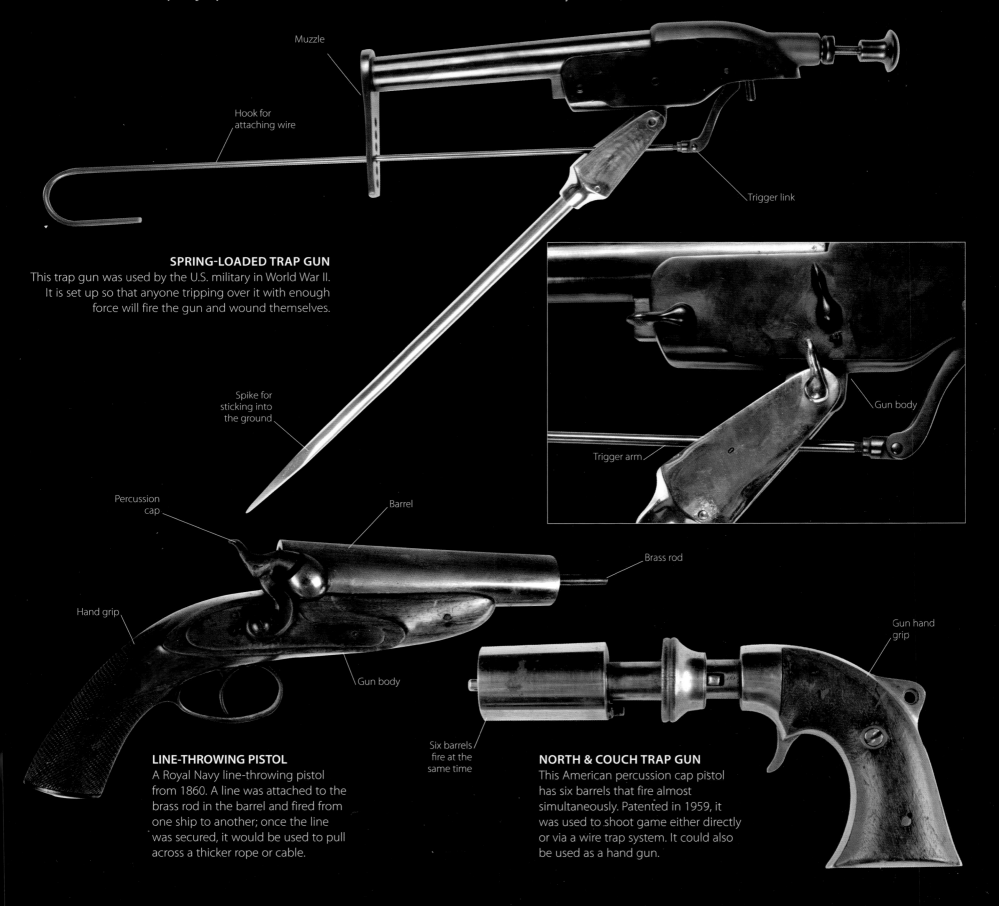

Muzzle

Hook for attaching wire

Trigger link

SPRING-LOADED TRAP GUN
This trap gun was used by the U.S. military in World War II. It is set up so that anyone tripping over it with enough force will fire the gun and wound themselves.

Gun body

Trigger arm

Spike for sticking into the ground

Percussion cap

Barrel

Brass rod

Hand grip

Gun body

Gun hand grip

Six barrels fire at the same time

LINE-THROWING PISTOL
A Royal Navy line-throwing pistol from 1860. A line was attached to the brass rod in the barrel and fired from one ship to another; once the line was secured, it would be used to pull across a thicker rope or cable.

NORTH & COUCH TRAP GUN
This American percussion cap pistol has six barrels that fire almost simultaneously. Patented in 1959, it was used to shoot game either directly or via a wire trap system. It could also be used as a hand gun.

COMBINATION WEAPONS

Weapons that combine a firearm with a blade or a club—or all three—have a pedigree that goes back to the sixteenth century. Until the advent of practical repeating firearms toward the middle of the nineteenth century, guns (unless they were multiple-barreled) could only fire one shot before reloading. As a result, weapons makers were concerned with giving the user an additional means of dispatching an opponent (or defending himself against said opponent). The introduction of repeating arms didn't completely end this trend; in the late nineteenth century, there was a vogue for revolver/dagger or knife combinations, and the famous (or infamous) French "Apache" managed to combine a revolver with a knife blade, in addition to a set of brass knuckles, in a single weapon. More recent combination weapons include "drillings" (a double-barreled shotgun with a rifle barrel—usually of European manufacture); combination guns (one shotgun barrel, one rifle barrel), and the survival guns (incorporating a small-caliber rifle and a shotgun) developed by the air forces of several nations as hunting weapons for downed aircrew stranded in remote areas awaiting rescue.

TURKISH GUN-SHIELD
Engraved across its entire surface and partly inlayed with gold and silver, this shield, which is 16 inches in diameter, incorporates a percussion-cap gun in a wooden mount on the reverse side, with a 5-inch protruding barrel. Pulling a string discharged the gun.

One of four muzzles

Gun Barrel

ETHIOPIAN SHIELD
Some Persian shields have spikes in their center to use in combat. The one barrel protruding from the middle of this shield looks like a spike at a distance. Only at close (shooting) range is it recognizable as a gun barrel.

INDIAN SHIELD WITH PISTOLS
The innocuous-looking "aged" shield hides four barrels behind its bosses, which swivel away to shoot a deadly deluge of bullets. It dates from the nineteenth century and is composed of hand-hammered steel.

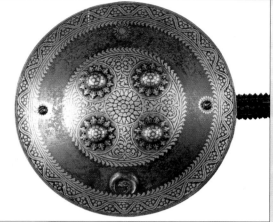

Koftgari decorated
hammer

INDIAN COMBO

Talk about multitasking: this nineteenth-century weapon—custom-made for an Indian prince—incorporates a sword; a shield; a single-shot, percussion-cap pistol; and a 12-inch needle dagger. It is made of steel with gold inlay and brass embellishments.

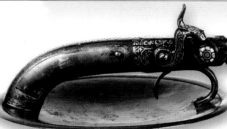

Blade folds against
sword sheath

Phoenix-head club

NINETEENTH-CENTURY COMBO

Another unusual nineteenth-century multiuse weapon—this one of European origin—includes a knife blade, a single-shot pistol, and a shaft reinforced with metal for use as a club.

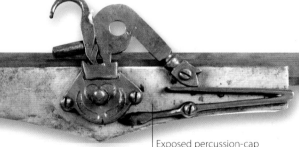

INDIAN MACE/PISTOL

In the nineteenth century, an Indian gunsmith fitted this mace—which may have been made more than two centuries earlier—with a percussion-cap gun.

Exposed percussion-cap
mechanism

TRUNCHEON GUN

This nineteenth-century British weapon combines a truncheon (club) with a decorated head with a percussion-cap pistol. It uses the firing system devised by British gunsmith John Day for his celebrated cane guns.

Trigger with trigger
guard

COMBINATION WEAPONS CONTINUED . . .

ROYAL NAVY BOARDING AX
Dating from the late eighteenth century, this British weapon combines an ax and a percussion pistol. The handle contains the gun mechanism and the bullet is fired through the top of the ax head.

BATON-DAGGER
This lethal weapon is just less than 19 inches long and combines a baton with a concealed spikelike dagger. It was made in China in the nineteenth century.

FLICK-DAGGER LIFE-PRESERVER
This combination weapon has a malacca cane shaft, with weighted ends decorated with a decorative cord binding. The dagger is retained by a spring catch and released with a flick of the wrist. It was made in Britain around 1850.

INDIAN MAHOUT CORNAC GUN
This rare matchlock Cornac gun dates from around 1800 and was used in elephant warfare. The short barrel and butt design allowed the mahout to continue to direct the elephant while firing.

Curved bayonetlike spike

ARAB SLAVE WHIP
This nineteenth-century slave whip has a shaft inlaid with mother-of-pearl, which contains a screw-in spike dagger.

Neat, spike-bladed dagger

FLINTLOCK PISTOL AX
Probably made in France in the late eighteenth century, this navy pistol has a small ax head on the end of the barrel, which would have been used for boarding enemy ships. It is often called a "rat-tail."

COMBINATION WEAPONS CONTINUED . . .

PERSIAN PISTOL DAGGER

This Persian pistol doubles up as a dagger—the blade is hidden in the grip. Its gently angled shape would have made it difficult to aim accurately, but also easy to conceal. It has a percussion-cap mechanism and some brass decoration

Dagger hidden in the grip

Slit tor crossbow band

CROSSBOW AND RIFLE COMBINATION

This is a Hodges catapult gun, made in England in the mid-ninteenth century. The weapon worked both as a rifle and a catapult. The two brass projections on the muzzle allow for attachment of the elastic band to fire the crossbow. It was intended to be used for hunting.

Trigger

POCKET-KNIFE PERCUSSION PISTOLS

Examples of an American pocket-knife pistol (above) and one made by the London firm of Unwin & Rodgers (at right). Pocket-knife pistols were popular in the late nineteenth century.

Folding blades

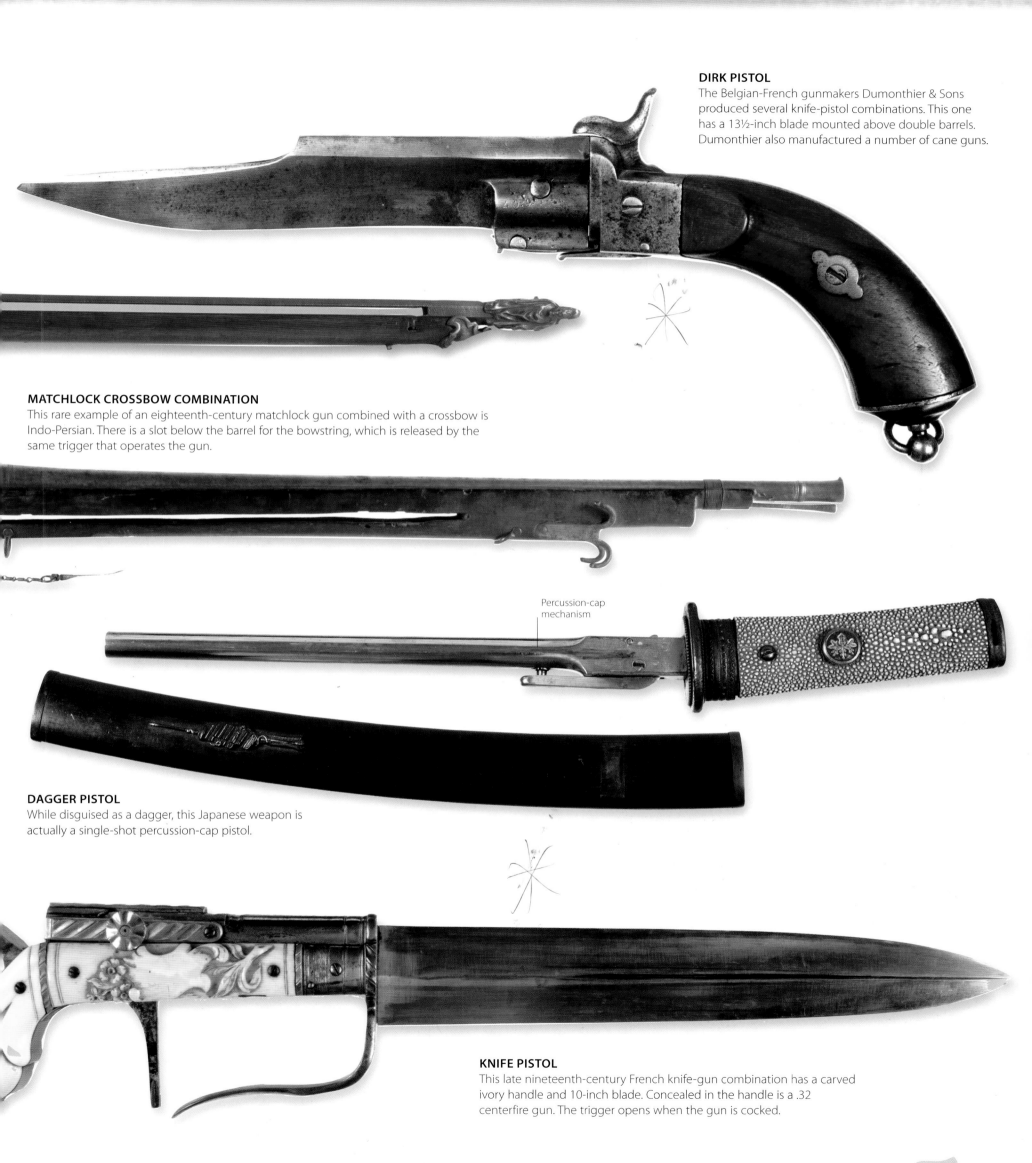

DIRK PISTOL

The Belgian-French gunmakers Dumonthier & Sons produced several knife-pistol combinations. This one has a 13½-inch blade mounted above double barrels. Dumonthier also manufactured a number of cane guns.

MATCHLOCK CROSSBOW COMBINATION

This rare example of an eighteenth-century matchlock gun combined with a crossbow is Indo-Persian. There is a slot below the barrel for the bowstring, which is released by the same trigger that operates the gun.

Percussion-cap mechanism

DAGGER PISTOL

While disguised as a dagger, this Japanese weapon is actually a single-shot percussion-cap pistol.

KNIFE PISTOL

This late nineteenth-century French knife-gun combination has a carved ivory handle and 10-inch blade. Concealed in the handle is a .32 centerfire gun. The trigger opens when the gun is cocked.

COMBINATION WEAPONS CONTINUED . . .

Pistol barrel

CUTLASS PISTOL
Dumonthier (see previous page) also made this single-shot, .31 percussion-cap pistol with a cutlass blade; the pistol barrel and blade are forged from the same piece of metal.

COMBO PISTOL DAGGER
This Belgian pistol (in formidable .80) includes not one but two knife blades—a 6½-inch straight blade that slides forward from the frame, and an 8-inch curved blade concealed in the buttstock. In addition, the trigger guard is lengthened and reinforced to parry the sword or knife-thrust of an attacker.

Trigger guard doubles as a hilt

APACHE
One of the rarest and yet most famous combination weapons of the nineteenth century was the "Apache," so-called because it was supposedly used by Parisian gangsters who took the name of the warlike Native American nation. (Firearms historian Charles Edward Chapel considered its name "a gross libel on American Apache Indians.") The "Apache" combined a revolver (usually 7mm pinfire), a folding blade of about 3½ inches, and a "brass knuckle" grip. Given the shortness of the blade and the fact that the pistol component didn't even have a barrel, it's effectiveness as either a firearm or a knife is pretty doubtful.

Revolver cylinder

PISTOL-KNIFE
A tiny pistol-knife combo that was made in the U.S. in the nineteenth century.

LE CENTENAIRE
Also reputedly popular with the criminal Apache gangs of Paris, this combination knuckleduster and single shot .22 pistol was made in France in 1889. It was also called a Coup-de-poing pistolet "Walh."

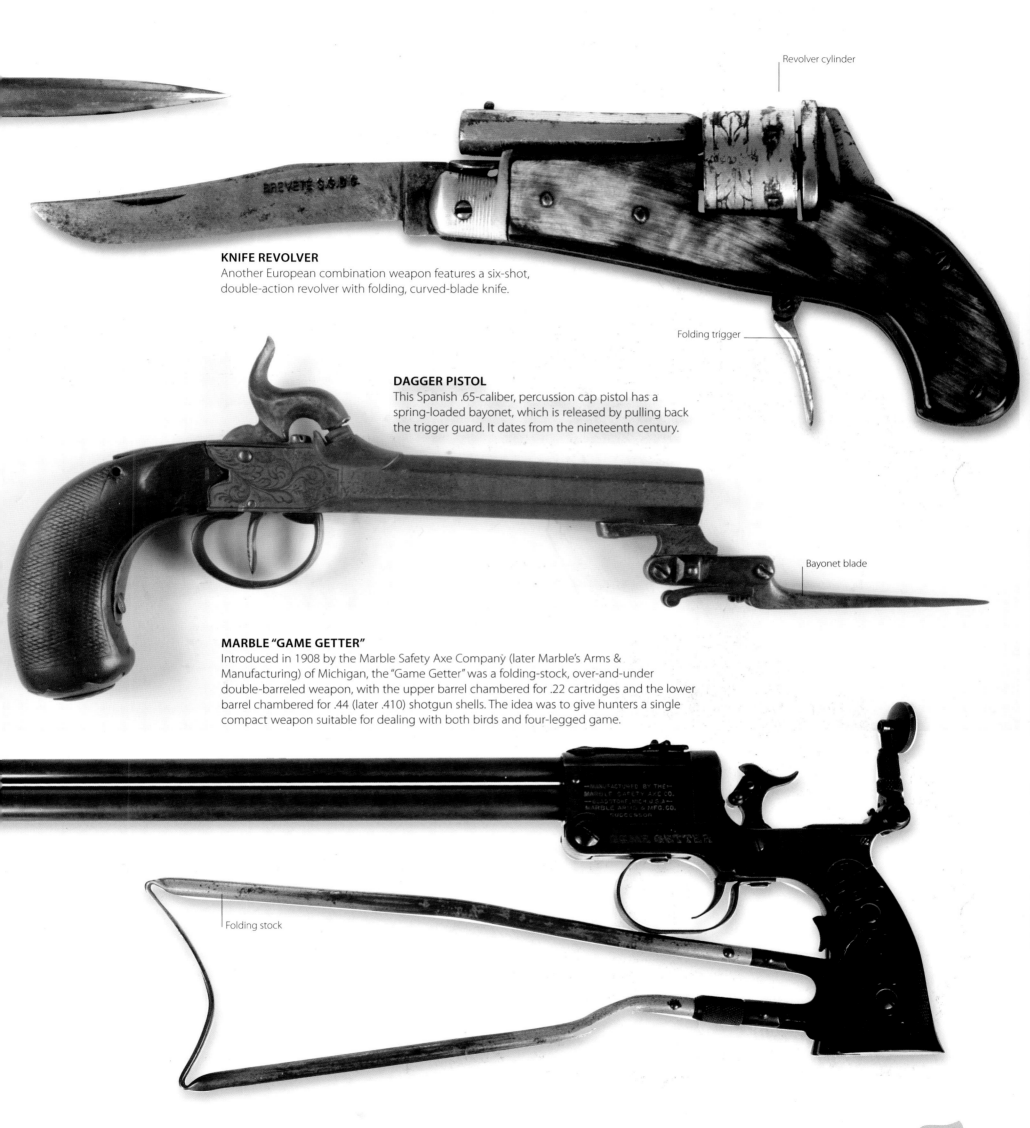

Revolver cylinder

KNIFE REVOLVER
Another European combination weapon features a six-shot, double-action revolver with folding, curved-blade knife.

Folding trigger

DAGGER PISTOL
This Spanish .65-caliber, percussion cap pistol has a spring-loaded bayonet, which is released by pulling back the trigger guard. It dates from the nineteenth century.

Bayonet blade

MARBLE "GAME GETTER"
Introduced in 1908 by the Marble Safety Axe Company (later Marble's Arms & Manufacturing) of Michigan, the "Game Getter" was a folding-stock, over-and-under double-barreled weapon, with the upper barrel chambered for .22 cartridges and the lower barrel chambered for .44 (later .410) shotgun shells. The idea was to give hunters a single compact weapon suitable for dealing with both birds and four-legged game.

Folding stock

THE WORLD AT WAR

20TH CENTURY & BEYOND

Mass conflict led to the development of a wide range of new weapons

Modern Warfare

Automatic weapons timeline
Arms makers long dreamed of a weapon that fired continuously at the touch of a trigger. Manually operated rapid-fire weapons first appeared in the nineteenth century.

1861
Gatling gun

1885
Maxim machine gun

World War I (1914–18) saw deployment of modern automatically firing machine guns alongside primitive trench-fighting knives. To a great extent World War II (1939–45) was fought with similar weapons. Automatic pistols, already in widespread use during the earlier conflict, replaced the revolver as the standard military sidearm. Submachine guns, such as the German MP40 "Schmeisser" and the cheap and simple Ppsh 41 used by the Soviet Red Army, joined the infantry's arsenal. The years preceding World War II had seen experimentation with semiautomatic, or self-loading, rifles to replace bolt-action models, but only the U.S. Army made such a weapon—the M1 Garand—its standard rifle during the war itself. Germany developed the MP44 Sturmgewehr (assault rifle), an innovative weapon that combined the rapid-fire capabilities of the submachine gun with the range and power of the rifle. Tanks and armored vehicles became increasingly important, too, with developments accelerating after World War I.

US TANKS ADVANCING
Sherman tanks lead this World War II cavalcade. These tanks were initially intended as a support for infantry rather than as offensive weapons.

1917
Thompson submachine gun

1932
Vickers heavy machine gun

1936
M1 Garand
semiautomatic rifle

1938
MP40 submachine gun

1941
MP41 assault rifle

1941
Ppsh-41 submachine gun

1957
M14 selective-fire
semiautomatic rifle

WEAPONS OF WORLD WAR I

World War I was a conflict of mass firepower, with the recently developed machine guns and other artillery capable of dealing death from long distances. But when orders were given to leave the trenches of the Western Front and advance on the enemy, infantrymen soon became engaged in episodes of desperate close-quarters combat. Famous battles such as those of the Somme (1916) and Passchendale (1917) consisted of many infantry advances, where edged weapons and pistols would have found a place along with rifles.

EDGED WEAPONS

By the outbreak of the "Great War," swords were mostly considered ceremonial weapons in European armies—except for sabers, which were still issued to cavalrymen. However, the mounted forces of the warring armies didn't have much opportunity to wield their sabers.

Although the first clash between the British and German forces—at the Battle of Mons, in August 1914—was a cavalry action, the war on the Western Front in France and Belgium quickly settled into static trench warfare in which cavalry played little part. (The British Army, however, kept large reserves of cavalry in hopes that it could exploit breaches in the German lines.)

BAYONETS AND TRENCH KNIVES
Every infantrymen had a bayonet for his rifle—hence the classic images of soldiers going "over the top" and advancing, bayonets fixed, into the no-man's-land that separated opposing trenches. Even if the World War I infantryman survived a hail of machine-gun fire to reach the enemy's lines, however, using the bayonet was an awkward business in the close confines of a trench. So soldiers increasingly turned to knives in hand-to-hand fights, and several armies developed purpose-built "trench knives" or "trench daggers" like those shown on these pages.

World War I soldiers also improvised edged weapons to meet trench-fighting conditions—weapons that would have been recognizable to medieval warriors. Some sharpened the edges of spades to a bladelike sharpness. Others attached knives to poles to create twentieth-century versions of the pike or halberd.

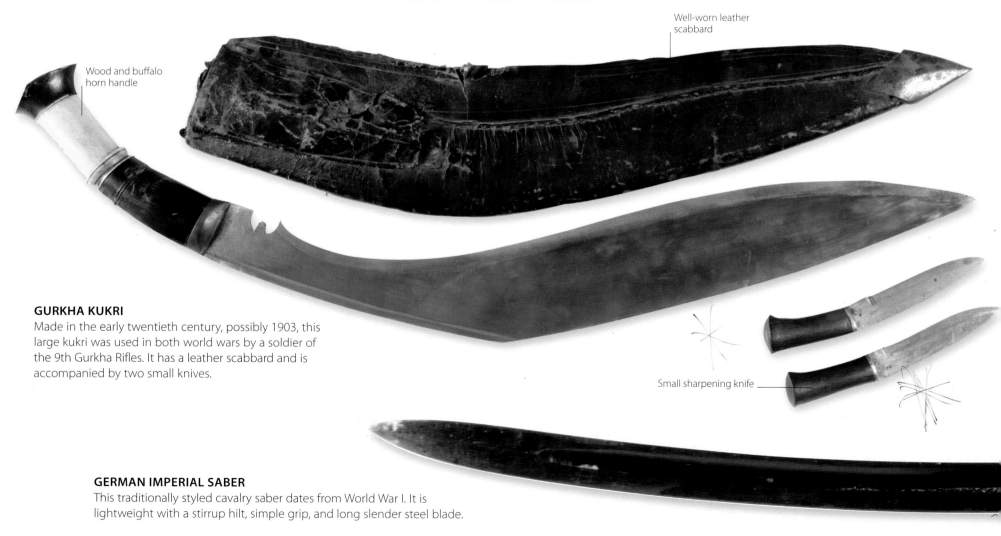

Well-worn leather scabbard

Wood and buffalo horn handle

GURKHA KUKRI
Made in the early twentieth century, possibly 1903, this large kukri was used in both world wars by a soldier of the 9th Gurkha Rifles. It has a leather scabbard and is accompanied by two small knives.

Small sharpening knife

GERMAN IMPERIAL SABER
This traditionally styled cavalry saber dates from World War I. It is lightweight with a stirrup hilt, simple grip, and long slender steel blade.

Metal scabbard

US 1918 TRENCH KNIFE
The original 1917 U.S. trench knife was found to be too fragile and was replaced with the model shown here, which had a handle of solid brass.

Solid brass "knuckle-duster" handle

"Skull-crusher" pommel

Triangular stiletto-style blade

Leather scabbard

Handle shaped like a "knuckle-duster"

US 1917 TRENCH KNIFE
In 1917, the U.S. Army developed a small fighting knife designed especially for close combat. It was a triple-threat weapon, featuring a triangular stabbing blade, a handle that doubled as a set of "brass knuckles," and a heavy "skull-crusher" pommel cap.

Leather belt hook

Metal sheath

GERMAN COMBAT KNIFE
The compact *grabendoch* (trench dagger) was widely issued to front-line German troops during World War I. This model has a blade of about 5¾ inches and an overall length of about 10 inches.

Strong blade with a single cutting edge

Stirrup hilt

EDGED WEAPONS OF WORLD WAR I CONTINUED . . .

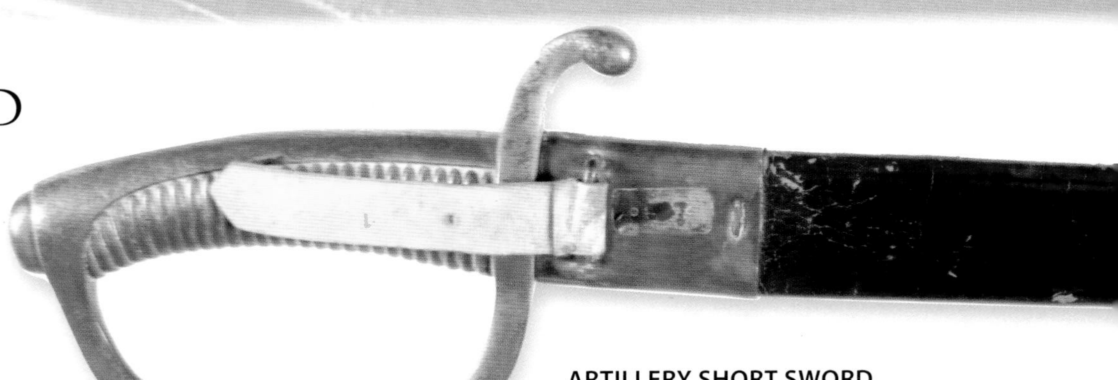

LEBEL BAYONET

This bayonet was produced in 1916 for use with the 8mm French Lebel Model 1886 bolt-action rifle. The metal grip was produced in both nickel and brass, as supplies of the metals dictated.

ARTILLERY SHORT SWORD

This neoclassical-style sword dating from 1816 was issued to a French foot soldier for used as a sidearm and a tool for clearing undergrowth.

Long, triangular blade

Strong, protective sheath

"THEY SHALL NOT PASS."

—General Pétain, Battle of Verdun, 1916

Glass lenses

Canvas mask

Charcoal filter

Instruction booklet

CORRECT USE OF GAS MASK EQUIPMENT

US GAS MASK

Poison gas was one of the special horrors of World War I. Both the French and the German armies used irritant gases (i.e., tear gas) early in the war, but gas warfare entered a more deadly phase during the Battle of Ypres in April 1915, when the Germans wafted chlorine gas toward British trenches. Soon both sides used gases, mainly delivered by artillery shells. Some gases (like mustard gas) disabled victims; others (like phosgene) were often immediately fatal. Early countermeasures were crude—such as holding urine-soaked cotton wadding over the nose and mouth—but as the war went on, increasingly effective gas masks, or "respirators," were developed. The one shown here was issued to U.S. troops.

GAS! GAS! QUICK, BOYS! – AN ECSTASY OF FUMBLING,
FITTING THE CLUMSY HELMETS JUST IN TIME,
BUT SOMEONE STILL WAS YELLING OUT AND STUMBLING
AND FLOUND'RING LIKE A MAN IN FIRE OR LIME.

Dulce et Decorum Est, Wilfred Owen (1917)

Sawtooth blade

Uniform tassel

MAUSER PIONEER BAYONET
Dating from World War I and before, this bayonet was made for use with a Mauser rifle. It has a sawtooth blade and a scabbard made from leather and silver.

Wooden handle

Protective quillon

BAYONET AND SHEATH
Weyersberg, Kirschbaum & Co. (WKC) began making swords in Solingen, Germany, over two hundred years ago. They made this bayonet in the late nineteenth century, and it went on to be used during World War I.

STEYR-MANNLICHER BAYONET
This wooden-handled bayonet was made for the Steyr-Mannlicher M1895 bolt-action rifle. It is marked "FG GY" indicating it was made in Hungary; bayonets for this rifle were also made in Austria.

HANDGUNS OF WORLD WAR I

In World War I, pistols were carried chiefly by officers and noncommissioned officers (NCOs). They remained a standard cavalry weapon and were prized for use in close combat by frontline infantry. They also were carried by tank crews, aircrew, and support troops as a defensive weapon in conditions that made the use of a rifle impractical. From the early years of the twentieth century, other handguns also found a role as police weapons and for home defense. Many designs had been around for years.

THE REVOLVER

By the time World War I began in 1914 the automatic pistol was finally winning acceptance among the world's armed forces.

Switzerland and Germany, for example, had adopted the 9mm Luger, while the United States (which would enter the war in 1917) adopted the Colt .45 automatic in 1911. Many military officers, however, believed (with some justification) that automatics weren't reliable or rugged enough to withstand the rigors of muddy, dusty, and damp combat conditions. The British Army remained strongly devoted to the revolvers made by the Birmingham firm of Webley & Scott, which first entered service in the 1880s; the French used the Lebel revolver, and the Russians, the Nagant.

GERMAN REVOLVER
Despite the official adoption of the Luger, many German cavalrymen of World War I carried the more reliable six-shot, .44 revolvers like the one shown here.

Ring attached to trooper's clothing via lanyard

Slide moves back to load cartridges

STEYR
The Steyr 9mm automatic was the standard pistol of the Austro-Hungarian armies in World War I and many later found their way into the Wehrmacht in World War II. Like the "snail drum" Luger, this particular pistol was captured during the Allied campaign against German and Italian forces in North Africa.

.455 Eley caliber, six-shot cylinder.

CONTRACT COLT NEW SERVICE REVOLVER
This was the largest swing-out cylinder, double action revolver produced by Colt. It is estimated that 356,000 were manufactured in many different variations in the 46 years (1897–1943) they were produced. .

GLISENTI M1910 AUTO

Manufactured by the firm of Real Fabbrica d'Armi Glisenti, the Model 1910 automatic was a mainstay of Italian forces in World War I. The M1910, however, had an overly complicated firing system that required the use of a weaker version of the 9mm round, which limited its range and stopping power.

Short recoil, slide exposed

Magazine release

GLESENTI 1884 REVOLVER

This Italian10.35mm revolver has a folding trigger that unfolds when the hammer is cocked. The more common variant models have a trigger guard and fixed trigger.

2ND MODEL NAMBU PISTOL

Named for its inventor, Colonel Nambu Kirijo, Japan's foremost weapons designer at the time, the Nambu pistol was pefected in 1915. It was widely used by Japanese officers but was never officially adopted by the military. Although it looks very like the German Luger, there is no similarity in the way it works.

8mm 8 round detachable box magazine.

SWISS ARMY LUGER

The Luger model adopted by the Swiss Army were 7.65mm-caliber while the German P08 model, adopted in 1908, fired the 9mm parabellum round, which remains, almost a century later, the most popular caliber for automatic pistols and submachine guns. The Luger was undoubtedly an excellent weapon, but its legendary status—it was a coveted souvenir among Allied troops in both world wars—exaggerates its overall performance.

BERGMANN-BAYARD M1910

Designed by Danish gunmaker Theodore Bergmann and his associates, the Bergmann-Bayard M1910 was a 9mm automatic that could take either a six- or ten-round magazine. Besides being the official Danish sidearm, it was adopted by the armies of Belgium, Greece, and Spain. This handgun model was also widely used by the Danish resistance movement during the German occupation of that country in World War II.

Detachable 7.65mm magazine

PISTOLS TO THE END OF WWI

SCHEINTOD HAHN GAS REVOLVER
Dating from the late nineteenth century, this German revolver has five barrels and a folding trigger. It shoots 410 shotgun shells.

Folding trigger without a safety guard

Cylinder takes twelve rounds

L'EXPLORATEUR MITRAILLE
Made in France by Francaise d'Arms & Cycles de Saint Etienne, this "Explorer" double-barrel 6mm revolver takes twelve rounds and shoots two at a time. It was made for the colonial market between 1900 and 1913.

Sliding ramrod

EUROPEAN SIX-SHOT REVOLVER
An early twentieth century example of a six-shot revolver with a sliding ramrod on the side.

Wooden grip

GERMAN ARMY REVOLVER
Made in 1893 for use as a service weapon, this single action, six-shot, .44 revolver is marked "Erfurt," which is the location of the German government's arsenal at the time.

CHINESE PISTOL

Dating from the early twentieth century, this is a 7.63 caliber automatic with a Mauser-type hammer. The Chinese made several copies of Mausers, one of the most famous being the Hanyang C96.

Ribbed grip

BROWNING PATENT PISTOL

This is the M1910 or "New Model" Browning. It is a six-shot 9mm. It was made very early in the twentieth century and its hard rubber grip, decorated with fine checkering, indicates it was made prior to World War II. The FN stands for Fabrique National d'Armes de Guerre.

Lanyard hook

HUSQVARNA M1907 PISTOL

Made by the Swedish firearms manufacturer Husqvarna Vapenfabriks Aktiebolag in the early twentieth century, this is a .38 caliber self-loading, semiautomatic service pistol. It is marked as pistol number1549, issued to Infantry Regiment No. 17.

TRENCH WARFARE

In 1897, a Polish-Jewish financier named Ivan Bloch (c. 1832–1902) published a book titled *The War of the Future*. Bloch contended that given the combination of mass conscript armies and weapons like machine guns and quick-firing artillery using explosive shells, any European conflict would degenerate into a war of attrition fought by soldiers burrowing into the earth for protection. His theory was ignored or scoffed at.

Not much more than a decade after his death, he was proved a prophet. Yet trench warfare was not new in 1914. During the American Civil War (1861–65), the effectiveness of the rifled musket was such that both sides learned the value of "digging in." Photographs of the Union Army's lines around Petersburg, Virginia, in 1864–65 are eerily similar to photographs of the Western Front in France and Belgium fifty years later.

SCANT PROTECTION
The shallow, hastily excavated trench of these Allied soldiers would be useless in the event of a direct hit by artillery but offered some protection from sniper fire.

"...NO PEACE FOR MEN, ONLY MURDER, CRUELTY, BRUTALITY"

James T. Farrell, *Studs Lonigan: A Trilogy*

THE WESTERN FRONT

When World War I broke out in Europe in August 1914, the French Army still believed that a spirited offense over open ground would always overwhelm the enemy. In the opening months of the conflict, the French managed to hold the German attackers on the Marne River and save Paris from capture, but their tactics cost hundreds of thousands of lives. Thereafter the French and their British allies established a line of trenches that stretched nearly 500 miles from the English Channel to the Swiss border, separated from the German trenches by a no-man's-land that in places extended no more than a few hundred feet or even less between the opposing forces.

WEAPONS OF TRENCH WARFARE

Previously, infantry had generally been the decisive factor on European battlefields, but in World War I artillery achieved preeminence. At the Third Battle of Ypres in 1917, for example, British artillery fired 4.7 million shells over three weeks. Intended to "soften" the enemy in preparation for an infantry assault across no-man's-land, the bombardment was ineffective. Dug deep into the ground, the Germans were able to emerge with their machine guns intact and ready to scour the advancing Allied infantry. In an effort to break the deadlock on the Western Front, the British developed a new weapon—the tank, a tracked, armored "land battleship." Tanks had some success, especially at the Battle of Cambrai (November 20–December 7, 1917), but did not prove a decisive factor in the war. For their part, the Germans sought to break the deadlock by developing tactics based around small groups of *strosstruppen* (literally, "storm troops") armed with new weapons such as flamethrowers and submachine guns for use in clearing Allied troops from their bunkers.

Bolt system

Top of receiver

Lowered back sight

Front sight

Buttstock

Magazine

GRENADE
Grenades are filled with explosives that are activated when the pin is pulled. This gives the user a few seconds to throw it at the enemy.

PERISCOPE RIFLE
This Enfield rifle has been fitted with a periscope to allow for remote firing over the top of the trench. A system of rods and mirrors allows the operator to fire without having to reveal himself to the enemy artillery.

Barrel with protective wrapping

"Pineapple" design

Raised lever sight

LEWIS LIGHT MACHINE GUN
Developed in 1911, this .303, gas-operated weapon was fed by a tubular 50-round top-mounted magazine, and it had a distinctive "shroud" to cool the barrel. It was widely used to arm Allied aircraft, and a .30 version was developed for U.S. forces.

Pistol grip

Barrel shroud

Bipod support

MORTARS
Sometimes called "the infantryman's artillery," compact, mobile mortars were developed during World War I to give supporting fire to riflemen in both offense and defense operations.

Barrel slide

"Knuckle-duster" handle

Mortar tube

BERGMANN-BAYARD M1910
This Danish 9mm automatic could take either a six- or ten-round magazine. Besides being the official Danish sidearm, it was adopted by the armies of Belgium, Greece, and Spain. It was later used by the Danish resistance during the German occupation in World War II.

US 1917 TRENCH KNIFE
In 1917, the U.S. Army developed a knife for close combat. This triple-threat weapon had a triangular blade, a "knuckle-duster" handle, and a skull-crushing pommel cap.

Front legs

MAUSER PIONEER BAYONET
Dating from World War I and before, this bayonet was made for use with a Mauser rifle. It has a sawtooth blade and a scabbard made of leather and silver.

Firing pin at base of tube

Footplate

INFANTRY RIFLES OF WORLD WAR I

From the turn of the twentieth century, military rifle technology advanced at a slower pace than that of other weapons. The World War I infantryman in most armies went into battle carrying a rifle with a design pedigree dating back to the mid-nineteenth century.

IF IT AIN'T BROKE . . .

There were valid reasons for this relative conservatism. Bolt-action rifles were sturdy, and mechanically simple, and they were also accurate over long distances—typically up to 500–600 yards. The main trend in rifle development before World War I was simply to make infantry rifles shorter and lighter. This meant there was a blurring of the nineteenth-century distinction between rifle and carbine; examples include the U.S. Springfield M1903, British SMLE (Short Magazine Lee-Enfield) and German KAR-98.

Although a well-trained soldier could get off about 15 shots per minute with bolt-action rifles at this time, weapons designers had also begun to work on semiautomatic rifles to increase the volume of infantry firepower. (Operating by means of recoil or from the energy of the gas created as a fired cartridge left the barrel, semiautomatic rifles—also known as autoloading rifles—fire once for every pull of the trigger.)

From the mid-1890s onward, the military establishments of Denmark, Mexico, Germany, Russia, and Italy experimented with semiautomatic rifles, but none of those developed at the time saw widespread use. Experimentation continued, but adoption of the semiautomatic rifle was slowed by the same concerns over replacement of revolvers with automatic pistols—the relative complexity of semiautomatic rifles compared to bolt-action rifles, and the fact that most semiautomatics fired a lighter, shorter cartridge. In addition, officers worried that troops armed with rapid-fire rifles would expend their ammunition too quickly.

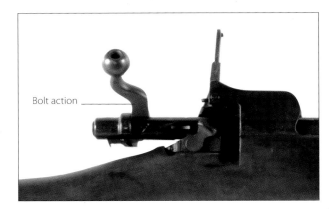

Bolt action

MANNLICHER-CARCANO
Although they bear the name of the Austro-German gun designer Ferdinand Ritter von Mannlicher, the Mannlicher-Carcano series of 6.5mm carbines and rifles—the mainstay of the Italian armed forces from 1891 through World War II—were actually based on a Mauser design. (The "Carcano" designation is for Salvatore Carcano, a designer at the Italian government arsenal at Turin.) The Model 1941 rifle is shown here. The Mannlicher-Carcano gained postwar notoriety in 1963, when Lee Harvey Oswald used a ML carbine he'd purchased through the mail to assassinate U.S. president John F. Kennedy.

STEYR-MANNLICHER M.95 RIFLE
This bolt-action rifle has a straight-pull bolt, allowing for very rapid firing. It was made in Austria between 1895 and 1921 and was nicknamed "Ruck Zuck" ("right now" or "very quick") by German troops.

Straight-pull bolt

Long-distance elevator sight

Bolt system named after its
designer James Paris Lee

BRITISH LEE-ENFIELD M1917 MARK III

With a design incorporating lessons learned in the Boer War (1899–1902), the first version of
the .303 SMLE (Short Magazine Lee-Enfield), the Mark III, entered service with the British
Army in 1907. The SMLE's action gave it a high rate of fire relative to other rifles of the time,
and it had a 10-round magazine. When German troops came under British fire early in World
War I, the British put up such a sustained, rapid fire that the Germans believed they were
under attack by machine guns.

EDDYSTONE ENFIELD

When the United States entered World War I in April 1917, it adopted a rifle based on the
British Enfield. This was the U.S. Rifle Model 1917—an Enfield with an action and magazine
modified for U.S .30 cartridges. Often called an Eddystone model rifle, it was one of many
made at the Remington Arms Eddystone Rifle Plant, Pennsylvania, during World War I.

6-round magazine

VETTERLI-VITALI

During World War I, the Italian Army modified numbers of its elderly
Model 71 carbines—originally single-shot, 10.4mm weapons—into
more feasible 6.5mm rifles fed by the same 6-round magazine used
by the Mannlicher-Carcano M1891.

Bayonet

KAR-98

The 7.92mm KAR-98 (for karabiner, model 1998) was the standard German infantry
rifle in both world wars. It used the classic forward-locking Mauser bolt action,
weighed 8½ pounds, and had an integral 5-round box magazine.

Muzzle sight

Attachment for sling

Detail of bayonet
mounting

INFANTRY RIFLES OF WORLD WAR I CONTINUED . . .

GERMAN ARMY RIFLE
This model 71/84 army rifle was developed by Mauser during World War I and manufactured at Spandau, Germany. It has an eight-round, tubular magazine.

Elevator sight

CAMEL RIFLE
A camel gun, or jezail, from the Middle East and used during World War I. This highly decorated gun has the very long barrel typical of jezails.

Lever to draw back and release the sling

Grenade in place on sling

GRENADE CATAPULT
Catapults were first used in Greece in the first century BC and were often used to defend castles during medieval times. This simple but effective grenade catapult was used by troops in the trenches in World War I to hurl hand grenades at their opponents.

Powerful springs

MOSIN-NAGANT M91/30/59

Magazine holds
five cartridges

Drawing on design elements provided by the Russian Colonel Sergei Mosin and Belgian Leon Nagant, the 7.62mm, bolt-action Mosin-Nagant would, in various models and upgrades, remain the standard Russian (and later Soviet) infantry rifle from the early 1890s until around 1950.

Mirror to reflect image
to mirror below

Magazine

PERISCOPE RIFLE

A system of mirrors and linked rods made a periscope and remote firing mechanism that allowed this rifle to be used without the operator having to put his head above the top of the trench. It is not clear who developed periscope rifles, but they were widespread by the end of 1914. Other developments included a periscope for a machine gun.

Mirror to reverse
the image

Trigger operated by a
series of linked rods

TWO HUNDRED YARDS AWAY HE SAW HIS HEAD;
HE RAISED HIS RIFLE, TOOK QUICK AIM AND SHOT HIM.
TWO HUNDRED YARDS AWAY THE MAN DROPPED DEAD;

The Sniper by Scottish poet W. D. Cocker

MACHINE GUNS OF WORLD WAR I

Although first used in large numbers in the Russo-Japanese War (1904–05), it was during World War I that the machine gun changed warfare forever. It remains a principal military weapon in the twenty-first century.

The concept of an automatic weapon—one that would fire continuously for as long as the operator pulled back the trigger—goes back to at least 1718, when Englishmen James Puckle proposed a multicylinder "defense gun." Several manually operated rapid-fire guns were introduced in the mid-nineteenth century. Some, like the U.S. Gatling gun were relatively successful. Others, like the French Mitrailleuse, were not. The first modern machine gun, the Maxim gun, appeared in 1885 (see also sidebar). Despite

competition from weapons like the British Gardner gun and the Swedish Nordenfeldt gun, the Maxim design was adopted by a number of nations from the 1880s through the early 1900s. Appearing at the high point of European imperialism, the Maxim and other rapid-fire guns proved useful in slaughtering indigenous peoples in colonial conflicts, prompting British writer Hilaire Belloc to rhyme sardonically:

"Whatever happens, we have got
The Maxim gun, and they have not."
Then came World War I. Although the British Army had been among the first to adopt the machine gun, it went into action underequipped with the weapon and underestimating its effects, while the French were convinced that "the spirit of the attack" would overcome automatic fire. The

German Army did not labor under these misapprehensions, however, and the Allies suffered accordingly—but would rapidly catch up in the firepower sweepstakes.

As many historians have noted, most brilliantly John Ellis in *The Social History of the Machine Gun*, the devastation wrought by the machine gun in World War I had a psychological as well as a physical aspect. The machine gun reduced killing to an industrial process. It represented the nexus of the Industrial Revolution and the age of mass warfare. Future British Prime Minister Winston Churchill—who spent ninety days as an infantry officer in the trenches of the Western Front—was certainly thinking of the machine gun when he wrote, in a postwar memoir, "War, which used to be cruel and magnificent, has now become cruel and squalid . . ."

FRENCH CHAUCHAT
One of World War I's worst weapons, France's Chauchat automatic rifle was poorly made from substandard components, and it was fed by 8mm Lebel rifle cartridges from a crescent-shaped magazine—an inaccurate and unreliable system for an automatic weapon. When U.S. troops arrived on the Western Front, they were equipped with large numbers of this weapon rechambered for the American .30 round. In addition to its inherent faults, most of these guns were mechanically clapped-out from years of service. American soldiers and marines—who called it "Cho-Cho"—considered it worse than useless, and usually left the it behind when going into action.

Pistol grip

Crescent-shaped magazine

Drum magazine

Sights

Barrel mouthpiece

Stand

LEWIS LIGHT MACHINE GUN
The British Army went into World War I using a couple of American machine-gun designs, including the Lewis Light Machine Gun. Developed by U.S. Army officer Noah Lewis in 1911, the .303, gas-operated weapon

was fed by a tubular 50-round top-mounted magazine, and it had a distinctive "shroud" to cool the barrel. It was widely used to arm Allied aircraft, and a .30 version was developed for U.S. forces.

GERMAN SPANDAU MAXIM
Officially the Maxim LMG 08/15, the "Spandau" got its nickname from one of Imperial Germany's arsenals. The 7.92mm, water-cooled, belt-fed weapon was the standard armament for German aircraft from 1915 on, after the development of the "interrupter gear," which synchronized the weapon's firing rate with the revolution of the aircraft's propeller, allowing the gun to shoot safely through the plane's propeller arc.

SIR HIRAM MAXIM

Born in Maine in 1840, Hiram Maxim became a prolific inventor at an early age, patenting—among other items—the proverbial "better mousetrap." While attending an industrial exhibition in Paris in 1881, a friend told him that if he really wanted to make a fortune, he should "invent something that will enable these Europeans to cut each other's throats with greater facility." Maxim took these words to heart, and a few years later he unveiled the gun that would bear his name. Fed by a continuous belt of ammunition (initially .45, later .303), the Maxim gun was recoil-operated; the operator cocked and fired the weapon, and the recoil ejected the spent cartridge and chambered a new round. Because the rapid rate of fire—up to 600 rounds per minute—could melt the barrel, he surrounded it with a jacket filled with water. (Later "air-cooled" machine guns would use a perforated metal jacket.) The Maxim design was soon adopted by several nations, including Britain, and reportedly, turn-of-the-twentieth century Maxims were being used by the Chinese Army in the Korean War more than a half-century later. Maxim took British citizenship and, in 1901, was knighted for his services.

Muzzle attachment

COLT VICKERS

Shortly before World War I, the British Army adopted the Vickers gun as its standard heavy machine gun. A .303 water-cooled gun based on the basic Maxim design, the weapon's biggest drawback was its weight, which was 83 pounds with its tripod. This meant it typically required a crew of six to eight men to carry and operate it.

MARLIN MACHINE GUN

When the U.S. entered World War I in April 1917, the U.S. Army contracted Marlin Arms to produce a version of the .30 Colt-Browning Model 1895 machine gun, which was already in use by the Navy. Designed by the John Browning (see page 00), the gun had a big disadvantage in infantry combat: The gas system used a piston that moved back and forth below the barrel, so it could be fired only from a fairly high tripod mount—thus exposing the crew to enemy fire. Because of the piston's tendency to hit the ground below, troops nicknamed it the "potato-digger."

High tripod mounting

Tripod back foot

Regulator piston

Upper part of cartridge receiver

This version takes .303 cartridges

HOTCHKISS PORTATIVE MACHINE GUN

Produced by the French in the early twentieth century, the Hotchkiss M1909 was a light machine gun that used 8mm Lebel cartridges. Many other countries adopted it, including Britain, where a version was produced for .303 rounds. Known as the Mark 1, this machine gun was also used in the U.S.

GANGSTER WARFARE

In January 1920, Prohibition—a federal ban on the "manufacture, sale, or transportation" of alcohol—went into effect in the United States. Intended to stop the crime and social ills associated with drinking, this "noble experiment" backfired badly. People still wanted to drink, "bootleggers" were willing to make or smuggle alcohol, and organized crime, seeing a chance to make rich profits, stepped in to control the trade in illicit hooch. Through the 1920s and beyond, gangsters fought each other and the authorities using a variety of powerful weapons, forcing law-enforcement agencies to catch up in the firepower stakes. Prohibition ended in 1933, but the Great Depression saw the rise of a new breed of outlaw, "motorized bandits" such as the Barker Gang, John Dillinger, and "Pretty Boy" Floyd, who roamed the roads of the Midwest and Southwest committing crimes.

GANGSTER PAYBACK
Commanding an estimated annual income of $100 million a year, Chicago gangster Al Capone could afford to set up this soup kitchen for the unemployed in 1929.

"I HAVE BUILT MY ORGANIZATION UPON FEAR"

Al Capone, June 23, 1926

THE TOMMY GUN

The most iconic weapon of the 1920s is surely the Thompson Submachine Gun. Much to the embarrassment of its inventor, John T. Thompson, who had developed it for military use, the weapon was eagerly taken up by gangsters in Chicago and other cities and put to deadly use in their battles with rival gangs and with the authorities. (Given the lax gun-control laws of the era, criminals could easily obtain weapons—even automatic ones.) The Thompson soon earned a variety of nicknames, including the "Tommy Gun," the "Chicago typewriter," and the "chopper."

Perhaps the Thompson's most notorious application came in the "St. Valentine's Day Massacre" of 1929, when members of Al Capone's gang murdered seven associates of a rival concern in a Chicago garage. The power of the Thompson's .45 ACP rounds at close range was such that several of the victims' bodies were reportedly cut nearly in half. The success of the Thompson in outlaw hands led many law-enforcement agencies, including the FBI, to purchase the weapon themselves; the Thompson would be part of the "G-Men's" arsenal for decades. Most local police forces, however, remained armed solely with revolvers and shotguns, and so were at a distinct disadvantage when gangsters came to town.

PISTOLS IN POCKETS

Another weapons development of the 1920s was the widespread adoption of "pocket pistols" by criminals. These were small automatic pistols, usually in .22 or .25 caliber, which, as the name implies, could be easily concealed in a coat pocket, an ankle holster, or tucked behind the belt in the small of the back. They were handy weapons in case a bootlegging deal went bad, or in last-ditch struggles to escape the police.

Magazine holds 20 rounds

Trigger guard

BROWNING AUTOMATIC RIFLE
The gas-operated, .30 Browning Automatic Rifle (BAR) was introduced in 1918 and did limited duty in World War I. It was used by the FBI against gangsters in the 1920s as well as by the criminals themselves, sometimes in cut-down form.

Wooden buttstock

THOMPSON
The Thompson submachine used a delayed-blowback operation developed by U.S. Navy officer John Blish. It fired the same .45 ACP cartridge as the Colt M1911 pistol and fed either from a 50-round drum magazine or a 20- (later 30) round box magazine. Hollywood forever linked the "Tommy Gun" with U.S. gang wars of the 1920s in the public mind, but the weapon also first saw military service during the decade.

Additional front grip

Box magazine

Six-shot cylinder

Leather holster

LILIPUT PISTOL
The Liliput series of automatic pistols made by Waffenfabrik August Menz in Germany was aptly named—this one measures 3½ inches long and was made in 1927. To keep the weapon as small as possible, Menz chambered it for the rare 4.25mm round. (Other, slightly larger Liliput models used a 6.35mm round.)

COLT POLICE POSITIVE
By the 1920s many U.S. policemen and private armed guards carried .32 or .38 Colt "Police Positive" revolvers. The name came from a new safety feature, introduced in 1905, which separated the hammer from the firing pin, thus preventing accidental discharge.

Handgrip

GAS BILLY CLUB
Federal Laboratories Inc. of Pittsburgh produced this combination billy club/tear-gas launcher for police use in the mid-1920s.

Diminuitive pistol

Lever trigger

Cylinder takes 24 rounds

Long barrel

MITRAILLEUSE
This defensive weapon was fitted to a window or barricade, and the firer pulled a string attached to the lever to fire and advance each of the 24 bullets. Al Capone's gang are said to have mounted it on boats used to bring in illegal booze from Canada in case they encountered U.S. Customs patrols.

WEAPONS OF WORLD WAR II

The weapons of World War II (1939–45) were broadly similar to those of World War I in that they were all devices for launching projectiles at high speed. However, infantrymen as stationary sharpshooters largely gave way to highly mobile, self-sufficient assault troops armed with self-loading, automatic assault rifles. Submachine guns, too, were widely distributed and produced a storm of fire on the battlefield, even though some, such as the British Sten gun, were somewhat crude weapons developed for mass manufacture. In the context of these maneuverable, rapid-fire weapons, it is perhaps surprising that hand guns, both revolvers and the more recent automatic pistols, remained in high demand on all sides and were used on an unprecedented scale during the conflict.

EDGED WEAPONS

In World War II, edged weapons were used most widely in the Allied struggle to push back the tide of Japanese conquest in the Pacific. The Japanese military's code of Bushido placed great emphasis on close-in fighting, and U.S. troops fighting on the Pacific islands often faced Japanese Banzai charges—wild onrushes of infantry led by officers brandishing swords, which were inevitably referred to as "Samurai swords" by their American opponents. (In fact, some Japanese did carry swords that had been passed down in their families for generations.) Japanese troops were also expert at infiltrating American positions at night. This usually led to grim hand-to-hand fights in which the Marine Corps fighting knife, the legendary Ka-Bar, proved its worth. Knives were also utilized in all theaters of the war by Commandos and other special forces, and by operatives of agencies such as the U.S. OSS and the British SOE for assassinations and "silent elimination" of sentries. Undoubtedly the most famous of these weapons was the Sykes-Fairbairn Commando Knife.

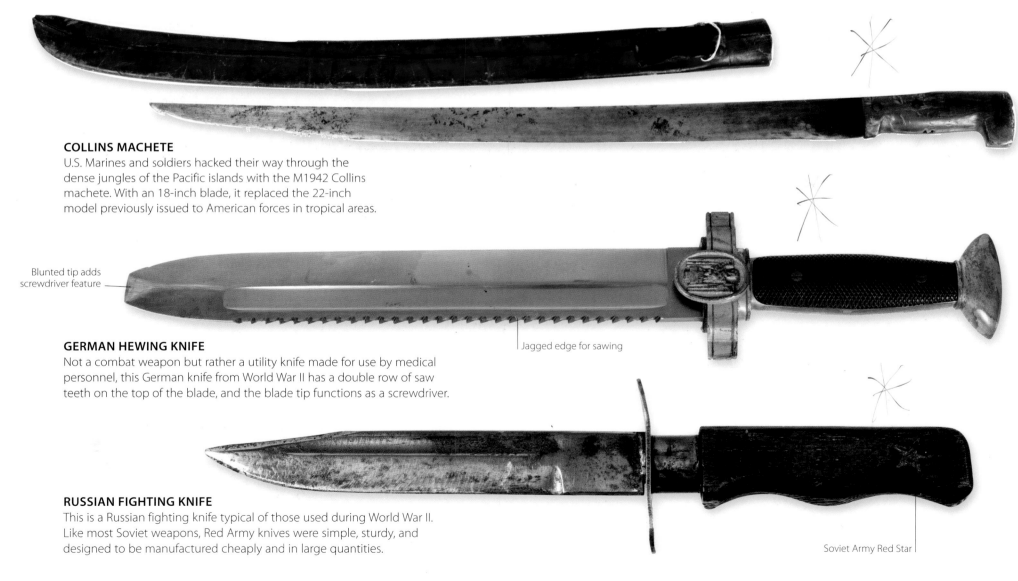

COLLINS MACHETE
U.S. Marines and soldiers hacked their way through the dense jungles of the Pacific islands with the M1942 Collins machete. With an 18-inch blade, it replaced the 22-inch model previously issued to American forces in tropical areas.

Blunted tip adds screwdriver feature

GERMAN HEWING KNIFE
Not a combat weapon but rather a utility knife made for use by medical personnel, this German knife from World War II has a double row of saw teeth on the top of the blade, and the blade tip functions as a screwdriver.

Jagged edge for sawing

RUSSIAN FIGHTING KNIFE
This is a Russian fighting knife typical of those used during World War II. Like most Soviet weapons, Red Army knives were simple, sturdy, and designed to be manufactured cheaply and in large quantities.

Soviet Army Red Star

W. E. FAIRBAIRN AND ERIC SYKES

While serving as a police officer in Shanghai, China, in the early 1900s, William Ewart Fairbairn became one of the first Westerners to achieve proficiency in Asian martial arts. (Ironically, in light of later events, he initially trained with a Japanese instructor.) Fairbairn eventually rose to command the Shanghai Municipal Police, and together with his colleague Eric Sykes, began training his officers in hybrid hand-to-hand fighting techniques they named the "Defendu System." With the coming of World War II, Sykes and Fairbairn were recalled to Britain, where they began teaching their system to the newly formed Commandos. During this time, the duo designed the famous dagger-style knife that bears their names. With the U.S. entry into the war, Fairbairn left for America to train the OSS; Sykes stayed on to work with SOE and SIS (Secret Intelligence Service).

Who Dares Wins
The motto of the British Special Air Services, the phrase has been adopted by other elite units, including those in France and Australia.

The army commandos 1940–45

United we conquer

SYKES-FAIRBAIRN

One of the most famous knives of World War II, the Sykes-Fairbairn Commando Knife was widely used by U.S. and British special forces. Developed by two experts in hand-to-hand combat (see above) it was a lightweight, stainless-steel weapon. The slender 7½-inch blade was designed especially to slip between the ribs of an opponent.

"KA-BAR WAS THERE."

—advertising slogan of the Union Cutlery Company's branded USMC knife

KA-BAR

Officially the "USN Fighting Knife, Mark 2" but universally known as the Ka-Bar after an advertising slogan of its manufacturer, the Union Cutlery Co., the Ka-Bar was the official fighting knife of the U.S. Marine Corps in World War II. Its famously tough construction made it an excellent utility knife as well as a fighting weapon.

Shovel with pick attachment

ENTRENCHING TOOL BAYONET

Issued to British troops in World War II, this tool enabled soldiers to entrench themselves speedily into a self-made foxhole using the sturdy spade and pick. The weapon was designed to be transportable in an infantry soldier's standard backpack.

Spike bayonet

EDGED WEAPONS OF WORLD WAR II CONTINUED . . .

MAUSER BAYONET
This Belgian Mauser bayonet dates from 1949. The steel flash guard on the top of the hilt is clearly visible in this inset picture.

Elegant slightly curved blade

BAYONET DAGGER AND SHEATH
This bayonet dagger was made in France for Nazi troops in 1944, during the time that Germany occupied France. It has a wooden handle and a 10-inch blade with a flat spine tapering into a double-edged tip. A blood groove is carved just below the spine. The smooth metal scabbard has a small ball at its tip—a ball finial—to protect it from denting as a result of constant knocking.

GERMAN MAUSER BAYONET
This bayonet was made by Simpson & Co. Suhl in Germany in the late nineteenth or early twentieth century. However, its accompanying sheath is an E.u.F. Hörster and dates from the 1940s.

Hook to attach bayonet to leather belt holster

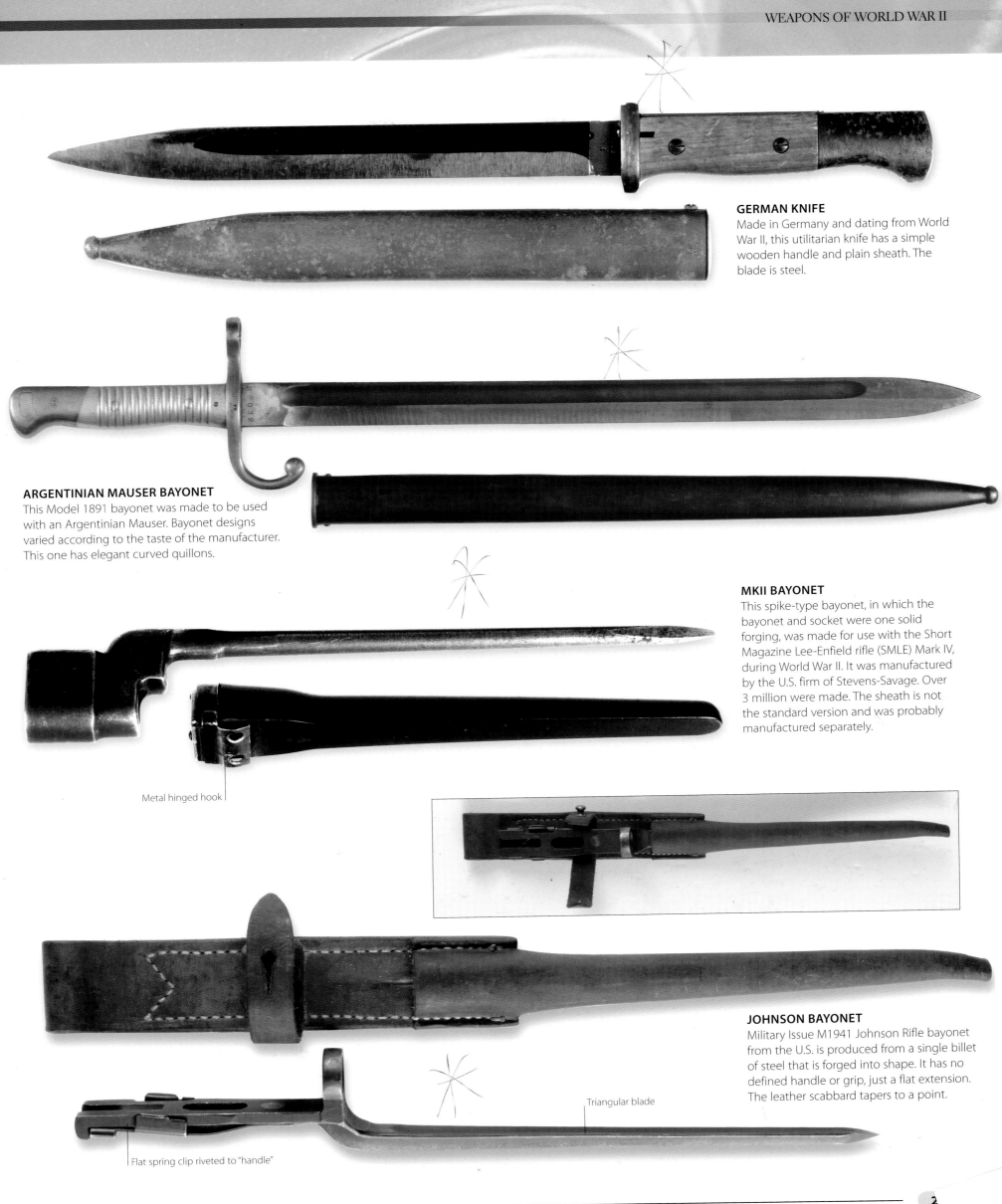

GERMAN KNIFE
Made in Germany and dating from World War II, this utilitarian knife has a simple wooden handle and plain sheath. The blade is steel.

ARGENTINIAN MAUSER BAYONET
This Model 1891 bayonet was made to be used with an Argentinian Mauser. Bayonet designs varied according to the taste of the manufacturer. This one has elegant curved quillons.

MKII BAYONET
This spike-type bayonet, in which the bayonet and socket were one solid forging, was made for use with the Short Magazine Lee-Enfield rifle (SMLE) Mark IV, during World War II. It was manufactured by the U.S. firm of Stevens-Savage. Over 3 million were made. The sheath is not the standard version and was probably manufactured separately.

Metal hinged hook

JOHNSON BAYONET
Military Issue M1941 Johnson Rifle bayonet from the U.S. is produced from a single billet of steel that is forged into shape. It has no defined handle or grip, just a flat extension. The leather scabbard tapers to a point.

Triangular blade

Flat spring clip riveted to "handle"

AXIS PISTOLS OF WORLD WAR II

With little room for improvement in revolver design, the interwar years saw automatics become the standard sidearm in most armies. The Soviet Union adopted the Tokarev, which the great weapons writer Ian Hogg described as a "[Colt] M1911 with a distinctive Russian accent." In Japan, the Nambu series of automatics (named for Colonel Nambu Kirijo, the nation's foremost weapons designer), chambered for 8mm, came into use. The Walther P38 gradually replaced the Luger in the Wehrmacht (German Army) during World War II.

NAMBU M14

The Nambu Type 14 was first produced in 1925, the fourteenth year in the reign of the Emperor Yoshito—a naming convention used for some other Japanese military weapons. This 8mm automatic was the principal Japanese military pistol of World War II, but because Japanese officers were required to personally purchase their sidearms, a variety of pistols saw service.

Enlarged trigger guard

Safety catch

SPANISH PISTOL

This 9mm pistol is a copy of an Astra 600 and was also made in Spain, probably during World War II or soon afterward. "Astra" is the trademark of the Spanish firearms company Astra-Unceta y Cia. The 600 was made in Spain for the Germans during World War II.

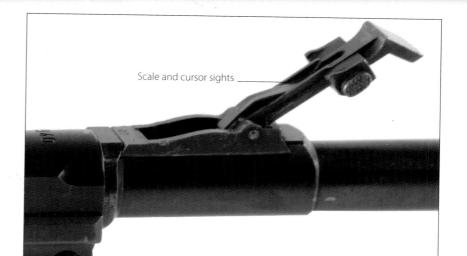

Raised sights

Scale and cursor sights

ARTILLERY LUGER

The German Artillery Luger was developed from 1900 as a weapon for self-defense. Some later versions had very long barrels. This one from the 1930s has a barrel 12 inches long.

THE HOUSE OF BERETTA

In 1526 the Venetian Republic contracted with gunsmith Bartolomeo Beretta of Gardone for a quantity of arquebuses. That deal was the start of a gunmaking dynasty that has endured for nearly half a millennium; the modern firm of Fabbrica d'Armi Pietro Beretta is still largely owned and run by Bartolmeo's descendants. The firm's reputation for high quality and excellence in design has made it one of the world's foremost manufacturers of weapons for military, police, and sporting use. While it produces every kind of gun from shotguns to assault rifles, Beretta's pistols are held in especially high regard. This respect was dramatically underscored by the U.S. Army's 1985 adoption of the 9mm Beretta M92SB/92F as its standard sidearm, replacing the venerable Colt .45 M1911.

BERETTA M1934 AUTO

The blowback-operated 9mm Beretta M1934 was Italy's standard sidearm in its wars in Africa in the 1930s and in World War II. The M1934 was mainly army-issue; a 7.65mm version, the M1935, was used principally by the Italian navy and air force.

Magazine release

NAMBU M94

Many experts consider this Japanese automatic to be the worst military pistol of modern times. The poorly designed cocking mechanism allowed the weapon to fire accidentally if any pressure was put on it.

Single-action trigger with concealed hammer

Magazine release button

Long barrel

Jointed arm in closed position

LUGER WITH DRUM MAGAZINE

Although the Walther P38 largely replaced the Luger as the standard German service pistol, the latter still saw much service in World War II. This particular pistol—fitted with a 32-round drum magazine—was taken from a German general following the Allied capture of the North African city of Tunis in May 1943. The so-called "snail drum" magazine was never popular because it had a tendency to jam.

Trommel-Magazine 08

AXIS PISTOLS OF WORLD WAR II CONTINUED . . .

Slide

Trigger guard

WALTHER P-38 PISTOL

This semiautomatic German military and police sidearm is of a type used from 1938 up until the reunification of Germany in the 1980s. It was made in February 1944 at the Spreewerke plant.

Magazine release

WALTHER P38

A military adaptation of the PP (Polizei Pistole, or Police Pistol) series of pistols developed by Carl Walther Waffenfabrik in the 1920s, the 9mm P38 was adopted by the German Wehrmacht in the 1930s to

replace the more expensive and complicated Luger. The P38's action was designed so that as long as the safety was on, it could be carried while cocked and ready to fire when the safety was disengaged—a highly desirable feature in a service pistol.

Detachable box magazine

Muzzle is hinged

Slide is removable

CZECH CZ VZ38 PISTOL

Manufactured in 1939 by Ceska Zbrojovka in Strakonice, Czechoslovakia, this is a semiautomatic, double-action pistol with an eight-round feed mechanism. The original was designed as a 6.35mm, but it was somewhat unsuccessfully altered to take the 9mm Short round, which made it large and unwieldy.

Muzzle hinge

Manual safety lever

JAPANESE TYPE 26 REVOLVER

Adopted by the Imperial Japanese Army in the twenty-sixth year of the reign of the Meiki emperor (1893), this 9mm, six-shot revolver borrowed many elements of Western design and bears similarities to both Smith & Wesson and Webley revolvers. It remained in service into World War II, when it was issued to reserve and home defense units.

CZ27 AUTO

A refinement of a German design, the Ceska Zbrojovoka Model 1927 (CZ27) was a straight blowback-operated 9mm with a 9-round magazine. Following its occupation of Czechoslovakia, Germany diverted the production of that nation's excellent arms industry, including the Ceska Zbrojovoka plant at Strakonice, for its own use.

ALLIED PISTOLS OF WORLD WAR II

Throughout World War II, U.S. forces continued to carry the Colt M1911—and would do so for four decades after the war's end. Having used Webley revolvers during World War I, the British continued to use them in World War II, although quantities of the Browning High Power 9mm automatic were issued to British forces.

Magazine release

Manual safety lever

SWEDISH M40 PISTOL

When the outbreak of World War II led Germany to suspend export of the Walther HP pistol, which neutral Sweden had just adopted as its service pistol, the Swedish government licensed a 1935 design from Finnish designer Almo Lahti. The 9mm M40, as it was known in Swedish service, looked like a Luger but used a firing system closer to that of a Bergmann-Bayard, with an added kick to ensure proper action movement in cold temperatures.

TOKAREV TT-33

Developed by Feodor Tokarev, a former Czarist officer turned Soviet gun designer, the Tokarev pistol was introduced in the late 1920s and adopted as the standard Red Army sidearm a few years later. Known as the TT (from "Tula-Tokarev," Tula being one of the principal Soviet arsenals), the pistol's firing system was essentially a copy of the one used in John Browning's Colt M1911 .45, chambered for the 7.62 round. The original model, the TT30, was later replaced by the TT-33.

ALLIED PISTOLS OF WORLD WAR II continued . . .

ENFIELD NO. 2 MARK 1* REVOLVER

This revolver is based on the No. 2 Mark 1 but with the hammer spur and single-action lockwork removed to enable it to be used in small spaces, such as inside a tank. It was made between 1938–57 and has a .38-caliber, six-shot cylinder.

Spurless hammer

ENFIELD NO. 2 MARK 1* REVOLVER

This version of the Mark 1* revolver has a barrel measuring only 1¾ inches. It only operates as a double-action gun and is only suitable for close-range firing. It is a very limited edition, commando model.

Spurless hammer

ENFIELD NO. 2 MKII REVOLVER

This spurless, .38-caliber, double-action six-shot revolver is intended for close combat. It is very similar to the Mark 1* and only varies in that its grip is plastic rather than wood to make it easier to grasp when firing rapidly.

Plastic grip

Removable side plate

CZECH CZ VZ45 PISTOL

Produced between 1948 and 1952, in the postwar communist Czechoslovak Republic, this is a modernized version of the VZ36–a personal protection pistol. The intention of the update was to make manufacturing the pistol more straightforward and to improve the trigger action.

WEBLEY 7.65 AUTO
While Webley & Scott was best known for revolvers, it produced several fine automatics over the years. This 7.65mm model was one of fifty especially made for the City of London Police (who traditionally do not carry firearms) for use in case of invasion during the dark days of 1939–41, when Britain fought Nazi Germany virtually alone.

WEBLEY MARK VI
This variant of the Webley Mark VI (introduced in 1916) is chambered for the .22 round and fitted with a special cylinder. It was used to train British troops in pistol shooting during World War II. (The use of the .22 cartridge allowed firing on relatively compact shooting ranges.)

WEBLEY MARK IV
Introduced in 1899, the Webley Mark IV revolver remained popular with British forces—especially the aircrew of the Royal Air Force—during World War II. Originally .455-caliber, World War II–era Mark IV's were more commonly of .38 caliber. The pistol here is shown in subdued "wartime" finish.

"THERE WAS NEVER A GOOD WAR, OR A BAD PEACE."

—Benjamin Franklin

WORLD WAR II RIFLES

When World War II broke out only one nation, the U.S., had already adopted a semiautomatic rifle—the M1 Garand (see sidebar)—as its standard infantry arm. The tempo of rifle design quickened, however, when the militaries of other nations realized that in modern warfare, a high rate of fire at short range was often more important than long-range accuracy.

In 1942, Germany developed the 7.92mm Fallschirmgewehr (Paratroop rifle) for its airborne forces. This could fire in both single-shot and fully automatic modes. Two years later came the MP44. This was another 7.92 selective-fire weapon, but it was intended to combine the functions of the rifle, submachine gun, and light machine gun. A truly revolutionary piece of technology, the MP44's alternate designation, Sturmgewehr, would provide the name for an entirely new class of weapon—the assault rifle.

Bayonet extended

RUSSIAN CARBINE M1944
The Mosin-Nagant Carbine M944, introduced toward the end of World War II, was the final iteration of the Mosin-Nagant series. Its most distinctive feature was an integral bayonet that folded into the stock.

Rear sight

JAPANESE PARATROOP RIFLE
Because the standard 7.7mm Arisaka rifle was too long for use in airborne operations, the Japanese military developed a special version for paratroops that could be broken down into two pieces for the jump and then reassembled on landing. However, relatively few of these rifles saw service.

Rotating bolt

JAPANESE TYPE 38
Introduced in 1905—the thirty-eighth year of the Emperor Meiji's reign, and thus named the Type 38—this 6.5 bolt-action rifle was the standard Japanese service rifle until the introduction of the Type 99 thirty-four years later. It was also produced in a carbine version.

Bolt handle

Integral wire monopod

JAPANESE TYPE 99 RIFLE
Firing a more powerful round (7.7mm) than the earlier 6.5 Type 38 Arisaka rifle, the Japanese Type 99 rifle first entered service in 1939. The Type 99's most distinctive features are an integral wire monopod and a set of rear sights that (very optimistically) were intended for use against aircraft.

JOHN C. GARAND

Born in Quebec in 1888, John Cantius Garand (pictured at left) moved to New England with his family as a child. Here he worked in textile mills and machine shops. His passion was for weapons design, however, and during World War I he submitted a design for a light machine gun to the U.S. Army. It was adopted, but put into production too late to see service. His obvious talents led to a position as an engineer with the U.S. government arsenal at Springfield, Massachusetts.

There, in the early 1930s, he developed a gas-operated, 8-shot, .30 semiautomatic rifle that beat competitors to win adoption by the U.S. Army in 1936. (The Marine Corps also adopted the rifle, but shortages led the marines to fight their first battles of World War II with bolt-action M1903 Springfields.) The M1 Garand gave U.S. forces a big advantage in firepower during that conflict; General George S. Patton described the rifle as "the greatest battle implement ever devised."

The M1 Garand remained the standard U.S. infantry weapon through the Korean War (1950–53); the rifle that replaced it in the mid–1950s, the M14, was essentially a selective-fire version of the M1. As a government employee, Garand earned no royalties on his design, although almost 6 million were eventually produced. A resolution to grant Garand a special bonus of $100,000 failed to pass Congress. He died in Massachusetts in 1974.

M1 GARAND

Despite its undoubted success on the battlefield, the M1 Garand was not without its drawbacks. The rifle's magazine fed only from an eight-round stripper clip, so in combat it could not be topped off by inserting individual rounds into the magazine. And when the clip was emptied, it was ejected upward with a distinctive "clang!" sound that could betray the firer's location to the enemy.

"YOU CANNOT INVADE THE MAINLAND UNITED STATES. THERE WOULD BE A RIFLE BEHIND EACH BLADE OF GRASS."

Japanese Admiral Isoroku Yamamoto

Folding stock

Webbing sling

M1 CARBINE

In the run-up to World War II, the U.S. decided to develop an "intermediate" weapon for use by officers and NCOs, armored crews, truck drivers, and support personnel—one that would be more compact than the M1 Garand rifle but more effective in combat than the M1911 pistol. The result was the M1 carbine, a lightweight (5½-pound), semiautomatic weapon firing a special .30 cartridge. The M1 was followed by the M2, which was capable of full-auto as well as semiauto fire, and a folding-stock version of the M1 (the M1A1, shown here) was developed for airborne troops. Although more than 6 million such carbines were issued before production ceased in the 1950s, the combat verdict was mixed; the weapon proved handy in street fighting in Europe and in jungle fighting in the Pacific, but many thought that it was too delicate and that the pistol-strength .30 carbine cartridge was too weak.

RIFLES OF WORLD WAR II CONTINUED . . .

Magazine of
steel-cored bullets

BOYS MARK I ANTI-TANK RIFLE
Named for Captain Boys, who was one of its designers, this British rifle was introduced in 1937. It fired a .55-caliber, steel-cored bullet at a speed of 3,250 feet per second and was capable of piercing ¾ inch of tank armor from 250 feet away. It has a five-round detachable box magazine. It was used in France, Norway, and the Far East until it was replaced by the PIAT.

BREDA PG AUTOMATIC RIFLE
The Breda is a 7mm gas-operated automatic rifle with a 40-round detachable magazine. It has the distinction of being the first automatic rifle to have a selector, enabling the operator to choose to fire a burst of four rounds, as well as single shots or longer bursts. Less than 300 of these rifles made it into production and 200 of them went to Costa Rica. The one shown here was made in Rome in 1935.

Detachable magazine

PHILIPPINE HUCK GUN
Used extensively by Philippine guerrillas during World War II, this gun is fired by pulling the barrel back against the firing pin. It was made by Richardson Industries Inc., Connecticut.

Folding sight

MANNLICHER-CARCANO CARBINE/GRENADE LAUNCHER
A true rarity from World War II, this weapon was a combination 6-shot carbine and grenade launcher. While most infantry rifles of World War I and World War II could fire grenades from a cup fitted into the barrel, this gun had a permanently attached grenade launcher on its right side.

Grenade launcher

MORTARS OF WORLD WAR II

Sometimes called "the infantryman's artillery," compact, mobile mortars were first developed during World War I to give supporting fire to riflemen in both offense and defense operations, and they remain in service in many armies today.

Typically produced in 60mm, 80mm, and 120mm versions, the mortar is just a tube that delivers plunging fire by launching a grenadelike projectile with a propelling charge in its base.

Lever trigger

MODEL 35 BRIXIA MORTAR
This Italian mortar has a pad for sitting on and protecting the soldier's back when it is being carried. It launched a tiny 2½-ounce explosive less than 600 yards and was far too complex, so it was not much used.

AIRBORNE MORTAR
This British 2-inch Mark 8 Mortar has a 14-inch barrel and a small baseplate for use by airborne troops. Based on a Spanish 5 centimeter model, it was put into production in 1938.

RIFLE GRENADES
A selection of rifle grenades that would be fired from a launcher attached to a rifle.

Small baseplate

MORTARS OF WORLD WAR II CONTINUED . . .

Explosive in container

Standard "pineapple" casing

Bright red casing

GRENADES
This selection of grenades includes a Mills bomb style grenade (far left), a Breda model 39 (left), and a storm trooper's stick grenade (above).

FRENCH MODEL 37 MORTAR
Used by French infantry, this model 37 has the usual sights, baseplate, and front bipod. It fires 50mm mortars.

"KNEE MORTAR"
This is a Japanese model 89 grenade launcher, which got its nickname due its unfortunate habit of shattering the thighbones of unwary users. It fires a 50mm shell or a type 91 hand grenade and has a rifled barrel.

BRITISH PIAT

Standing for projector, infantry, antitank, this weapon when into production in 1942. An internal spring drove a spigot into the projectile, launching it and recocking the mortar. It was an effective weapon: A British soldier was awarded the Victoria Cross after using it to stop two German Tiger tanks in Italy.

GRANATWERFER 36 MORTAR

This mortar used a trigger to fire the 50mm round, rather than relying on drop fire. It was widely used during the early years of the war and became the standard equipment of every Nazi rifle platoon, until superseded by a larger mortar.

FINNISH MORTAR

This is a small hand-held 47mm mortar used by the Finns against the invading Soviet forces in 1939–40. It would have had a strap for slinging it over a soldier's back.

Ceremonial Weapons of WWI & WWII

By the turn of the twentieth century, the sword had ceased to have any real usefulness on the battlefield (in the Western world at least) and was increasingly relegated to a ceremonial role, remaining—as it had for many centuries—a symbol of the officer's authority. Other purely ceremonial weapons that endured into the twentieth century include the officer's swagger stick and the field marshal's baton. Another custom that endured into the era of the World Wars was the presentation of ceremonial weapons—usually richly decorated swords or pistols—to honor victorious commanders. In the buildup to World War II until 1945, all Japanese officers were required to wear a sword. However due to high demand, the swords were not made by traditional swordsmiths.

Weapons of WWI

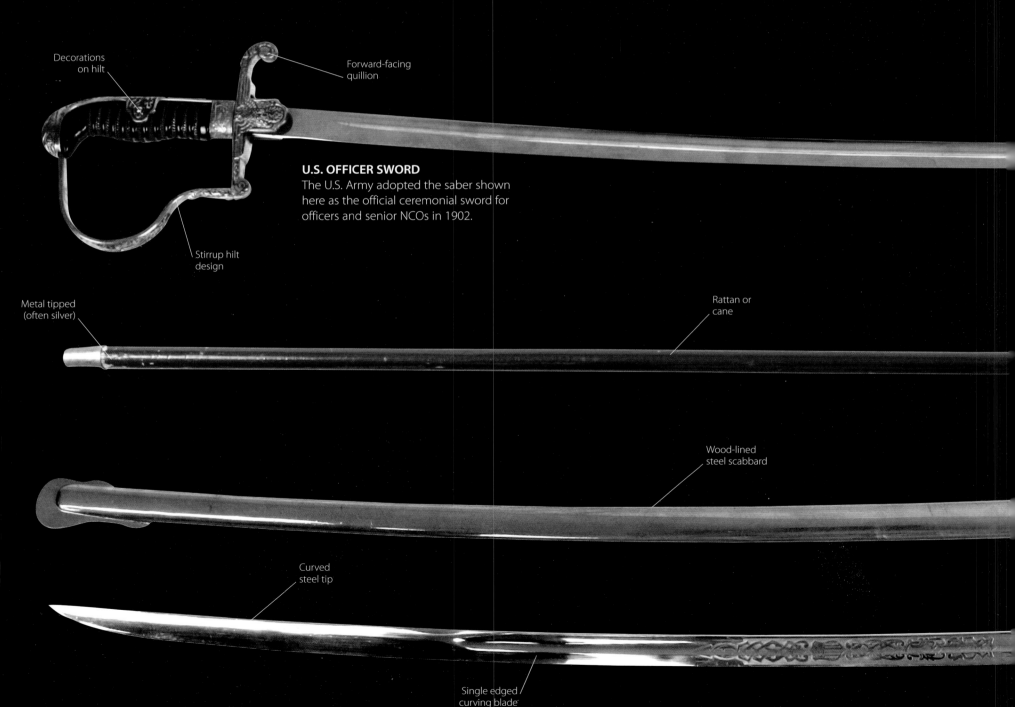

Decorations on hilt

Forward-facing quillion

U.S. OFFICER SWORD
The U.S. Army adopted the saber shown here as the official ceremonial sword for officers and senior NCOs in 1902.

Stirrup hilt design

Metal tipped (often silver)

Rattan or cane

Wood-lined steel scabbard

Curved steel tip

Single edged curving blade

TOTALITARIAN SYMBOLS

Both Fascist dictator Benito Mussolini, who seized power in Italy in 1922, and Adolph Hitler, head of the Nazi Party that gained control of Germany in 1933, had an intuitive understanding of popular psychology and the uses of propaganda. Along with mass rallies, rousing films, and other propaganda elements, both Fascist Italy and Nazi Germany used the symbolism of weaponry as a tool to cultivate fervent militaristic spirit in their citizens and to bind them more closely to an all-powerful state.

One such practice was the widespread distribution of elaborate ceremonial blades, especially daggers. In Nazi Germany, each branch of the military, paramilitary groups, party organizations like the Hitlerjugend (Hitler Youth), and even civilian organizations like police and firefighting formations had its own unique knives or daggers to be worn with dress uniform. Often these weapons were engraved with "patriotic" mottos—such as the Hitler Youth knives, which bore the inscription Blut und Ehre ("Blood and Honor").

While the alliance that eventually defeated Italy and Germany—the Soviet Union, the U.S., and Great Britain—did not fetishize the blade, their leaders also, on occasion, recognized its role as a symbol of courage and martial prowess. During the Teheran Conference in November 1943, for example, British Prime Minister Winston Churchill presented Soviet leader Josef Stalin with a magnificent custom-made presentation sword—the "Sword of Stalingrad"—on behalf of King George VI and the British people in commemoration of the Soviet victory in that epic battle.

GERMAN POLICE BAYONET
The hilt of this German Police bayonet is in the form of an Eagle, symbol of the Weimar Republic, Germany's government from the end of World War I until the establishment of the Third Reich in 1933.

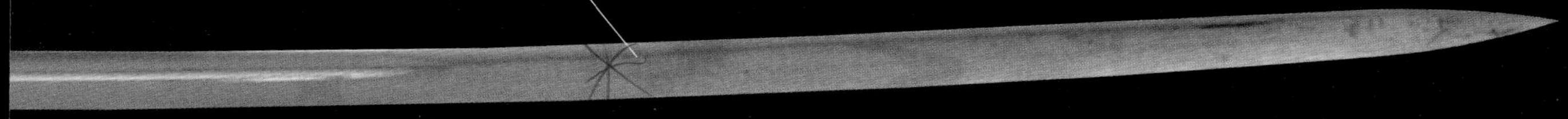

Engraved steel pommel

Curved quillion

Steel-edged blade with wide single fuller

Finely curved blade

SWAGGER STICK
Officers and sometimes NCOs of various armies (and the U.S. Marine Corps) often carried swagger sticks like the one shown here. Typically about 2 feet or less in length, they were short canes, often covered in leather and metal-tipped. The swagger stick's origin is obscure; they may have derived from the "pacing sticks" used to space out soldiers in marching ranks—or to mete out corporal punishment. By the twentieth century the item became merely a symbol of rank.

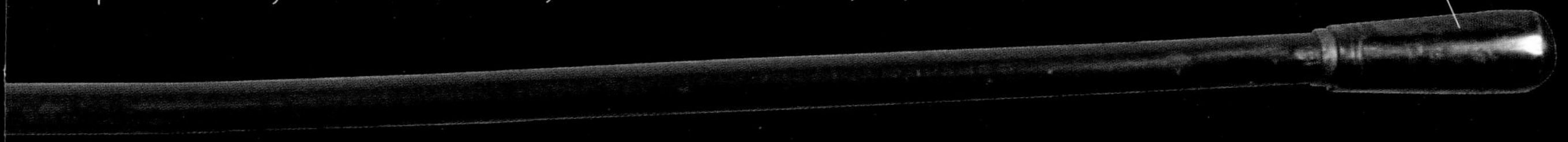

Rubber cover

GERMAN ARMY OFFICER'S SWORD
With a single-edged 32¼-inch blade, the Heer Mannschaftsabel (officer's sword) was the standard dress sword of the German Army from around the turn of the twentieth century through World War II. Most were manufactured by firms in the Westphalian city of Solingen, a city renowned for its fine-edged weapons since the late fourteenth century.

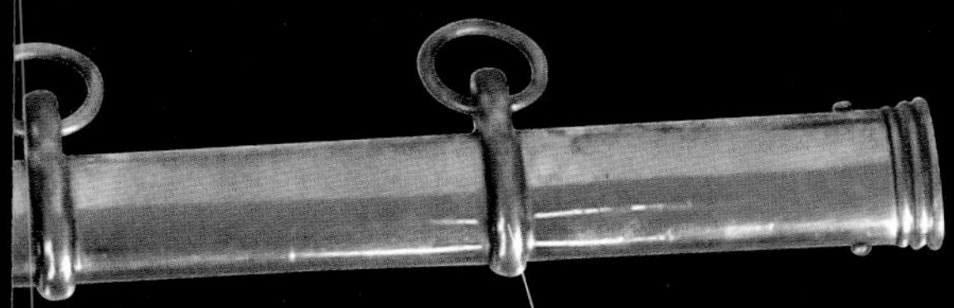

Very finely pointed tip

Rings for securing to uniform

Leather grip

Ceremonial tassle or embroidered wrist strap

Hilt has D-shape ring with two branchea

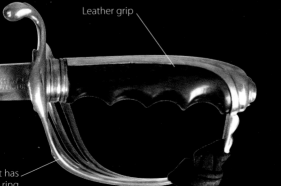

WEAPONS OF WWII

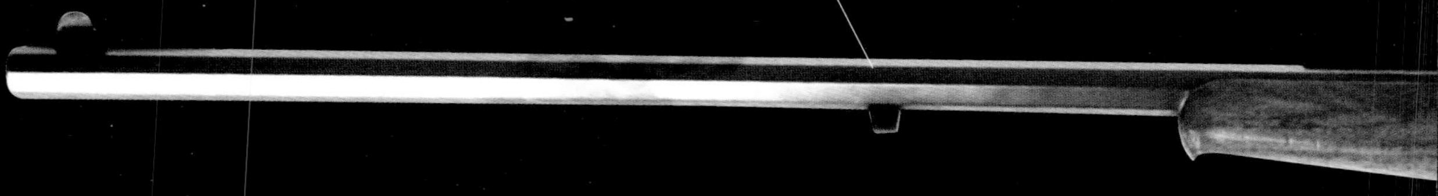

Heavy barrel to reduce swaying motion

LUFTWAFFE SWORD
Made in Solingen, this Luftwaffe officer's dress sword bears the Nazi swastika on both its pommel and the base of its hilt. It is shown here with its scabbard.

Swastika engraved on blade

LUFTWAFFE/ARMY DAGGERS
These daggers were worn by officers of the Luftwaffe [above, the 1937 Model] and Wehrmacht [right]. Some naval daggers had a pommel decorated with both the eagle of Imperial Germany and the Nazi swastika.

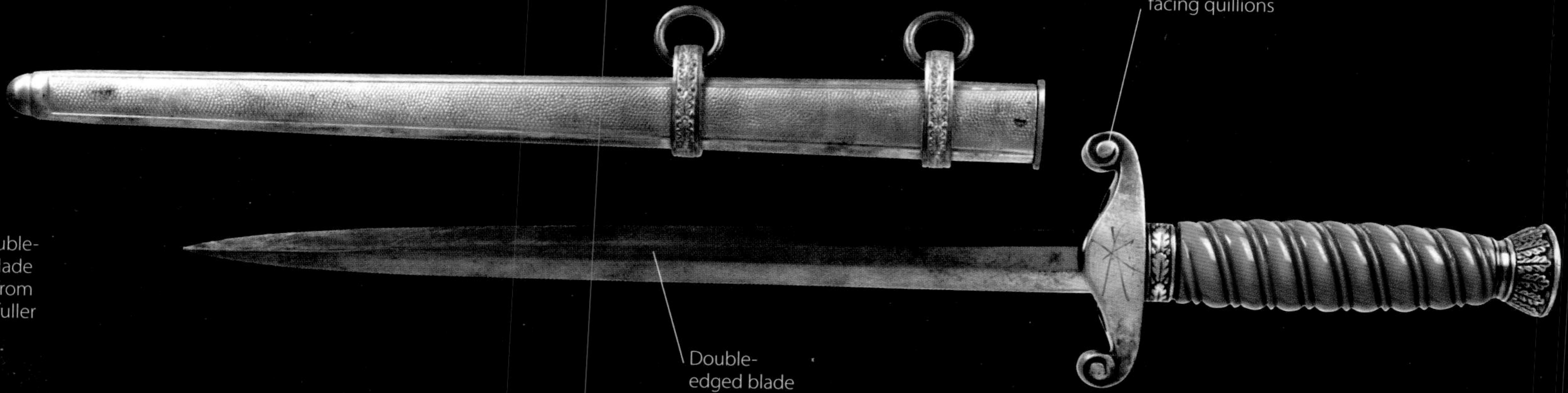

Scrolling forward-facing quillions

Steel double-edged blade leading from narrow fuller

Double-edged blade

ITALIAN FASCIST PARTY KNIFE
Only members of Italy's Fascist Party, in power from 1922 until the overthrow of dictator Benito Mussolini during World War II, possessed this blade. It is shown with its steel scabbard.

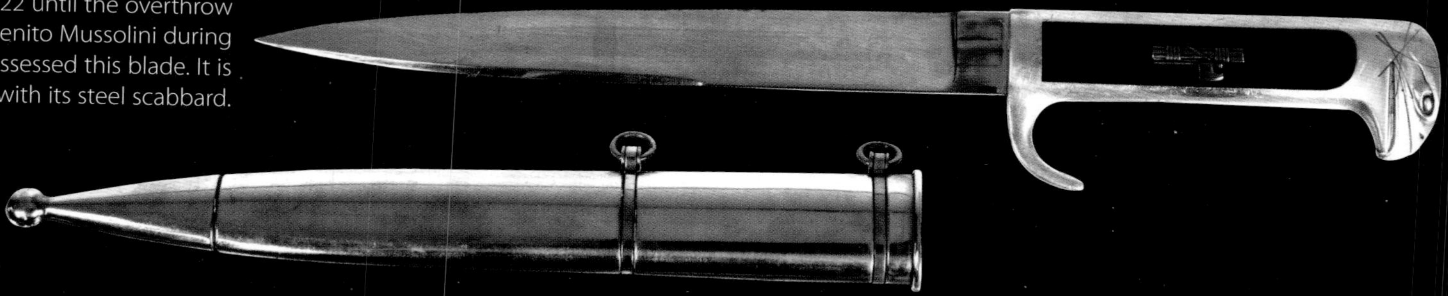

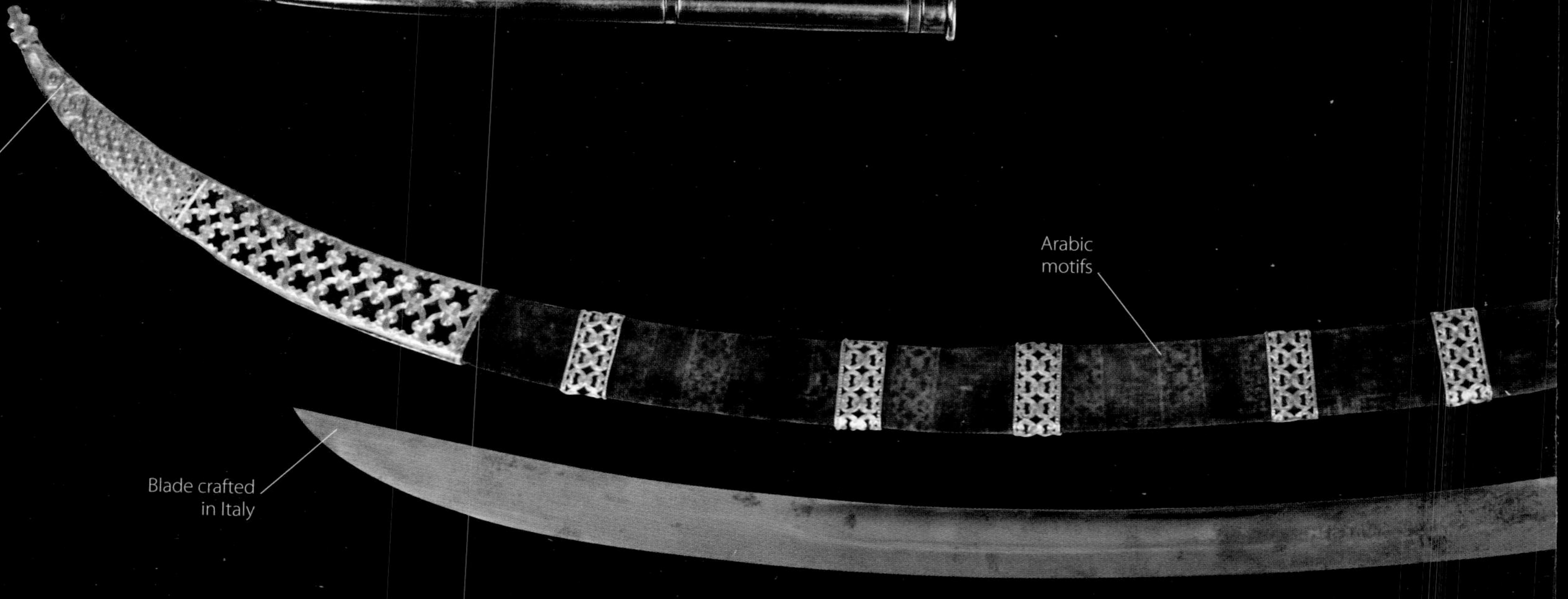

Intricate goldwork

Arabic motifs

Blade crafted in Italy

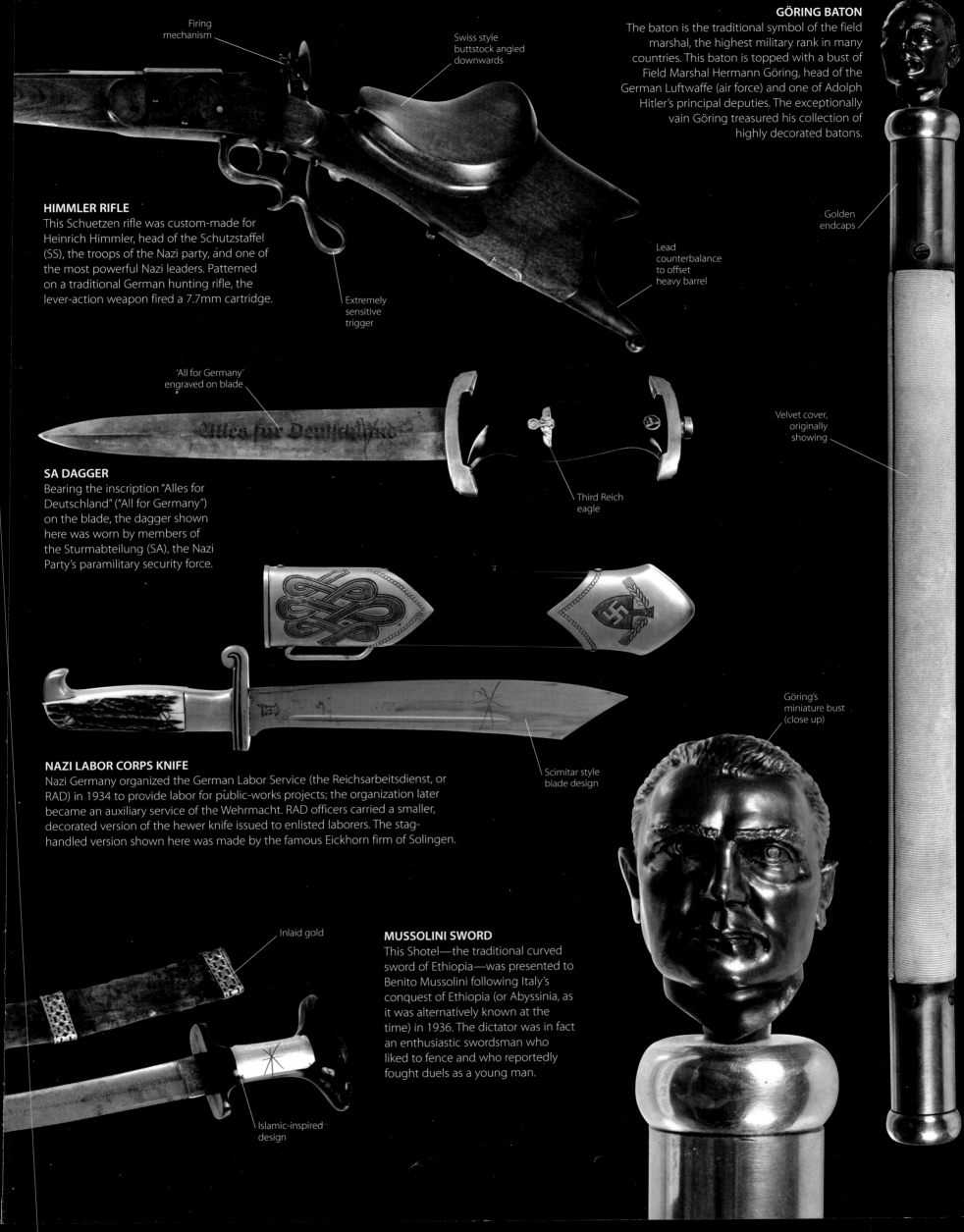

HIMMLER RIFLE

This Schuetzen rifle was custom-made for Heinrich Himmler, head of the Schutzstaffel (SS), the troops of the Nazi party, and one of the most powerful Nazi leaders. Patterned on a traditional German hunting rifle, the lever-action weapon fired a 7.7mm cartridge.

Firing mechanism

Swiss style buttstock angled downwards

Extremely sensitive trigger

Lead counterbalance to offset heavy barrel

GÖRING BATON

The baton is the traditional symbol of the field marshal, the highest military rank in many countries. This baton is topped with a bust of Field Marshal Hermann Göring, head of the German Luftwaffe (air force) and one of Adolph Hitler's principal deputies. The exceptionally vain Göring treasured his collection of highly decorated batons.

Golden endcaps

Velvet cover, originally showing

Göring's miniature bust (close up)

'All for Germany' engraved on blade

SA DAGGER

Bearing the inscription "Alles for Deutschland" ("All for Germany") on the blade, the dagger shown here was worn by members of the Sturmabteilung (SA), the Nazi Party's paramilitary security force.

Third Reich eagle

NAZI LABOR CORPS KNIFE

Nazi Germany organized the German Labor Service (the Reichsarbeitsdienst, or RAD) in 1934 to provide labor for public-works projects; the organization later became an auxiliary service of the Wehrmacht. RAD officers carried a smaller, decorated version of the hewer knife issued to enlisted laborers. The stag-handled version shown here was made by the famous Eickhorn firm of Solingen.

Scimitar style blade design

Inlaid gold

MUSSOLINI SWORD

This Shotel—the traditional curved sword of Ethiopia—was presented to Benito Mussolini following Italy's conquest of Ethiopia (or Abyssinia, as it was alternatively known at the time) in 1936. The dictator was in fact an enthusiastic swordsman who liked to fence and who reportedly fought duels as a young man.

Islamic-inspired design

MACHINE GUNS OF WORLD WAR II

Not only were machine guns used by infantry during World War I, they were also developed to be fitted to aircraft (and used against them from the ground), armored cars, and tanks. In the interwar years, weapons designers developed even more powerful machine guns, like John Browning's .50 M2, which fired a cartridge the size of an old-fashioned Coca-Cola bottle. Even before World War I had ended,

however, several nations sought to package the punch of the machine gun in a weapon that could be carried by an individual infantryman. By World War II, this policy had led to the development of the British Bren gun and the U.S. BAR (Browning Automatic Rifle). These weapons were typically magazine-fed. The German Wehrmacht, however, made a belt-fed light machine gun, the 7.92mm MG42. This

formed the foundation of Germany's infantry squad in World War II. Following the war, the concept of the "squad automatic weapon" evolved into guns like the U.S. military's Vietnam-era M60 and the M249, the latter based on a Belgian design.

"Gramophone"-shaped drum led to its nickname of "record player"

SOVIET DEGTYAREV DP MODEL 1928
This light machine gun was adopted by the Soviet Army in 1926 and became one of their most important weapons in World War II. Manufactured at Tula Arsenal in the USSR, it features a 42-round detachable drum and takes 7.62-caliber cartridges.

BROWNING M1919
During World War I, John Browning designed this .30 machine gun for aircraft use; designated the M1919, it arrived too late to see World War I service. However, the weapon was used by the U.S. Army Air Corps (later the U.S. Army Air Forces) into the early days of World War II, when it was largely replaced by the formidable .50 M2.

250-round belt feed

VICKERS-BERTHIER MARK 3
The Vickers-Berthier was a light machine gun, designed by the Frenchman Adolphe Berthier in Britain and licensed by Vickers. The first version was built in 1928, with improvements made in 1929 and 1931. The Mark 3—a slightly heavier weapon—was built specifically for the Indian Army in 1933.

The length of the barrel is just under 24 inches

RPD MACHINE GUN

The Ruchnoy Puleyot Degtyaryova (Degtyaryova's hand-held machine gun) was developed from 1943 to replace the DP (opposite). A 7.62mm light machine gun, it became the standard weapon for the Vietcong during the Vietnam War and is still widely used in Africa and some Asian nations.

Foregrip

100-round belt stored in a drum

BROWNING AUTOMATIC RIFLE

Another Browning design, the gas-operated, .30 Browning Automatic Rifle (BAR) was introduced in 1918, too late to perform more than limited duty in World War I. However, it remained in U.S. service, with some modifications, through the Korean War (1950–53). In most respects it was an excellent weapon, capable of fully automatic fire and, in the hands of an experienced user, single shots. Disadvantages included its weight (19½ pounds) and its magazine capacity of only 20 rounds—low for a full-auto weapon.

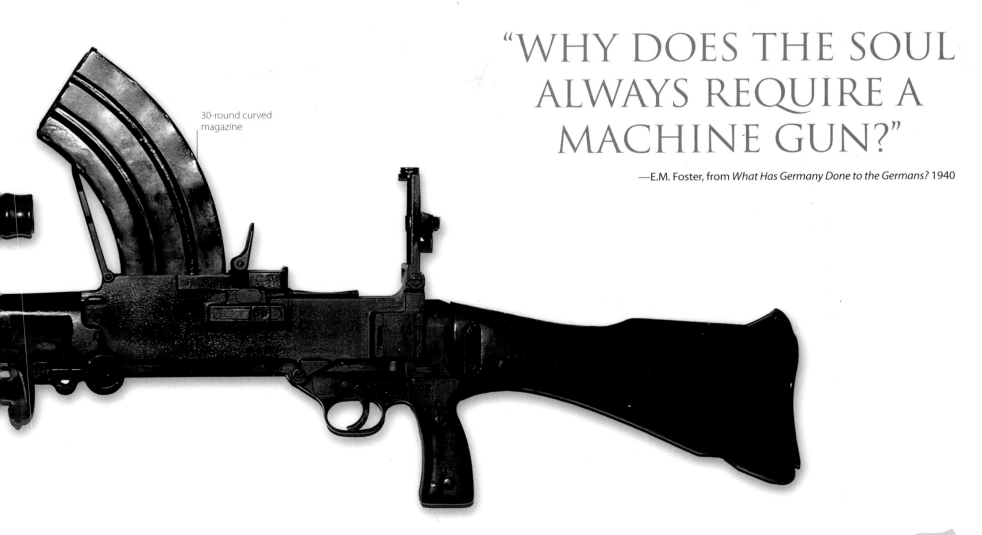

30-round curved magazine

"WHY DOES THE SOUL ALWAYS REQUIRE A MACHINE GUN?"

—E.M. Foster, from *What Has Germany Done to the Germans?* 1940

MACHINE GUNS OF WORLD WAR II CONTINUED . . .

JAPANESE AIRCRAFT CANNON
While the British Royal Air Force (RAF) and the U.S. Army Air Forces (USAAF) armed their fighters and bombers mostly with machine guns, the air forces of other nations preferred automatic cannons, usually 20mm weapons firing explosive shells rather than bullets. Such as this 20mm Japanese aircraft cannon.

The barrel is 51 inches long

GERMAN SOLOTHURN S18-1000
This 20mm anti-tank gun was produced in Switzerland by the German-owned Rheinmetall Company. It was considered for adoption by the U.S. Army, but was eventually used by Italy, Hungary, Finland, and Germany during World War II.

Quick change barrel

Integrated cooling fins

JAPANESE TYPE 96 LIGHT MACHINE GUN
Designed by Japanese General Nambu, this was based on the Hotchkiss used in World War I, and intended to replace the Japanese Type 11 machine gun. However, production proved slow and it never completely lived up to expectations. It has a 30-round detachable box magazine of 6.5mm cartridges.

Barrel shroud

GERMAN MG42
One of World War II's most effective weapons, the 7.92mm, belt-fed German MG34 and its wartime replacement, the MG42, were distinguished by their versatility. Equipped with a bipod, they went into action in an infantry support role. Tripod-mounted, they proved an excellent defensive weapon; and they could be fitted on tanks and other vehicles as well. The MG series' high rate of fire—up to 1,200 rounds per minute—and their distinctive sound led Allied troops to nickname the weapon "Hitler's Zipper."

SUBMACHINE GUNS OF WORLD WAR II

As World War I ground to a bloody stalemate on the Western Front, soldiers of the warring nations began to acknowledge the many inadequacies of the standard infantry rifle—its length, weight, and above all its relatively slow rate of fire. As a result—and inspired by the success of the machine gun—weapons designers developed the submachine gun. This infantryman's firearm sacrificed the rifle's long-range accuracy in favor of a smaller weapon that could be fired from the hip or shoulder, and which could unleash a rapid volume of fire in close combat. Refined in the interwar years, the submachine gun

figured prominently in World War II, and even today—when the assault rifle has largely subsumed its functions—submachine guns retain a role in antiterrorism and various other specialized operations.

THE SUBMACHINE GUN'S ORIGINS
The Italian Army introduced a proto-typical submachine gun in 1915, but pride of place in the weapon's development really goes to Germany, which, three years later, adopted the Bergmann MP18/1 designed by Hugo Schmeisser. This was a blowback-operated

weapon that fired a slightly modified version of the 9mm parabellum round used in the Luger pistol. The MP18/1 originally used the 32-round "snail drum" magazine also developed for the Luger, but postwar versions used a side-mounted box magazine. The MP18/1 arrived too late and in too few numbers to change Germany's fortunes on the Western Front. Around the same time the Bergmann was being developed, U.S. Army colonel J.T. Thompson designed the now-legendary gun that bears his name

Bent barrel for shooting around corners

Front sight

Curved magazine

MP44
Officially the MP (Machinenpistole) Model 1944, aka the Sturmgewehr (Storm, or Assault, Rifle) Model 1944, this gun represented the cutting edge of small-arms technology as World War II headed to its bloody close. Gas-operated, the selective-fire weapon used a short (kurtz) version of the standard 7.92 German cartridge, feeding from a detachable 30-round magazine. (Although designated "44," the first models were issued in 1943.) The Soviet AK-47 design,, the world's most popular assault rifle, is a direct descendant. The MP44 shown here was issued with a special curved barrel—useful for shooting around corners in street fighting.

SUBMACHINE GUNS OF WORLD WAR II CONTINUED . . .

Stock folds over the top
of the receiver

Curved magazine

PPS SUBMACHINE GUN
Developed by the Russian weapons designer
Alexei Sudayev, this machine gun and its various
versions were used extensively by Soviet Union
troops during World War II. It was particularly
favored by reconnaissance units and support
service personnel. It has a curved, 35-round box
magazine and a perforated barrel jacket.

Folding stock

Simple tube barrel

STEN
Simple and cheap to manufacture and easy to use, the STEN submachine gun and
its numerous variants were a mainstay of British and Commonwealth forces
throughout World War II. Its name derived from the initials of its designers, R.V.
Shepard and H.J. Turpin, combined with those of Britain's Enfield National Arsenal.
The 9mm, blowback-operated submachine gun—which fed from a 32-round, side-
mounted detachable magazine—saw service everywhere from Normandy to New
Guinea. The Australian version was known as the AUSTEN, from "Australian STEN."

Magazine

Trigger guard

REISING
The U.S. .45 Reising gun (named for its designer, Eugene
Reising) was a selective-fire, delayed blowback-operation
weapon used by the U.S. Marine Corps early in World
War II. Issued in a full-length, wooden-stock version as

well as the folding wire-stock model shown here, the
Reising's locked-breech firing system was susceptible to
fouling from dirt and moisture, so it proved ineffective
and unpopular in the jungle campaigns on Guadalcanal
and other islands.

WORLD WAR II AND AFTER

Most nations had adopted some form of submachine gun before the advent of World War II, although military conservatives often derided the weapon as "cheap and nasty" and lamented its relative lack of accuracy and "stopping power" (most submachine guns fired a pistol-strength cartridge rather than a rifle round, the latter being too powerful for the submachine gun's firing system.) The weapon proved its worth, however, in all theaters of World War II, especially in street-fighting in Europe and in close-quarter battle in the Pacific islands.

The Soviet Union in particular liked the weapon so much so that it produced millions of PPSh41/42/43 models, and even equipped whole battalions with them. While technically crude compared to German submachine guns like the MP40, the PPSh series (short for Pistolet-Pullemet Shpagin) were rugged and reliable in the brutal conditions of the Eastern Front, easy to use even by minimally trained Red Army soldiers, and could be produced quickly and cheaply. Chinese copies of the Russian design, like the Type 50, saw extensive service in the Korean War (1950–53), in which U.S. troops dubbed them "burp guns" from their distinctive sound.

Bolt recoils into buttstock

FRENCH MAS
The 7.65mm MAS (from Manufacture d'Armes de St. Etienne) Model 1938 submachine gun was the French army's principal World War II submachine gun. It was an unusual weapon in that the trigger had to be pushed forward to put the weapon in safety mode and the bolt recoiled into a tube inside the buttstock.

Barrel lacks insulation

Stock folded against body

MP40
Although popularly known as the "Schmeisser," this German submachine gun, officially the MP (Machinenpistole) Model 1940, was not developed by the great German weapons designer Hugo Schmeisser. More than one million were manufactured for Wehrmacht use during World War II, and the 9mm, blowback-operated, metal-and-plastic MP40 is generally considered the first standard-issue infantry weapon to use no wood in its construction. Its excellent reputation is reinforced by the fact that many Allied troops used captured MP40s in preference to their own issue submachine guns.

SPECIALIZED WEAPONS OF WWII

The special battlefield conditions of World War II required specialized infantry weapons. The appearance of the tank as a major battlefield presence led to the development of rocket-propelled weapons to allow infantrymen to deal with enemy armor. In the brutal conflict between the Soviet Union and Nazi Germany on the Eastern Front, both armies fielded sniper units armed with specially adapted rifles. While World War II saw the widespread use of radios for communication, the venerable flare pistol continued to be used for signaling when radio silence had to be observed. A grimmer type of weapon were the brutal devices used in Nazi Germany's POW and concentration camps.

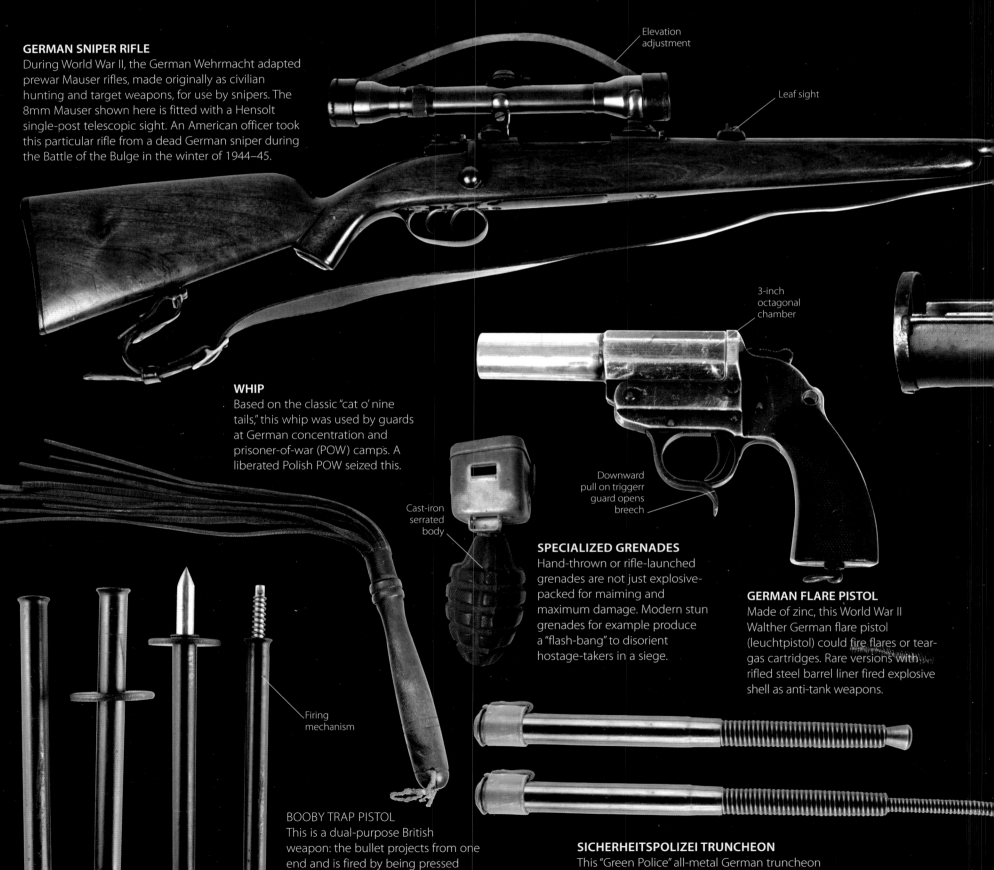

GERMAN SNIPER RIFLE
During World War II, the German Wehrmacht adapted prewar Mauser rifles, made originally as civilian hunting and target weapons, for use by snipers. The 8mm Mauser shown here is fitted with a Hensolt single-post telescopic sight. An American officer took this particular rifle from a dead German sniper during the Battle of the Bulge in the winter of 1944–45.

Elevation adjustment

Leaf sight

3-inch octagonal chamber

WHIP
Based on the classic "cat o' nine tails," this whip was used by guards at German concentration and prisoner-of-war (POW) camps. A liberated Polish POW seized this.

Cast-iron serrated body

Downward pull on triggerr guard opens breech

SPECIALIZED GRENADES
Hand-thrown or rifle-launched grenades are not just explosive-packed for maiming and maximum damage. Modern stun grenades for example produce a "flash-bang" to disorient hostage-takers in a siege.

GERMAN FLARE PISTOL
Made of zinc, this World War II Walther German flare pistol (leuchtpistol) could fire flares or tear-gas cartridges. Rare versions with rifled steel barrel liner fired explosive shell as anti-tank weapons.

Firing mechanism

BOOBY TRAP PISTOL
This is a dual-purpose British weapon: the bullet projects from one end and is fired by being pressed against the user's body. Used as a booby trap it fires when stepped on.

SICHERHEITSPOLIZEI TRUNCHEON
This "Green Police" all-metal German truncheon dates from the twentieth century. A flick of the wrist throws out a coiled steel spring extension.

THE LIBERATOR

Although not produced especially for the OSS, the "Liberator" pistol has—rightly or wrongly—long been associated with that organization. The Liberator was simplicity itself: A single-shot pistol firing a .45 ACP round through a smoothbore barrel. Made of 23 pieces of stamped metal, it came in a cardboard box with ten cartridges (five of which could be stored in a compartment in the grip), a wooden rod for ejecting spent cartridges, and a wordless, comic strip-style sheet with assembly instructions. About a million of these guns were made by the Guide Lamp Division of the General Motors Corporation in 1942. The weapon was nicknamed "the Woolworth gun," after the discount store where all items sold for five or ten cents. (The actual unit cost was about U.S. $2.00.) With an effective range of about six feet, the Liberator was really a weapon designed to allow the user (if he or she were brave and lucky) to obtain better weapons. This gun was apparently intended for mass distribution to resistance fighters in Axis-

occupied Europe and Asia, the idea being that they would be used on stragglers and sentries, whose weapons would then be captured and added to the guerrilla group's arsenal. In keeping with its clandestine nature, the gun had no manufacturer's stampings or other telltale markings and it weighed about one pound. While they may have been originally intended mainly for distribution in Nazi-occupied Europe, there is not much evidence many were actually used there, but guerrillas fighting Japanese forces in the Philippines apparently used some Liberators to good effect.

In the early 1960s, the CIA revived the idea of a no-frills, single-shot pistol in the form of the so-called "deer gun," or "zip gun," a successor to the Liberator and a 9mm weapon the U.S. distributed to anticommunist guerrillas in Southeast Asia.

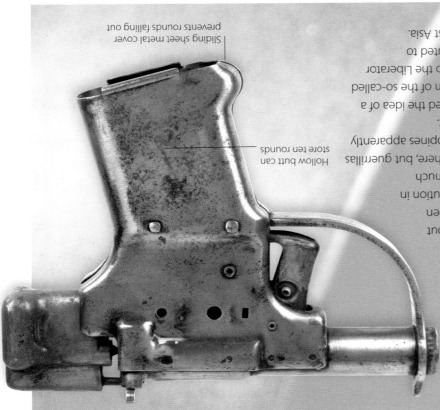

Sliding sheet metal cover prevents rounds falling out

Hollow butt can store ten rounds

DEADLY MUSIC
Made in 1965, this fully functional silver flute was adapted to fire a .22 round. A brass screw on one of the keys functions as a trigger.

Brass screw trigger

DEADLY TOOLS
The tire gauge and screwdriver shown here are replicas of actual weapons produced for Allied operatives in World War II. Each is a single-shot .22 pistol.

Trigger and cocking mechanism

.22 round discharged from here

LOZENGE-CASE GUN
An agent of Italy's Fascist government reportedly used this pistol, disguised as a tin of throat lozenges, to assassinate an American intelligence operative in Switzerland during World War II. (As a neutral nation, Switzerland was a hotbed of espionage and intrigue throughout the conflict.) To fire the weapon, the assassin opened the lid and pressed on one of the "lozenges," which served as a trigger.

Concealed barrel

Lozenge strip disguising trigger

WEAPONS OF ESPIONAGE CONTINUED . . .

BELT-BUCKLE PISTOL

Made for a Nazi soldier during World War II, this belt buckle conceals a miniature 22-caliber pistol. Another variation comprised two 7.65mm barrels with lockwork hidden behind a Nazi Party belt buckle. The barrels were two inches long and such tiny weapons meant the wearer needed to get very close to the victim to have any hope of success..

SPRING GUN
This easily concealed weapon is typical of those used by the U.S. OSS in World War II.

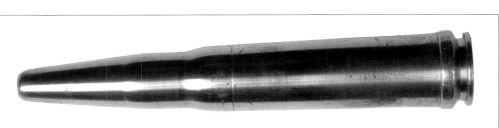

AMERICAN MACHINE GUN SHELL
Carefully hidden inside this .50-caliber machine gun shell is a minute spring-loaded .22-caliber gun dating from the mid-twentieth century.

Pen exterior forming a handle

Blade

PHILIPPINES

SILVER PEN DAGGER
Writing implements, such as this American silver-cased pen, were used in espionage during the World War II and Cold War eras for hiding weapons.

THE COLD WAR
When World War II gave way to the Cold War, the OSS gave way to the Central Intelligence Agency (CIA). The CIA continued to use one the most effective OSS weapons, the .22 Hi-Standard automatic pistol. With a design similar to the civilian Colt Woodsmen pistol, the Hi-Standard was equipped with a silencer developed by Bell Telephone Laboratories. In keeping with the agency's doctrine of "plausible deniability" in

covert operations, the Hi-Standards in the CIA's arsenal were manufactured without any markings that would indicate their American origin. The CIA also developed a range of highly unusual weapons; reportedly, the agency worked on an exploding seashell in an unsuccessful attempt to kill Cuban dictator Fidel Castro, who was an avid skin-diver.

The KGB, the postwar version of the Soviet Secret Police, had its own arsenal of unusual weapons, including a 4.5mm gun

disguised as a lipstick. Issued to female agents, this was nicknamed "the Kiss of Death." KGB agents also used poison pens, and wallets concealing gas-firing cartridges. The KGB also developed for Bulgarian agents the umbrella with a pointed end and laced with poison (ricin) that was used to jab and assassinate Bulgarian dissident Georgi Markov in London in 1978. So devious was this method of murder that only when Markov's body was exhumed did Western intelligence discover the truth.

WEAPONS OF ESPIONAGE CONTINUED . . .

PALM GUNS

A selection of so-called palm guns were designed to be concealed and operated in the palm on the hand. They were often used as covert assassinations weapons as well as self-defense firearms by agents during World War II and into the Cold War era as well.

RAZOR PISTOL
The handle of this American twentieth-century safety razor has been used to conceal a small pistol.

LIPSTICK GUN
This highly decorative lipstick case conceals a tiny weapon designed for self-defense. This is an American version fired by twisting its knurled ring a quarter-turn. The most famous lipstick pistol was the KGB's "kiss of death" for female agents, which contained a 4.5mm single-shot pistol encased in rubber.

ZIPPO LIGHTER PISTOL
There are various different designs for pistols hidden within lighters. They were usually fired by fully opening the case. Zippos were often chosen because their popularity as lighters meant they were unlikely to attract special attention. They were also better made than other lighter models.

PIPE PISTOL
Another variant on the "smoking gun" is this American pipe containing a spring pistol. It is a simple device with a spring-operated firing mechanism. The mouthpiece is removed for loading and firing.

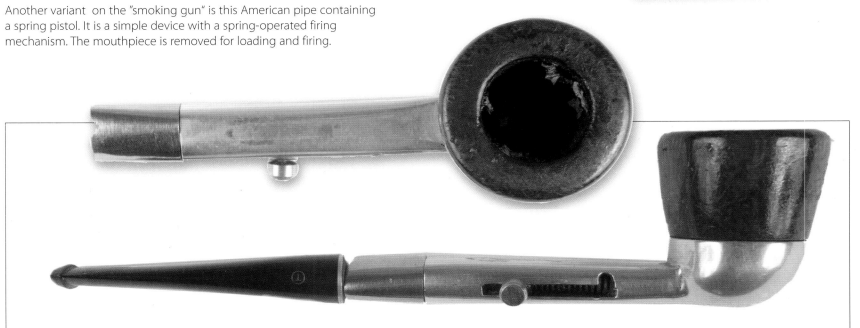

CHEMICAL & BIOLOGICAL WAR

The use of chemical and biological agents in warfare—whether against enemy forces, animals, or civilian populations—stretches back to early use of poisons. But despite the fear that they inspire, such weapons have proved difficult to use effectively, then and now, because spores (like those that cause anthrax) and toxins (like botulin, which causes botulism), and other agents often disperse unpredictably and can be just as deadly to the "attackers" as to the "defenders." Because they are relatively inexpensive to produce, chemical and biological weapons are sometimes called the "poor man's weapons" and as such they are attractive to terrorist organizations. The possibility of a chemical or biological attack by a terrorist group or "rogue state"—with theoretically countless deaths—remains terrifying in the twenty-first century.

GAS ATTACK
In World War I, mustard gas, phosgene, and chlorine were all released on the battlefield to incapacitate the enemy. Primitive gas masks could offer some protection but only if conditions were otherwise favorable.

"AS UNDER A GREEN SEA, I SAW HIM DROWNING"

Wilfred Owen, "Dulce et Decorum Est," 1917

EARLY EXAMPLES

Arrows have long been tipped with poisons, and there are plenty of medieval accounts of attackers using catapults to hurl the dead bodies of diseased humans, horses, or other animals into castles or fortified towns to spread disease. But one of the most notorious episodes of deliberate biological warfare came in the aftermath of the French and Indian War (1754–63, known as the Seven Years' War in Europe), which gave Britain control of most of North America. When the Native American leader Pontiac led a revolt against the new British overlords, the British commander at

Fort Pitt (now Pittsburgh, Pennsylvania), Sir Jeffrey Amherst, arranged for blankets used by smallpox patients at the base to be given to local Native Americans. A smallpox epidemic quickly spread throughout the region.

MODERN TIMES

In World War I, both sides resorted to chemical warfare in the form of gases, and German agents are also known to have tried to introduce anthrax among cavalry horses in Romania. In World War II, a secret unit of the Japanese Army, Unit 731, attempted to spread diseases like cholera and plague among

Chinese civilians. While the facts are in dispute, some historians believe Unit 731's activities caused hundreds of thousands of deaths in China. In the Cold War, both sides stockpiled biological agents like anthrax and ricin (an extremely deadly poison derived from the castor bean). In 1972, concern over the dangers of germ warfare led to an international treaty forbidding their manufacture and use. However, in the 1980s, Iraqi dictator Saddam Hussein used chemical weapons against Iraq's own minority Kurdish population. In one documented episode, as many as 5,000 Kurds may have died in one 1988 chemical attack.

Folding rear sight for grenade launcher

Launcher mounts onto forestock

Rifle foresight

Rifle trigger [grenade trigger to right]

Rifle grenade launcher tube

M4 RIFLE WITH GRENADE LAUNCHER
This U.S. Army asssault rifle has a mounted grenade launcher fired by a propellant charge. Such models were designed to replace stand-alone launchers.

Bulb-shaped body

CHEMICAL GRENADE
Hand grenades with chemicals are used for incendiary, screening, signaling, training, or riot control.

Inner mask decreases fogging

Impermeable rubber-coated canvas

Filter allows air and sweat to pass through

AGENT ORANGE USED TO FLUSH OUT VIET CONG
The U.S. military sprayed millions of gallons of Agent Orange and other herbicides on trees and vegetation during the Vietnam War. Several decades later, concerns about the health effects from these chemicals continue.

NUCLEAR, BIOLOGICAL, CHEMICAL SUIT
This NBC suit is designed to enable the military to fight while exposed potentially to hazardous materials

Offers several days' protection

POST–WORLD WAR II WEAPONS

The most significant development in firearms in the decades after World War II was the proliferation of rugged and versatile assault rifles, especially the Soviet Kalashnikov (AK47). With over 70 million dispersed globally, these cheap but deadly weapons fuelled ongoing geo-political, civil, and ethnic conflict in the world's most unstable regions, including Afghanistan. Recent decades have seen civilian and military engineers experimenting with "caseless" ammunition and even rocket propulsion to replace conventional ammunition and firing systems, but most contemporary firearms remain based (albeit in highly evolved forms) on designs and systems introduced decades ago or even in the nineteenth century. Self-loading pistols from the 1950 (including those shown here) gained popularity with security forces combating the growing threat of international terrorism.

HANDGUNS

Pistol design stayed somewhat static until the 1970s, when the rise of global terrorism led to the development of a new generation of automatics, most chambered for 9mm. Designed to meet the changing needs of law-enforcement agencies and antiterrorist military units, these pistols could be carried safely, used in close confines (such as airplane passenger cabins) with minimal danger to hostages or bystanders, and had a high magazine capacity. One of the first pistols that met these criteria was Germany's Heckler & Koch VP70. It was also the first pistol that had plastic in its construction.

In 1983 the Austrian firm Glock AG introduced the first of its extremely successful Glock series of automatic pistols, with magazine capacities of up to 19 rounds. Glocks are composed mostly of plastic, which led to fears they could pass through metal detectors, but these fears have proven unfounded.

Cylinder holds six rounds of ammunition

EASTERN EUROPEAN REVOLVER
This revolver dates from post World War II. Revolver design by then was fairly universal: there is not much developmental difference between this and the classic British service revolver introduced back in World War I.

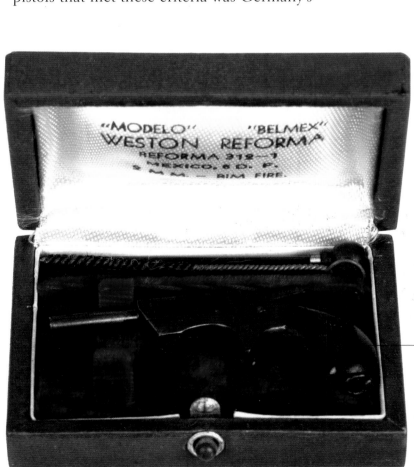

One cent coin to indicate scale of Weston pinfire pistol

2 ¼inch Belmex rim fire pistol

WESTON MINIATURE
Although Tom Weston is perhaps the best-known twentieth-century maker of miniature guns, the details of his life are sketchy. The Mexico City resident was apparently a leading collector and seller of antique firearms when, in the 1930s, he engaged Mexican craftsmen to make tiny but fully functioning guns. These unique weapons, produced mainly in the 1950s and 1960s, are prized by collectors of firearms curiosa. Shown here is a 2mm "Reforma" single-shot pistol.

RUSSIAN MAKAROV

Another version of the Russian standard side-arm issued in the 1950s. This has a 3-inch barrel and weighs one pound. It took powerful ammuntion that tested the blowback design of the time.

PM (*PISTOLET MAKAROVA*) SEMIAUTOMATIC

This self-loading pistol (Pistolet Makarova or Makarov's Pistol) is a semiautomatic. The result of a design competition to replace the Tokare TT-33 and Nagant M1895 revolver, it was produced by a team led by Nikolay Fyodorovich Makarov and became the standard side-arm for the Soviet Union's military from 1951–91.

Vent holes for combustion gases released within barrel

Butt holds eight-round removeable magazine

Small ("Microject") rocket

GYROJET PISTOL

Americans Robert Mainhardt and Art Biehl developed one of the most unusual and innovative firearms of recent decades, the Gyrojet pistol, in the early 1960s. The Gyrojet was actually a pistol-scale rocket launcher, firing a 12mm (later 13mm) projectile burning a solid propellant. MBA Associates, the company Mainhardt and Biehl set up to manufacture the weapon, also produced a carbine version. According to some sources, the U.S. military became interested in the Gyrojet concept because it seemed to promise a "jam-free," recoilless infantry weapon, but it proved impractical in tests under combat conditions. Gyrojet weapons never found much of a civilian buyership because of the expensive ammunition.

No removable magazine (rounds pushed down from open "bolt")

Slide mounted safety catch

BERETTA M9 SEMIAUTOMATIC

The Beretta is a conventional short-recoil design and has been the U.S. Military's official side-arm since the 1980s. The slide top is cut away to allow single rounds to be inserted by hand in the event of the magazine being damaged or lost.

POST-WORLD WAR II HANDGUNS CONTINUED . . .

TAURUS PT92 SEMIAUTOMATIC PISTOL
Made in the old Beretta factory in São Paulo, Brazil, this short-recoil pistol with a double-stack magazine is a reproduction of the Beretta 92. Like the Beretta, it has an open-slide design where the upper portion of the slide is cut away exposing much of the barrel.

SIG P226 SERVICE PISTOL
This is a full-sized, service-type pistol made by SIG Sauer. It is chambered for the 9×19mm Parabellum, .40 S&W, .357 SIG, and .22 Long Rifle. It is essentially the same basic design of the SIG P220, but developed to use higher capacity, staggered-column magazines in place of the single-column magazines of the P220.

92FS BERETTA SEMIAUTOMATIC PISTOL
This was the version that replaced the Colt M911A1 as the official handgun of the U.S. military in the 1980s. This particular model was also the gun wielded to such dramatic effect by actor Bruce Willis in the highly charged "Die Hard" movie franchise.

WALTHER P99 SEMIAUTOMATIC PISTOL

The Walther PP (short for police pistol) series pistols are blowback-operated handguns. Energy comes from the movement of the spent cartridge case pushed out of the chamber by rapidly expanding powder gases. The PP dates back to 1929 with German and Nazi forces being issued with them. Hitler killed himself with his PPK variant.

HECKLER & KOCH USP

This Universal Self-Loading Pistol was Heckler & Koch's answer to the Glock. Heckler & Koch is a German defense manufacturing company that produces various small arms. Another handgun that was built to be easily modified , it could be configured in several different ways, making it popular as a modern special forces pistol.

DESERT EAGLE

Made by Magnum in the U.S. this is a semiautomatic pistol capable of handling very powerful ammunition. It is gas-operated (unlike most other self-loading pistols, which use short recoil or blow-back systems) and has a modular design, which means it can accept sets of components for different ammunition as well as barrels of varying lengths. The Desert Eagle was designed by Bernard C. White of Magnum Research, who filed a U.S. patent application for a mechanism for a gas-activated pistol in January 1983.

GLOCK 9MM DUTY PISTOL

This semiautomatic pistol was produced for the Austrian army just after World War II and had to fulfill 17 criteria, including having fully interchangeable components. Called the Glock 17, it has undergone some changes since, but remains widely used and well-respected.

POST-WORLD WAR II WEAPONS CONTINUED . . .

INFANTRY WEAPONS

The most successful infantry weapon of the post–World War II era is the AK47 assault rifle, often called the Kalashnikov after its chief designer (see sidebar). Simple construction with few moving parts made this rifle easy to maintain and use, even by relatively untrained troops or guerrilla fighters. The AK47 remains ubiquitous in the twenty-first century, with probably more than 100 million units of the weapon and its variants produced as of this writing.

The postwar years saw the armies of most nations adopt selective-fire assault rifles. The majority of such rifles were chambered for the 7.62mm round; for example, the Belgian FN FAL, introduced in 1950 and adopted by more than 50 nations. An exception was the M16, adopted by the United States. It took 5.56mm rounds and was based on the Armalite rifle designed by Eugene Stoner in the 1960s. In recent years, many armies have adopted rifles with smaller cartridges, often in "bullpup" designs, which place the magazine and action behind the trigger guard. Just as the assault rifle was an outgrowth of the World War II German Sturmgewehr, the belt-fed squad automatic weapons now used by many armies are an evolution of the German MG42.

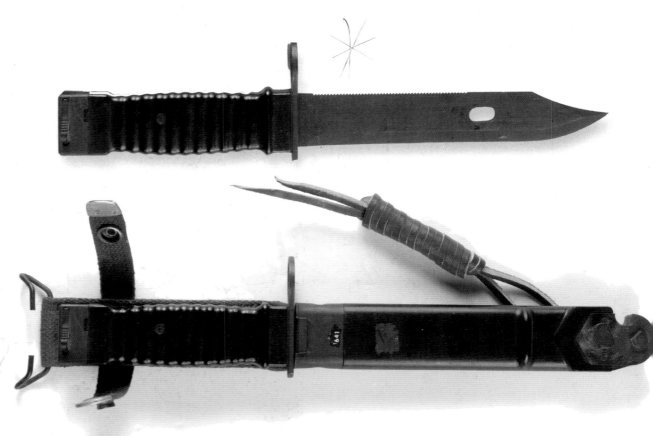

GERMAN BAYONET
This rare bayonet was designed to be used with the Stoner 63 assault rifle, an American modular weapons system designed by Eugene Stoner in the early 1960s. The rifle was used by the American army from the 1960s to the late 1980s.

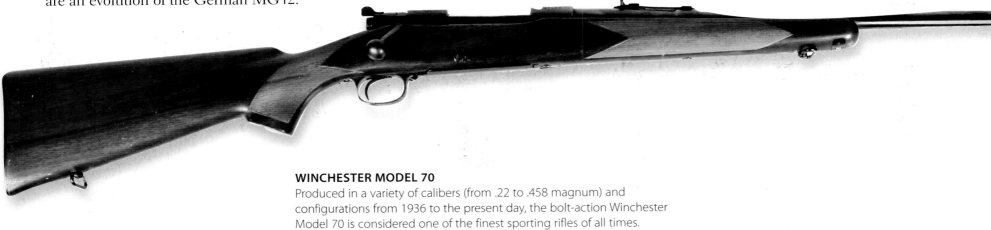

WINCHESTER MODEL 70
Produced in a variety of calibers (from .22 to .458 magnum) and configurations from 1936 to the present day, the bolt-action Winchester Model 70 is considered one of the finest sporting rifles of all times.

Bayonet folds into the forestock

SKS CARBINE
During World War II, Soviet weapons designer Sergei Simonov worked to develop a semiautomatic rifle firing a "short" version of the standard 7.62mm Soviet round. The result was the SKS-45 carbine, a gas-operated weapon that fed from a 10-round box magazine and featured an integral bayonet that folded into the forestock. The SKS was a highly successful weapon and it was produced in large numbers in China and other nations until it was largely replaced by the AK47.

M. T. KALASHNIKOV

Born in Kurya, Siberia, in 1919, Mikhail Timofeyevich Kalashnikov had no formal technical education; instead, he received hands-on training as a railroad "technical clerk." Seriously wounded in 1941 while serving as a tank commander with the Red Army, Kalashnikov began working on weapons designs during his convalescence. He designed a couple of submachine guns, but as the Red Army already had successful submachine guns in production, they weren't adopted. Kalashnikov then turned his talents toward the development of a weapon known, in Soviet terminology, as an "Automat"—the same assault-rifle concept pioneered by the Germans with the MP44. (The German weapons designer Hugo Schmeisser and some of his associates, who had been captured and pressed into Soviet service at the end of World War II, may have contributed to Kalashnikov's work; this is still debated.) In 1947 the Automat Kalashnikov (AK) Model 47, debuted, and the Red Army adopted the weapon in 1951. Kalashnikov rose to the post of chief weapons designer for the Soviet military, produced other weapons (such as the 5.54mm AK-74). He won every award possible in the Soviet Union and, later, the Russian Federation. In 2004, he endorsed his own brand of vodka. He is still alive at this writing.

Curved magazine

AK47

Perhaps the AK47's greatest virtue is its reliability under tough combat conditions: During the Vietnam War, Vietcong guerrillas reportedly retrieved AK47s that had been hidden for days in muddy rice paddies, but which fired perfectly. In contrast, the U.S. M16—while a technically superior and, in some respects, more lethal rifle—has to be kept meticulously clean to avoid jamming. The model shown here is a Chinese version.

Wood forestock

I WANTED TO INVENT AN ENGINE THAT COULD RUN FOR EVER. I COULD HAVE DEVELOPED A NEW TRAIN, HAD I STAYED IN THE RAILWAY. IT WOULD HAVE LOOKED LIKE THE AK-47 THOUGH.

–Mikhail Kalashnikov

POST WORLD WAR II WEAPONS CONTINUED . . .

Telescoping buttstock

M4A1 CARBINE

This version of the M4 family of carbines has a tactical grip and a holographic sight. The M4s are a development of the M16 rifle but are generally shorter and lighter. The M4A1 is gas-operated with a telescoping buttstock. It is capable of fully automatic fire, as well as the selective fire and three-round bursts of the standard M4.

M4 CARBINE

Until recently the M4 carbine was built solely by Colt, but the U.S. army have taken ownership of the design, which will allow other companies to make new improved versions. The military makes much use of these weapons in operations worldwide.

Magazine and action are
behind the trigger guard

STEYER AUG

Designed in the early 1970s, the AUG (Armee Universal-Gewehr or universal army rifle) is th standard small arm of the Austrian army and police. It is a 5.56mm assault rifle with a bullp design and an interchangeable barrel.

Integral bipod

Box magazine

M249 LIGHT MACHINEGUN
This is the U.S. version of the world-renowned Minimi, made in Belgium. Gas-operated and air-cooled, it also features a quick-change barrel, which is a useful option in case of overheating, jamming, or other problems.

Selector makes it easy to change the firing rate

MP5 SUBMACHINE GUN
The MP5 is made by famous gunsmiths Heckler & Koch. It was designed in the 1960s and has since appeared in many different versions. It is a 9mm fed from a box or curved magazine containing up to 30 rounds.

MP5K
This shortened version of the MP5 was introduced in 1976 with the intention of producing a weapon for close-quarters combat and special services. It lacks a buttstock and the bolt and receiver are shortened. The barrel is also much shorter, stopping after the foresight.

Vertical foregrip

POST WORLD WAR II WEAPONS CONTINUED . . .

UZI SUBMACHINE GUN

The first UZI was designed by Major Uziel Gal of the Israeli army and it gave rise to a family of similar weapons, some known as machine pistols. The UZI was the first submachine gun to use a telescoping bolt. It has found widespread use as a personal defense weapon as well as in armies of all nations.

Stock folds under body

STERLING SUBMACHINE GUN

The British Sterling submachine gun was brought into service late in World War II and continued to be used by the British army until 1994, when it was replaced by the L85A1 assault rifle. Initially called the Patchett after its designer, George William Patchett, it proved itself a reliable and accurate weapon, performing well in difficult conditions.

RESOURCES

ABOUT THE BERMAN MUSEUM

Since the Berman Museum of World History opened its doors to the public in April of 1996, thousands of visitors have enjoyed its unique and varied collection of art, historical objects, and weapons. Located in the Appalachian foothills in Anniston, Alabama, and next door to the seventy-five-year-old Anniston Museum of Natural History, which is affiliated with the Smithsonian, the Berman Museum's reputation and collection have grown exponentially since its inception. The Berman Museum's holdings number 8,500 objects and it has 3,000 items related to world history exhibited in its galleries. Among the many rare and fascinating objects from around the world, there are items such as an air rifle from Austria, military insignia from German and Italy, a scimitar from the Middle East, and graphically carved kris holders from Indonesia. The Museum attracts both a global and regional audience. All who visit can appreciate the historic significance of the collection and gain greater awareness and respect of other cultures.

Its five galleries—Deadly Beauty, American West, World War I, World War II, and Arts of Asia—exhibit items spanning a period of 3,500 years. A focal point of the Deadly Beauty gallery is the elaborate Royal Persian Scimitar, circa 1550, created for Abbas the Great, King of Persia. The American West gallery covers approximately 200 years (c. 1700–1900), emphasizing the United State's political, economic, social, and cultural structures, and their influences on settling the West.

The World War galleries use objects from the Museum collection to explore the causes and conditions of both wars, the historical significance of the countries involved, and the resulting political, economic, cultural, and social changes brought about by each war. A rare piece of equipment in the World War I gallery is the Tanker's Splinter Goggles, used by tank personnel to protect their eyes and faces from metal splinters from machine-gun fire. Exhibited in the World War II gallery is the M1942 "Liberator" Pistol, as well as a large collection of Adolf Hitler's tea and coffee service, purported to have come from the last bunker that the Führer occupied. The Arts of Asia exhibit features an extensive and ever-growing collection of Asian textiles, ceramics, sculpture, jade, and metal.

The Berman Museum of World History is home to the vast and eclectic collection of Colonel Farley L. Berman and his wife, Germaine. Farley Berman, a lifelong resident of Anniston, Alabama, served in the European theater during World War II, and in the occupation force afterward. There he met Germaine, a French national. They were married and spent the next fifty years traveling the world acquiring historic weapons and artifacts, paintings, bronzes, and other works of art. Berman's self-trained collector's eye recognized the importance of items that were perhaps seen as ordinary, and he made it his mission to preserve a few. The Bermans established contacts—and a reputation—in numerous auction houses and among antique dealers in Europe and America.

The Bermans freely shared their collection with the public long before the City of Anniston constructed the Museum facility. Hundreds of military dignitaries and others were invited to their home for personal tours of their collection. Colonel Berman could best be described as a colorful storyteller and was notorious for firing blank rounds from his collection of spy weapons when guests least expected. He advised aspiring collectors to purchase good reference books, spend some years reading, and visit a range of museums before acquiring.

During the early 1990s, several large museums expressed interest in receiving the Bermans' collection. They were disappointed when Germaine proposed that the collection remain in Anniston. Colonel and Mrs. Berman's collection stands as the core of Berman Museum. Since the Museum's opening, many have recognized its importance and have contributed their own personal treasures to this impressive collection.

BERMAN MUSEUM OF WORLD HISTORY

www.bermanmuseum.org
840 Museum Drive, Anniston, AL 36206

mail: P.O.Box 2245, Anniston, AL 36202-2245 USA
phone: 256-237-6261

GLOSSARY

A

ACTION Generally speaking, the overall firing mechanism of a gun

ATLATL A spear-throwing device

ARQUEBUS Shoulder-fired matchlock musket

ASSEGAI A South African throwing spear, most famously used by Zulu warriors

B

BAGH NAKH Indian claw daggers with three to five curved blades

BALL A synonym for bullet

BLUNDERBUSS A short, smoothbore musket (occasionally a pistol) with a flared muzzle

BOLT In reference to crossbows, a short dartlike projectile, also known as a quarrel

BOLT-ACTION A gun (typically a rifle) whose action is operated by manipulating a bolt, either by drawing it back ("straight pull") or on a rotational axis

BORE *See* **GAUGE**

BUCKSHOT Lead pellets fired by shotguns

BUTT, OR BUTTSTOCK The part of a gun braced against the shoulder for firing

C

CALACULA A Fijian club with a saw-toothed blade

CALIBER The diameter of a cartridge, expressed in fractions of an inch (e.g., .38, .45) or millimeter (e.g., 7.62mm, 9mm)

CARBINE A short-barreled, compact musket or rifle, originally carried by mounted troops or, in modern times, by soldiers whose primary jobs (vehicle crews, for example) made it impractical to carry a full-size rifle

CARTRIDGE The cased combination of bullet, powder, and primer used in modern firearms; prior to the introduction of the metallic cartridge, the term referred to bullet and powder wrapped in paper for ease of loading muzzle-loading weapons

CENTER-FIRE A type of cartridge with the primer sealed in a cavity in the center of its base

CHAIN MAIL Personal armor made of many links of iron or steel riveted together

CHAMBER The part of a gun in which the cartridge is seated before firing

CHASSEPOT Nineteenth-century French bolt-action rifle

CHUKONU Chinese repeating crossbow

CLIP A metal strip holding a number of cartridges for insertion into a gun

COMPOSITE BOW A bow using bone or other material to reinforce wood.

CROSSBOW Type of bow using laterally fixed "limbs"

CROSSGUARD *See* **GUARD**

D

DAGGER Short knife used for stabbing

DARRA GUNS Guns produced by the gunsmiths of Darra Adem Khel (then part of India, now part of Pakistan)

DERINGER The original weapons made by Henry Deringer; the imitation was spelled with an additional r

DERRINGER Short, extremely compact and concealable pistol

DHA HYMYUNG A Burmese dagger

DHA LWE A Burmese sword

DHAL A Persian shield

DOUBLE-ACTION A pistol (either revolver or automatic) in which a single, long trigger pull both fires the weapon and brings a cartridge into the chamber in readiness for firing. *See also* single-action

DYAK Sword used by the Dyak people of Borneo

F

FIGHTING KNIFE, OR COMBAT KNIFE Edged weapon intended for use in hand-to-hand combat rather than as a tool

FIRING PIN The part of a gun's firing mechanism that strikes the cartridge's primer

FLINTLOCK Gun-firing system utilizing a piece of flint striking against a piece of steel to strike sparks for ignition

FU PA (Chinese "tiger fork") Three-pronged head metal head on a shaft

G

GAS-OPERATED Term used to describe a gun that taps excess gas from the weapon to operate the action

GATLING GUN A multi-barreled gun fed from a hopper, developed during the American Civil War and still in use in an eletctrically operated version

GUARD Vertical projections on a sword or knife, separating the hilt from the blade. Also known as crossguard

GAUGE For shotguns, the equivalent of the term "caliber," in this case expressed as fractions of a pound, e.g., 12-gauge; synonymous with bore

GRABENDOCH German term for "trench dagger"

GRIP General term for the handle of a sword or knife

H

HANDGUN Originally used to refer to any firearm that could be carried and used by an individual; in modern usage it refers solely to pistols

HILT The portion of a sword grasped by the user, usually consisting of the guard, grip, and pommel

HOPLITE Armed artillery soldier of Ancient Greece

HOWDAH PISTOL A powerful British pistol used by elephant riders to fend off tigers

J

JAMBIYA An Arabian curved dagger that was mostly decorative but it was also an effective fighting knife

JIAN A Chinese short sword

K

KATANA Traditional sword of the Japanese samurai

KINDJAL A curved double-edged fighting knife of the Cossacks

KOFTGARI A form of decoration consisting of gold-inlaid steel

KORA The national sword of Nepal

KRIS, OR KERIS A traditional knife of Malaysia and Indonesia

KUBA Deadly weapon of the Kuba people from West Africa

KUKRI, OR KHUKURI A Nepalese fighting knife

KULAH KHUD Indo-Persian helmet

L, M, N

LEVER-ACTION A gun that uses a lever, pushed downward and then upward by the firer, to load and eject cartridges

LUK Bend in a kris

MAGAZINE The part of a gun containing cartridges in readiness for firing; in rifles, the magazine is often charged (loaded) by a clip

EMAIN-GAUCHE A dagger held in the left hand, used in conjunction with a sword in European swordfighting during the Renaissance

MAMELUKE SWORD A curved sword used by the slave-soldiers of Islamic armies, its pattern later adopted for ceremonial use in the West

MATCHLOCK Early firearms which used a slow-burning match to provide ignition

MERE *See* patu

MUSKET Generally, a smoothbore, shoulder-fired infantry weapon, in use in the West up until the widespread introduction of rifles in the mid-nineteenth century

MUSKETOON A short-barreled musket

MUZZLE The opening of a gun's barrel

MUZZLE-LOADING Used to refer to a gun that loads by the muzzle

NIMCHA A curved, North African blade of varying lengths

P,Q

PALLASK A double-edged sword designed to penetrate the chain-mail armor worn by mounted soldiers of the Ottoman Empire

PARTISAN *See* patu

PATU A short-handled war club that was the principal weapon of the Maori people of New Zealand

PERCUSSION CAP A capsule containing a fulminating agent

PESH-KABZ A curved Persian knife used to penetrate chain-mail armor

PIHA KAETTA A traditional knife of Sri Lanka (now Ceylon); mainly a ceremonial weapon

PINFIRE An early type of self-contained cartridge, no longer in common use

PLATE ARMOR Personal armor made of overlapping plates of iron or steel

POMMEL The often knoblike projection atop a sword or knife

PRIMER The part of a cartridge which, when struck by the firing pin, ignites and fires the main charge

PUMP-ACTION A gun whose action is operated by a sliding mechanism, usually mounted below the barrel

QUARREL *See* bolt

QUILLION Sword separator between blade and hilt that can be either straight or curved; see guard

QUIVER Basketlike container for carrying arrows

R

RECEIVER Generally speaking, the part of a gun incorporating the action, as distinct from the stock and barrel

RECOIL The backward pressure exerted when a gun is fired

RECOIL-OPERATED A type of semi- or fully automatic gun that uses recoil to operate the action

RIFLING The process of boring cylindrical grooves into a gun barrel to stabilize the bullet in flight, thus increasing accuracy

RIMFIRE A type of cartridge in which the primer is evenly distributed around the rear of the base

ROUND Synonym for cartridge, usually used to refer to magazine capacity, e.g., twenty-round.

S

SABER, OR SABRE Curved sword typically used by cavalry

SAFETY The part of a gun's action designed to prevent accidental firing

SALAMPUSA An iron-bladed sword used by the warriors of the Salampasu people of Africa

SCABBARD Receptacle for carrying a sword

SCIMITAR Catch-all term for curved-bladed swords of Middle Eastern origin

SELF-LOADING Used to refer to guns that will fire once with each trigger pull without the need to reload; the term is synonymous with semiautomatic

SEMIAUTOMATIC *See* self-loading

SNAPHANCE, SNAPHAUNCE A type of lock, an ancestor of the flintlock

SHEATH Receptacle for carrying a knife

SHOTGUN Smoothbore, shoulder-fired weapon, typically firing buckshot; most commonly used in hunting but also in combat

SINGLE-ACTION A revolver that has to be manually cocked before each shot; single-action automatics require cocking only before the first shot is fired; see also double-action

SMOOTHBORE A gun with an unrifled barrel. *See* rifling

SODEGARAMI The Japanese sleeve grabber that was used by police to immobilize criminals

STOCK Any part of a gun which is gripped with the hand before firing, e.g., forestock; see also butt

T,U

TORADOR An matchlock musket that was used in India for hundreds of years

TANTO A Japanese dagger used by the Samurai

THUMBSCREW A torture device that compressed the thumb or other fingers using a screw

TREBUCHET Medieval catapult

TRIGGER The part of a gun's action pulled back by the firer's finger to discharge the weapon

TULWAR, OR TALWAR All-steel Indian curved saber

UMKHONTO South African spear

W,Y,Z

WHEEL LOCK Firing mechanism that used the friction of a spring-powered metal wheel against iron or flint for ignition

YARI A Japanese straight-headed spear

YATAGHAN A major blade weapon of the Ottoman Empire from the fifteenth through the nineteenth centuries

ZWEIHÄNDER The longest sword of the European Renaissance; from the German for "two-hander"

INDEX

ACKNOWLEDGMENTS

Moseley Road Inc would like to thank the following people for their assistance and patience in the making of this book—
Thunder Bay Press: Peter Norton, Lori Asbury, Ana Parker, JoAnn Padgett, True Sims, Dan Mansfield, and Melinda Allman;
The Berman Museum of World History: Adam Cleveland, David Ford, Susan Doss, Evan Prescott, Sara Prescott, Quinton Turner and Kira Tidmore; the design and editorial teams for being enthusiastic and creative under intense pressure, and last but not least Tina Vaughan's husband and children, Tim Streater, Dylan, and Tomos, who put up without their wife and mother for three long months; and Dill, for coping so admirably without Adam.

PICTURE CREDITS

Unless otherwise noted, all silhouetted weaponry images are from the Berman Museum of World History, Anniston, Alabama, with the exception of the following:

KEY : *a*=above; *al*=above left; *ar*=above right; *b*=below; *bl*=below left; *br*=below right; *c*=center; *cl*=center left; *cr*=center right
1 Shutterstock/zimand; 2-3 Shutterstock/Adam Michal Ziaja; 10-11 Shutterstock/Rohit Seth; 12-13 Shutterstock ; 14*al* Shutterstock/Diego Barucco; 14*ar* Courtesy Wikipedia; 14*b* Shutterstock/E Petersen; 15*a* istockphoto/Mark Kostich; 15*bl* Shutterstock/arindambanerjee; 15*br* Shutterstock/I Pilon; 18 Shutterstock/mountainpix; 19*a* © BrokenSphere/Wikimedia Commons ; 19*cl* Shutterstock/Zelenskaya; 19*c* Shutterstock/Terry Davis; 19*cr* Shutterstock/Yuriy Boyko; 19*b* Shutterstock/chungking; 20*a* Shutterstock/Nastya Pirieva; 20*cr* istockphoto/Henning Mertens; 20*b* Courtesy Wikipedia; 21*b* Courtesy Wikipedia; 22-23*bg* Shutterstock/Rohit Seth; 22*al* Shutterstock/BasPhoto; 22*ar* Shutterstock/azzzim; 23*cr* Courtesy Wikipedia; 24-25*bg* Shutterstock/Rohit Seth; 24*a* The Walters Art Museum, Baltimore; 24-25*c* Shutterstock/Dja65; 24*cl* Courtesy Wikipedia; 24*cr* & *b* The Walters Art Museum, Baltimore; 25*a* The Walters Art Museum, Baltimore; 25*cra* Shutterstock/ADA_Photo; 25*br* Courtesy Wikipedia; 26-27 Shutterstock/Edward Bruns; 28-29 Courtesy Wikipedia/Musée du Château de Versailles, France; 30-31, 32-33, 34-35, 36-37*bg* Shutterstock/Edward Bruns; 36*al* Shutterstock/ermess; 36*ar* Shutterstock/Ruben Pinto; 38-39, 40-41*bg* Shutterstock/Edward Bruns; 43*br* Shutterstock/William Attard McCarthy; 44-45*bg* Shutterstock/Edward Bruns; 46-47*bg* Shutterstock/Edward Bruns; 48*cl* Courtesy Wikipedia/John Antoni/The British Museum, London; 48*b* Courtesy Wikipedia/Sailko/National Archaeological Museum of Athens; 49*c* Courtesy Wikipedia/Thomas Quine; 54*al* Courtesy Wikipedia/Bullenwächter; 54*ar* Courtesy Wikipedia/Simon Burchell/The British Museum, London; 54*bl* Courtesy Wikipedia/deadkid dk/Museum of the Mausoleum of the Nanyue King, Guangzhou; 56-57*bg* Shutterstock/Edward Bruns; 56*a* Courtesy Wikipedia/Daderot/Yunnan Provincial Museum, Kunming, Yunnan, China; 56*cb* Shutterstock/Olemac; 57*a* Shutterstock/ermess; 57*cb* Shutterstock/CreativeHQ; 58-59*bg* Shutterstock/Edward Bruns; 59*c* Courtesy Wikipedia/McLeod/National Museum, Copenhagen; 62-63, 64-65, 68-69, 70-71, 74-75, 76-77, 80-81, 82-83, 84-85, 86-87, 88-89, 90-91, 92-93*bg* Shutterstock/Edward Bruns; 94 istockphoto/Duncan Walker; 96-97, 98-99, 100-101, 102-103, 104-105, 106-107*bg* Shutterstock/Edward Bruns; 109*ar* Courtesy Wikipedia/Tretyakov Gallery, Moscow; 110-111, 112-113*bg* Shutterstock/Edward Bruns; 114-115*b* Courtesy Wikipedia; 116-117, 118-119*bg* Shutterstock/Edward Bruns; 120-121 Shutterstock/Elen 418; 122-123 Library of Congress, LC-DIG-ppmsca-01657; 124-125, 126-127, 128-129, 130-131, 132-133, 134-135, 136-137, 140-141, 142-143, 144-145, 146-147, 148-149, 150-151, 152-153, 154-155, 156-157, 158-159, 160-161, 162-163, 164-165, 166-167, 168-169, 170-171, 174-175, 176-177*bg* Shutterstock/Elen 418; 178-179 Shutterstock/IntraClique LLC; 180-181 Library of Congress, LC-DIG-pga-01839; 182-183*bg* Shutterstock/IntraClique LLC; 184-185*bg* Shutterstock/IntraClique LLC; 184*a* Courtesy Cedar Hill Cemetery, Connecticut; 184*bl* Library of Congress, HAER CT-189-A-4; 184*br* Library of Congress, LC-USZ62-110403; 185*bl* Library of Congress, LC-USZ62-136377; 186-187, 188-189, 190-191, 192-193, 194-195, 196-197*bg* Shutterstock/IntraClique LLC; 198 Library of Congress, LC-DIG-pga-01855; 200-201*bg* Shutterstock/IntraClique LLC; 200*cl* Courtesy Wikipedia; 202-203*bg* Shutterstock/IntraClique LLC; 203*a* Courtesy the Berman Museum of World History, Anniston, Alabama; 206-207*bg* Shutterstock/IntraClique LLC; 206*a* Courtesy Wikipedia; 208-309*bg* Shutterstock/IntraClique LLC; 208*a* Courtesy Wikipedia; 214-215, 216-217*bg* Shutterstock/IntraClique LLC; 219br Jupiterimages; 220-221*bg* Shutterstock/IntraClique LLC; 220*a* Courtesy Wikipedia; 224-225, 226-227, 239-231, 232-233, 238-239, 240-241, 242-243*bg* Shutterstock/IntraClique LLC; 244-245, 248-249, 250-251, 252-253, 254-255, 258-259, 260-261, 262-263 Shutterstock/James Thew; 263*al* Courtesy Wikipedia; 264 Courtesy NARA; 265*a* Jupiterimages; 266-267, 268-269, 270-271, 272-273, 274-275, 276-277*bg* Shutterstock/James Thew; 277*a* Courtesy Wikipedia; 278-279, 280-281, 286-287*bg* Shutterstock/James Thew; 286-287*b* Shutterstock/Marafona; 287 top Shutterstock/Olemac; 287*c* Jupiterimages ; 288-289, 290-291*bg* Shutterstock/James Thew; 290*a* Shutterstock/Zimand; 294-295, 296-297, 298-299*bg* Shutterstock/James Thew; 300 Library of Congress; 301*a* Shutterstock/RCPPhoto; 301*c* The Vietnam Center and Archive, Admiral Elmo R. Zumwalt, Jr. Collection; 301*cr* Shutterstock/Konstantnin; 301*br* Shutterstock/Aaron Amat; 302-303*bg* Shutterstock/James Thew; 303*al* Shutterstock/Tereshchenko Dmitry; 303*ar* Shutterstock/zimand; 303*br* Shutterstock/Vartanov Anatoly; 304-305*bg* Shutterstock/James Thew; 304*al* Shutterstock/Vudhikrai; 304*c* Shutterstock/Michael Coddington; 304*bl* Shutterstock/Jaroslaw Grudzinski; 305*al* Shutterstock/MISHELLA; 305*ar* Shutterstock/Vartanov Anatoly; 305*c* Shutterstock/Nomad_Soul; 305*b* Shutterstock/zimand; 306-307*bg* Shutterstock/James Thew; 307*ar* Courtesy Wikipedia; 307*c* & *b* Shutterstock/vadim kozlovsky; 308-309*bg* Shutterstock/James Thew; 308*a* Shutterstock/Vartanov Anatoly; 308*c* & *cr* Shutterstock/Sergii Figurnyi; 308*b* Shutterstock/Rodionov; 309*a* Shutterstock/zimand; 309*c* Shutterstock/Vartanov Anatoly; 309*bl* & *br* Shutterstock/zimand; 310*bg* Shutterstock/James Thew; 310 Shutterstock/CreativeHQ; 311 Shutterstock/Adam Michal Ziaja

ARNPRIOR PUBLIC LIBRARY

105763

DISCARDED

DATE DUE / DATE DE RETOUR

OCT 0 8 2013	SEP 2 0 2021
NOV 1 6 2013	NOV 1 2 2021
DEC 0 7 2013	MAR 0 4 2022
JAN 3 0 2014	JAN 1 1 2024
FEB - 5 2014	
MAR 0 8 2014	
APR 2 4 2014	
OCT 0 9 2014	
JUN 2 3 2015	
DEC 1 0 2015	
OCT 2 7 2016	
FEB 2 5 2017	
APR 2 6 2017	
JUN 2 0 2017	
MAY 0 9 2018	
MAR 2 1 2020	

CARR M^cLEAN   38-297